Aneurin Bevan:

the Creator of the National Health Service

*I Beryl gyda
Cofion cu
D Ben Rees*

Aneurin Bevan:

The creator of the National Health Service

D BEN REES

MODERN WELSH PUBLICATIONS

First Edition April 2024

Copyright © D Ben Rees 2024 and Modern Welsh Publications

This book is copyrighted under the Berne Convention

No reproduction without permission. The publishers would like to thank the Welsh Book council editorial department and in particular to Huw Meirion Edwards, Arwel Jones, Harri Roberts, and to Dr Pat Williams, Angela Lansley, David Fletcher, of the Modern Welsh editorial team. I owe great debt to Nicholas Thomas-Symonds for his foreword and also Graham James, who remembers Bevan from his youth and for his recollections. They add immensely to the book. Designing the book jacket: Cinnamon Design of Liverpool.

All rights reserved

Presented to Niklaus Thomas-Symonds, MP for his foreword to this book

ISBN 978-1-7393373-3-9

Typeset by Palimpsest Book Production Ltd, Falkirk, Stirlingshire

Printed and bound in Great Britain

Published by Modern Welsh Publications, Allerton, Liverpool

Aneurin Bevan in a pensive mood.

Ellen Wilkinson

Hugh Dalton

Contents

A Foreword by Nicklaus Thomas-Symonds, MP	ix
Recollections of Graham James: Ebbw Vale, Nye Bevan and myself	xii
An introduction to Aneurin Bevan the politician	xv
Tredegar and the family	1
Primary school to coalface	17
Education in London and prominence in Tredegar (1919–1929)	39
Off to Westminster	72
The young MP's vision (1929–1935)	86
The amazing marriage of Aneurin Bevan and Jennie Lee	110
Bevan continues to oppose the political establishment (1935–1945)	131
Political obstacles stand in the way of the proposed National Health Service	158
Achieving the goal: creating a National Health Service	182
Minister of Housing	204
A brave stand and socialist ideas	216
Aneurin Bevan and Wales	227
Aneurin and the Bevanites (1951–1955)	242
The new Aneurin in British politics	255
The final days of the political giant	274
An assessment of Aneurin Bevan as a politician	290
Bibliography	321
Index	337

Sir Stafford Cripps

Industrial Town of Ebbw Vale

Foreword to "Aneurin Bevan: Creator of the National Health Service": Dr D. Ben Rees

The Rt Hon Nick Thomas-Symonds, Chair of the Aneurin Bevan Society, Member of Parliament for Torfaen , and Shadow Secretary of State for International Trade

As I was growing up in the South Wales, in Blaenavon, at the head of the Eastern Valley, it was my grandmother, Olwyn Thomas, who inspired me to become Torfaen's Member of Parliament, proudly representing my home. As I railed against Conservative Governments of Margaret Thatcher and John Major closing industries and leaving communities of talented people bereft of opportunities, she told me that, whilst discussion was all well and good, if I wanted to make a difference, I should go into politics. She pointed to politicians whose achievement had changed people's lives. The name that she came back to again and again, was that of the South Wales Valleys politician whose achievement had transformed lives for her generation – and for generations to come.

I knew the name "Nye Bevan" from my earliest years, even though his life had been – cruelly - cut short twenty years before I was born. For my grandmother, his monumental achievement in creating the National Health Service had provided her and her community with reassurance that if they ever needed healthcare, it would be there for them. As the leaflet that Prime Minister Clement Attlee's Labour Government sent to every household in the country stated: "It will relieve your money worries in time of illness." This was not in any sense overstated: this was the reality of what the new NHS meant for working families across the United Kingdom.

Nye, of course, understood the enormity of the change he was bringing about. When he introduced the National Health Service Bill in 1946, he concluded his speech with characteristic eloquence:

> "I myself, if I may say a personal word, take very great pride and great pleasure in being able to introduce a Bill of this comprehensiveness and value. I believe it will lift the shadow from millions of homes. It will keep very many people alive who might otherwise be dead. It will relieve suffering. It will produce higher standards for the medical profession. It will be a great contribution towards the wellbeing of the common people of Great Britain."

Nye saw the provision of universal healthcare as the means to a more fulfilled society, of people freed from worry who could fulfil their potential. In his book, *In Place of Fear,* he put it beautifully: "Society becomes more wholesome, more serene, and spiritually healthier, if it knows that its citizens have at the back of their consciousness the knowledge that not only themselves, but all their fellows, have access, when ill, to the best that medical skill can provide."

In recent years, the NHS has – once again – demonstrated its enduring value. Our magnificent NHS staff showed a courage and commitment to caring for patients during the pandemic that drew people out onto their doorsteps to applaud them. Yet, at the same time, the NHS faces intense pressures: underinvestment by the Conservatives since 2010 and a backlog of cases caused by the necessity of prioritising covid patients are taking their toll. I will be campaigning for a new UK Labour Government to tackle this and continuing to make the case for the value of the central principle of a healthcare system available on the basis of need, not ability to pay.

There is a particular importance to this in the twenty-first century. For those, like my grandmother, who can remember what our healthcare system was like before the NHS came into being on 5 July 1948, are becoming fewer and fewer. The patchwork healthcare system provided inconsistent coverage, by postcode, and between the sexes. It favoured men as wageearners, and led to a society where conditions were, too often, not caught early enough, and, even when they were, care could be inadequate. That is what makes this biography, by D. Ben Rees, so timely. As we approach the seventy-fifth anniversary of the NHS, a new book gives the opportunity to, once again, appreciate the contribution of the post-war Minister of Health and Housing to our national politics.

D. Ben Rees' characterisation of Nye as "The Greatest Welshman of All Times" captures his significance. Millions of people, from Nye's contemporaries to future generations, have benefited from the NHS, living longer and healthier lives. Indeed, a passion for Nye and his remarkable life runs through the pages of this book: it is clear that the author has a deep affinity with his subject. As my first knowledge of Nye came from discussions with a family member, so it is for D. Ben Rees. As he puts it: "Ever since my youth, Aneurin Bevan has been a hero in my mind, mainly because an uncle of mine, Evan Rees, a seaman and a bachelor, would talk about him every time he returned home from his faraway journeys."

As in my own biography of Nye, D. Ben Rees seeks to put Nye's achievements in historic context as he is placed alongside Winston Churchill and David Lloyd George, both of whom became Prime Minister and led the country in times of war and peace. This book argues, convincingly, that "Bevan [was] in the same league as David Lloyd George and Winston Churchill." As I have previously argued, Churchill and Bevan were "two of the greatest orators in British politics, rivals with opposing ideologies who produced moments of intense hostility but also held an underlying, if sometimes grudging, respect for each other." Lloyd George's social reforms, including the National Insurance Act of 1911, mark him out, like Nye, as an architect of progressive change.

Nye did not reached the top of British politics in the sense of becoming Prime Minister. Yet, of those who have not held the highest office in the land, Nye achieved the most, and, arguably, more, than many who have actually occupied Number Ten Downing Street. Yet such a record still needs to be defended, and D. Ben Rees' work will be an important aspect of that. Each new biography opens up the possibility of attracting new audiences, and I am delighted to see that this the book is available in Welsh and English.

Whilst not every new reader will be familiar with Nye, the modern-day political landscape would have been all too familiar to him. Once again, we survey the economic mess caused by the values of a Conservative Party that favours the wealthiest. Once again, as in Nye's time, it is working people who are paying the price. Even in tough times, though, Nye was optimistic. Speaking at the Labour Party Conference in Blackpool in 1949, he told delegates that the Labour Movement should "raise its head high and look at the stars."

That was because, as Nye considered what had been achieved since the election victory of 1945, he knew that Labour Governments change lives for the better. That is the lesson of Nye's life: he was a man of power who used it to help people. I hope that, in producing this biography, D. Ben Rees will contribute to more and more people becoming familiar with what Nye achieved and how he was able to do it. This year, 2022, marks a hundred years since the Labour Party first became the Official Opposition at Westminster. In the century since, Labour has only been in power for thirty-five years, on its own or in coalition. It falls to my generation of Labour politicians to take inspiration from Nye, secure power, and change lives for the better once again.

Rt Hon Nick Thomas-Symonds MP
Abersychan, Torfaen, October 2022.

Recollections of Graham James: Ebbw Vale, Nye Bevan and myself.

My life

I was born in 1938 at 18 Mount Pleasant Square, Ebbw Vale. The Square was a collection of houses not far from the centre of town. Six were single storey, the rest two-storey. There was a road all the way round and through the middle, between the houses. Sometime during my early childhood, we moved across to live on the other side of the road and now had to cross that road to reach the outside lavatory. Toilet paper was made of squares of the daily newspaper, held with string, an early example of recycling. There was no bathroom: to have a bath, we carried the metal bathtub in from outside and set it up in front of the open fire.

My first school was Willowtown Elementary School followed by Pontygof Boys' School for one year in 1948, crossing the busy main road with traffic going down to the Steelworks. I failed the 11+ exam and attended Willowtown Secondary Modern School until I was 13 when I passed to go to Ebbw Vale Junior Technical School. I stayed there until I was 16.

I had hoped for an apprenticeship, but was not accepted for any I applied for. After signing on a few times, I managed to find work in the Steelworks as a scrapboy then moved into office work within the packing department. Off then to National Service from 1956 to 1958. On my return, it was back to the packing department. A short while later, I was offered a job in the production office.

Me leading the Providence members
parade on the Whit Walk 1952

Over the next couple of years, I enrolled in various evening and WEA courses. I applied to Coleg Harlech to study Economics, Industrial Relations and English, living and studying there from 1960 to 1962. I was secretary of the college's National Association of Labour Students Organisation and attended its national conference in Hull. I led a group of college students to canvas in the Montgomery by-election in 1962. During the campaign, I met Jim Griffiths, George Thomas and Megan Lloyd George. My contact with D Ben Rees was through 'Aneurin', the political magazine he was editing at the time, while a student at Aberystwyth University.

From Harlech I went to Smethwick and taught as an unqualified teacher before completing a teacher training course over three years in Wolverhampton. I then taught at Yate, Bristol for 8 years before moving to my first headship. My second headship came 8 years later. During this time, I married, raised my family, maintained a keen interest in sport (both playing and watching) and remained involved with my local church, being a member of the Local Ministry Team and being a Bishop's Visitor to church schools in Gloucestershire for 16 years.

Ebbw Vale

The Ebbw Vale of my childhood was a typical valley town with a strong community spirit. There were rows upon rows of houses built on the sides of the mountains.

The main source of employment was the Richard Thomas and Baldwin Steelworks (later British Steel) which at one time employed around 10,000 people. There was social and welfare provision for employees, consisting of a social club, bowls, and tennis, as well as rugby and football teams.

Ebbw Vale had a well-respected rugby team in the top section of Welsh rugby. The Ebbw Vale cricket team also played at the Welfare Ground - later Eugene Cross Park. Glamorgan C.C.C. played matches there. Ebbw Vale soccer team played in the Welsh League. At one time, there were four cinemas in the town. The town also had a Male Voice Choir and a choral society.

At Christmas time, staff of RTB would perform a pantomime for children of employees at The Palace (a cinema). I remember going to several of these as a child.

The churches and chapels were very active and took part every year in a Whit Walk. They also had their own identity and held their Anniversary Services as well as the annual outings to places such as Barry Island and Porthcawl.

Nye Bevan was one of us and his presence in the House of Commons made Ebbw Valians aware that he was representing us and speaking for us. His gift of oratory and his pride in his background made him popular both locally and on the national stage. Although he is internationally celebrated as the founder of the National Health Service, to local people, he was passionately committed to the welfare and interests of the working people of his local area

My earliest memory of Nye Bevan is from the late 1940s when I would have been about 10. I remember walking alongside him and Jennie Lee when he was on his way to speak at an open air meeting at the Mountain Top between Ebbw Vale and Tredegar, now commemorated with the Aneurin Bevan Memorial Stones. Later, I recall going to the Workman's Hall in Ebbw Vale on General Election night in 1950 or 1951 to await the results coming in - no TV coverage then. Around 1 - 2am, when the result had been announced, he came to the Workman's Hall to be greeted with delight by jubilant local people.

Some years later, in the late 1950s, I attended a meeting with a colleague, John Evans, where Nye was speaking of the attempt to discipline him over some matter. He was quick to point out to those who intended to discipline him that they had already suspended 'Standing Orders' and could therefore do nothing. Nye always knew the rules and was able to point out when they weren't being followed.

Aneurin Bevan

An introduction to Aneurin Bevan the politician

Since my youth, Aneurin Bevan has been a hero of mine. My early admiration undoubtedly stemmed from the fact my uncle Evan Rees, a seaman and a bachelor, talked about him every time he returned home from his faraway journeys. Uncle Evan stayed with my aunt in the village of Llanddewi Brefi and was totally mesmerised by the noted orator. Coincidentally, Uncle Evan died of the same illness as Aneurin a year later, in 1961. In 1960, I was a student at the Theological College in Aberystwyth. While there, my friend Arfon Jones and I published a socialist magazine embracing Welsh nationalism – we named it after Aneurin.[1]

Publishing a journal in memory of Aneurin Bevan

The magazine proved to be a breath of fresh air within the Labour Party in Wales. We had wonderful support from trade unions and officials including Tom

---

[1] An academic study may be found on the magazine by Andrew Edwards, 'Aneurin: reinventing Labour: the voices of a new generation', *Llafur,* vol. 9, no. 1 (2004), 71–84.

Jones, Shotton and Ron Mathias, Cardiff, not forgetting the Labour Party's regional secretary Cliff Prothero in the Cardiff office, Charles Street. Another Labour pioneer whose support we secured was David Thomas of Bangor; then there were James (Jim) Griffiths, MP for Llanelli and Dr Huw T. Edwards, a true friend to Aneurin Bevan, who wrote a beautiful eulogy in English for the journal.[1]

First biography on Aneurin and the review by Saunders Lewis

Aneurin Bevan became an important part of my life. In 1962, at the start of my Christian ministry in Abercynon, it was pure delight to be reading the first volume of Aneurin Bevan's biography by his successor in Ebbw Vale, Michael Foot. In this now rare 510-page volume Bevan is portrayed most favourably by his admirer. I also remember reading Saunders Lewis's fair review on the biography in the then new magazine *Barn*, in December 1962. It made a great impression on me, and I kept a copy, because Saunders Lewis says thus in his detailed analysis:

> What a shame that a Welshman didn't write him a biography. Aneurin Bevan had the gift of a genius . . . But he does not know Aneurin Bevan's background. The account of his mother and father are pitifully inadequate. The author doesn't know about the life of the Welsh non-Conformist chapels in the South Wales industrial areas.[2]

Saunders goes on to give example after example of Foot's failure to place this genius of a politician in his rightful background in Tredegar and the coalfields of South Wales. He refers to the London Labour College, and says:

> That was the generation who turned away from Welsh Mabon Unionist towards Marxism. Mabon's emphasis on the worth of the independence of the local societies within the Trade Unions was rejected. That would have been part of Mabon's Welshness, from his commitment to the Welsh culture and the Eisteddfodau, and that was an anathema to the Marxists. That is a key in understanding Aneurin Bevan's hatred of the Welsh language and culture.[4]

---

1 Huw T. Edwards, 'A pen portrait of the late Aneurin Bevan', *Aneurin*, vol. 1, no.2, 4.
2 Saunders Lewis, 'Aneurin Bevan', *Barn*, Number 2, December 1962, 35.

There is much truth in what Saunders Lewis says, but he forgets to mention that Aneurin Bevan was himself the product of the Eisteddfod movement, and that Welsh was not an unfamiliar language to him.[1]

In fact, as a young lad in Sirhowy Vale he found himself in the heartland of Eisteddfod life.[2] His father David Bevan took him under his wing. He taught Aneurin the art of translating from Welsh to English and vice versa.[3] He wrote articles in both languages and competed in the Eisteddfodau.[4] Aneurin, and a group of friends including Morgan Lewis, would often leave Sirhowy Primary School's yard without permission, wandering off to trespass on private land. Their behaviour attracted plenty of complaints from furious locals and helped give the school a bad name. At least six unruly children of the same period were in school with him.[5] It's no wonder he often got the cane; his behaviour effectively deprived him of a formal education.[6] He had to educate himself, and that is exactly what he did.

At the close of his review, Saunders Lewis says thus:

> It's a shame that nobody takes Welsh politics seriously enough to study Aneurin Bevan's career from a Welsh perspective.[7]

No truer word was ever written. I would go a step further and say that, in 60 years, nobody has written a biography of him in Welsh This was my motive for preparing in the Welsh language a biography of him that appeared. in January 2020. It was widely praised in few reviews. It deserved more of them. They never came to my annoyance. This book is my effort to produce a biography in English which should be well received for I have spend hours upon hours, days upon days and weeks upon weeks to produce it for April 2024.

---

1 NLW, Box 1/4. The papers of John Lloyd Williams (1888–1982), Member of Parliament for Kelvingrove, Glasgow (1945–1950). John Lloyd Williams (native of Pantperthog, near Corris) met with Aneurin Bevan in Cardiff in 1917. They were both miners. Lloyd Williams mentions that Aneurin, like others (for example Noah Ablett) could recall every line from John Morris Jones's translation of Omar Khayyam's poem. Aneurin and Lloyd Williams were students at the Central Labour College in London. It was there Lloyd Williams recognised his gift of being able to read Marxist literary classics in French and German.
2 Edith Passey, 'Memories of Aneurin Bevan: My Uncle', *Blaenau Gwent. Forum Journal*, Number 6, December 2009, 30.
3 *Ibid*.
4 Anonymous, 'Nye the Man they Idolised', *Western Mail*, 7 July 1960, 4.
5 Peter Morgan Jones, 'An Unruly Pupil', *Blaenau Gwent Forum Journal*, Number 6, December 2009, 26. Other unruly children like him were Rees Price, Daniel Reed, Godfrey Edwards, Absalom Price, John Medlicott, Thomas Saunders (who ran after certain girls with a knife) harmed Rose Peter
6 *Ibid*, 27. Another of Aneurin's generation is mentioned, namely David Parker, who delighted in throwing stones and earth clods at girls.
7 Saunders Lewis, 'Aneurin Bevan', *ibid.*, 35.

Comparing two politicians brought up in Monmouthshire

Aneurin should not be shunned for his Welshness, and the best way to prevent the temptation is to compare him to another important Monmouthshire politician: Roy Jenkins. Born in Abersychan in 1920, Jenkins was the son of Arthur Jenkins, a miner leader who left the coalfields to concentrate on the Labour movement.[1] Arthur Jenkins joined Monmouthshire Council, first as an employee and then as a councillor (where he served alongside Bevan in the twenties). In 1935, he became the Member of Parliament for Pontypool. On the matter of Welshness, one can see Roy Jenkins did not have the same knowledge of the natural Welsh culture of the valleys as Aneurin Bevan. It was this culture which was so much part of the lives of its citizens: the drinking clubs, rugby, pubs and nonconformist chapels. Saunders Lewis' concludes: He had no traumatic reason to turn his back on the scenes of a singularly happy childhood; but if the introverted Welsh culture of pub, rugby club and chapel had meant anything to him – why should it?[2]

To Bevan, these mentioned institutions were very familiar to him.

It was Oxford and Balliol College – and the snobbery of his mother, Harriet (née Harris) Jenkins – which changed Roy Jenkins's life. He was granted opportunities which the young lad of Tredegar had no hope of achieving. The universities of Oxford and Cambridge would open their doors widely to any young lad who supported Labour, thus Roy Jenkins left the valleys far behind him. Although he delighted in the fact that he was the child of a Labour home, he did not work for the cause like Bevan did.[3] Bevan was a pioneer of the first rank in Tredegar, placing the Labour Party as he did as a priority for his compatriots.

Roy Jenkins belonged to the generation of politicians who came to the bosom of the Labour Party because of their times at Cambridge and Oxford Universities. These same people became 'ravenous monsters' to Bevan. One who troubled him more than anyone else was Hugh Gaitskell, who fell under the spell of Labour intellectuals at Oxford. Neither did Bevan have anything to say to Douglas Jay, Patrick Gordon Walker or Roy Jenkins. Some of the others who had been in the same colleges, such as Harold Wilson and Richard Crossman, became followers of Bevan during the forties and fifties. To Bevan, there was little difference between

---

1 At the beginning of his career in Westminster, Roy Jenkins became an admirer of Bevan. He says, 'But although I was given an Attlee label, the two senior ministers who attracted me were Stafford Cripps and Aneurin Bevan'. See. Roy Jenkins, *A Life at the Centre* (London, 1991), 83.
2 John Campbell, *Roy Jenkins: A Biography* (London, 1983), 9.
3 *Ibid*, 8. 'He did not, as a boy, help with Arthur's constituency work, or go canvassing any more than Hattie did. He was deliberately distanced from that. As soon as he was old enough to form an ambition, he knew that he too should go into politics, which meant without question Labour politics.'

Labour's governing elite and the Tories. One of the few Tory leaders who did not attend Oxford or Cambridge was Winston Churchill.[1] In 1941, when Roy Jenkins attempted, for the second time, to stand as Oxford Union President, Aneurin and J. Bahadoor Singh, an Indian who had defeated Jenkins a year earlier, came to help him with a topic which was close to Bevan's heart: *'That this House does not want to hear of the Conservatives again.'* The debate was won, but the youth of Abersychan lost the leadership contest by 94 votes to 85.[2] Rather than becoming a disciple of Aneurin's, Roy Jenkins became a friend, disciple and political heir of Gaitskell. Bevan could not stand the right-wing tendency within the Labour Party. In 1951, Gaitskell, now Chancellor, cut health spending to pay for the war in Korea, imposing charges on the previously free dentures and spectacles. Bevan had no option but to resign.[3] Harold Wilson, then President of the Board of Trade, and John Freeman, the War Office Under Secretary, also resigned their posts but remained Labour MPs. These resignations cast a shadow on the remainder of the fifties for the Labour Party. The Welshman from the valleys. Roy Jenkins insisted on looking at his options carefully. As Bevan compiled articles for *Tribune*, the leftist paper which was important for the Welsh socialists of Monmouthshire (Ebbw Vale as well as Pontypool), he believed Jenkins would follow him into the political wilderness. Roy, however, was afraid of upsetting his father, not to mention the Premier Clement Attlee and Roy's newfound hero Hugh Gaitskell.

The immortality of Aneurin Bevan

Bevan immortalised himself as Minister for Health and Housing, with health being at the forefront of his achievements. The National Health Service still stands as the single most important achievement by any politician in twentieth century British politics. How true are these words uttered by a cultured Welshman: Looking back, he is seen as the single most expositor of Democratic Socialism which Wales ever produced.[4]

Bevan set his heart on battles which were relevant to every region of Britain: unemployment, poverty and injustice. He had been deprived of much of Welsh

---

1 Campbell, Roy Jenkins, 10
2 *Ibid*, 15–16.
3 According to Woodrow Wyatt, there was nothing in October 1950 which could have prevented Bevan from succeeding Attlee as leader of the Labour Party. What actually stopped him was his resignation, as he was a politician who loved Britain and who was incredibly British and proud of it., but he also was ready to rebel before apologising. See Woodrow Wyatt, 'A Magic Personality', *Sunday Times*, 10 July 1960.
4 'Aneurin Bevan (1897–1960)' [in] *Cydymaith i Lenyddiaeth Cymru*, (ed. Meic Stephens) (Cardiff, 1986), 42.

culture – his father did not listen to his wife and teach him Welsh. The Labour politician Cledwyn Hughes reminded him of the essentials in his charming way; however, it was May Harris of Ammanford who rightly identified the struggle of so many Labour politicians like Bevan. In 1943, she argued, that these socialists, namely Aneurin Bevan and her uncle Jim Griffiths, needed to be taught about Wales, its history, its culture and its problems. Then she says:

> We cannot expect an opinion nor any co-operation from them until they know more. How? Oh dear! Meetings, articles, propaganda – and all of it clashing against terrible prejudices on their side, because they'd fed on Marx and some comfortable, if vague ideas concerning nationalism.[1]

About the same time, Dr Ceinwen Thomas and Dr D. J. Davies, Pantybeiliau, Gilwern, unorthodox nationalists whose articles appeared in the the weekly Welsh language paper *Y Faner*, asked Aneurin to work for the campaign started by Plaid Cymru for the establishment of a Secretary of State for Wales. He was asked to support Welsh-medium forms to enable Welshspeaking farmers and others to claim subsidies. Housewives in the Cambrian Mountains should be provided with Welsh-language food ration books; if not, the books should at least be bilingual. There were appeals for more Welsh on the radio, and for Welsh-speaking Army personnel to be put in battalions together and not into entirely English-speaking ones.[2] Bevan politely responded to the linguist scholar Ceinwen Thomas on 6 March 1941, thanking her for having contacted him. His answer is significant and shows that Bevan, like many others, sees the nationalism of Plaid Cymru in the same light as he did the nationalism of Europe. One of the reasons for the witness of the student magazine Aneurin twenty years later was to show the dangers of such a standpoint. Here is his answer in full to Ceinwen Thomas:

> I fully appreciate what you say, but I would like to point out that although the utmost cultural autonomy and encouragement should be given to Wales, I am anxious as I am sure you are, that we should not stress those aspects of Welsh nationalism which would tend to create an irrational resurgence of National feeling which has already proved so disastrous in Europe.[3]

---

1 NLW. Papers of Gwynfor Evans. C1/3. Box 1 (May–December 1943). Letter of Mrs May Harris, 12 New Road, Ammanford to Gwynfor Evans, Llangadog, no date, but sometime in 1943.
2 NLW. Papers of Gwynfor Evans. C1/3. Box 1 (May–December 1943). Letter of Mrs May Harris, 12 New Road, Ammanford to Gwynfor Evans, Llangadog, no date, but sometime in 1943.
3 *Ibid*. Letter of Aneurin Bevan to Dr Ceinwen Thomas, dated 6 March 1941.

It is easy to understand the stance he took, and one of the tragedies of twentieth century Wales is that he ignored the pressing need for leadership in what Dr Ceinwen Thomas and others were worried about. After all, he was a politician of such intellect – the greatest health minister that Britain had seen in the twentieth century. Britain is unlikely to see a health minister of his calibre again. Subsequent appointees have had to live in his shadow, including the incumbents who have faced the Covid-19 crisis. Aneurin Bevan always had plenty of ideas; his vision was to improve the world and the lives of the ordinary people. He felt warmly towards Welsh culture, despite being denied the opportunity to be a fluent Welsh speaker. His agent, Ron Evans, sent a letter to the secretary of the Literary Society of Tafarnaubach in his constituency regretting the fact that Bevan couldn't attend the Annual Eisteddfod on 9 October 1959 because of the General Election. He took pride instead in knowing he was the Honorary President of the Tafarnaubach Eisteddfod.[1]

His speeches and sayings are memorable and it is clear his Welsh socialist philosophy steered his life from cradle to grave. In 1956, at a speech in Manchester, he said he did not wish to be leader of the Labour Party if that party was not socialist in its outlook. He knew that trade union leaders were against this viewpoint, and he had to battle both inside and outside his party with his advanced ideas; in the end he had to compromise. But through it all, Aneurin Bevan became a symbol of what it is to be a Welshman, bringing with him the convictions and principles of Welsh Nonconformity at its best.

Every Labour leader who came after Hugh Gaitskell, namely Harold Wilson, James Callaghan, Michael Foot, Neil Kinnock, John Smith, Tony Blair, Gordon Brown, Ed Miliband, Jeremy Corbyn and Sir Keir Starmer, speaks of Aneurin Bevan with admiration. Michael Foot became his biographer, Neil Kinnock was born in the same town, and Blair, Brown and the others have always championed him. There is a superficial similarity between Corbyn and Bevan; however, Bevan's oratory skills far exceed those of Corbyn and Sir Keir Starmer. Corbyn was never an intellectual but became leader of the Labour Party because there was no one from left or right to outshine him. Andy Burnham had not developed his skills then; he is much more mature in 2022 than he was in 2014. David Cameron, Theresa May and even Boris Johnson would have been slated had they faced Aneurin Bevan at the despatch box in the House of Commons. Bevan's oratory skills meant he succeeded David Lloyd George as the hero of Westminster debates. Members of Parliament of every persuasion would make sure they attended when Bevan was speaking, entranced as they were with his rich use of language, his unbelievable rhetoric and his sonorous Welsh accent. He could be impatient and, frequently

---

1 National Library of Wales (NLW). Papers of Ron Evans, Aneurin Bevan's agent, correspondence 1959–1970. Letter of Ron Evans on behalf of Bevan to the Secretary of the Eisteddfod at Tafarnau Bach, dated 9 October 1959.

exploded with anger, his words flowing like a torrent. His temperament hadn't much changed since he was a child in Tredegar. On one occasion he fell out with his parents and told them he was leaving his home in Charles Street. He duly packed his bag and opened the door, only to feel the chilly, frosty air hit his face. He stayed where he was for a moment, paralysed. Next minute, he felt his father's hand on his shoulder, commanding him gently, 'Come back to our living room, Aneurin – there's a chair waiting for you by the fire.'[1]

The story told by one of his admirers is a symbol of his tempestuous career. Bevan ventured to leave the Labour Party fold more than once, was thrown out twice, and came very close to being sacked at least twice again. Despite this, the Labour Party meant a great deal to him. The miners, steelworkers and farm servants were his people, the backbone of the Labour Party in the Tredegar of his youth. He could not turn his back on his own people, nor depart for any other party. The Labour Party leaders knew that and, because of his passion, there was a comfortable seat waiting for him in the heat of every intense debate – unfortunately it was not a leader's seat.

Comparing Aneurin Bevan with other politicians

In fact, the trade union barons made sure Aneurin Bevan didn't get that seat after Attlee's era. Bevan had personally experienced the poverty and misery that made life most difficult in the interwar years. This meant he told the union leaders and Labour technocrats the truth, sharing sobering facts. He was looked upon as a colourful, charismatic figure, but he was much more. He became an integral part of Britain's politics. After David Lloyd George's death in 1945, Bevan became the Welsh nation's hero. He was a true descendent of Keir Hardie, although he didn't mention him a great deal. They were similar pioneers, but Bevan was more of a senator than Hardie. One of his disciples in the fifties, Desmond Donnelly, MP for Pembrokeshire, compared him to Charles James Fox, the great late eighteenth-century Whig statesman and renowned orator. Others agreed. Not only were the two men quite alike in looks, but both were able to debate with verve in the House of Commons. This is what Donnelly says:

> If you read Fox's speeches and compare them with Bevan's, there is a striking similarity of style. There is the same curious sentence construction, with the point at the end. The same persecution mania was possessed by both men. Bevan, like Fox, was also a natural aristocrat. Although the miner's cottage

---

1 NLW. Papers of Desmond Donnelly. B15, 1960.

with its earth floor in Tredegar was a different starting point from the gracious rooms of Holland House.[1]

It is a shame Bevan did not publish more books; his only volume of essays is *In Place of Fear*. It is, at times, is wonderful as is his attack on the appeasers in *Why Not Trust the Tories?* From *In Place of Fear*, it's clear Bevan wasn't a Marxist thinker: the book reveals a politician who can put over his ideas clearly and forcefully. The novelist Emyr Humphreys pays Bevan this compliment as a Welsh nonconformist:

> In this sense the Welfare State is the most enduring contribution to the reforming aspirations of Welsh nonconformity to the British nation state. Indeed, Bevan's state of open rebellion and unstinting honesty made him a more sympathetic product of the Welsh nonconformist conscience than Lloyd George.[2]

The novelist and robust Welshman, Emyr Humphreys (who lived till he reached his centenary) hit the nail on the head. Bevan was more the product of nonconformist conscience than Lloyd George ever was, and whenever he failed, he readily acknowledged this. That is why, throughout his Westminster career he felt he was a lone politician. He admitted this to some of his early friends like John Strachey, and his wife Jennie Lee knew of his depression from lack of true friends. By the end of his tormented life, he acknowledged he had to accept discipline and co-operate with people to whom he did not have much to say. By then, the left-wing Messiah had come to the end of his tether. This is the opinion of the historian Keith Laybourn. He believed that Bevan had changed his view fully by the time of the 1957 Labour party conference in Brighton, criticising as he did the accepted idea of doing away with nuclear weapons. He realised that no foreign minister could, in the name of the UK government, walk nakedly to the great hall of the United Nations with the aim of trying to get the world into some order. Ultimately, one had to go there and be in possession of the horrible, deadly arms to be able to bargain with USSR and China.[3] His language was as muscular as ever, but the address and his capitulation was a cause for regret to his supporters. Aneurin Bevan, of all people, was ready to relinquish there and then all the speeches and rallies at which he had championed the uncompromising principles of the left. To his most loyal supporters, it all brought about misery, disbelief and a sense of alienation. Aneurin Bevan's influence and that of the left diminished overnight within the Labour Party.

---

1 *Ibid.*
2 Emyr Humphreys, *The Taliesin Tradition: A Quest for the Welsh Identity* (London, 1983), 213.
3 Keith Laybourn, *A Century of Labour: A History of the Labour Party* (Stroud, 2001), 104.

Bevan's failure to understand Hugh Gaitskell

Hugh Gaitskell, the product of a well-to-do middle class family, had proven to this son of a miner from the terraced house in Tredegar that his background and education at private school and Oxford University had given him advantages over a politician who was far more intelligent, knowledgeable and appealing in his speeches than the Oxbridge graduate could ever be. At New College, Gaitskell was taught by the socialist G. D. H. Cole, who encouraged him to join the Labour movement. In the party, Cole believed, Gaitskell could make his mark and he was proved right. While G. D. H. Cole became Gaitskell's mentor, Aneurin's Hitler-like headmaster at Sirhowy Primary School was caning him – on his hand and legs and back. Never had there been such a gap in experience between two politicians in the same political party in the twentieth century. And yet, like Gaitskell, Bevan carved his name in Britain's history, perhaps more than any other postwar politician from Wales. By the time he and his compatriots finished their work during what was a most difficult time in every sense, Britain had the most advanced welfare state in the world. Sweden's socialists followed the model as did Denmark and Norway (many years later).[1]

Aneurin commended the help of the Marshall Plan in order to rebuild Western Europe following the war, and he himself was very active within the inevitable limitations which existed after the Second World War. He could not support one of the great powers any more than the others. His wish was to see world politics

---

1 Donald Sassoon, *One Hundred Years of Socialism: The West European Left in the Twentieth Century* (London, 1996), 142

'moving from the division of two "blocks" around the USA and the Soviet Union'.[1] For him, there was a 'third block' which embraced the neutral countries; Bevan was the instigator of many of these ideas, which resulted in Marshal Tito of Yugoslavia embracing him.

In his huge work with the National Health Service, he insisted Wales be a separate unit from England, as was Scotland. The civil servants attempted to place North Wales with Liverpool and South Wales with Bristol.[2] Bevan was against such arrangements, which is why he established the so-called Health Board for Wales in 1946.

Bevan takes the platform at the National Eisteddfod in Ebbw Vale

During his visit to the Ebbw Vale National Eisteddfod in August 1958, Aneurin Bevan delighted in his nationality and the Welsh and Welsh-speaking culture. I shan't forget his speech on the evening of Sunday 3 August, during the Singing Festival, nor, for that matter, Paul Robeson's contribution. He mentioned that Monmouthshire's characteristics were Welsh, that there were Welsh fables to be found as part of that region's culture, and that he welcomed the reunification between Monmouthshire and Wales. He was also proud what his Labour friend Cledwyn Hughes had done in partnership with Peter Thomas to invite the local authorities to contribute annually towards the costs of staging the National Eisteddfod of Wales It had come about, as Bevan mentioned in his speech, because of the partnership of his friend Cledwyn Hughes and the then Secretary of State for Wales, the Conservative Peter Thomas.[3] Bevan prided himself on supporting the idea which was going to assist the National Eisteddfod of Wales. After his death, in 1960 the career of the rebel, the brave man, the incomparable orator whose name would live for ever, came to be analysed. The lady who ran the mountain pub where Aneurin and Jennie would go after hours of walking in the Blaenau Gwent hills maintained he kept his country spirit over the years. 'He was one of the lads' she said. 'They would be willing to die for him in these parts. Putting Bevan down was considered worse than putting one of the family down.'[4] A perfect picture of her most famous customer hung on the wall. At the pub, Aneurin would rather discuss agriculture with those who lived in the uplands than domestic or international politics. At the end of his colourful career, his standpoint combined the essence of the right (as in keeping nuclear weapons) but also

---

1 Nicklaus Thomas-Symonds, 'Golwg ar Aneurin Bevan', *National Library of Wales, Circular Letter of the Welsh Political Archive, Manifesto, 48,*16.
2 NLW. Papers of Gwilym Prys-Davies, Box 1.
3 D. Ben Rees, *Cofiant Cledwyn Hughes: Un o Wŷr Mawr Môn a Chymru* (Talybont, 2017), 59–60.
4 Martin Johnes, *Wales Since 1939* (Manchester and New York), 121.

the priorities of the left, that is, putting home issues first. But he was still Aneurin Bevan, the rebel who remains respected today by Welsh folk. The parliamentary member and philosopher Bryan Magee was ready to say at the end of Bevan's time that he was blessed with genius.[1] A politician who had the opportunity to notice him from the very first day he frequented Parliament until his death was Clement Attlee. He liked Aneurin from the opening day in 1929 for his gallantry, his gifts, his compassion, his anger and more than any of these, for his empathy with ordinary folk in their anguish, in their worries and in their doubts. Attlee did not see much of Karl Marx or Noah Ablett in him; he saw far more of Keir Hardie, Bruce Glasier and William Morris in the young Bevan. Attlee said of him:

> He embraced the poetry, the artist, the compatriot; one saw the natural aristocrat in Nye; he had seen enough of the evil of capitalism during his childhood to be able to understand why Bevan hated it.[2]

This will be seen in abundance in this biography of Aneurin Bevan.

---

[1] Bryan Magee, *Confessions of a Philosopher: A Journal through Western Philosophy* (London, 1997), 277.
[2] Kenneth Harris, *Attlee* (London, 1983), 149.

CHAPTER I

Tredegar and the family

Aneurin Bevan was born in the mining town of Tredegar, a town overflowing with enthralling history and an example of an area which was anglicised in a short period of fifty years at the end of the Victorian era. The town is located in the Sirhowy Valley next to Rhymney Valley, where the Welsh language maintained a much stronger hold on its people. There is a road from the lowest part of Rhymney town over the mountain and down to Tredegar and, from the beauty of the uplands, the stroller may see a large part of western Gwent. One can look down the valley, over Abertyswg to Cwmsyfiog and Aberbargoed. Moreover, the Blaenau Gwent region is rich with rivers, some of them immortalised by Dylan Thomas in his masterpiece *Under Milk Wood* – rivers like the Little Ebbw and Great Ebbw as well as the Rhymney and Sirhowy rivers.

Getting to know Tredegar

Tredegar is easily recognisable with its iron clock in the middle of the town. The clock was erected in memory of the Duke of Wellington; from it, the town's streets spread out in four directions. The town is a thousand feet above sea level, and much of its history is linked to another family of very wealthy soldiers, namely the Tredegars, two of whom were prominent in the Crimean War. The Tredegar family owned thousands upon thousands of acres in Monmouthshire, Glamorganshire and Breconshire. Much of this land was desolate, but some of it boasted productive, profitable coalfields. The family showed great generosity towards Tredegar and, at the beginning of the twentieth century, donated a large piece of land for a park. It was there that young Aneurin Bevan and his contemporaries enjoyed swimming and playing cricket – a game which was very close to the heart of this lively lad.

The Tredegar family also owed hundreds of houses in 65 streets including Queen, Morgan, Temple and Castle, plus Islwyn Terrace, Penuel, Pencoed, Harcourt, Heathfield and Arnold Place.[1]

Briefly we can refer to the importance of Tredegar in the realms of religion and Welsh literature. During the first half of the nineteenth century, Welsh speakers flocked in their thousands to the Monmouthshire valleys. Between 1801 and 1841, the population of Monmouthshire exceeded that of any other county in Wales and England. The vast majority of those incomers were Welsh speakers from Breconshire, Carmarthenshire, Cardiganshire, North Pembroke, Montgomeryshire and Glamorganshire. These immigrants brought their denominational zeal with them. If they came from Pembrokeshire, they built Baptist chapels; if they were from Llanidloes and Llanbryn-mair in Montgomeryshire, then they built and supported the Methodist Wesleyan Church; and if they were from Ceredigion and Carmarthenshire, they favoured Welsh Independent Chapels or those of the Welsh Calvinistic Methodists. Saron Chapel, Tredegar opened in 1820, its handsome building erected by immigrants from Carmarthenshire.

The Influence of the Blue Books

These nonconformists stood together as one when the three volume *Y Llyfrau Gleision (Blue Books)* was published in 1847. In the House of Commons, a busybody politician called William Williams – the Member of Parliament for Coventry and a fluent Welsh speaker originally from Llanpumsaint in the Carmarthenshire countryside – asked that an inspection be made concerning the state of elementary education in Wales and the provision of teaching English to working-class children. Three English-born and English-educated barristers were duly appointed by the government of the day, namely Lingen, Symons and Johnson, to undertake the inspection. The three of them did a thorough and detailed analysis of the situation; however, they were at a great disadvantage because they were monoglot Englishmen, and furthermore prejudiced churchmen of their times. The Welsh folk and the children who frequented the nonconformist chapels were much more conversant in Welsh rather than English and, as a result of unsubstantiated evidence, these commissioners reported back that Welsh speakers were as a whole an irresponsible, ignorant, then a superstitious group of people.

Without doubt, there was an element of truth in the accusations, but the blame was almost entirely laid on the shoulders of the nonconformist leaders and lay

---

1 *Western Mail*, 29 December 1915, 1.

folk as well as the Welsh language speakers.[1] Two of the most prominent campaigners against the report were connected with Tredegar.[2] The first defender of the Welsh was the Revd. David Rhys Stephen ('Gwyddonwyson' 1807–52). A fine orator, he was brought up in Tredegar with the Welsh Baptists. He was ministering in Manchester as an exile at the time of the report, but he travelled throughout Wales, fiercely debating and condemning its findings. The other nonconformist firebrand was the Evan Jones better known as Ieuan Gwynedd, minister of Saron Welsh Independent Chapel since July 1845.[3] Ieuan Gwynedd represented the nonconformists at their very best. Articulate and seriously minded despite suffering constantly from TB, he was an asset to the chapel witness. His life was all too short, but his legacy as a supporter of women's rights is now greatly appreciated by historians and socialists.

Tredegar was blessed with a host of mighty nonconformist chapels and powerful preachers who came from all over Wales to strengthen the radical welsh witness. Powerful propagandists such as Samuel Roberts, from Llanbryn-mair, and Dr Owen Thomas, of London, and later Liverpool, visited local ministers and preached in Tredegar and the surrounding districts of Rhymney, Tafarnaubach, Hengoed and Bedwellty. The gregarious Robert Ellis ('Cynddelw' 1810–75) ministered for fifteen years with the Welsh Baptists, from 1847 to 1862 at Sirhowy. He was a most multi-gifted gentleman, with a strong constitution, wit, and an unique social vision.[4] Indeed, he verged on being a genius, despite being twenty years of age before he learnt to read and write his native tongue. He, with the assistance of William Williams ('Caledfryn') and William Roberts ('Nefydd') were prominent Liberals within a radical, religious as well as the humanitarian societies of the day.

These men were Tredegar's strongest characters until the birth of Aneurin Bevan. Everyone was afraid of Caledfryn's ready and extremely biting tongue.[5]

The preservation of culture became a priority for these nonconformist chapel

---

1 To his great disappointment, Aneurin Bevan's home town was named after Tredegar, the home of the Morgan family who created a huge estate around Coedkernew (Coedcernyw) on the outskirts of Newport. Tredegar town, thirty miles to the north, was named after Tredegar iron works which was established in 1799 on land given on lease by the Tredegar estate.

2 Ben G. Owens, 'David Rhys Stevens ('Gwyddonwyson') 1807–52' in *Y Bywgraffiadur Cymreig hyd 1940* (London, 1953), 866–7

3 Geraint H. Jenkins, 'Ieuan Gwynedd: Eilun y Genedl' in *Brad y Llyfrau Gleision*. (Gol. Prys Morgan) (Llandysul, 1991), 101–124; S. J. Jones, 'Ieuan Gwynedd: Ei Fywyd a'i Waith' (Unpublished MA dissertation University of Wales, 1931); National Library of Wales, The Papers of Ieuan Gwynedd; Brinley Rees, *Ieuan Gwynedd, detholiad o'i ryddiaith* (Caerdydd, 1957) (Llyfrau Deunaw); C. Tawelfryn Thomas, *Cofiant Darluniadol mewn Rhyddiaith a Chân, i'r Diweddar Barch Evan Jones (Ieuan Gwynedd)* (Dolgellau, 1909).

4 J. T. Jones, 'Robert Ellis' ('Cynddelw'; 1810–75), *Y Bywgraffiadur Cymreig hyd 1940*, 196–7.

5 Gwilym Rees Hughes, 'Astudiaeth o Feirniadaeth Newydd a Glasurol Caledfryn' (PHD Thesis University of Wales 1975); Gwynne Jarvis, 'Cysylltiadau Llenyddol Caledfryn a'i Waith fel Bardd a Beirniad' (MA dissertation University of Wales, Aberystwyth, 1976).

leaders in Tredegar as for the rest of Wales. They had mixed views about the Welsh language; English was the language of commerce and was thus a necessary means of communication. Music was important to these chapel-minded steelworkers and miners, shopkeepers and craftsmen along with literature, and especially poetry. One literary figure born in Tredegar was William Williams ('Myfyr Wyn' 1849–1900). He was a blacksmith by profession, based at Sirhowy steelworks. A volume of his poetry was published under the title *Gwreichion yr Eingion* in Tredegar in 1877.[1]

A gathering of Welsh language poets in Tredegar and Sirhowy would meet together regularly , they included Joseph Bevan ('Gwentydd'), Ezekiel Davies ('Gwentwyson'), Evan Powell ('ap Hywel Llyfr Wyn'), John Davies ('Ossian Gwent') and William Thomas, ('Islwyn'), one of Gwent's most famous poets in the nineteenth century. Ossian Gwent was an excellent lyricist, a member of the cultured working class.

The violent clash between the Irish and Welsh in the town

During the second half of the nineteenth century, there was further migration, this time from England and Ireland. As the years progressed, there were frequent skirmishes between the Welsh and the Irish; 1882 was a year of devastating violence in the town.[2] The fighting began on the evening of Saturday 8 July and continued throughout the following afternoon and evening. Some of the unruly Welsh threw stones at the homes of the Irish, with the drunken contingency managing to break windows and even front doors.[3] Having destroyed the doors, some went into Irish homes and threw the furniture and other valuable items onto the street. The authorities had no choice but to call on the Royal Welch Fusiliers to come in haste from Newport, Cardiff and even Pembroke Dock in Pembrokeshire to maintain order on Tredegar's streets. By the time the first soldiers arrived, at least seventy houses belonging to the Irish community had been badly damaged, and over a hundred other homes had suffered slightly less intimidating attacks. After the violence, most of the Irish families decided to move to Cardiff where they were provided with shelter in a workhouse.[4] According to the authorities, one reason for the violence

---

1 D. Myrddin Lloyd, 'William Williams ('Myfyr Wyn'; 1849–1900)', *Y Bywgraffiadur Cymreig hyd 1940*, 1019.
2 Jon Parry, 'The Tredegar Anti-Irish Riots of 1882, *Llafur*, vol. 3, no. 4, 20– 23.
3 H. O. 144/100/A18568. Letter by Chief Constable of Monmouthshire to the Home Office.
4 Attention is drawn to the incident by one of one of the early Irish historians in Britain. See John Denvir, *The Irish in Britain* (Liverpool, 1891), especially chapter XXLV.

was that Irish men were perceived to be taking work from the local Welsh workers in the steel and coal mining industries – the Welsh could be as prejudiced against incomers as any other nation. This war song, full of prejudice, was often sung in Tredegar and indeed all over South and West Wales:

> O claddwch y Gwyddelod
> Naw troedfedd yn y baw,
> Ac arnynt rhowch yr helaeth
> O ffrwyth y gaib a'r rhaw,
> Ac arnynt rhoddwch feini
> A rheiny o dan sêl, Rhag ofn i'r diawled godi
> A phoeni'r oes a ddêl.[1]

Translated it means:

> Oh bury ye the Irish
> Some nine feet under the soil, Upon them put a-plenty
> Of stuff from pick and shovel,
> And on them place the boulders
> And seal them nice and tight, In case the blighters worry
> The age to come with fright.

Living conditions for Welsh, English and Irish miners and steelworkers were primitive and basic. In fact, many Welsh families were tempted to emigrate in search of a better life than Tredegar could offer.[2] Among those who left was James D. Davis who became a key politician in the United States and another celebrity in Tredegar's political gallery. James Davies (that was the spelling of his surname when he lived in Wales) was just seven years old when he left Tredegar for the United States of America, a country he hardly knew of its existence.[3] James' father and his grandfather had suffered enough humiliation at the steelworks. They worked day after day for a small salary, and would comfort each other by saying to each other, 'Don't expect life to be a gift to you' Than the other would say:' What you own is what you have to work for with your own hands.'

---

1 Quoted in J. Geraint Jenkins, *Drefach Felindre and the Woollen Industry* (Llandysul, 1976), 25.
2 Charles Evans Hughes's father was a native of Tredegar and the son stood for the 1916 election for the Presidency of the United States. He was beaten by 4,000 votes.
3 Suzanne Twiston-Davies, 'James J. Davis – Iron Puddler and Senator of Pennsylvania', *Transactions of the Honourable Society of Cymmrodorion*, 1983, 184–185.

Tredegar family emigrates to the United States of America

James Davies was born on 27 October 1873. Growing up in Tredegar with his brothers, life was sweet. He felt like a bird in a nest, and he would be woken up every morning by the songcall of his mother. It was her voice which was his sheer delight. He would play with his friends from morning until night before he entered the primary school. This idyllic Welsh world was smashed to pieces when the grandfather persuaded the family to emigrate in search of a better life. In April 1881, a year before the Irish riots in Tredegar, the Davies family arrived in New York. Due to the fact James' father could not read or write; his surname was spelt by an immigration official as Davis. That is how the bright lad James J. Davis was known from then until the day he died.[1] As his mother shed tears over Tredegar and Sirhowy when she arrived in New York, her treasures were stolen at the dockside by thieves who saw their opportunity. Witnessing his mother's grief made James determined to succeed in the new world for his mother's sake. He left school at eleven and went to work as an iron puddler in Sharon, Pennsylvania. Like many Welsh exiles, James Davis became successful in the political arena. President Harding chose him as Secretary for the Labour Service, and he continued in the job under both Presidents Coolidge and Hoover. James was later elected Senator for Pennsylvania and when he died on 22 November 1947, numerous Welsh flags was seen hovering in the sky over erous settlements connected with his life in the United States. In the same way as there was Prime Minister material in Aneurin Bevan, it was possible for many to see James J. Davis as a potential President of the United States. His epitaph read thus:

> I have been a puddler of iron and I would be a puddler of men. Out of the best part of the iron, I helped build a stronger world.[2]

While families like the Daviess were leaving Tredegar, other families were moving to live in the town, and that is what happened to Aneurin Bevan's family on his father's side.

---

1 W. Arvon Roberts, 'Cyfunydd Archdderwydd America', *Y Casglwr*, Number 121, Winter Edition, 2017, 17.
2 James J. Davis, US Secretary of Labor, *The Iron Puddler, My Life in the Rolling Mills and what became of it* (Pennsylvania, 1922).

The attraction of Tredegar to Bevan's family

Aneurin's grandfather hailed from Breconshire and his grandmother Margaret was born in Carmarthenshire (in 1822). According to 1861 Census, his grandfather was employed at the steelworks.[1] They had four children. William, born in 1847 in Merthyr Tydfil, later worked as an iron miner like his father. Sometime between 1847 and 1853, the family of three moved from Merthyr to Tredegar where another son, John was born in in 1853.[2] Then a daughter called Ann was born in 1856 and Aneurin's father David came along in 1860. His mother's family had also moved to Tredegar, and it was there that Phoebe Prothero was born in 1864. She married miner David Bevan in 1889 and the couple went on to have ten children, all born at home at 7 Charles Street (the family later moved to 32 Charles Street). The majority of the children were given Welsh names: Blodwen, Myfanwy, Aneurin, Iorwerth, Idris and Arianwen. The others were named David John, William George, Margaret May and Herbert Luther. David John died aged eight, and Herbert Luther also passed away during his childhood. Iorwerth and Idris were twins, but Idris died at birth.[3] Aneurin Bevan was born at 32 Charles Street and was named after the Welsh language poet Aneurin Fardd (Aneurin Jones) who edited the magazine *Bedyddiwr* (Baptist) while living in Monmouthshire. It was published it in the cellar of the Half Way Inn in Pontllanfraith.[4] Aneurin Fardd travelled around Wales visiting eisteddfodau as both a bard and adjudicator. Eventually, the poet emigrated to the United States, spending time in New York before moving to California. He died in Los Angeles.

A portrait of David Bevan, a cultured miner

It is doubtful that David and Phoebe Bevan ever met Aneurin Fardd but they knew of him. The information was basically presented to them through David's literary circles, his relationship with the Baptist chapels and his membership of the Cymmrodorion Society. David Bevan, the staunch nonconformist, was a Welshman through and through, according to the standards at the beginning of the twentieth century. Phoebe pressed him to speak Welsh to the children at home but this did not happen as confirmed in the 1911 Census. David Bevan admitted sadly that he

---

1 Research into the 1861 Election by the author.
2 *Ibid.*
3 Michael Foot, *Aneurin Bevan: A Biography, Volume I: 1897–1945* (London, 1962), 19.
4 Saunders Lewis, 'Aneurin Bevan', *Barn*, Number 2, December 1962, 35.

was the only fluent Welsh speaker in the home.¹ This was a sad acknowledgment when one considers his commitment to Welsh culture and his love of the lyrics of the poet John Ceiriog Hughes (1832–1887). He taught his brood to sing and play the piano, praising them and pressing a sixpence into their hands whenever they performed well on stage at the penny readings at Carmel, and other town chapels, where these little eisteddfodau were regularly held. His father passed onto Aneurin a lifetime love and interest in music; however, he himself was never a natural musician. David Bevan, on the other hand, was an enthusiast at every local eisteddfod, and also competed in the literary competition. He won prizes for penning lyrics in praise of creation and the town of Tredegar, which was so close to the hills of Monmouthshire. When his favourite Aneurin was born on 15 November 1897, there were fields at the far end of Charles Street and a charming, clear river nearby, which was brimming with fish.² The miners' houses were usually whitewashed every spring or were sometimes in pink.³

Aneurin was an adventurous child, by the time he started primary school, he and his friends were climbing Bedwellty mountain and Cefn Man-moel. The neighbouring farms with their Welsh names were a stark reminder of the days when the Welsh language was spoken by the majority of the local population. The landscape remained important to him throughout his adult life.

When the Anglican traveller Reverend William Coxe travelled to Tredegar at the beginning of the nineteenth century, he needed the aid of a Welsh speaker to help him converse with local people whose first language was Welsh.⁴ Aneurin Bevan grew up knowing Welsh speakers were once in the majority in his area. He never had any difficulty in pronouncing the rather lovely sounding place names around his town, such as Troedy-rhiw-gwair, Pen-rhiw-ffawyddog, Pen-yr-heol-las, Croespen-maen, Argoed and Pont-y-Coedcau. He noticed the adults were ready to place an English name such as Blackwood on the village rather than the Welsh version of Coed Duon. David Bevan was an avid reader (he received several Welsh periodicals) and a great lover of culture. He could frequently lose himself in the

---

1 Thomas Jones, one of Rhymney's brightest sons, said of his family: 'From what I understand, we spoke Welsh at home until I was six years old, but as the children went to school, the language of the family turned to English, keeping Welsh solely for the purposes of religion.' This was a pattern to be found in almost every family in Blaenau Gwent. See Mary Wiliam, 'Myfyr Wyn, Aneurin Bevan a fi: atgofion plentyndod ac astudio, tafodaiaith yn Sirhywi, Sir Fynwy', *Llafur Gwlad*, no.135, February 2017, 18–21. Thomas Jones's quotation comes from pages 19–20.
2 T. I. Ellis, *Crwydro Mynwy* (Llandybie, 1958), 32.
3 *Ibid*.
4 *Ibid*, 43. The natives wore red shirts like the Garibaldi soldiers of Italy, not to compliment him but because the shirts were warm and comfortable, thus keeping the atrocious cold weather and running noses at bay. These shirts could be worn for a whole year without having to wash them. They were shirts suitable for the cold winds of the mountains and especially for those who dug in the very depths of the earth, or the 'Black Land', as it was called.

poetry of Aneurin Fardd, Ceiriog, William Thomas (Islwyn) and his fellow minister, Reverend Evan Rees (Dyfed).¹ David realised early on that he had children who were ready to follow in his footsteps, particularly Aneurin, and later, Arianwen. Working down the mines was not an easy job, but he would get much consolation from the congregational singing and music in the home, in the poems he wrote (some of them love poems to Phoebe), from Welsh and English literature, and especially the work of local bards.

He made sure he bought *Tannau Twynog* when it was published in 1904. The volume of poems was by Thomas Twynog Jeffreys (1844–1911) of Rhymney, someone he personally socialised with. In fact, David Bevan would travel from Tredegar to buy his best footwear at Twynog's shoe shop at 97 High Street, Rhymney. He would quote the verse in Welsh to be found in the shop window:

Pawb sydd am eu traed yn sych,
Yma cewch esgidiau gwych.
Rhai i blant, ac i bob oed,
*Fel bo hyd a lled y troed.*²

This verse can be translated:

All those who wish for feet that
are dry Come here for excellent
shoes to try. Some for children,
for every estate, As length and
width of foot dictate.

David Bevan had a wide circle of Welsh-speaking friends in Tredegar and Sirhowy. One of these was Alderman Ben Phillips (1848–1908), who was originally from Whitland in West Wales but became an important Monmouthshire politician.³ He was the first chairman of Tredegar District Council, a member for Sirhowy on the county council and subsequently became the chair of Monmouthshire Council. He lent tremendous support to primary and secondary education and to the success

---

1 Edgar Phillips, 'Aneurin Fardd: 1822–1904' in *Bywgraffiadur Cymreig hyd 1940*; Meurig Walters, *Islwyn – Man of the Mountain* (The Islwyn Memorial Society, 1983); Hugh Bevan, 'Islwyn, bardd y Ffin' in *Beirniadaeth Lenyddol: erthyglau wedi'u dethol a'u golygu* gan Brynley F. Roberts (Caernarfon, 1982), 100–110; R. L. Griffiths, 'Coffáu Islwyn ac adnewyddu'r ddelw ohono, *Barn* 185 (1978), 337–8; Beti Rhys, *Dyfed: bywyd a gwaith Evan Rees, 1850–1923* (Denbigh, 1984).
2 A conversation with his granddaughter, Mrs Jeffreys Jones, at her home in Ystrad Mynach in 1964.
3 Alderman Ben Phillips (1853–1908), Hawthorne House, Sirhowy, *Pontypool Free Press*, 7 February 1908, 5. Aneurin Bevan knew his sons, Dr Nat Phillips, Abergavenny Mental Hospital and T. W. E. Phillips, a solicitor in Tredegar.

of the Liberal Party. As far as his religion goes, he was active with the Welsh Independents, being secretary of Ebeneser Chapel, Sirhowy.[1]

One key figure of the Monmouthshire coalfield was William Thomas, Sirhowy, who was district secretary to the Tredegar Miners' Federation. For thirty years, he acted as check weigher at the Bedwellty Colliery. He supported the Wesleyan Methodist Sunday school and was superintendent for a quarter of a century. He was known as a chapel-orientated Liberal, although by the end of his life, he favoured the Labour-Liberal coalition, or the Lib-Lab as it was called.[2]

Another colourful character was Henry Bowen (1842–1917), a miner whose Welsh background meant everything to him. Truth be known, he never mastered the English tongue. He was a Liberal all his life, and he could be very reactive in his ideas at times.[3] It was within the mining sphere and the Welshspeaking world that David Bevan came to know him. Bowen was sincere and loyal in his nonconformist religion, and opposed dictatorship, either in the colliery or in distant lands. Bowen did not try and stay within the Lib-Lab group; however, he did have a particularly keen interest in the Cymmrodorion Society of Tredegar and was the deacon of Adulam Baptist Chapel. Another prominent Welshman with the Cymmrodorion was David Aggex, an elder at Penuel, Presbyterian Church of Wales in Tredegar.[4]

David Bevan, Henry Bowen, David Aggex and others like them rose early – David Bevan would catch the 5.30 a.m. train to the Tŷ Trist Colliery, the first of its kind to be sunk adjacent to the farm of the same name. By the end of the nineteenth century, Tredegar was a busy place and boasted many thriving collieries. In 1891, the population of Tredegar had increased to 18,497 and the town had swallowed up the small villages of Troed-rhiw-gwair and Georgetown. Trefil depended on the quarry and remained separate. The Anglican church had a massive infrastructure, but even then, it could not compete with the huge number of chapels being built by every nonconformist denomination: there were some thirty nonconformist chapels in the town. Two were enormous, in size (each could easily seat 1,000 people) and membership: Penuel, the Calvinistic Methodist massive temple and Siloh, the Welsh-language independent chapel. With the iron industry in decline since 1857, coal mining had taken over as the main form of employment. By the end of the century, Tredegar, along with Newport, was one of the biggest towns in the county.

---

1 *Ibid*.
2 'Death of W. Thomas, Sirhowy', *Monmouth Guardian and Bargoed and Caerphilly Observer*, 15 September 1916.
3 Susan E. Demont, 'Tredegar and Aneurin Bevan: A Society and its Political Articulation, *1890–1924*', Unpublished PhD., University of Wales, Cardiff, 1990, 66. This dissertation is an important study and I have read it carefully.
4 *Ibid,* 80.

Economic success

1897, the year of Aneurin Bevan's birth, was a year of glad tidings for Tredegar. The town's Steel and Coal Company managed to secure an agreement with the Northern Ireland Railway Company to export 600,000 tons of the best steam coal, and on top of that, Abertysswg coal pit had been sunk in the Rhymney Valley.[1] Tredegar Steel and Coal Company owned four profitable pits: Tŷ Trist, Whitworth, Bedwellty and Pochin. By 1906, every one of them was making a massive profit for the company.

The Religious Revival of 1904-6

Between 1904–1906 Wales and Merseyside witnessed the religious revival associated with the young miner from Loughor near Llanelli, Evan Roberts.[2] Having previously worked at a pit in the Loughor area, Roberts was studying for the Christian ministry with the Calvinistic Methodists at a preparatory college in Newcastle Emlyn. He underwent an emotional religious conversion at Blaenannerch chapel some four miles from Cardigan in 1904 and within two months 'the divine flame of fire', as it was called, was to be heard in chapels of the mining communities of South Wales.[3] . David Bevan thought the world of Evan Roberts, and was disappointed that the mystic revivalist did not visit some of Tredegar's chapels. Instead, Bevan took some of his children, including Aneurin, along to the prayer meetings which were held in Penuel and other chapels. There were fervent prayers in these meetings and wonderful emotional hymn singing. The Welsh revival had been a phenomenon which Bevan would mention from time to time, but he himself had not come under its spell. At least, he does not mention the phenomenon, as Jim Griffiths does in his book Pages from Memory. The experiences in Ammanford to him and his brothers especially Gwilym who was converted and the other brother D R Griffiths the poet known as Amanwy is amply analysed.

---

1 *Ibid,* 19 June 1897.
2 You find important facts and dates relating to the life and ministry of Evan Roberts by D. M. Phillips, *Evan Roberts, the Great Welsh Revivalist, and his work* (Dolgellau, 1923).
3 D. Ben Rees, *Chapels in the Valley: A Study in the Sociology of Welsh Nonconformity* (Upton, 1975), 151–173; idem, *The Revival of 1904–5: The Visit of Evan Roberts to Anglesey in 1905* (Llangoed, 2005), 107; C. R. Williams, 'The Welsh Religious Revival, 1904–5', *The British Journal of Sociology,* iii (London, 1952), 242 ff.; Basil Hall, 'The Welsh Revival of 1904–5, a critique (in) *'Popular Belief and Practice, Studies in Church History'* (Editors: C. J. Cumming and Derek Baker), Vol 8 (Cambridge, 1972), 291–301; David Jenkins, *The Agricultural Community in south west Wales at the turn of the Twentieth Century* (Cardiff , 1971), 219–244.

A by-election

During the revival, a by-election was held in the West Monmouth constituency. It was a Liberal seat, and one of the party's prominent politicians, William Harcourt, was duly elected as Parliamentary Member in 1895.[1] Harcourt didn't have much interest in the electorate, and only met his supporters in the mainly English-speaking constituency (only 30% of the electorate could speak Welsh) once in eighteen months. In comparison, around 70% of Rhymney residents were Welsh speaking, but only 28.1% of Tredegar's population could converse in Welsh by 1901 (this fell to 19.7% in the 1911 Census). When David Lloyd George, one of the rising stars of the Liberal party, visited Monmouthshire in 1895, he made his anguish about the dismal state of the language clear. He voiced his sharpest comments about the town of Tredegar. To him, it was a half-English town, its inhabitants showing virtually no enthusiasm for Welsh causes and ideals. He wrote back to his wife Margaret in Criccieth, 'Here the people have sunk into a morbid football ism.'[2]

There were exceptions to the rule – individuals like David Bevan – but they were in the minority. Monmouthshire was looked upon as being part of England rather than Wales, and it was a great disappointment to Lloyd George that a branch of Cymry Fydd had not been established in Tredegar – a movement which had been founded by London Welsh folk in 1886 along the same lines as of Young Ireland.

Lloyd George was expecting a great deal from Tredegar's up and coming sons and daughters. Many of the local Liberals attended the tumultuous meeting in Newport in January 1896, where divisions appeared in the ranks of the Liberal Party between the representatives of the anglicised districts such as Tredegar, Cardiff, Newport, Barry, Swansea and the remainder of Welsh speaking Wales, , that is the heartland of . West, Mid Wales, and Northwest Wales where Lloyd George was a hero.[3]

In 1904, the miners found they had a more conducive representative in Sir William Harcourt's successor, the Liberal Tom Richards (1859–1931).[4] Richards was a miner

---

1 Ian Machin, 'Sir William Harcourt, 1827–1904' in *Dictionary of Liberal Biography* (chief editor Duncan Brack) (London, 1998), 164–67. 'Harcourt was defeated at Derby General Election, (July 1895), but once again a Liberal was ready to stand down in his favour, and West Monmouthshire became his new constituency.'

2 Kenneth O. Morgan, *Lloyd George Family Letters* (Cardiff, 1972), 91.

3 See 'Cymry Fydd' in *Cydymaith i Lenyddiaeth Cymru* (Ed. Meic Stephens) (Cardiff, 1986), 117–18. Further details may be found in William George, *Cymry Fydd: Hanes y Mudiad Cenedlaethol Cyntaf* (Liverpool, 1945) and Kenneth O. Morgan, *Rebirth of a Nation: Wales 1880–1980* (Oxford, 1981).

4 An important article for the background and the period was written by Professor David Smith, 'Leaders and Led' in *Rhondda Past and Future* (Rhondda (no date), 37–65.

and an agent, and a pioneer of the South Wales Miners' Federation from its inception in 1898. His chapel-orientated character combined several appealing characteristics for the majority of Tredegar's Liberals: he was a fluent Welsh-speaker, he promoted Temperance, he was a member of Monmouthshire Council, and he was one of the main leaders of the South Wales Miners' Federation.[1]

Aneurin Bevan's mother

David Bevan was fortunate in his family life, in particular in his wife, Phoebe Prothero. It was Phoebe who did the organising and the disciplining at home and she was ambitious for her children, despite the lack of resources to support them.

Phoebe's father was John Prothero, a happy-go-lucky character born in a relatively affluent home at Glasbury, Breconshire in 1818.[2]

John Prothero married Margaret, who hailed from the same county and who had been born in 1826. They had four daughters: Mary Ann was born in 1849 and Alma followed in 1855. The family of four moved from Breconshire to Tredegar between 1855 and 1860 and lived at 8 New Pits Street. Elizabeth was born in the town in 1860 and Phoebe in 1864. By 1871, Mary Ann Prothero was working at the coal mine while Alma was doing labouring work; Elizabeth and Phoebe were still at school.[3]

It appears that John Prothero was a blacksmith, and as in the case of Jim Griffiths' father in West Wales, there was plenty of work for them. Blacksmiths were needed for fitting horseshoes and putting nails in miners' shoes. Phoebe Prothero had quite a comfortable home background, with her ancestors hailing from Herefordshire. In fact, her great grandfather had served as sheriff of that county. As a mother and wife, Phoebe was well liked by her neighbours. She was a determined lady with a strong mind and outlook. Phoebe ruled the family with a combination of love and discipline. None of her children, not even Aneurin, dared to argue with her. A typical valleys housewife, she got up at five in the morning to get her chores done. She kept the home clean, prepared nutritious meals, washed the dirty coal-covered clothes daily and ironed them to perfection. None of the children went without enough to eat, even during the most dreary and difficult of days. On top of all this, she was well-dressed and found time to make clothes for everyone in the home; she was what is commonly known as a seamstress and was extremely skilled.

Phoebe employed young girls as apprentices during the early years of her marriage.

---

1 J. H. Morris and L. J. Williams, *The South Wales Coal Industry 1841– 1875* (Cardiff, 1958); Philip N. Jones, *Colliery Settlement in the South Wales Coalfield, 1850 to 1926* (Hull, 1969).
2 Michael Foot, *Aneurin Bevan: A Biography, Volume I: 1897–1945*; ibid, 18.
3 *Ibid*.

A half dozen apprentices would be seen in the best room, learning the art of sewing and preparing patterns and other ambitious plans, as well as producing skirts that sold extremely well. As the family expanded in number, she had to curtail the amount of material she bought and sold. Eventually, Phoebe gave up on her business commitments and concentrated fully on her duties as a mother and housewife. Her one great aim was that each child born to her and David should be dressed in their Sunday best for the chapel services and Sunday school activities. In this way, she set the standard for all other mothers in the street.

Phoebe would buy food wisely, investing in a big joint of bacon, and a tub of butter weighing twenty pounds, in order to save money. She enjoyed the occasional shopping trip to Bristol, Newport or Cardiff. She had a comfortable utility room full of clothes she had bought for the family. In 1906, David and Phoebe made the vital decision to move from number 32 to 7 Charles Street. Their existing home just wasn't big enough for their growing family and they'd saved sufficient money in the meantime to be able to buy number 7 for the sum of £130. Their new home had seven rooms and David Bevan built an extra room for George Prothero, Phoebe's brother. He was a 52-year-old bachelor.[1] George also worked down the mines, and by paying for his lodging, he was able to contribute substantially to the family weekly bills.

David Bevan was in his element in his new larger home, for he loved gardening and loved to look after the dozen hens who provided eggs for breakfast. He also gained some cash by mending his family as well as his neighbours shoes. David Bevan improved the new house in the first year by adding a bathroom and toilet and then placed an organ into the front room for the purpose of a family hymn-singing session on a Sunday night. He would invite every one of the family to gather round the organ to sing the hymns of Zion, both in Welsh and in English. Every Sunday morning and evening, he would walk to Carmel Baptist Chapel in Dukestown with a few of his eldest children. Bevan was always in his element when he was walking home in the company of some of the deacons and discussing, with deep understanding, the message of the preacher. In a nutshell, this sums up Aneurin Bevan's upbringing in the Nonconformist tradition.

Phoebe made sure that each of her children had a duty to perform; Aneurin was asked to slice and butter the bread. She also insisted each child arrived promptly at the dinner table and did not bring street gossip with them from their friends. Ministers, deacons and town leaders looked forward to the occasional invitation to lunch or tea at 7 Charles Street. Mrs Phoebe Bevan had the gift of producing a spread and baking the most delightful delicacies while her husband had the gift of entertaining the dignitaries.

---

1 Census of 1911, research by the author. Michael Foot uses the word uncle for him. *Ibid*, 19

Phoebe ruled her family, as the book of Proverbs states, with calmness. Like the protestant hero Martin Luther, she believed cleanliness was indeed next to godliness. It was a cause of regret to her that some of the youngest children, Aneurin included, had to sleep three, sometimes four in a bed. To her that was a sign of poverty that she detested.

The background of Phoebe Bevan

Phoebe Bevan

Phoebe left school at the age of nine, and so wasn't very literate.[1] She turned the pages of the family Bible with awe; however, the scriptures was a difficult task to read, and on occasion, impossible to understand. Her one wish in life was that her children would have better educational advantages than she or her husband had received. In that respect, David and Phoebe were sorely disappointed in the education that most of their children received. Their son Aneurin Bevan received a disappointing time in the primary school. Bearing in mind his unbelievable prowess as politician and a minister of state, it is a tragedy that Aneurin was not better

---
1 Michael Foot, *ibid*, 19.

served. His education stemmed from his home and the Sunday School. He he spent hours at his local library with his father. Father and son were avid readers. More than anything, David made sure Aneurin Bevan was brought up in the ambience of the chapel, Sunday school and the world of the Welsh *eisteddfod*. It is sheer folly to forget that background, the Welsh language and its culture.[1] The same thing could be said of Aneurin Bevan, the boy, as was said of another great politician, David Lloyd George: Religion was the chief intellectual interest among the villagers at large. They were nearly all Nonconformist Methodists, Baptists or Independents. The extempore sermons of their local preachers were their weekly treat and subsequent theme of discussion and analysis. Their most familiar songs – and singing has from prehistoric times been the favourite artform and pastime of the Welsh – were their Welsh hymns, set to poignant, nerve-tightening tunes, plaintive or exultant, but never staled or prosaic, and sung in parks with adventurous harmonies.[2]

This was the heritage experienced by Aneurin Bevan, and he became a symbol of what it is to be a Welshman and a socialist.[3] As a man, Bevan helped to put Tredegar on the map. In 1846, one of the Blue Book deputies asked a schoolboy in the town what was the capital of Great Britain, and he answered 'Tredegar'.[4] This was far from the truth in 1846; however, by 1946, the boy's answer would have been quite acceptable if one considered the contribution of the gifted men of that town, and specifically the boy who was born at 32 Charles Street, Tredegar.

---

1 This is a sentence relating to the period with regard to Aneurin Bevan in *Cydymaith i Lenyddiaeth Cymru*, (Cardiff ,1986), 41: 'He was brought up in Tredegar, within the atmosphere of the chapel and the eisteddfod; and he was named after Aneurin Fardd (Aneurin Jones; 1822–1904), but he was a man who developed a dual relationship with his native country.'
2 Thompson, Malcolm , David Lloyd George (London, 1948), 52.
3 Kevin Williams, 'The End is not Mine', *Planet*, 127, February/March 1998, 38.
4 Siân Rhiannon Williams, 'Y Brad yn y Tir Du: Ardal Ddiwydiannol Sir Fynwy a'r Llyfrau Gleision' in *Brad y Llyfrau Gleision, ibid*, 125–145. The reference is on page 135.

CHAPTER 2

From primary school to coalface

At the beginning of the twentieth century there were eight schools in Tredegar and Sirhowy.[1] The choice was narrower for the Bevan children because their parents were nonconformists, so the school in Earl Street was Catholic and the priests would not grant places to non-Catholic children. The probable choice for the parents lay between the school in Earl Street and Sirhowy. The school in Sirhowy was built in 1877 with an endearing teacher called Lilah Lewis looking after the infants while the headmaster of the primary school was William E. Orchard.[2] When Aneurin Bevan became a pupil, it was a large school of 291 boys and 276 girls, with 325 children attending the infant school alone. Aneurin went to this school because his brother and sister, William and Blodwen, had gone there before him and it was an easy to walk from their home in Charles Street to its buildings. Sadly, none of David Bevan's children achieved any real success at this primary school except for Myfanw. She won prizes at the Sirhowy school and gained a scholarship to the grammar school. William left school at eleven to follow in his father's footsteps down the mines, while Blodwen found a job of work knitting and needlework under the eagle eye of her mother. Aneurin's experience at Sirhowy Primary School was most unfortunate of them all. Few of the teachers saw in him the talent that was so much part of his DNA, his make-up and background. From the moment the headmaster William Orchard set eyes on him, he took an instant dislike of his presence and, in the years that followed, he regularly admonished the boy and cruelly mistreated him.

The blue-eyed boy with the jet-black hair became a source of ridicule, both to the headmaster and to a few of the staff. Yet, one has to admit that Aneurin some-

---
1 *Kelly's Directory of Monmouthshire* 1901) on the website ancestry.com
2 *Ibid.*

times deserved to be rebuked but not the severe punishment he received. His biggest problem was that he often could not obey at once the voice of authority. Headmaster and pupil became increasingly hostile to one another, to the point where it became at times physical. One afternoon, Orchard placed his fist on Aneurin's chin, and immediately got a fierce response. Aneurin stamped his heavy heeled clog on the headmaster's foot, He felt the pain from the delicate corns.[1] Orchard wailed in pain, while Aneurin was send out from the class. He hurried as quickly as he could from the school to the security of his home in Charles Street.

Constant friction between headmaster and young Aneurin

One day in the classroom, the headmaster pointed his finger at a boy who looked underfed and with an unkept shirt and jersey clothes that betrayed his home. He was of poor means and the Headmaster abruptly asked him why he hadn't attended school the day before. The boy answered shyly and humbly that it was his brother's turn to wear the shoes, as they only had one pair between them. When Mr Orchard heard this explanation, he gnashed his teeth and poked such fun at him that the majority of the children joined in the sarcastic laughter. But one boy in the class had no smile on his face and that was Aneurin Bevan. He took the inkwell from his desk and threw it with all his might in the direction of the headmaster's desk. Fortunately, he missed the target, but the monstrous deed sent William Orchard into a rage.[2] Bevan was ordered to go immediately to the headmaster's room where he was subjected to the older man's angry homily and was caned a dozen times. Bevan entered the room red-faced – he had a ferocious temper – and he warned the headmaster not to take the path of utter retribution, lest he and his friends decide to plan a night-time campaign to pester him and his family. William Orchard realised he was dealing with a Jekyll and Hyde character. He decided the best course of action was to ignore Aneurin Bevan and send him home as soon as he could. He did not think about their future teacher-pupil relationship, and there was no respect between the two of them while the boy remained at Sirhowy School. The headmaster hoped his unruly pupil would leave the school as soon as the law allowed. For his part, Bevan felt utterly defeated and frustrated by the school system;

---

1 Michael Foot, *Aneurin Bevan, Volume 1, 1897–1945*, (London, 1962,) 20.
2 *Ibid*. The biographer Michael Foot tells us of another story in this sentence: "Later again he throws a snowball with a stone in it at the monstrous, redfaced Orchard, even after lamenting to his friends that he had again missed the target." See also Tessa Blackstone, 'The boy who threw an inkwell: Bevan and Education' in *The State of the Nation: The Political Legacy of Aneurin Bevan* (Ed. Geoffrey Goodman) (London, 1997), 156–178

in fact, school was a daily horror for him.[1] He looked at the building and its teachers, and especially the headmaster, as his personal enemies rather than his mentors or friends. Not one of them was able to inspire him to make the most of his talents and ability.

Aneurin Bevan realises he needs to be educated

By the time he was eleven, Bevan realised he needed educating. He came to believe the only way out of his dilemma and his educational boredom was to teach himself. He did this by reading as widely as possible. Through the committed help of his father and his Sunday school teachers, Aneurin had learnt to read and he soon saw the value of this skill. He learnt to write, but not like his sisters. His handwriting was messy, his words looking like crows' feet, his lines and sentences uneven. As for arithmetic, it was simply irrelevant to him. He never completely mastered the subject of economics in his entire life.

A strong bond between father and son

As a child, Aneurin Bevan had a huge regard for his bookish father, and the two of them would frequently go for walks in the hills surrounding Tredegar. During this time, his father started to feel uncomfortable with what he regarded as the 'Ungodly Trinity,' namely the Established Church and its alien bishops, the brewers who got rich on the back of the gullible and uneducated, and the greedy capitalists, that is the comfortable squire or the bloated factory or colliery owner who became rich through the efforts of miners and workers. David Bevan believed his concerns should be shared by his fellow miners. He came to think very highly of the South Wales Miners' Federation, or 'the Fed' as it was called in Tredegar and District. He became the treasurer of the lodge, recognising the enemy was none other than the Tredegar Iron and Coal Company. For years as a Welsh nonconformist, he, like the majority of miners of his background, had supported the Liberal Party. In 1906, he voted for Tom Richards, a miners' leader who united the new supporters of Labour and the party that had been in power in Wales for decades , the Liberals.[2] David Bevan also sought to rub shoulders with the early socialists, but for many years, their witness proved rather timid, respectable and weak within his home town. Then during Aneurin's childhood, David came under the influence

---

[1] Michael Foot, *ibid*, 20 'Aneurin hated school with an abiding hatred.'
[2] David Martin, 'Ideology and Composition' in K. D. Brown (ed.) *The First Labour Party, 1906–1914* (Kent, 1985), 17–20

of the Clarion movement campaigns. The campaigners visited mining towns and villages in Monmouthshire. David bought the *Clarion* newsletter, enjoying its spirit of optimism, the debates and its emphasis on brotherhood, humanity and the new order. He particularly liked articles by the editor Robert Blatchford, For the first time, his eyes – and Aneurin's – opened to the inequalities around them.

At school Aneurin could stand up for his rights and he could play well with his friends. By the time he was nine, he was in possession of a strong body and sharp mind. To his headmaster, however, he was not among his favourites. To him Bevan was a complete failure. Mr Orchard kept him in the same class for two years. It was psychologically hurtful to see his contemporaries move up to a higher class simply because they had not questioned the authority of Mr Orchard. This hurt his pride and confidence even more. On top of everything, he also suffered greatly from a stammer. We don't know why nine-year-old Bevan could not get his words out as all the other children could.[1] Many a theory has been put forward by those who have studied his early years. His second biographer Michael Foot theorised it was possible that the treatment he had received at school, that is the constant bullying of his headmaster, had, in fact, brought on the stammering.[2] However, according to his mother, it was her brother, John who was responsible, for he also had a stammer. Aneurin and his brother William often stayed with him, and when they arrived home, both would mimic John's speech, and particularly his stammer, incessantly. In the case of Bevan, the mimicking became part and parcel of his pronunciation. In his sister Myfanwy's opinion, her brother was a terribly lonely child in his schooldays, who outside his home didn't have many close friends. Bevan's frustration at school, along with his rebellious nature, resulted in frustration and mental torture; this, in turn, led to him struggling to speak the simplest of sentences without stammering.[3]

Starting work as a young boy

Aneurin Bevan received a reprieve when he left school at eleven to start earning a living. This said, we cannot but wonder at the fact that he lost out on these key years in his development. His biographers list the facts, but only Nick Thomas-Symonds wonders at his lost education and the failure of William Orchard and others to bring out the best in him.

The treatment of Bevan at school is rather unusual when you look at the lives of a few of his contemporaries the bright and gifted youngsters of his era. An

---

1 Michael Foot, *ibid*, 21
2 *Ibid*.
3 *Ibid*, 21–2.

example would be the miner's son Ness Edwards – who became Member of Parliament for Caerphilly in 1939 – who was born on 5 April 1897 (the same year as Aneurin Bevan) in a terraced house in Castle Street, Abertillery. He attended primary school like Bevan and left at thirteen to work at the Vivian coal mine in Abertillery. No mention is made of him being treated as vengefully as Bevan at Sirhowy, a few miles from Abertillery.[1] But when we look at another politician who belonged to an earlier generation, i.e. Morgan Jones, Member of Parliament for Caerphilly from 1921–1939, we see a glaring difference.[2] He was born thirteen years before Bevan in Bargoed, and was the fifth of seven children. Morgan Jones received his education in the primary schools of Gelligaer and Hengoed and won a scholarship to Lewis School, Pengam, one of the best schools in the southeast. There, on 3 August 1897, a few months before Aneurin's birth, Morgan Jones was accepted to the same grammar school as Neil Kinnock attended years later. It is clear William Orchard wrecked Aneurin's education. The headmaster of Hengoed primary school took much more interest in Morgan Jones than Orchard did in Aneurin Bevan. In contrast, it was Jones' headmaster who suggested he consider being a teacherpupil at Gilfach School, Bargoed and afterwards persuaded him to seek a place at Reading University. In a letter of introduction, Jones' headmaster said that he was commending Jones as one who showed necessary skills and what he calls 'aptitude of fondness of his work.'[3] The comparison with Morgan Jones makes it abundantly clear how Aneurin Bevan was punished by Sirhowy School. Nobody there had recognised his strength of character, the personal attributes which bore fruit when he arrived as a young Member of Parliament in Westminster. What might he have achieved had he had the opportunities that Morgan Jones of Bargoed received years earlier than him? Then consider how Archibald Lush, a close friend from Tredegar, had gone on to study at Jesus College, Oxford. So, by eleven years of age, Aneurin Bevan had left school and found work in Davies the butcher's shop on Commercial Street for a wage of two shillings and sixpence a week.[4] This meant long hours walking the streets of Tredegar, carrying a basket full of meat to the customers. He would call with the parcels on his bike and deliver the meat directly to the customers' homes. In doing this, he got to know the town like the back of his hand. His wages were a tremendous boost to him and for the first time in his life, he could afford to buy interesting comics like *Magnet*, *Gem* and *Popular*, and occasionally buying some other comic that caught his attention.[5] Before long, his

---

1 Wayne David, *Remaining True: A Biography of Ness Edwards*, (Llanbradach, 2006), 2. Like Aneurin Bevan, Ness Edwards went to work with his father and older brother down the mines.
2 Dylan Rees, Morgan Jones, 'Educationalist and Labour Politician,' *Glamorgan,* vol. XXXI, 1987, 66–83
3 *Ibid*, 66.
4 Michael Foot, *ibid*, 22
5 *Ibid*.

father tired of seeing him read what he called 'rubbish' and began to intervene. His crafty son devised a cunning way of hiding the comics under Sirhowy bridge, but tired of this when others heard of his hideout and stole his comics before he had chance to read them. David Bevan pointed his son in the direction of Tredegar's well-stocked library which catered mostly for miners. Here he was able to read widely and the volumes of Rider Haggard, Nat Gould, Hall Caine and Seton Merriman pleased him no end. Despite Bevan's thirst for knowledge, no one – not his contemporaries, his former teachers or his family – saw anything out of the ordinary in the little butcher boy. Neither David nor Phoebe Bevan considered for a moment persuading their son to sit an exam to gain a scholarship to grammar school. Seemingly, neither parent had faith enough in their son's abilities. Neither did they possess enough money for him to sit an 11+ exam, and so therefore there was no alternative for Aneurin Bevan but to face the toil and strain of physical work. He decided to follow the footsteps of his father, his oldest brother and his uncle, and he left the butcher's shop to be a slave worker in Tŷ Trist colliery, which is an odd name at best as it means 'house of sadness'! On the threateningly dark morning of 15 November 1911, Aneurin Bevan left his home with his brother William (Bill) wearing colliers' clothing.

The work he faced in the mine was to be far more challenging than distributing meat from his basket or standing behind the counter until midnight on busy Saturday nights.

Beginning life as a young miner

The miners were woken every morning (except Sunday) at half past four by the so-called 'knocker-up'. They would get dressed, eat breakfast and leave for the mines.[1] Bevan , Bill and their father were joined on their trek through the streets by hundreds of other miners all heading for the same pit. Mining was hard work, with a long time spent daily underground. When his father David Bevan started as a collier, he was expected to work 60 hours a week, including Saturday afternoon. In 1890, a 53-hour week was introduced, which is what Aneurin Bevan would have been working. A further changed occurred in 1919 when the working week was reduced to 47 hours. Another bonus was the introduction of better working conditions in the collieries. His wages were substantially better than at the butcher's shop, but the work was far more physical with many dangers, including being kicked by horses. Some days water flowed into the colliery, or a tram might escape from the hands of the miners and career uncontrollably towards any miners who happened

---

1 *Ibid*, 24.

to be in its path. He proudly brought home ten shillings at the end of the first week, and he would hand it all over to his mother. In return, he would get back sixpence: tuppence to spend on comics, tuppence for chocolate, and tuppence for any cake which was to his liking.[1]

Aneurin Bevan continued to attend Sunday school; however, his parents were starting to hear some distressing stories about his behaviour there, especially relating to the theory of evolution. It seemed that whenever the topic for the Sunday lesson was discussed, he would introduce the Darwinian concepts like survival of the fittest. The Baptist Chapel was in the evangelical tradition, so unsurprisingly there was an inevitable strong-minded opposition to his Darwinian arguments. His parents suggested it might be better for him to attend the more liberal-minded English Congregational Chapel Sunday school on Commercial Street. But before long, and as an ardent admirer of Charles Darwin, Bevan was again disrupting the lesson, and there were many protests from a well-loved teacher and few of the other pupils concerning him.[2] One loyal teacher even protested to the minister of the Church. He insisted that while Bean should have as much freedom to air his liberal heretical views, it should not be to the annoyance of other Biblical students. He said he would resign if they allowed Aneurin Bevan to dominate the proceedings, even though he and everyone else at Sunday school sympathised with his terrible stammer.

Early socialists in Tredegar

At Tŷ Trist colliery, Aneurin Bevan struck up a friendship with Lewis Halloway (1853–1915), a committed trade unionist, and it was through him he came to know of the efforts that were taking place to form the Independent Labour Party in the town.[3] This was a left-wing movement with a tinge of revolutionary fervour, and there were socialists of conviction within the branches who were disrupting the political order which brought so much power to Liberalism and Conservatives. Aneurin, his brother and father would discuss these new developments around the dinner table, especially about the commitment of Walter Conway (1875–1933), a miner like them, but one who was brought up in the workhouse. It is very likely that Conway was one of the main pioneers of the Labour movement in Tredegar. By 1915, he had been appointed as the secretary of the Medical Aid Society of Tredegar. He remained with the Society for years; a society that had a huge influence on Aneurin and his vision for the National Health Service in years to come.[4]

---

1 *Ibid*, 25.
2 *Ibid*, 25–6.
3 Susan E. Demont, 'Tredegar and Aneurin Bevan', 82.
4 *Ibid*.

Witnessing days of travail in the mining industry

Aneurin took pride in the lives and battles of the South Wales miners, and this was another topic of conversation around the dinner table. There was much excitement in the South Wales minefields during those years, and especially so in the Rhondda Fawr. There the Liberal politician DA Thomas who became through the patronage of the House of Lords the Baron Rhondda. He ruled the huge Cambrian combine of collieries around Tonypandy with an iron fist on the question of the miners' pay. He lived in Llanwern House, near Newport.[1] He was elected in 1888 as the Liberal MP for Merthyr and, although he had great wealth, his home was quite minimal, according to his daughter, the suffragette Margaret Haig Thomas. She later mentioned how mean her father could be at his home:

> The house was a joyful one, but there was not much in the way of comfort there. There was only one truly comfortable chair outside the study![2]

Even as a lad working on the coalface, Aneurin Bevan realised the government of the day was likely to use its strength to teach the Welsh miners a hard, bitter lesson. From his reading of the newspapers he realised that the reactionary Liberal leaders such as Lord Rhondda, Judge Bryn Roberts (known as a great enemy of the trade unions), Winston Churchill (then Home Secretary) and the Chief Constable of Glamorgan, Captain Lionel Lindsay. were all preparing for a violent struggle. Churchill called for soldiers to be deployed to Tonypandy, in the heart of the Rhondda Valley, to keep order. Some eight hundred policemen were sent to the Welsh valley from London's Metropolitan Police, and a good many soldiers were instructed to immediately travel to Tonypandy to reprimand the miners. Chief Constable Lionel Lindsay was not a pleasant individual: he was a mixture of a fervent, reactionary Tory and irascible imperialist. He had spent his apprenticeship in Egypt with the British Army and held the miners in exactly the same contempt as he did of the ordinary Egyptians. The South Wales miners were exactly 'wogs' to him and he believed they should be treated as the scum of society. The young Aneurin warmed to the unof-

---

1 Both he and Lloyd George had discussed the burning topic of a free Wales; but it has been acknowledged that D. A. Thomas was a keen 'Free Wales' man. But he changed his viewpoint, and on 16 January 1896 in Newport, one of the stormiest and unruly political meetings in the history of Welsh politics took place. This is the day that the movement known as Young Wales ended its existence as a forceful movement for home rule for Wales. The 'Conquerors' went for lunch with D. A. Thomas in a nearby hotel and the 'Losers' to hear Lloyd George testifying in a meeting that it was to be a matter of 'war until the end'. Read more about the event in William George, *Cymru Fydd: Hanes y Mudiad Cenedlaethol Cyntaf*, (Liverpool, 1945), 39– 47.
2 T. I. Ellis, *Crwydro Mynwy,* (Llandybie, 1958), 126

ficial miners' leaders, men of ability who served the Rhondda miners, like Noah Ablett and Noah Rees. He also took a great deal of interest when the Unofficial Reform Committee came into being in order to entice the more moderate miners' leaders within the Fed to be more militant. The committee, which was in favour of reforming the Fed, had been inspired a great deal by Marxism.

Bevan as a young man

This is the period when the pamphlet *Miner's Next Step* appeared. Noah Ablett (1883–1935), a natural intellectual, was one of the main authors.[1] He had, at one time, thought of becoming a candidate for the nonconformist ministry but he discarded the idea, instead embracing syndicalism, an unique phenomenon in the South Wales mining valleys, which Ablett considered to be a 'scientific labour union'. The word 'syndicalism' has French origins; however, this particular brand of unionism had been attractive for thirty years in the Rhondda and obviously influenced Aneurin Bevan's politics. He read widely on the subject, understanding its truth: the worker should have a stake in industrry and not only his employer, they should as trade unionists take strike action to secure victory, and individuals were needed to concen-

---

1 It was mainly written by Noah Ablett with the help of a small group of thinkers who were part of the Plebs League and the Cambrian Combine Strike in 1910–11, and who were active on the Unofficial Reform Committee. See 'The Miners' Next Step' in *Gwyddoniadur Cymru* (ed. John Davies, Menna Baines, Nigel Jenkins and Peredur Lynch) (Cardiff, 2008), 672–3; Alun Page, *Arwyddion ac Amserau*, (Llandysul, 1979),171. The account of the Cambrian Strike of 1910 is to be found on pages 33–36.

trate on Trade Union affairs and not on a parliamentary career . Aneurin Bevan, Arthur Horner and others of their generation in Wales greatly appreciated and admired the intellect of Noah Ablett. For Bevan, Ablett was much more important to him than the Merthyr MP Keir Hardie (1856–1915).[1]

J. Keir Hardie, M.P.

Bevan admires Noah Ablett more than Keir Hardie

Hardie was the instigator of the socialist organisation called the Independent Labour Party formed in Bradford in 1893. In 1900, he was nominated as Labour candidate for Merthyr Tydfil and the Aberdare constituency and became the first Member of Parliament to win in the colours of the Labour representation committee in 1900 in the South Wales coalfields. Hardie the Scot had a commitment to Christianity, to Wales, to the need for self-government and to socialism. For a period, he was a

---

1 Keir Hardie, the Scotsman, had fought for the first time for Labour in Mid Lanark in 1888 when he secured only 617 votes. See Roy Gregory, *The Miners and British Politics, 1906–1914* (Oxford, 1968), 91

natural leader.[1] Aneurin Bevan didn't mention him much, and there is no record of him going to hear Hardie speak, as Jim Griffiths and his comrades from Ammanford did at Cwm-caegurwen in 1908. The truth is that it wasn't Noah Ablett who won the South Walian miners over to the ranks of the Labour Party, but the former miner from the Ayrshire coalfields. Keir Hardie, more than any of his contemporaries, was the instigator of a huge change in British politics. Besides Arthur Henderson and Ramsay McDonald, who were also effective evangelists for the cause of the Labour Party, there was no one comparable to Hardie. But, of the three men, it was Hardie who won for the Labour Party (and the Independent Labour Party) the kind of support which snowballed constantly in the South Wales coalfield from 1900 until the end of the First World War.[2] Inevitably, not every miners' leader and parliamentary candidate who stood for Liberal-Labour supported Keir Hardie. One of those who had difficulty was Tom Richards, an endearing mining leader, who represented West Monmouthshire at Westminster. The truth was that he was much more ready to support a Liberal than he was to praise a Labour member in Parliament . He always spoke highly of Lloyd George and supported him every time he had the opportunity. Richards was fearless enough to condemn his fellow trade union members who moved from Liberalism to the Independent Labour Party. For him, they were turning their backs on the hero of the Welsh nation, namely David Lloyd George.

The Labour Party's struggle to exist in Tredegar

The Labour Party in its infancy recognised the situation as being a particularly difficult one. There were dozens of constituencies where the working classes, who were in the majority, were refusing to give Labour a chance to represent them. They would much rather show practical support for the Liberal Party. It was Watkin Lewis, a Welsh speaker who was born in 1876 and was a native of Sirhowy, who was one of the earliest Labour representatives to win a seat on Tredegar District Council.[3] He worked as a miner at the Navigation pit, and he took on responsibility as the clerk of the local miners lodge. Walter Conway, another socialist who has been referred to already, was an integral part of the culture of the Monmouthshire

---

1 See Kenneth O. Morgan, *Keir Hardie: Radical and Socialist* (London, 1997), chapter viii, 'Leader of the Party' (153–177); R. Silyn Roberts, James Keir Hardie, Y Genhinen January 1916. Hardie is mentioned as learning the Welsh words of the National Anthem of Wales with the title of *Hen Wlad fy Nhadau*.
2 The historian Kenneth O. Morgan goes as far as to say that Aneurin Bevan had underlined Keir Hardie's yearning for disarmament in the fifties, *ibid*, 287.
3 Susan E. Demont, *ibid*, 89. Lewis was a keen Congregationalist and he would refuse to attend the Miners Union's meetings on Sundays as he wished to keep the Lord's Day 'holy'.

coal mining valleys as was Aneurin himself.[1] One had, in the valleys of Rhymney, Sirhowy and the town of Abertillery, the values of middle-class culture at its best, namely the Sunday school movement and its classes where the Bible was taught to children as well as to adults. When the relationship between Aneurin and the Sunday school teachers worsened, Aneurin decided to establish his own Sunday school which met at the Workers' Hall to discuss some of the deep fundamentals of the Christian faith. The strong fellowships and debates of the young socialists were also held on Sunday afternoons, which in turn became an integral part of the Pleasant Sunday Afternoon movement. Here, hundreds of working men congregated together to hear quality speakers address them with inspiring addresses.

The purpose of these meetings was to enlighten and educate the attendees. Other activities were held under the auspices of the Cooperative Movement, which helped the Workers' Education Association (WEA) and became in 1919 a partner with the Labour Party . The branch of the Independent Labour Party which was established in Tredegar in 1911 is key to the understanding of socialism as a centre-point of the political culture at the time. The great debates took over from the serious discussions and propaganda posters were prepared for the visits of Keir Hardie, Bruce and Katherine Glasier and others wellknown ILP leaders.[2]

Radical tradition of the period

It was most difficult for these early socialists to overtake the strength of the Liberal radical tradition which garnered support for Lloyd George, and which harnessed a good deal of endorsement within the South Wales Miners' Federation, in particular from representatives of the Monmouthshire collieries. In 1907, men like William Brace, Tom Richards, Alfred Onions, Ted Gill and Frank Hodges supported Lloyd George rather than Keir Hardie. The political culture asked for open-mindedness, with individuals from various viewpoints joining in emotionally charged discussions. A row broke out within the free churches of Monmouthshire – the nonconformists – between those ministers who emphasised personal salvation and others who preached the social gospel. In 1908, the ILP prophet the Revd R. J. Campbell delivered his message and his new theology in Abertillery. David Bevan and his son were at the meeting and, on a personal level, David was totally bowled over by Campbell. The visit forced the Monmouthshire valleys' nonconformists to discuss the nature of their ministry. A public debate in Abertillery followed between two

---

1 *Ibid,* 93. Walter Conway (1875–1933) was one of the founders of the Independent Labour Party in Tredegar.
2 . *Ibid.* Conway chaired the meeting for Katherine Glasier in 1912 in Tredegar and Aneurin was seen attending.

local Baptist ministers, J. T. Evans and J. Morris Evans. Towy Evans had been a huge influence on Ness Edwards in terms of supporting a personal gospel while J. Morris Evans always emphasised the social gospel in the pulpit.[1] J. Morris Evans had spent his youth in the United States and he believed personal salvation was possible within a reformed economic and social order, free of poverty and austerity. His message was anti-capitalist and on the path of Christian socialism. In their chapel-based small-mindedness, the deacons of the Baptist Chapel, King Street, Abertillery dismissed their minister, but the Labour movement and the socialist organisations such as the ILP came to the rescue of Morris Evans. After a long bitter battle between the reactionaries and the socialists he was not forced to leave his pastorate. The convinced members of the Labour movement were keeping an eye on the chapel elders and deacons who could make life hard for an astute Christian socialist minister. The chapel hierarchy was well defeated in Abertillery.

The New Era Union was established in the Monmouthshire valleys in July 1909, supported by at least hundred miners who gave a shilling a month. The Union was committed to providing educational support, social work and spiritual guidance and was keen to promote discussions and debates. David and Aneurin Bevan expressed their interest in the proposed programme. There was a fundamental difference between the Plebs' League, a movement which largely favoured Marxism, and the New Era Union which favoured open debate on Christianity and democratic socialism in Tredegar. Representatives from both camps shared the same platform and expressed opposing opinions. Frank Hodges, the trade unionist, delivered his notable lecture on "Social Democratic Religion" and received a huge ovation. The New Era Union remained in force until the Great War. In fact, between 1909–1914, Christian socialism was far more powerful in the valley coalfields of Monmouthshire than Marxism ever was. During this period, Frank Hodges and Sydney Jones, who exerted a huge influence on young Aneurin, were tutors at Sirhowy and the surrounding districts. When the Plebs' League came to Tredegar during the First World War, under the patronage of the National Council of Labour Colleges, Walter Conway seized the chance to arrange adult classes on the subject of Marxism. The young miner Aneurin Bevan joined the class and learnt a huge amount from the self-taught tutor to reinforce his own wide reading and personal study.

---

1 The Reverend Towy Evans took a great interest in the young socialist, Ness Edwards. See Wayne David, *Remaining True: Biography of Ness Edwards* (Llanbradach, 2006), 2.

A troublemaker in the collieries

From his first day underground in the darkness and the dust, Aneurin Bevan became known as a difficult and troubled young miner. According to Michael Foot, he worked like a tiger (his detractors insisted he was lazy, but this was simply not true).[1] An official at the Tŷ Trist colliery referred to him as 'that bloody nuisance, Bevan'.[2] He moved from colliery to colliery, often with his eldest brother . Many of the clerks in the colliery management offices complained that he was a constant 'trouble maker'. Bevan was subject to both the criticism of the over-men who had no time for him and the admiration of his brother Bill and his mates. Eventually, a quarrel led to Bevan and his brother moving to Bedwellty New Pits where they worked alongside one another, something which was important to them. They were earning more than many miners; however, not everything was rosy there. One day, Aneurin decided to take the morning off in order to introduce the complex debate concerning Marxism to the officials, telling them in no uncertain terms that the miners had earned their pay after a specific number of hours and anything their labour produced after that was pure profit for the company. He had many an argument with the deputy manager. One day they met each other on top of the pit, with Aneurin adamant that he was going home in protest against those who were running the Bedwellty New Pits. There was nothing for it but to leave Bedwellty and seek work at Whitworth colliery with the everloyal Bill Bevan at his side. Even there, it wasn't long before Bevan got into trouble. After an emotional debate just before Christmas, he refused to secure a second-hand piece of timber to hold up the roof, instead insisting on using new wood. The deputy manager was furious, but was wise enough to wait for a foolproof opportunity to get rid of Aneurin Bevan, that is when he refused to empty a tram full of rubble. The young agitator presented his problems to the members of the colliery lodge and secured their backing and that of the South Wales Miners' Federation, who asked firmly that the Tredegar Iron and Coal Company find work for him elsewhere. The company decided to send him to Pochin colliery, which was considered to be the largest of them all. Aneurin's tenure there wasn't without its quarrels, this time with the manager, Thomas Reynolds. When Reynolds first met him, he greeted him with these words:

> 'Oh here is the famous Aneurin Bevan! The son of David Bevan, so I understand. I used to know him well.'

---

1 Michael Foot, ibid, 29
2 *Ibid*.

'Indeed,' answered Aneurin, 'you know a man better than yourself.'[1] Aneurin Bevan saw the coal industry at its worst during the seven years he was a working miner at the coalface. He was especially concerned about the lack of communication and poor relationship between the owners and miners, and the waste of resources he witnessed around him. Bevan was not happy with the way the miners were paid and the greedy competition that existed between them as to who might get the best wages. He knew from first-class experience how hard everyone of them had to work in order to earn those wages.

Appreciating the Miners' Federation

Aneurin became more convinced of the worth of the South Wales Miners' Federation and appreciated the great friendship between coalface miners who faced death every day of their lives. Despite his stammer, his voice could be heard as clearly as anyone else's in the lodge meetings, as could his daily protests when timid Trade Union leaders accepted the awful working conditions. By the middle of the First World War, Bevan was a proud trade unionist who could not be ignored. He became chairman of Pochin Number 1 Lodge and, in his spare time, he read widely, spellbound by the works of H. G. Wells, Jack London, James Connolly, Daniel de Leon and Eugene V. Debs. He walked the mountains with his friends, sharing with them what he'd learnt in the Plebs' League classes of Sydney Jones and Walter Conway in Tredegar, Sydney Jones in Pontllanfraith and Blackwood. One of his fellow members there was Harold Finch (later the Member of Parliament for Bedwellty), who would always maintain that Bevan was the star of the class. It was in Finch's class that Aneurin began to question his belief as a Christian and the doctrines of Calvinism in which he'd been steeped as a child.

In 1916, Aneurin Bevan persuaded Bill his brother to join him in the extramural adult class at Tredegar. The knowledge he gained there spurned his brother Bill Bevan to serve as a local councillor. Other miners who became prominent in the Labour movement or went into local government as a result of the education they received in the classes included Fred Frances and J. J. Caldicott, who became vice-secretary of the Labour and Trades Council in Tredegar.[2]

---

1 *Ibid*, 33.
2 S. E. Demont, *ibid*, 175.

Chairman of the miners' lodge

As chairman of the miners' lodge, young Bevan showed a gift of leading others, discussing and standing up for miners' rights and convincing the majority of trade union members to support him. Whenever he witnessed some obvious injustice in the colliery, he would discuss the matter that very evening at the end of the class with the tutor Walter Conway. After their conversation, Aneurin would feel more confident about protesting and fighting for the miners' rights. His stammer remained a constant blight, until one day, he asked Walter Conway's advice on how to conquer it. Conway answered in a flash, 'If you can't say it, then you don't know it.'[1] Years later, Bevan acknowledged it had been the best advice he'd ever been given. Walter Conway was a kind mentor in his eyes and, unlike many others, he supported Conway's pro-war stance on the First World War, that is he wanted to see Britain conquer Germany.[2] Bevan wasn't a pacifist like his friend Ness Edwards of Abertillery; however, both future politicians suffered for the stand they made, as did so many stalwarts who belonged to the Independent Labour Party (at this point in his life Bevan didn't have much to say to the party). He set about organising all the lodges of the Tredegar Company pits into one big lodge. His idea was to centralise the power of the miners in relation to Whitworth, Pochin (pits 1 and 2), Tŷ Trist (pits 1 and 2), Bedwellty New Pits, Oakdale and Markham, plus McLaren and Abertysswg in the Rhymney Valley, to create one huge lodge. This is how the Tredegar Combine Lodge came into existence. As Oliver Powell said, 'the man who created the lodge was Aneurin Bevan.'[3]

Dedication to the lodge

The existence of one powerful central collieries lodge made sense against a tremendously determined company which stood for capitalism. Bevan had previously attended the unofficial conference where the official leaders of the Fed were severely criticised for being so timid and co-operative. Union leaders at Tredegar pits accepted every decision made by the owners without protest. That was the situation, until Bevan

---

1 Aneurin Bevan, 'The Best Advice I Ever Had,' *Readers' Digest,* November 1953.
2 At least a thousand Tredegar lads and men volunteered for the First World War, amounting to ten percent of the population. Walter Conway was enthusiastic about the war, as was Member of Parliament, Tom Richards. He called Germany a nation of 'sneaks and assassins' from a recruiting platform. With him on the platform was the pit manager and W. Stephen Davies, the most important manager of TIC company. See S. E. Demont, 137.
3 *Ibid*, 221. Foot does not refer at all to Oliver Powell.

decided to take action in 1917–1918. He learnt so much about the reality of the relationship between employer and employee in Sydney Jones's Marxist class in Blackwood (he was after all the only Tredegar miner who attended that particular adult education class).[1] Bevan was elected vice-chair of the new centralised lodge, and he was keen to start discussions with the management over better working conditions and a raise in the weekly wages. Bevan however refused to be a member of the deputation to the colliery management lest his presence spoilt their visit. The veteran Labour stalwart Alfred Onions, pioneer of the movement in Monmouthshire, was distressed that eight thousand miners had come out on strike That is why he couldn't agree at all with Bevan's leadership.[2] Bevan made sure that the lodge organised every aspect of its planning thoroughly, making constant contact with similar lodges and committees within the other valley collieries in order to win support. Bevan was sent to spread the word in the Ogwr and Garw valleys in Glamorganshire, and he ventured forward confidently with his crusade. His view was to let the miners decide whether they should hold a conference to discuss their opposition. The MP for Bedwellty, Clem Edwards, was angry with Bevan that he had gone so far.[3] He was not in favour of unofficial action-taking, which is why he was not fully supportive of the attitude expressed in the pamphlet The Miners Next Step which was written by Noah Ablett and those he brought together in Tonypandy .. But Bevan did not worry about his neighbouring Labour MP Clem Edwards's viewpoint, and by the time the miners of Glamorgan and Monmouth understood the crux of the situation, it was quite obvious that there was support and a great deal of sympathy with the attitude and situation of the Tredegar miners. Some forty thousand miners by then were ready to support the strike.[4] When the strike began, that number grew even further to some fifty thousand miners. At the end of the three-week strike, over forty thousand miners were freely supporting the bitter struggle for improvement.[5]

---

1 Bevan became a regular delegate to the district meetings from his own Combine Lodge Executive and a frequent attender at the lectures given by Sidney Jones, Noah Ablett and other resident or visiting Marxist scholars.' See Michael Foot, *ibid*, 36.

2 Alfred Onions had held a position as Treasurer of the South Wales Miners' Federation, had fought in the name of the miners as a parliamentary candidate and was a true friend to Thomas Richards. But to the fervent socialists, he was a traitor, as one of the Rhondda's syndicalists W. F. Hay said of him: 'A bitter day of reckoning is coming for those who like Hartshorn, Brace, Richards, Onions etc, have seized upon, misled, and betrayed the most important industrial movement of modern times.' See *The Rhondda Socialist,* April 1912. Quoted in Roy Gregory, *The Miners and British Politics* (Oxford, 1968), 135.

3 Clem Edwards was the candidate who followed Sir Alfred Thomas as representative of the Liberals in East Glamorgan. Clem Edwards had succeeded in becoming a barrister in 1889 and had worked with Ben Tillet at the time of the famous London dock strike in the same year. He campaigned for eight-hour days for the miners. See Roy Gregory, *ibid*, 132.

4 Susan E. Demont, 'Tredegar and Aneurin Bevan', 206.

5 *Ibid*, 213.

It wasn't easy for anyone. The miners had long-abandoned the Federation's leadership and the large colliery structure was under the heel of the local coal-owners as well as the moderate trade unionists who were led by the Lib-Lab politicians. One should not give Aneurin Bevan too much attention, even though he was full of energy and willing to travel long distance to gain support for the Tredegar struggle. He wasn't chosen as part of the deputation for the Federation Conference in Cardiff because he could be a loose cannon, a young lad with no family of his own to support. Fellow comrade Harold Finch, who himself had been campaigning at Bedwellty, described him as a very 'raw' youth who was 'stuttering and spluttering about the place'.[1].

Difficult days during the First World War

Aneurin Bevan's story in relation to the First World War demands a discussion, not least because there are various versions of the narrative. At home, his nonconformist parents were most suspicious of the destructive war and his mother refused point blank to buy war certificates – she called them 'money tainted with blood'.[2] At the colliery, Aneurin would hear of the miners' quarrels about the war and government goings-on, often repeated in the daily press through the rhetoric of Lloyd George. At the Independent Labour Party, he would hear propaganda concerning the underhandedness of the Treasury which held the country's purse strings. By 1917, Bevan was among a minority of miners who viewed the war as the capitalists' war rather than his own war as a Welshman and a socialist. It concerned him that hostilities were dragging on and that Britain and her allies were not able to have the upper hand on Germany and the central powers. On 7 December 1916, David Lloyd George had become Prime Minister – the first ever Welsh-speaking Welshman to hold the title. The politician from Dwyfor managed to get the top role with the aid of two prominent Welshmen. David Davies, the MP for Montgomeryshire, persuaded backbench Liberals to support Lloyd George.[3] Thomas Jones was a civil servant from Rhymney who championed Lloyd George's talents among the leaders of the Labour movement.[4] But many prominent Welsh folk believed that 'Lloyd George's War' had negated all the religious institutional values which had been

---

1 *Ibid*, 214.
2 Michael Foot, *ibid*, 32.
3 David Davies was the one who presented a report to the Prime Minister in which he foresaw the crumbling of the Tsar's reign, as Thomas Jones testifies. See Thomas Jones, *Lloyd George* (London, 1951), 104.
4 *Ibid*, 164–88.

importat to the world of Liberalism.[1] In that respect, Aneurin Bevan was not far from the mark, the Conscription Act which was passed in 1916 angered him and millions of other citizens.[2]

In her doctorate essay, Susan Demont showed that Michael Foot's report of the antagonism between the War Office and Aneurin Bevan was factually wrong.[3] It is clear that Bevan had to appear before a Medical Board at Tredegar Town Hall on 22 April – and the verdict of that board was that he was medically fit for enrolment. After that meeting, he was given three warnings. David Griffiths, an officer of the Tredegar Combine Lodge, sent him a card on behalf of the medical tribunal. However, there was some doubt. Nobody knew whether Pochin colliery had reached their quota, and so future correspondence was suspended for the time being – the *call-up notices,* as they were called. However, according to his biographer, he was arrested at that time. His sister, Blodwen had thrown the first warning note he had received into the fire. Bevan couldn't care less, as he had received a word from a recruiting officer that the colliery's quota was thirty – he was number thirty-one. Aneurin Bevan at that period was on an evangelistic rally for the cause of socialism in West Wales, and when he returned home, his sister Margaret May, whom he loved dearly, was seriously ill. That night, two policemen called to arrest him. Though deeply concerned for his sister, Bevan accompanied them to the police station in Tredegar. It was a stormy night for his parents, with their Margaret fighting for her life and their son in the cells. But according to the press, he faced the court on 7 June, a week after the strike had come to an end. He spent two nights in a cell, and then appeared in court at Ebbw Vale, when he was ordered to stand trial in Tredegar on 18 June. He was defended by Gordon Edwards, a solicitor from Newport, and two members of the Tredegar Combine Lodge who spoke for him. The case centred round the question of the Pochin colliery quota, something Bevan spoke about. Had the quota been filled before the authorities had sent the third warning, the so-called blue paper? As an officer of the Federation Lodge, he was excused service, but not everyone saw this as a fair defence. The second reason was more genuine, in that Bevan was by now suffering from nystagmus in his eyes, and it was that condition which in the end let him off the hook. The chair of the magistrates, Alderman T. J. Price, decided to delay proceedings for another month, so the Bench could do some more fact-finding.

---

1 K. O. Morgan, *Rebirth of a Nation: Wales 1880–1980* (Oxford, 1981), 165.
2 See Michael Foot, *Aneurin Bevan, ibid,* 32–33 also Vincent Brome
3 This is the material that Susan Demont used: *Merthyr Express,* 22 June, 20 July 1918 and *Western Mail,* 19 June and 16 July 1918.

Facing the authorities

And so, on 15 July, the court was convened to discuss the case. His solicitor regretted Bevan's absence on that day. He was in full vigour persuading other mining areas in Glamorganshire to support them in Monmouthshire. The authorities showed sympathy towads the situation in Bevan's household as well as wisdom, as they could see that he could be a difficult rebel if he were forced to participate in a military camp. But he was able in the end to opt out of military service because of his eye ailment, he was able to produce a medical certificate confirming he had nystagmus. After all, Bevan was enjoying the opportunity that had come his way to study and read widely during the First World War. At Cardiff in 1917, he had met fellow miner John Lloyd Williams (who during Attlee's first administration of 1945–50 was the Labour Member of Parliament for Kelvingrove constituency in Glasgow). Williams was most enamoured to hear a Tredegar miner who could recite word for word, in Welsh, of Sir John Morris-Jones translation of Omar Khayyam's poem. It is incorrect to say Aneurin Bevan did not understand any Welsh; as a youngster he had committed this lengthy poem to memory. The two young miners spent time at the Central Labour College, and it was there, according to John Lloyd Williams, that Bevan also learnt to read some French and German.[1]

Frustrated at the warfare on the continent of Europe

By 1918, Bevan had grown to dislike the nasty and bloody warfare on the European continent. He really enjoyed learning by rote the works of the poet-soldier Siegfried Sassoon. Bevan's wish was not to raise his hand to fight in a capitalist war. Both his temperament and his outlook were totally at odds with the war. He made it quite clear to everybody that he wouldn't voluntarily wear military apparel, that it was better for everyone just to leave him where he was, ruffling feathers on behalf of the needy in his home town. He was extremely clever in comparing himself with many of his comrades who were of the same background and ideas. Bryn Roberts went to jail for his pacifist views, as did Ness Edwards. Bevan was closer

---

[1] NLW The papers of John Lloyd Williams (1888–1982), Member of Parliament for Labour in Kelvingrove, Glasgow from 1945–1950. Box1/4. Born in Pantperthog near Corris in 1888 and died in Bow Street, Ceredigion on 31 December 1982.

to Arthur Homer in his standpoint.¹ The key thing for him was to have capacity and freedom to use his hands for his comrades and his town through the Labour Party. He hoped to have the opportunity to stand as a Labour representative in the near future.

Welcoming the Armistice

Aneurin Bevan welcomed the end of the Great War at eleven o'clock on the eleventh day of the eleventh month, that is in November 1918. To him, the Allies had won the day because there were more of them, that there was a charismatic Welshman as leader, and they had more resources, with Britain being supported by 32 nations.² Although the Russian Revolution had not been celebrated on the streets of Tredegar, Bevan knew Russia's involvement until 1917 had been an important factor in the task of conquering Germany. He didn't tire of reminding his fellow-organisers that between nine and ten million people had died as a result of the hostilities and some 30 to 40 million had been wounded – a large percentage suffered daily serious physical and mental wounds. One thing which was crystal clear to him, as well as his his parents and his family was that he had been extremely fortunate to havebeen spared the bloodshed of the battlefield.³ The warfare had been terribly cruel on the continent of Europe because of the tanks, the big guns, the explosions and the nerve gas. Bevan couldn't understand why so many miners had enlisted to spend their days wading through mud and instructed to kill. He learned how the son of the West Monmouthshire MP Tom Richards had been the hero of Pilckem Ridge battle on 31 July 1917, when the shepherd-bard, Ellis Humphreys Evans, known today as Hedd Wyn of Trawsfynydd, was killed.⁴ No wonder Tom Richards was elected unanimously when a General Election was called in December 1918. He organised only one meeting in Tredegar where he championed the victory of the

---

1 The allied countries were Britain, France, Belgium, Russia (up until 1917) Italy, America (after 1917) Serbia, Romania, Greece, British dominions and colonies, the Arabs, Japan, China, the new countries of South America against the central powers, namely Germany, Austria, Hungary, Turkey and Bulgaria. See Emyr Price, *Cymru a'r Byd Modern ers 1918* (Cardiff, 1980),
2 Michael Foot, *Aneurin Bevan, ibid,* 34. I believe that Oliver Powell, a friend of his, has said it all in these words: I believe there was a terrific lot of wire-pulling, you see 'let him go, get him out of the way, he will be less trouble outside the bloody tent than in'. See Susan E. Demont, 'Tredegar and Aneurin Bevan', *ibid,* 222.
3 D. Ben Rees, 'Hedd Wyn (1887–1917) and the First World War' in D. Ben Rees (Ed.), *Hanes Gŵyl Hedd Wyn and the Black Chair, Bardd Fugail y Rhyfel Mawr/Poet-Shepherd of the Great War* (Talybont, 2018), 1–6.
4 'His impudence, his cheek, his brass was colossal,' says Lewis, one of the leaders of the Blackwood Socialists who marvelled at the spectacle.' See Michael Foot, *Aneurin Bevan, Volume 1, 1897–1945* (London, 1962), 36.

Great War and attacked the President of the Miners' Federation of Great Britain for his mean attack on David Lloyd George. Bevan was perturbed whilst listening to him and he decided there and then that he and his friends had to change the atmosphere completely within the constituency and in Tredegar itself. He had plenty of grit, as noted by young socialists in Tredegar district. He would have to arm himself better than he had done in the First World War in the inevitable battle of socialism against capitalism.

CHAPTER 3

Education in London and prominence in Tredegar (1919–1929)

By 1918, there was a great deal of dissatisfaction across Britain from the wounded soldiers, unemployed workers and much frustration by ordinary members of the Labour Movement with the British establishment.[1] By the general election of 1922, it was obvious Lloyd George's Liberals were losing votes over heavily to Labour in industrial areas. Moreover, many Welsh and English intellectuals and radicals were leaving the Liberals to join the ranks of the Labour Party. Since 1922 Labour has been the dominant political party in Wales, the result of solid campaigning for democratic socialism in the industrialised communities of North and South Wales over hundred years ago.

The consequences of the First World War

In the mining communities, young idealistic socialists like Aneurin Bevan realised that one had to take action within the square mile and do so among young people like himself, who were living in distressing times in closely-knit communities. Change was happening within these long-forgotten communities in terms of religious and cultural traditions. Priorities too had changed after four years of war and a pandemic (the Spanish Flu) which had brought sudden death to around 50 million lives globally. The consequences of the First World War was to weaken family structure. Before the war, the man of the house left all household duties to his wife, but

---

1 . In the city of Liverpool, the police went on strike in 1919 and the army had to be drafted in as well as officers from other cities in order to keep the peace. See. Herman Mannheim, *Social Aspects of Crime in England between the Wars* (London, 1940), 156

wartime saw thousands of women standing in for men: in factories and in the community.¹ These women workers were ready to express themselves by voting and a minority ready to support Labour organisers of the calibre of Elizabeth Andrews of Ton-Pentre, in the Rhondda who was appointed in 1918 to bring women within Wales into the growing political party. The war had convinced women like Andrews that the socialists had something more relevant to offer them than the Liberals ever had. The same women who helped gain the vote for their sex in 1918 and 1928 were obviously a wil,ling to vote for the Labour Party in general and local elections from 1922 to 1929. For Aneurin Bevan, the Labour Party meant more than just winning an election. When a party branch was established in Tredegar, he became an active member. Prior to that, he had been influential within the Trade and Labour Council and, in April 1914, he was invited to be one of the four Tredegar Labour Party candidates for the local district council and fought the West Ward as best as he could. Bevan found himself at the bottom of the poll; however, many a socialist who voted for him saw in the young Aneurin a budding politician of originality and with huge potential. His great wish was to make the Labour Party an integral part of the everyday lives of most of those who joined its ranks. A strong sense of fellowship and community activities was, after all, what the Welsh language nonconformist chapels had achieved. In the communities. Bevan also believed the Labour Party and its members ought to be fully committed to the cause of fairness and human rights, show respect for all workers, and be ready to voice their concern for an 'honourable' wage. The ideal was that socialists should be, at all times, active and intelligent people. Aneurin believed the key to success in life was education, yet it had been lacking in his own formative years and in the lives of most of his contemporaries. The education he had received at Sirhowy School was scanty and poor; however at Tredegar Miners library he had recognised his ammunition. Many a leftist historian interpreted Labour, both before and after the First World War, as an ideology which looked to Westminster's Parliament as a means of addressing ongoing concern.² Rather than crushing and belittling communities, it could instead be a power house where the concerns of the working class were voiced by Labour Members of Parliament and one day achieve a formidable victory at the polls. Within the Labour movement, the miners, more than most trade unionists, believed they needed dedicated individuals of conviction to represent them in the House of Commons. Lloyd George had betrayed them badly by refusing to implement the Sankey Report of 1919 which suggested nationalisation of the mining industry.

---

1 H. A. Mess, *The Message of the COPEC* (London, 1924), 39.
2 John Saville, 'Notes on Ideology and the Miners before World War 1', *Bulletin of the Society for the Study of Labour History*, No. 23, 1971, 25–7.

Bevan wins a scholarship to the Central Labour College

In terms of education, Bevan had a reprieve when the Central Labour College re-opened in October 1919 with its hero Noah Ablett at the helm as chairman of governors. The South Wales Miners' Federation was the chief financial supporter of the college, assisted nobly by the National Union of Railwaymen. They were was happy to pay for eight to twelve scholarships for the most talented miners from the South Wales coalfield. To secure a scholarship, a miner had to take an exam; if successful, they were required to pledge their service to the Labour movement on completion of two years intensive training in London. In the year 1919, there were two hundred applications for just eight scholarships. Among the successful candidates were four outstanding young men: Aneurin Bevan of Tredegar, Jim Griffiths of Betws, Ammanford, Ness Edwards of Abertillery and Bryn Roberts of Rhymney.[1] The students varied both in age and background. Griffiths was a Welsh-speaker, a 29-year-old miner who was married to a Hampshire lass called Winifred and was well-used to attending adult education classes, especially the ones held weekly at Tŷ Gwyn (White House) in Ammanford.[2] Ness Edwards and Aneurin were close friends and shared many of the same ideals, having been brought up attending the Baptist chapel. At 22 years of age. they would spend hours discussing the distressing situation in the South Wales coalfield in the guest room of Ness Edwards' home at Castle Street, Abertillery. Ness, a fully fledged supporter of the Plebs League, took an oath rejecting the idea of going to war. Aneurin disapproved of this and did not go along with the oath. Ness joined the so-called NoConscription Fellowship, but was soon imprisoned, spending time in Dartmoor jail before escaping. For months, he hid in the caves of Llangynidr over twenty miles from his home. Eventually, the severity of the weather meant he had no choice but to give himself up to the military authorities. Edwards had to spend the remainder of the war at the notorious prison of Wormwood Scrubs.[3]

---

1 Aneurin Bevan was on cloud nine after he gained his scholarship. His friend Harold Finch mentioned how he came knocking on the door of his home in Blackwood to see whether his scholarship results had come through. When he heard the good news, i.e. that he had gained a scholarship to the Central Labour College, he made his way back to Tredegar as if he had gained a fortune. See Michael Foot, *Aneurin Bevan, Volume 1, 1897–1945* (London, 1962), 37

2 James Griffiths, *Pages from Memory* (London, 1968), 20–6

3 The details regarding Ness Edwards and his friendship with Aneurin Bevan may be seen in Wayne David, *Remaining True: A Biography of Ness Edwards* (Llanbradach, 2006), 4, 6, 45–7, 62–7, 69, 73, 79, 83–4, 86, 93 and 102.

The educational provision at the Central College

In September 1919, Aneurin Bevan headed to the Central Labour College full of excitement and expectation. He was fortunate in already having a circle of friends there, including Ness Edwards and Bryn Roberts. In fact, at least half of the students assembled in the college came from the South Wales coalfield. They were young miners of the same background and political beliefs as Bevan. The college was located at 11 and 13 Penywern Road, Earl's Court – two houses which had been amalgamated to form one property. In 1919, the principal was W. W. Craik, who had succeeded Dennis Hird, by then in ripe old age and on the verge of retiring from his long and valid contribution to adult education. A gifted teacher in the Labour college in London was Alec Robertson, a headmaster from Glasgow, and fondly remembered by Jim Griffiths, even more than by Aneurin Bevan. Robertson lectured on sociology, industrial and political history and economics. Another knowledgeable tutor from the Rhondda Valleys was none other than W. H. Mainwaring, who had been involved in the preparation of the *Miner's Next Step* in 1912. The students of Bevan's time also benefited from the fellowship and learning of Alfred J. Hacking, a scholar who had been educated at Exeter College, Oxford.[1]

How Clara Dunn helped Bevan to overcome his stammer

Guest lecturers were common and the *Daily News* cartoonist and cartographer J. F. Horrabin became a popular one. Voice teacher Miss Clara Dunn was another and taught the students how to project their voice so the audience could hear them easily.[2] She did a marvellous job in helping Aneurin Bevan overcome his speech impediment. Had he not met Clara Dunn during his college days, it is certain he would not have become one of the finest orators the Labour movement has ever had. Bevan depended entirely on the coaching technique and skill of Clara Dunn and was ever thankful for her invaluable help and support. While his stammer did not disappear completely, Clara Dunn's patient coaching freed him, to a great degree, from his debilitating problem and soon he was mesmerising his fellow students with his superb oratory.

The Central Labour College was proud of its emphasis on ideology. *'Y Bolshies yw y Gorrah!'* meaning 'The Bolshies are the Best!' was its slogan, according to John

---

1 D. Ben Rees, *Jim: The Life and Work of the Rt. Hon. James Griffiths. A hero of the Welsh nation and architect of the welfare state* (Liverpool, 2020), 75.
2 Michael Foot, *ibid*, 38. To the question, 'How did you cure the stutter, Nye?' he would respond with humour, by saying 'by torturing my audiences'.

Thomas, a prominent figure in the adult education movement in West Wales.[1]. He uttered the Welsh language slogan in Ammanford, hoping for better days ahead for the anthracite coalfield. When this did not happen, Thomas left for the North Staffordshire coalfield.

Bevan neglects the lecturing offered

According to Michael Foot, Aneurin Bevan did not turn up regularly to lectures. He was critical of the discipline at college, which belonged to the old order and, in his opinion, was something which had disappeared in the days of the First World War. It wasn't easy for many of the older students to put up with these obsolete old-fashioned college rules. Jim Griffiths and Bryn Roberts sought to obtain a key each so that they could open the door late at night and not disturb anybody. Griffiths was after all a married man, whose wife was lodging nearby. Naturally, he would visit her every night, or they would go to the theatre. Griffiths and Roberts wrote to the college principal about the matter.[2] Bevan the rebel ignored the rules entirely and ventured out every night to see the delights of London or speak at Hyde Park or Marble Arch.[3] He also longed deeply for his home in Tredegar and the hills of northern Monmouthshire.[4]

The set book for the syllabus was none other than Karl Marx's classic, *Das Capital* and W. H. Mainwaring was expected to delivere 35 lectures on Marx. Aneurin attended barely any of these well-prepared lectures . Unfortunately, he didn't have much faith in the tutor from the Rhondda (later, there were a few serious complaints about the standard of teaching pursued by W. H. Mainwaring). One student, D J Williams, who became Labour MP for Neath constituency years later, even attacked the syllabus as well as Noah Ablett, chairman of the governors.[5] Aneurin, however, accepted Ablett's view that the first ten chapters of *Das Capital* were all you needed to understand to become a potential coalfield leader. For many a Marxist scholar, those are considered to be the most difficult chapters of the three volumes.

---

1 John Thomas, 'The present and future prospects for the South Wales miners', *Communist Review*, January 1922, 8; Richard Lewis, *Leaders and Teachers: Adult Education and the Challenge of Labour in South Wales 1906–1940* (Cardiff, 1993), 152.
2 National Library of Scotland, Acc 5120, Box 2, 1920, the letter of Jim Griffiths and Bryn Roberts to W. W. Craik, dated 2 October 1920.
3 Michael Foot, *ibid*, 38.
4 'But even the London parks were poor substitutes for Welsh mountains'. See Michael Foot, *ibid*, 37.
5 D. J. Williams (who became Labour Member of Parliament for Neath, 1945–1964) launched the attack on the College and on Ablett in the magazine *Plebs*, December 1926

Ness Edwards' opinion of Aneurin Bevan

We have an interesting and memorable portrayal of Aneurin at college from his friend Ness Edwards. Aneurin's delight was to debate syndicalism and socialism with other students until the early hours. Then he would invariably sleep until lunchtime and miss a great many lectures. Ness Edwards described Bevan as a bumble bee bouncing from flower to flower. His ambition was to experience life in all its fullness, and he achieved this during his two years at college. In 1921, his first article – about Marx's and Engels's communist manifesto – was published. In it, Bevan described the manifesto as the brightest proclamation in socialist literature. He believed the chief reason for studying the document was for readers to be incited by the fire within its pages.[1] Michael Foot's comment is worth noting here: 'Bevan had caught it, and all the events he saw around him enflamed him the more.'[2]

No welcome for him or other students by colliery officials

One of the saddest chapters in the history of the South Wales coalfield is how many a bright young lad had to leave the Welsh valleys because the colliery owners and officials would seek revenge on them if they had been educated at the Labour College in London. Aneurin Bevan was frustrated that he was not welcomed back to the Tredegar collieries by those in authority. When Frank Phippen returned to the Rhondda in 1920, the owners of the colliery where he had worked refused to re-employ him.[3] It was an awful situation, because these ex-students were not eligible for unemployment benefits. The situation worsened. After returning to his colliery in the Rhondda, D. J. Davies was greeted with these words from the manager, 'Go and ask Lenin for a job.'[4] Bevan suffered the same treatment at the hands of the Tredegar Coal and Steel Company.[5] According to Glyn Evans of Garnant, by 1923, half the intelligent students who left the Central Labour College could not secure work, and South Wales Miners' Federation officials weren't ready to support them because so many loyal and bright colliers were out of work.[6] Even when the South Wales' Miners' Federation did secure jobs for these men who had been steeped in Marxism, the colliery's administrators would make sure they were given the worst

---

1 Michael Foot, *ibid*, 39
2 *Ibid*.
3 Richard Lewis, *Leaders and Teachers, ibid*, 163.
4 *Ibid*.
5 Michael Foot, ibid, 16–7.
6 Glyn Evans's article from the Labour College to the *Plebs*, 23 October.

jobs possible, for example, working in the worst seams underground and far away from the other miners. The only way to secure decent work for these returned miners was if they were selected by their workmates to represent them as check weighers. Some historians give the impression that the unfairness and persecution were less obvious at the collieries than in the railway industry, but that was not completely true.[1] The position of check weigher made the world of difference to Labour College students at the end of their leadership training. Unfortunately, by 1923, the jobs of the check weighers in most collieries had been filled and, despite the promise of helping the colliery in their need, a gifted handful had to leave the South Wales coalfield for other British collieries. Some left for the Midlands and the Kent coalfield in South-East England.[2] The beginning of the industrial depression was another nail in the coffin and the college closed in 1929 due to lack of funds. Noah Ablett's highly enthusiastic vision was forgotten. That same year Bevan returned to London to practice his oratory as an MP in Westminster.

Bevan receives more from college than he is willing to admit

I am ready to suggest for Aneurin Bevan's future career, the Labour College was an important experience and a form of training. I state this despite the man himself and Michael Foot seeming to disagree. Richard Lewis wrote:

> It is difficult to believe that Nye Bevan's career would have been seriously derailed if he had missed the chance of a sojourn at Penywern Road, and Arthur Horner's development was little impaired by his decision not to seek a scholarship.[3]

That is partly true. But one must also remember that he won a scholarship which was no mean feat, and that the Labour College was expecting its students to write essays, to give speeches to large crowds and take part in by-elections. As a student, Aneurin Bevan was invited to speak on a street corner in east London, during the dockers' strike. He was expected to attend House of Commons debates regularly so that he could keep with with the critical situation of the industry.[4] As many an

---

1 Brian Simon (ed.), 'The Labour College between the Wars' in *The Search for Enlightenment: The Working Class and Adult Education in the Twentieth* Century (London, 1990), 108. Brian Simon is the author of the essay.
2 Richard Lewis, *Leaders and Teachers, ibid,* 165.
3 *Ibid,* 166.
4 Gwilym Prys Davies, *Cynhaeaf Hanner Canrif: Gwleidyddiaeth Cymreig 1945–2005* (Llandysul, 2008), 38.

historian has pointed out, this unique college's value went beyond the lecture halls to the real-world experiences offered to the young socialists, that is the political, artistic and cultural life of London, as well as the engaging debates which lasted until the early hours. Students had an opportunity to read the volume of the German Marxist, Joseph Dietzgen, *Positive Outcome of Philosophy* (1906) and Karl Kautsky's socialist exposition of Thomas Moore's book on s *Utopia*. Bevan also read the works of American socialists and came to understand Russia's 1917 communist revolution as well as the continuation of capitalism in Europe and the USA. At college, he did not have to earn his daily bread and he had freedom to do what he wanted all day. In the evenings, he could mingle and talk with his fellow students who were equally keen about a future within the Labour movement. Ness Edwards read the three volumes of *Das Capital* three times over – a feat Bevan failed to achieve even once.

The Central Labour College left an indelible mark on Aneurin Bevan and his fellow students, who thereafter became prominent across South Wales constituencies, in local government and among a few of the most ambitious individuals that in years to come entered the House of Commons. These young miners had been fearless leaders before they arrived in London, stirring up protest and progress at home. They came from the same background and shared the same ideals. Aneurin, like Jim Griffiths, was delighted to accept the economic analysis of Marxist philosophy, but not the political viewpoints.

Jim Griffiths acknowledged in an interview that it was his chapel background as a Welsh Independent which accounted for his rejection of full-blooded Marxism.[1] Aneurin Bevan had a similar background; in fact, it was the Sunday school which had given him status and nurtured his oratorical skills. The training at the Central Labour College had expanded his experience and had been most valuable. By 1927, eleven of its former students were sitting together around the table in Cardiff as members of the Executive Committee of the South Wales' Miners Union ..[2] During the thirties, six former Labour College students entered the House of Commons: Aneurin Bevan, George Dagger (Abertillery) in his bow tie, Ness Edwards (Caerphilly), Jim Griffiths (Llanelli), Arthur Jenkins (Pontypool), the father of a bright up-and-coming Labour politician and E. J. Williams (Ogmore) who was well-rewarded by the Labour government. Their lecturer W. H. Mainwaring later

---

1 Mrs James Griffiths, *One Woman's Story* (Ferndale, 1979), 82; D. Ben Rees, *Jim*, 76.
2 Members of the South Wales Executive Miners' Committee as well as leaders of the Labour Party who had attended the Labour College up to 1927 included W. Coldrick (who became Member of Parliament for Bristol), George Dagger, Jim Griffiths , Ness Edwards Aneurin Bevan, D. J. Davies (one of the leaders of the South Wales Miners Union in the Rhondda), S. Jones, W. H. Mainwaring, Cliff Protheroe (Secretary of the Labour Party in Wales), Morgan Phillips (who became General Secretary of the Labour Party), John Lloyd Williams (MP for Glasgow Kelvingrove from 1945 to 1950), D. J. Williams (MP for Neath in 1945), Bryn Roberts, W. J. Saddler and E. J. Williams (MP for Ogmore).

represented miners in the Rhondda Fach (Rhondda East constituency). Noah Ablett's vision of training future leaders and tutors for the benefit of miners, railwaymen and their unions, not to mention the overall Labour movement had been realised.[1] Bevan was accurate when he described Ablett as 'a leader of great intellectual power and immense influence'.[2]

Condition and challenge of the coalfield

Aneurin Bevan belonged to a key industry in the life of South Wales and, and the North-East Wales counties of Flintshire and Denbighshire. In 1920, miners were at the height of their political strength with some 271,000 employed in the coalfields of the south. They were not going to give up the constant battle for better underground conditions, pay rises or shorter working hours, and neither were they going to allow their communities to disappear and die. They were in the vanguard of a better world for all residents of the surrounding communities. When the coal owners dragged their feet, the miners gave warning that a strike was imminent. Lloyd George's reaction, in 1919, had been to set up a Royal Commission to prepare a report on the matter of pay and working hours and to give further consideration to the business of nationalising the coal industry.

He appointed John Sankey as the chairman and the Commission's report proposed that the industry be nationalised in principle, but no clear viewpoint could be agreed upon on how to do that.[3] This was a good opportunity for Lloyd George to reject the policy of nationalising the industry. The failure to realise one of the main proposals of the Sankey Commission was a stumbling block for the next quarter century, and the Liberal Party suffered from such a blunder. Aneurin Bevan and his fellow students returned from the Labour College to their various districts ever more determined that the coal industry had to be nationalised.

---

1 Noah Ablett has not had the praise which he richly deserved, and Bevan was the first to acknowledge his greatness. See Aneurin Bevan, *Place of Fear*, London, 1952, 39–40. See also concerning Ablett, D. Ben Rees, *Jim, ibid*, 55, 59, 61, 64–5, 75–8, 89, 161 and 291; Michael Foot, *Aneurin Bevan, ibid*, 26–9; John Campbell, *Nye Bevan: A Biography*, London, 11; Dai Smith, *Wales! Wales!* (London, 1984), 130–132
2 Aneurin Bevan, *In Place of Fear* (London, 1952), 246.
3 . A valuable exposition on the Sankey Commission may be found in Henry Pelling, *A History of British Trade Unionism* (London, 1971), 159– 166.

The powerful ministry of the 'red minister of religion'

Aneurin knew as much as anybody that there had been a serious and well-organised militant spirit in Tredegar during the two years he had been in London. The community was loyal to the local miner leaders which had set up the Tredegar Vigilance Committee. Its chairman was none other than the Reverend J. J. Harrison, who was regarded as one of the most militant ministers of Welsh Nonconformity within Tredegar.[1] The usual name given to him by his friends and foes alike was the 'red minister'.[2] Under his leadership, the committee had managed to raise the enormous sum of two thousand pounds by Christmas 1920. Back from college, Aneurin Bevan was full of admiration for the 'red minister' and his clear leadership for the working-class cause. For his part, Harrison enjoyed being in the limelight and made sure he appeared on the Labour Party platforms in his splendid bright red tie to show his solidarity with the working class. He was invited to address the miners at an annual May Day rally, along with the more cautious middle-of-the-road Evan Davies MP and Morgan Jones, a full-blooded pacifist who was elected shortly afterwards as Labour MP for Caerphilly.

Under the guidance of Reverend J. J. Harrison's leadership there was valid co-operation between the chapels and churches, and with the emerging Labour Party. Labour College classes were held at his instigation and friends of the cause contributed to the *Daily Herald's* appeal for the town's children, many of whom were experiencing real hunger. In all, £2,878 was raised through various meetings, concerts, carnivals and other collections.[3]

Some of Tredegar's chapels decided to purchase shoes for those children who were on their electoral roll. This would enable them to attend Sunday school and the annual witness march through the town in the name of Christianity. Bevan was fully aware of the leadership provided by the chapels and in particular by the Reverend J. J. Harrison. In fact, he admired the fellow rebel, a man dedicated to the gospel witness but also enthusiastic about Christian socialism. In April 1921, Aneurin Bevan chaired a meeting of Tredegar miners. George Barker a militant trade unionist and the future MP for Abertillery came to address them on the possibility of another strike. One of the Monmouthshire miners who won a scholarship to the Labour College was Sam Fisher of Nine Mile Point Colliery, who

---

1 *Merthyr Express*, 10 December and 21 December 1920.
2 *Ibid*, 7 May 1921 edition
3 There is no mention of the Reverend J. J. Harrison by Michael Foot in his biography of Aneurin Bevan, but he was rescued from oblivion in Susan E. Demont's research PhD thesis, 'Tredegar and Aneurin Bevan: A Society and its Political Articulation 1890–1924', PhD, University of Wales, Cardiff, 1990, under 'Experience of the Labour Movement 1919–1926' and 'Strikes and lock out 1919–1921'.

decided to support and enjoy as much as he could the fellowship of Bevan. Some of the miners' leaders in Tredegar and Sirhowy weren't happy that the two mature students were present at the meeting rather than studying in London. A letter was sent to the headmaster W. W. Craik to express their surprise to see the students at home in Monmouthshire. Craik replied immediately that both had been given his permission to be there. Despite this, many of the colliery lodge officials weren't comfortable with Bevan. There was a strained relationship between him and many of those leaders who, in his estimation, were in the moderate camp like Evan Davies, their Member of Parliament. The leader of the moderate wing was usually the secretary of the lodge, David Griffiths, who was not rejoicing that Aneurin Bevan, 'the extremist' as he called him, had come back to town during term time to stir up trouble as he always did.[1] Bevan knew this group of influential local leaders were opposed to him. In contrast to his college friend Jim Griffiths, who was welcomed by the miners of Betws when he returned from the Labour College, Bevan did not receive a hero's welcome in Tredegar. Ten years later, the people of the Amman Valley held a concert in Jim's honour to celebrate his achievements as a trade union leader – he was elected then as the president of the South Wales Miners' Federation. Bevan never reached the higher ranks of the Miners Union as Griffiths did.

Aneurin often heckled by the local miners

At political and coal-focused meetings, Aneurin had to endure much torment. Some would shout loudly at him, 'Sit down, you Bolshevik!' Miners who had been involved in the First World War were consistently rude whenever Aneurin opened his mouth. Two influential Colliery Lodge officials, John Yandell and William Allen, tried to quell the outbursts, especially when the temperature of the meetings rose and a brawl seemed likely. It's important to remember that years earlier Bevan had been duly elected as chairman of the Tredegar Combine Lodge; yet even before going to college there was scarce welcome for him at these meetings. On one occasion, Bevan lost his temper:

> Well, now I will rule. I rule that the meeting is out of order. It is not a Combine Lodge meeting as there are many outsiders present, and you must look for another chairman.'[2]

---

1 *Merthyr Express,* 6 August 1921.
2 *Ibid*, 31 May 1919 edition.

Consequently, he left the stage like a bullet. To him, the enemy was the Tredegar Coal and Iron Company, but he knew there was a lot of antipathy towards him from the trade unionists who had been most supportive of the Great War, including members of his own union, who regarded him as a lucky miner who had escaped the horrors of Flanders and the trenches. He was twenty-three when he returned to Tredegar and still regarded by many of his co-leaders as an extreme socialist. There was no work and no welcome from the coal owners. To complicate matters, his father was now more or less an invalid so Aneurin had no option but to walk from one colliery to another looking for work. This he did with verve. His mother was most concerned with his affliction on his eye and felt that he should consider an alternative employment to that of mining .. The truth was the all-powerful coal company didn't want him anyway among its miners. Worse, Aneurin's own trade union was not prepared to fight his corner because his personal membership had been postponed while he was being educated in London.

Aneurin was out of work and on the dole for three long years, apart from a six-week period when he was employed to open up roadside dykes. His unemployment – a nightmare for him and his family – was an experience he never forgot for the rest of his life. Between 1921 and 1924, he received only two shillings a week as unemployment pay. His mother, Phoebe, and the rest of the Bevan family loved and cared for him during that period. He could not afford to attend a further education college in Newport as he did not have the resources . When he got a salary of two pounds a week , his unemployment benefits ceased .Bevan was in tears when he told his mother that soon the entire family would have to live on his sister wages. Arianwen was happy with the arrangement, but the experience would rattle her brother for the rest of his days. The colliery owners did not only deny him a week's work, but took pleasure from being able to dent his pride too. Clearly, they were ready enough to punish men who had courage to speak their minds or whom they regarded as Labour extremists. Aneurin Bevan never forgot the physical and emotional wounds inflicted on him. When he had the opportunity to address the government of the day from the back benches of the House of Commons, he did not rest on his laurels, but used his considerable oratorical skills to condemn every one of the Tory establishment figures and their Liberal poodles for their wickedness. He accused them of being determined to inflict punishment as often as tjhey could on the working class of Wales.

Tredegar's poor people would come daily to seek their MP's help at 7 Charles Street and the young Marxist became quite an authority on insurance and benefits, frequently arguing with the authorities on his constituents' behalf.[1] He fought for his ailing father's right to a health benefit and won the day. His mother was over

---

1 Michael Foot, *Aneurin Bevan, Volume 1, 1897–1960* (London, 1963), 45.

the moon, and advised him to take up a career as a barrister, promising the Bevan family's financial support for his studies at the Inns of Court. Phoebe realised more than anyone else in the family that Aneurin would be a wonderful advocate within a law court.[1] Alas, he did not listen to her plea, as he was not ambitious in that way. One would never hear him talk of a career or a calling; for his highest wish was to come to the aid of people who had been badly treated by the Tories. It was they, after all, who had stripped his family of a decent living and taken them to the brink of starvation.

Contemplating the option of emigrating

Bevan had contemplated emigrating to Australia or New Zealand or Canada like many other miners he knew well. James Williams of Charles Street was one such mining friend. In April 1927, Williams, his wife and their six children moved to New Zealand. As chair of the Tredegar Workers' Institute from 1919–1926, Williams was presented with a gold watch from the managing committee. Bevan's friend David Minton, of Blaina, did his utmost to persuade him to join him in moving to Australia. The men had been protesting outside Bedwellty workhouse on a really fine day when Minton addressed his loyal friend:

> Aneurin, this country has gone to the dogs. Come with me to Australia. I sold my house and I'm able to pay my debts and pay for a ticket for the boat. My home cost me six hundred pounds. I had a hundred and fifty for it. You and I can do better in the new country than here, as the only thing left is to rot in lying around doing nothing.[2]

Aneurin Bevan was fond of his friend – Minton was an example of the working class at its best, with his socialist principles, determination and innate intellect. On hearing Minton's appeal, Aneurin wept and became silent. He did not wish to say anything to deter or upset his friend. Later, he found enough strength to respond:

> David, I'm upset to see you go, but if that is how you feel, then you must go, and I wish you every luck. As for me, I'm going to stay to battle it out. You are older than I am and have lost your home, and it must be difficult to live here with your old memories. But if these young men leave, who is there who will put up a fight? And I cannot bear it seeing them winning.[3]

---
1 *Ibid.*
2 *Ibid.* 46–7.
3 *Ibid.*

Aneurin did not speak these words easily for his whole being was telling him to say farewell to his loyal friends and his loving family too. At home, he recounted the story to his father. After a few minutes of silence, David Bevan answered his son: 'I think you have made the right decision, but it will be a long, drawn-out battle.'[1]

The establishment of discussion political groups

In the winter of 1921–22, under Aneurin Bevan's supervision, a dozen young Tredegar socialists decided to set up a club along the lines of the National Council of Labour Colleges, which were doing splendid work in the Welsh valleys. W. W. Craik, J. P. Millar and others, were responsible for training young trade unionists, the most ambitious of whom became Members of Parliament. The NCLC was achieving a great deal among the working classes of Britain.[2] There was a similar success story in nearly every coal-mining town. When the Lodge meetings finished their official committee business, many Marxists and leftist socialists would meet up with their NCLC tutor who, invariably, would have been educated at the Labour College in London. This local class would eventually turn into a branch of the Independent Labour Party, or the Connolly Socialist Labour Party or even a branch of the Communist Party. Some of his friends at the Lodge tried to persuade Bevan to turn the class into a branch of the Communist Party but, although he was well versed in Marxism, he rejected the suggestion, as his friend, Oliver Jones testified.

His words were, 'You'll be cutting yourselves off the main flow of the Labour movement.'[3]

Bevan wanted to establish a discussion group in every colliery where members could talk about – and recommend – important writings on socialism and share their viewpoints. The work of Professor G. D. H. Cole and his unique vision of socialism, that is Guild Socialism, was discussed regularly as were the ideas of William Miller and the possibility of socialists taking direct action.[4] In Tredegar, this discussion group evolved into the Quest Club. Badges with a question mark were ordered and a constitution was prepared. Each member was expected to pay a weekly subscription to be set aside for any potential bad times, especially when a fellow

---

1 *Ibid*, 45
2 *Ibid*, 48. One of these Members of Parliament was Bernard Taylor, who was MP for Mansfield. In his early days as a collier, he was a tutor in his local Labour College tutorial class. Here is his testimony years later: *'The National Council of Labour Colleges has every reason to be proud of the work it did in the field of working-class education. It made knowledgeable socialists and equipped them with information that has stood them in good stead and made them more effective in their work for the Labour Movement.'* See Lord Taylor of Mansfield, *Uphill all the Way: A Miner's Struggle* (London, 1972), 102.
3 Michael Foot, *Aneurin Bevan, Volume 1, ibid*, 48.
4 *Ibid*, 49.

comrade might need assistance. The Quest Club met every Sunday afternoon at the Workers' Institute. Initially, members comprised young miners in their twenties, with the exception of Oliver Jones, a great influence on Bevan, who had been involved in the mining industry for years. These were truly militant lads who were engaged in a difficult propaganda battle with the colliery owners as well as middle-of-the-road trade union leaders. They were frequently scrutinised by the nonconformists, in particular by the lay preachers of the chapels – who were often criticised for their hypocrisy – and who in the main were in charge of the Band of Hope (for children), with its long history of promoting temperance. Matters pertaining to Monmouthshire County Council and the role of the local MP Evan Davies often appeared on their agenda. They discussed Christianity and other recognised religions practised locally. Karl Marx's philosophy became a way of life for them. They even adopted his famous words as their slogan: 'The philosophers have only interpreted the world differently; the point, however, is to change it.'[1]

Many a time, they would listen to a peroration from Aneurin Bevan in which his anger was directed at the Tredegar Coal and Iron Company. It was company owners and officials who, in his opinion, ruled the town and lorded it over everyone. The company owned the land and most of the workers' houses, while company representatives controlled the local council, the Medical Aid Association, the hospital committee and the Workers' Institute. Company officials and their families also dominated Tredegar's Chamber of Commerce. The Quest Club embarked upon a crusade to bring the self-important owners and officers of the company down a peg or two, while gaining more power for workers in Tredegar. The plan was to turn their efforts towards the colliery lodges, the ward Labour Party meetings and the Trade Council Chamber of Commerce, where they had lined up at least two hundred militant socialists to speak.

When Bevan announced that they could, in time, convince working-class organisations to support militant and uncompromising Labour, his friends rallied around his ideological vision. His first goal was to get more capable and committed Labour Party members elected on to the local district council, not as moderates but as visionaries who would argue for social justice. The council was, at the time, invariably controlled by the Independents or Liberals, who had failed to implement any substantial improvements. The Liberals were moderates who kept away from any burning topic to avoid confrontation and whose agenda was hardly revolutionary. Bevan thoroughly enjoyed his battle to become a Labour councillor in 1919, even though the local electorate's loyalty to the Liberals meant he failed to gain a seat.[2]

---

1 Bryan Magee, *Confessions of a Philosopher: A Journey Through Western* Philosophy (London, 1998), 211.
2 *Merthyr Express,* 22 June 1918.

Opponents of Aneurin Bevan and his own prejudices

Some of his supporters advised Bevan to contemplate standing for county rather than district council, but he refused: it was better to begin in Tredegar among his own people. You needed patience with the electors as well as stamina, he insisted, after finishing fourth on 8 April 1922. An opportunity would soon arise. Three other senior Labour candidates *were* elected, meaning the Labour Party now had four councillors out of sixteen on the district council. The local press immediately recognised the 'former student' Aneurin Bevan as a trouble maker, who bombarded the council clerk and chair with difficult questions and suggested social improvements which were unacceptable to most councillors. One of Bevan's greatest opponents at the colliery and the council was David Griffiths.[1] A bitter personal battle developed between the two men, each with their own supporters. During meetings of the combine lodge, both men would address the meeting, with the miners invited to decide who had won the debate. Bevan usually outshone his rivals and was bitterly disappointed that he always lost to the formidable Griffiths. David Griffiths never won the debate but he always won the vote of the miners.

Like every politician, Bevan had his prejudices and frustrations, one of which was his opposition to the Workers' Educational Association (WEA). He believed he had gained a lot from the National Council of Labour Colleges and owed a great debt to them, but viewed the WEA as an adult educational organisation which was void of any militant viewpoint, politically speaking. Its mission was simply to educate adults and not – like the Plebs League – to raise political concerns about the government of the day. As far back as 1918, even before going to the Labour College, Bevan had been against the idea of holding WEA classes in Tredegar.[2]

When he returned home after attending the Labour College, he and Sydney Jones had duly arranged a seven-week course on the subject of sociology for the Plebs League in Blackwood. The two men were the course tutors, but it was all a labour of love. The WEA paid its tutors, NCLC did not. The expectation from the Plebs was that those who worked on behalf of the Labour Colleges Council did so for free.

Bevan could be extremely confident and sometimes tended to be a little bombastic in his dealings with middle-class officials as well as Miners Union trade unionists. His friend and contemporary, Oliver Powell said this of him:

---

1 *Ibid*, 22 October 1921 edition.
2 E. Demont, 'Tredegar and Aneurin Bevan', 295.

> He (Bevan) was throwing his weight about and the people didn't like it at all. He was interfering and he had no standing with the union actually, but he was always on the platform, he was always on about the officials, he wouldn't let go. No, he was distinctly unpopular.[1]

Those who had been educated at the central Labour College were looked upon as extremists by some of the South Wales Miners' Federation officials, both at a local and national level. At a meeting, one student acknowledged they were 'rejects' as far as the townsfolk were concerned. It's uncertain what Aneurin hoped to achieve by being so irate. His pressing wish was to beat David Griffiths, but his behaviour spurred many who might otherwise have supported him to opt for his opponent. Similarly, the first time Bevan tried out for the job of check weigher at Tŷ Trist Colliery, he missed out because he was viewed as one of those people who delighted in stirring up trouble. Leaders of the masonic lodges criticised many of these so-called extremists who would drag collieries into such a situation that the company officials could not condone their stand. Bevan himself had not recently taken any part in the colliery, as he was giving his time to the unemployed. Local miners' agent, George Davies, admired him on one hand but feared him ever becoming a local councillor.

Eventually, Aneurin Bevan was elected and his work programme was a vast one. He took a detailed interest in the condition of the houses, water, health and every aspect of the town's life. Indeed, he was of the opinion that much of the town's housing was in a deplorable condition. According to the local paper, the *South Wales Weekly Argus,* he said:

> People were living in conditions not fit for criminals. No doubt horses, especially race horses, were housed much better than some of our citizens are being reared.[2]

Bevan fought vigorously for the establishment of a dynamic housing committee under the supervision of the district council, calling for as much government aid as was possible, especially as a result of the Wheatley Housing Act of 1924.[3] The Act had been a wonderful accomplishment of Labour's first term in office under

---

1 *Ibid*, 172–6.
2 The same story may be had in the *Weekly Argus* by the health officer for Tredegar in his annual report for 1928 when he says: 'Suffice it to say that nearly all housing evils, such as over-crowding, cellar dwellings, tent and van dwellings, and old dilapidated houses, are still with us'.
3 The action of the Labour Government of 1924 in bringing John Wheatley's Housing (Financial Provisions) Act 1924 into existence is still praised. See Nicklaus Thomas-Symonds, *Nye: The Political Life of Aneurin Bevan* (London, 2015), 42.

the leadership of Ramsay MacDonald.[1] David Bevan became very fond of the extremely religious Scotsman John Wheatley, who was associated with radicalism as well as the devotional spirit of the Catholic Church at its best.

The plight of the poor vexes him

The living conditions of the poor in his home town upset Councillor Bevan, who was still a young man. In January 1923, over a thousand unemployed miners went to protest against conditions at Bedwellty Workhouse and managed to imprison the guardians for two days and two nights in order to convince the rest of the country of the injustices suffered by its inmates. The Bedwellty workhouse came under the jurisdiction of the system established by the Poor Law. Following the First World War and the Great Depression, the workhouse represented poverty in Wales (and the UK) at its very worst. Most of Bedwellty's board of guardians empathised with the frightened and poor conditions of the patients within the large workhouse. It was a grim place: the stench of so many people in wards together, the monotonous diet and lack of activity. In the workhouse, the frail and very old had nothing to look forward to but a certain, painful death. The Conservative government accused Bedwellty's board of making payments which were far too generous for the unemployed. On 5 February 1927, the health minister Neville Chamberlain passed the so-called Board of Guardians Default Act.[2] Bedwellty Workhouse had received the sum of £1,024,000 in loans, leaving it with a massive debt of £976,520. Chamberlain wrote to the guardians saying they were far too merciful in their approach and cared too much about such distressing people. This meant in his opinion that they were over-spending unnecessarily. The battle of the guardians, as it became known, was between those who served on the board and the Tory establishment. Thirty of the fifty-four governors at Bedwellty were members of the Labour Party. Chamberlain appointed three commissioners to govern Bedwellty workhouse instead of the elected guardians; as a result, benefits to the poor were severely curtailed. It was a difficult time, and Neville Chamberlain succeeded in getting his own way in the House of Commons.

There was no-one of Aneurin Bevan's sympathetic compassion there to challenge him. The Bedwellty board was the third such organisation to have received Chamberlain's scorn and he became the laughingstock of intelligent left wingers within the ILP and Labour Party. Aneurin Bevan never forgot this difficult period in his life, the unnecessary suffering of the unemployed and those in the workhouse.

---

1 Bedwellty, *Gwyddoniadur Cymru yr Academi Cymreig*, 71.
2 Michael Foot says, *ibid*, t.107 – '*to the people of Ebbw Vale and Tredegar, the most hated and vindictive measure ever placed on the Statute Book*'.

It was a sad difficult world and, as Oliver Harris, a veteran of the Miners' Federation in Monmouthshire, said of Tredegar and Bedwellty:

> The Bedwellty poor are asked to live on less than one third of what it actually costs to feed, clothe and shelter some of the inmates of our workhouses.[1]

Bevan immersed himself body and soul in the battle of Bedwellty and in raising awareness among his fellow socialists of the evil that was in action in his neighbourhood. He saw Neville Chamberlain –a minister of state with privilege and wealth – doing his utmost to oppress the needy and the working class. Bevan became the unofficial leader of his district and town, indeed of his generation. It was cause for great joy for him to gain a place in the Labour Party's executive committee in the Ebbw Vale constituency and ultimately to be elected its chairman in 1923. Another pioneer was Eugene Cross, then a miner but who later became a highly respected officer at the Ebbw Vale steelworks. Neither he nor Bevan had much admiration for their MP Evan Davies, nor any confidence that he would stand up for his constituents. .

After the end of Labour's first session of government in 1925, Aneurin Bevan and Harold Finch travelled to the Labour Party Conference in Liverpool as miners' representatives.[2] While he did not get the opportunity to address the delegates, he was able to voice his opinion within the mining contingency. There was no way of silencing him, and the president of the miners' delegation, Stephen Walsh, asked who he was and where he came from. Harold Finch answered the question: 'Here is Aneurin Bevan of Tredegar.' 'Well', responded Walsh. 'My God, he's a smart boy.'

The death of David Bevan

One night in February 1925 it became apparent that David Bevan was battling for his life. Before the night was over, he had passed away in his son's arms.[3] According to the local press David Bevan was well known in the town 'because he was the father of Aneurin Bevan, chairman of the executive committee of Tredegar Combine Lodge, leader of the Labour movement in the electorate of Ebbw Vale, and a dedicated member of Tredegar Urban District Council.[4] Then his Welshness was mentioned, his skill as a literary figure and translator and his support of popular

---

1 *Ibid*, 81.
2 *Ibid*, 67.
3 *Ibid*.
4 *Ibid*.

culture – the culture which was responsible for keeping the Welsh way of life alive. This was very apparent at David Bevan's home. , he was a Welsh nonconformist par excellence. What does that mean? This was well-expressed by the longest-serving Welsh nationalist president and the first Plaid Cymru MP in Westminster, Gwynfor Evans:

> A great part of the secret of its nonconformity was its use of essential elements of the Welsh tradition; in its sermons, its hymns and anthems, in its appeal towards the mind and feeling, and in its use of the Welsh language. Without any help from neither government or privileged class, its people created a cultivated pattern of social living.[1]

That is a summary of the life and world of David Bevan who was accompanied on his final journey by his family, his coworkers, and the Baptists of the district. According to Michael Foot, Aneurin walked with the deacons to the cemetery on top of the hill, believing that there was no hope of ever again finding a friend like the one who had passed away in his arms. David Bevan was a huge influence on his son, and that is why Aneurin was so sympathetic to the values and Welsh heritage which had been passed on to him during such a depressing time in the life of the people. It was the age of the great migration. Half a million people were forced to turn their backs on their country between 1921 and 1939. Some 259,000 Welshmen and women had to leave the industrial valleys that Bevan loved passionately.[2] It was a period of change and poverty, where soup kitchens were set up in the chapel vestries. Old clothes were given to the people of the villages and towns, and scores of Welsh people in their choirs would sing in exchange for some money on the streets of London. It was a time when Wales the country and the Welsh nation meant hardly anything to the imperialists who were in charge of the United Kingdom. The editor of an English-medium magazine entitled *Welsh Outlook* wrote, after the election of October 1924, that it had all been very nearly hopeless because the supposed attention given to the *Land of Song* and the miners had been missing.[3] But in Tredegar, there was a man who was ready to fight in the name of his father's generation as well as his own. That man was Aneurin Bevan. Within the midst of his fervent supporters at the Query Club, he recognised an opportunity to effect political change in Blaenau Gwent, Wales, the United Kingdom and beyond.

---

1 Gwynfor Evans, Aros Mae (Swansea, 1971) , 273
2 Nicklaus Thomas-Symonds, Nye: The Political Life of Aneurin Bevan (London, 2015), ,59
3 Michael Foot, *ibi.*, 68.

Moving house and gaining a new job

The year 1926 had been a memorable one. After his father's death, Aneurin's mother and family moved from Charles Street to Beaufort House on Commercial Street where a front room was put aside on the first floor for Bevan to use as an office.[1] By now, he had literally jumped in and filled a gap, doing much unpaid work for the South Wales Miners' Federation. The local miners created a new job as disputes agent for him. The Fed wasn't ready or far-sighted enough to acknowledge the new post; however, the colliers at the combine lodge appreciated his dedication to their welfare. The miners of Tredegar were asked to vote, with 1,953 voting in favour of the new post and 621 against. The job, unique in the Monmouthshire coalfield, gave Bevan a task to accomplish and some financial resources to help him. Every miner belonging to the combine lodge was expected to pay a penny a week towards his wages of five pounds. These earnings were very good, as no miner would receive that amount for a week's work. A phone was placed in his office, and every miner who had a complaint knew where to go and who to ask for. Aneurin was in his element; day after day he debated with colliery officials and agents of the powerful Fed and similar institutions. His sister Arianwen agreed to act as his secretary and to be in charge of his busy office.

Aneurin Bevan was by now a well-known figure at the Miners Medical Aid Society in Tredegar and the miners' vision to form clubs to pay for a doctor before the end of the nineteenth century had been realised in the town. In the twenties, there was a local hospital where the Scotsman and doctor A. J. Cronin provided medical care. (Cronin later became a popular author and his novels *The Stars Look Down* and *Citadel* provide a fascinating glimpse into the mining communities in South Wales.).[2] The majority of the society's members paid weekly for the facilities. In return, they could receive the free services of a committed doctor like Dr Cronin and have a chance to see specialists who attended the local hospital when there was a need. Members also received glasses and medicines for free as the need arose. If a patient needed more specialist treatment, an examination was arranged at a hospital outside Tredegar within a few days, again free of charge. Patients would receive money to travel by taxi to that particular hospital, or transport could be provided by the Medical Aid Society. As a result of the efforts of miners in areas such as Tredegar, an embryonic form of health service was created in the Victorian

---

1 *Ibid*, 68
2 Nicklaus Thomas-Symonds, *Nye: The Political Life of Aneurin Bevan*, 39. The novel *Citadel* sold more than any other book by the London-based publisher Collancz in its entire history. The wife of Dr A. J. Cronin, namely Mrs (Dr) Agnes Mary Cronin (neé Gibson) (1898–1981), was a physician at Tredegar Hospital in the twenties.

era that did not exist in many areas in Wales. Aneurin wanted Tredegar's health system to be replicated in every town and district across the country; it was this vision which spurred him to create the National Health Service in 1948.

The General Strike of 1926

In early March 1926, Sir Herbert Samuel produced a report on the coal mining industry for the Royal Commission.[1] This time, the report did not advise nationalising the industry, but supported the owners' case to reduce wages, thus lowering the miners' living standards. The owners were not prepared to move an inch under the leadership Evan Williams, the Pontarddulais-born president of the Mining Association of Great Britain. The miners' leaders felt betrayed. They had a leader who would never compromise. There was no moderation to be had in the vocabulary of A. J. Cook of Porth, secretary of the Miners' Federation of Great Britain.[2] It was he who coined the slogan: 'Not a minute on the day, not a penny off the pay' – a saying his predecessor Frank Hodges would never have uttered.[3] Aneurin Bevan was one of Cook's greatest admirers. He counted him as a hero, as indeed he was to all Britain's miners, apart from a considerable number of them in the Nottinghamshire Coalfield.

For a long time, the miners had been asking for the nationalisation and financial assistance for the industry – there was no chance of it coming. The miners believed their union could depend on the support of others which belonged to the Trade Union Congress. The government failed to give clear leadership as had been expected, and all the talks came to an end on 2 May. There was no choice but to strike, which meant a General Strike lasting from 3–12 May. During this unique chapter in the history of the Labour movement, there were nine days of comprehensive press articles, analysis and of blaming both sides. Labour brought orators from up and down the country to address the striking miners at their collieries.[4] While it came as a surprise to the UK government that hardworking trade unionists in Wales would stand in solidarity, the determination to stick together provided consolation to Aneurin.

Local humanitarian and religious groups actively supported Tredegar's miners and their families; however, the mightiest and most influential support came from the combine lodge and its dispute agent. There were 236,000 miners in Wales in 1926, and the miners held at the beginning their own, but soon enough there were

---

1 D. Ben Rees, *Jim*, 94.
2 John Davies, Hanes Cymru (London, 1990), 531. 'Cook was utterly uncompromising and a genius as a ruffler of feathers.'
3 164 D. Ben Rees, *ibid*.
4 Michael Foot, *Aneurin Bevan*, 68.

examples of apathy, even idleness, on the part of some of the other trade unions. The government decided to put pressure on the miners by doing away with the Seven Hour Act of 1919 and renewing the so-called Special Powers Act. Aneurin Bevan frequently travelled to Cardiff, getting together with others to make the miners of South Wales a notable example to all the miners of Britain. Tredegar's executive committee was meeting daily at the Workers' Institute with Aneurin at the helm. An argument arose between him and the Inspector of Police, Robert Edwards, because the latter could foresee violence on the streets. His exact words were 'If there's any trouble here, we'll have the place running with blood.'[1] After all, Tredegar was famous for its riots.

Wasn't there one against the Irish and another in 1911 against the Jews? The tenor of Bevan's message to the police officer was this: if the police behaved as they ought to, there wouldn't be any violence on the streets of Tredegar. He was right and Inspector Robert Edwards had no reason to complain about the behaviour of those on the peaceful strike.

Burning the *Western Mail*

The only enemy Aneurin made during the strike was the Cardiff-based *Western Mail*. The paper defended the colliery owners every step of the way, badmouthing the good name of A. J. Cook and his team of speakers. Bevan was so angered by its propaganda that he led a march to Waunpound, a mountain which stands between Ebbw Vale and Tredegar, where he burnt two dozen copies of the *Western Mail*.[2] The 'funeral' sermon was delivered by Bevan himself, the miner's friend but no admirer of the so-called national newspaper. He thus made an enemy of the paper forever and made sure Tredegar library did not order a copy of the reactionary, anti-Labour paper during the year of the General Strike. Despite this, towards the end of Aneurin's life, the newspaper extended an invitation to David Llewellyn, a moderate Tory who became an MP for Cardiff North, to write a booklet entitled *Beloved Patrician*.

The 1926 strike lent added lustre to the militant spirit in the collieries. The miners' working conditions were difficult and depressing. Unemployed miners could not receive any benefits or help from guardians of the poor, but those very guardians could give aid to women and children with pay-outs of twelve shillings a week to a mother and four shillings per child. Educational authorities could give free school meals to the children and most did.

---

1 *Ibid*, 69–74.
2 *Ibid*, 71. He made sure that he had plenty of supporters to be able to destroy the *Western Mail*, namely the edition of 1 November 1926. See Nicklaus Thomas-Symonds, *Nye*, 44.

Important tasks for Aneurin Bevan

In Tredegar, Aneurin had at least two tasks to fulfil. Firstly, as chair of the huge Combine Lodge and of the Council of Action, he was chiefly responsible for handing money out to those who were on strike.[1] On top of this, he made sure each person associated with the mines – trade unionists and non-members alike – would receive financial assistance. Secondly, he turned the Council of Action into a movement to assist people who were in deep trouble. Under its auspices two soup kitchens were opened. Two Tredegar-based choirs went off raising funds all over the country, while there were free concerts, sports days, and brass and jazz bands from Cardiff and Newport to entertain the community. Some Tredegar shopkeepers were appalled and jealous of what Aneurin, his right-hand man Archie Lush and his committee could do. The matter was raised in the chamber of Tredegar District Council, where criticism was directed at what Councillor Aneurin Bevan had achieved without consulting with his fellow councillors or with local charities. Bevan had no difficulty in defending himself. They had to move quickly to implement his ambitious plans, he explained. Tredegar councillors should be focusing on what had been achieved, for example the soup kitchens were preparing food for at least fifteen hundred out-of-work men every day.[2]

Moreover, they had raised the funds for the food by their own efforts and had not asked a penny from the council. Some councillors were annoyed that Bevan's personification of the role of the Labour Party as a benevolent benefactor ignored the critical role of the council, that is the council chairman ought to be the committee chairman in such a scheme. Bevan realised every local government rule had been turned on its head but he was unperturbed: the various schemes and plans had been in his hands and he was content with the final results. The ordinary people who had been helped knew who their real friend was. One aggrieved councillor admitted: 'Aneurin Bevan has been too smart for us; we are absolutely whacked.' Indeed, one miner went further and said of him in a sarcastic tone:

> No wonder men like Mr Bevan urge us to stick it out. Mr Bevan goes to London and I go to the soup kitchen. I challenge that I have paid four times the amount he has into federation funds during the last ten years.'[3]

Many of Bevan's followers laughed at such crass enmity. Thereafter followed a powerful speech by Aneurin Bevan, the unofficial leader of the miners of Tredegar and district.

---
1 Nicklaus Thomas-Symonds, *Nye*, 44.
2 Michael Foot, *Aneurin Bevan*, 72.
3 *Merthyr Express,* 12 November 1926.

There was no time to lose, he said. Had they dragged their feet, they would not have had the tidy sum of £160 in the kitty. His committee was being supported by 80% of the population, and he invited the council or any of the dissatisfied miners to dare interfere with arrangements which were popular and acceptable. In order to maintain its authority, the council insisted two of its councillors be co-elected onto the welfare committee. Bevan merely asked, in all sincerity, how many 'shekels' were the two new ones ready to collect? The people he wanted around him were doers.

Bevan emerges as an effective administrator and orator

Bevan was master of the situation. He showed his gift as an administrator, as an orator , as a leader of the community. He was someone who could speak and also take action. According to Michael Foot:

> Tredegar survived the ordeal better than many towns, thanks to his energy in organising a whole series of activities, apart from the kitchen meals. He was not afraid to show his authority to others beside the police.[1]

However, it wasn't only in Tredegar that Bevan was cultivating some status for himself. He was making himself available for debates and emerging as a representative of the poor and needy in his beloved town and the mining villages that extended an invitation to him. At a Miners' Federation of Great Britain conference on 16 August 1926, Bevan joined Arthur Horner for the first time, to try and enlighten the miners as to their socialist vision. Aneurin Bevan was concerned, as was Jim Griffiths, at seeing the Communist Party double its membership in South Wales in 1926. A Miners' Minority Movement was being established and supported in many areas. The unofficial movement afforded opportunities to many miners and provided intelligent miners like Aneurin Bevan, Will Paynter and Arthur Horner (the last two being prominent Welsh communists of their time) the opportunity to provide strong community leadership. Indeed, the *Western Mail* correspondent pointed out: 'That even Napoleon had no greater influence with the guards than plain Aneurin Bevan has with sections of the Tredegar proletariat.'[2] This was a chance for them to get a platform for their syndicate ideas, even though Bevan made sure he kept the communists and communism at arms' length. Thus, it was the fiery leftist socialist general secretary Arthur Cook who had the last word at the August conference of the Miners' Federation of Great Britain.

---

1 Michael Foot, *ibid,* 72
2 *Western Mail*, 28 October 1926

Bevan admires the fighting spirit of Arthur Cook

It was at another conference on 7 October 1926 where Aneurin Bevan made a name for himself, when he won the argument that the strike should carry on and rounded on those who had gone back to work. Among a number of other suggestions, he called on the men who were defending the colliers to refrain from working, feeling they should concentrate on propaganda work within the Labour movement. Even though Arthur Cook was calling the safety men from their work, he had no choice but to accept that this time Bevan had the last word. In a vote, 589 of the representatives were in support of Bevan's argument, with just 199 against.[1]

Adopting the Fed's offer clearly showed how militant the Welsh had become; however, according to the secretary of the Safetymen's Union, the MFGB had no right to call on them to strike. The Minority Miners' Movement earnestly called on him, 'Fight, Arthur, fight like hell, the men are with you.'[2] But to be fair, neither Bevan nor anyone else needed to have said anything to Cook. The Labour movement had never seen a more committed agitator than him. He ventured all over Wales, England and Scotland, wherever there was a coalfield, urging the miners to keep together. Despite his pain and tiredness he refused to rest on his laurels. A leg injury – the result of being kicked in 1926 – continued to be problematic due to lack of care. Eventually, Cook's leg was amputated above the knee.[3] Within six weeks of returning to his office, he died on 2 November 1931. Cook had his obvious weaknesses, and his biographer, Paul Davies, has captured his contribution fairly:

> Compared with Ablett, Horner and Bevan – the most intellectually gifted Labour leaders to emerge from the South Wales coalfield – Cook appears unsophisticated, a man of instinct rather than ideology. His thoughts and energy were absorbed by day-to-day actions.[4]

Bevan was keeping a hawkish eye on every working class movement .He kept in touch with the Miners' Minority Movement, even when there was no branch in Tredegar. He attended the National Conference of the Miners' Minority Movement where 883 representatives came together to listen to Tom Mann, one of icons of the left. Having accepted the job of check weigher at Pochin colliery, Bevan's

---

1 Robin Page Arnot, *South Wales Miners: Glowyr De Cymru: A History of the South Wales Miners Federation 1914–1926* (Cardiff, 1926), 69.
2 Interview of Len Jeffreys (Crosskeys) which was held at Swansea University. Richard Burton Archive SWCC/AUD/ 272.
3 Robin Page Arnot, *South Wales Miners*, 69.
4 Paul Davies, *A. J. Cook* (Manchester and New York), 1987, 119–20.

presence meant a great deal. He was pulling hard on the Labour network, providing a forceful link to the Acting Council of the Combine Lodge, for he was an influential member of the district council and was one of most prominent leaders in the affairs of the Labour Party.

Oliver Powell shows his jealousy towards Bevan

The anonymous miner mentioned earlier wasn't the only one complaining how Aneurin Bevan's travel expenses to conferences and meetings were being paid through the generosity of less fortunate workers who were confined to their localities. Oliver Powell was also ready to criticise his friend:

> The hope of going to the conferences was far on the horizon, if we weren't prepared to pay the expenses from our own pockets, and have the Lodge pay for them.

Clearly, Powell believed Aneurin or Dai Griffiths, or one of the other officials at Tredegar and Bedwellty Lodge, were monopolising everything.[1] To him, Bevan was forever in some conference or other. For after all he would love to be elected a member of the executive committee of the South Wales Miners' Federation, but by the time of the Special Conference on 4–5 November, Aneurin was starting to get tired of the bickering from these few jealous but frustrated miners. He was also getting truly annoyed by Arthur Horner's viewpoint. Bevan called for a debate and an agreement. He was convinced the mine owners were the real enemies and, in the miners, the Fed had an 'army of socialists' who were ready to stand as one. He loved being alongside them in the workingclass struggle.

By 1926, Bevan was a key figure both locally and at Fed meetings, in part because of his skill as a speaker, but he was also known as a man of action who was always ready to listen to and support anyone who needed assistance. He was regarded as a hard-working politician who took great care to read the minutes of the council and all its committees in detail. Bevan was a realist, and he was never heard suggesting an amendment on any matter without there being any hope of achieving the purpose .Motivated at all times by his empathy for those struggling on the breadline, including those who were ill (TB was rampant at the time), or disabled or suffering from industrial injuries. His concern for others is the reason he was often seen walking to look at a particular landscape and road conditions. Then he would pop into the local slaughterhouse to ensure hygiene standards were maintained by

---

1 *Bevan's Tredegar: The Man and His Town* (HTV, 1965).

the proprietors or walk to the nearby dam or to the gas works. He was certain to attend every meeting or committee relating to housing, unemployment, the plight of the elderly or the need to buy more library books. Bevan persisted in his campaigning, disturbing many a councillor because he was meticulous and ready to follow every issue which affected his beloved town.

Aneurin Bevan made time for every cause; he was enthusiastic, ready to express his opinion and willing to prepare a written report after every visit he made and the meetings he attended. He had plenty of ideas and a sincere pride in the town of his birth. It was he who suggested a memorial be erected in Bedwellty Park to remember the Tredegar soldiers who paid the ultimate price during the First World War. He managed to persuade the council as a whole to care for Bedwellty Park, despite lack of support from a few vociferous councillors. The truth was obvious: the Labour Party had not yet gained the upper hand in Tredegar (as was the case in many South Wales towns) leaving Aneurin Bevan in the minority on the district council.

Bevan puts his hometown on the political map

Aneurin Bevan was a practical and committed councillor. He could also be stubborn when efforts were being made by other politicians to place Tredegar on the map. The town had produced many people who had made a name for themselves outside Wales, who deserved to be remembered. When an application was made to celebrate the life and work of politician James J. Davies(or Davis), who had been Labour Secretary and a candidate for the Vice Presidency of the United States of America, Aneurin argued against it on the grounds that Davies had held a job as Labour Secretary within a reactionary administration. For him, that was enough for the idea to be rejected and discarded by the civic leaders in Tredegar. One of the councillors asked in the council chamber: 'Can't we forget politics for a while?' Bevan answered like a shot: 'Our task here is to make people remember politics, not forget them.[1]'

Bevan a very powerful advocate in local government

Aneurin Bevan was accused by the councillors of other parties of talking too much in the council chambers, of being determined to get his name in the local papers and of his tendency to ignore the council chair's authority when debating on an issue . At school, as a Labour College student, and now as a councillor, Aneurin

---
1 Michael Foot, *Aneurin Bevan*, 87.

was in his element when he was challenging conventions, discipline, rules and the authority of those who were in charge of affairs. At times, his language could be inflammatory and he was easily given to emotional quarrelling. He was also criticised for nepotism, especially when he managed to get his brother a job as a caretaker at the local hospital and his sister a job as council clerk. He felt the criticism to the core, even though he was a strong character, but always supporting his own kith and kin. His own view was that every job was being filled by people who had convinced the select panel. Councillor W. W. Wakefield ventured to criticise him. Bevan responded by calling him 'an impudent old swine".[1]

Councillor Bowen and Aneurin Bevan were the two that brought contoversy to local government . Their arguments and debates created interest in local politics . Every time Bowen stood up, Bevan would follow; when Bevan was speaking and suggesting a plan, Bowen would be preparing to undermine his argument. Due to numerous other engagements, Bevan had missed many council meetings during the General Strike; while Bowen loved to criticise Bevan when he was present, he did not bother in his absence! There was always a robust and fierce debate between the two men. One of the best was on 3 September 1927 when Bevan said: 'Next April I hope the electors will exercise more care in selecting their representatives.' Councillor Bowen answered as chair of the council: 'I hope so too, and if so, you might not be here?' Bevan got upset and replied in fury: 'If that is the way you uphold the dignity of the council you had better shut up.' Bowen could not withhold his venom and immediately went for another attack: 'Such language as that towards the chairman of the council is very improper, but I am not surprised as it is coming from you.'[2]

Bevan's input to the South Wales Miners' Federation was key to his behaviour within the district council and he was extremely pleased to be offered a scholarship by the *Daily News* enabling him to travel to the continent Europe on behalf of the miners. It was his first trip abroad and he was joined by Arthur Jenkins of Pontypool. The men travelled to Germany, Poland and the surrounding countries to investigate the situation of the coal industry. Aneurin Bevan had always been on cordial terms with Arthur Jenkins, who was by then an Alderman and the most important figure at Shire Hall. Jenkins was disappointed that Prudential Insurance was ready to invest in Poland's coal mines, thus depriving the South Wales collieries of much-needed capital. Both men came to detest the Prudential for its economic stubbornness and lack of support to the South Wales coalfield.[3]

Bevan's biographers tend to regard him as a supporter of syndicalism from his youth. However, a fellow NCLC tutor, Len Jeffreys of Crosskeys, maintained that

---

1 *Merthyr Express,* 28 March 1924.
2 *Ibid,* 24 September 1927.
3 Michael Foot, *Aneurin Bevan,* 91–2

Aneurin Bevan had broken ties with the Miners' Minority Movement by the end of 1926 and that his days as a syndicalist had long come to an end. Susan Demont asks the question: 'Had he been a serious syndicalist?' She comes to the conclusion that he hadn't been, at least not in terms of syndicalism as an ideology understood by Noah Ablett.[1] To Ablett, there was no political party worth joining, and he more or less turned his back on electoral politics. Not so Aneurin Bevan. He fought constantly for a place as a district councillor, latterly with Monmouthshire County Council. By 1926, he was setting his sights on becoming a Member of Parliament. That said, Bevan was upset that a good friend of his, Fred Francis, had stood in Labour colours at elections in 1922, 1925 and again in 1928 and had lost each time. It wasn't easy for leftist activists such as Francis and Bevan to be elected in Tredegar; however, one thing was certain, neither of them wished to hand in the towel; they were not going to give up their ambition without a struggle. By 1928, at least five out of ten Labour councillors on Tredegar District Council were members of the Quest Club. To fellow miner John Lloyd Williams, who remembered him well from the Labour College, Bevan should have been more cautious in his criticism of many a Labour Party grandee. His college principal, W. W. Craik, was a useful influence on him from a left-wing Labour Party point of view.[2] Bevan came back to Tredegar fully believing that it was within that party that he had to win support for his future as a politician. Another friend, Will Coldrick of Abersychan, argued that the vast majority of students whom he met at the Labour College believed it was possible for the Labour Party to win a General Election soon. They spent hours discussing the prospects and a great deal of the discussion focused on the philosophy of socialism or labour-ism as propounded by the trade unions. Which of the two philosophies would appeal to conservatively minded Labour Party members in England was the ultimate question. In Wales, it was a different story because Nonconformity had made the Welsh electorate more ready to accept the passion and honesty of sincere left-wing MPs. They did not want revolutionary socialism but they were always content with passionate socialism.

Coldrick remembered Aneurin as a natural political debater who stood out among his generation as a potential genius. J. L. Williams explained the difference between the two most outstanding Labour College students like this: Jim Griffiths was 'an all-rounder' whereas Aneurin Bevan was the 'bright one'.[3] In the opinion of Williams, Bevan was on the verge of entering Parliament even before Griffiths. That is how

---

1 S.E. Demont, 'Tredegar and Aneurin Bevan', 316.
2 Concerning Bevan and the students, see W. W. Craik, *The Central Labour College 1909–29: a chapter in the history of the adult working-class education* (London, 1964) and Richard Lewis, 'The Central Labour College: Its Decline and Fall 1919–29', *Welsh History Review*, vol. 12, no. 1–4.
3 National Library of Wales: Papers of J. Lloyd Williams, boxes 1/4

so many of his contemporaries were looking upon him by 1926, as the 'bright young man in the labour movement '. We may see in the next chapter how he went about superseding the local Member of Parliament and taking his place as an impressive spokesman for the Ebbw Vale constituency in the House of Parliament.

Michael Foot

Nye and Jennie on their way to Westminster

CHAPTER 4

Off to Westminster

The General Strike of May 1926 and its immediate repercussions had a profound influence on the subsequent political career of Aneurin Bevan. He understood that protesting, striking and rebelling were essential tools of resistance, but recognised that miners of his conviction were desperately needed in Westminster to fight for the fundamental rights of the British working class. He also knew he faced a mammoth task in bringing Tredegar's Labour Party around to his way of thinking. It had been an arduous battle to win seats for a few left-wing candidates in local elections; it seemed the town's voters preferred moderate right-wing councillors to firebrand ones in the Bevan mould.

Difficulty in winning a seat for Labour in Tredegar

The truth was that the Tredegar electorate was most anxious to support middle-aged Labour figures of the calibre of David Griffiths and Sam Filer, while younger and leftist candidates consistently failed to win seats. With the exception of a few right-wing Labour councillors on the district council it was the members of the left who were the more active ones. Despite meeting regularly, in the eyes of the electorate they were wasting their time and were far too extreme. The electorate was often prejudiced against dedicated socialists. It was the same if a female dared to stand as a prospective councillor. Kathleen Vaughan, a middle-class woman of Irish background, had to face stubborn hostility when she stood as a councillor.

When she became leader of the women's section of the Labour Party in Tredegar, Bevan was thrilled for he recognised her talent.

Kathleen Vaughan had energy and ideas. Within two months, the Labour Party in the town had gained an extra sixty women and girls as active members.[1] She organised rallies and persuaded prominent Labour MPs like Philip Snowden, Charles Edwards and Rhys J. Davies to speak at a rally on May 1, successfully filling the town's Temperance Hall. She charged them with concentrating on the gospel of socialism, hoping they would be able to convince the more Liberalminded miners to consider carefully what the Labour Party might achieve with their support. Despite all this, Vaughan did not stand a chance when she stood for the district council. First, she was a woman and thus should be at home looking after her family. Secondly, – and even worse in the miners' view –she had leftist tendencies. But despite drawing plenty of attention from the Tory press, Kathleen never gave in and she stood again for a seat on Tredegar District Council in 1928, only to suffer a dismal defeat once more.

Bevan had the same difficulty

Aneurin Bevan had trodden the same path himself, and failed badly to be within the executive of the Miners' Federation. His natural ambition was to become a member of the executive committee that met monthly in Cardiff. To this end, he did try to become a delegate in 1924, but his friendly tutor Sydney Jones and other prominent trade unionists like Sam Garland of Oakdale colliery were unwilling to stand aside for their young friend despite acknowledging his intellect. This suited the Federation for Bevan had too much to say for himself. They achieved their goal,[2]. Here is the result of the election among the miners:

Sydney Jones (Blackwood)	4,724
Aneurin Bevan (Tredegar)	3,445
Sam Garland (Oakdale)	2,014

Sydney Jones was a left-wing leader in Blackwood who was very popular with the Sirhowy Valley miners. In 1927, Bevan stood against Jones for the third time; he lost again, this time by 896 votes.[3] . Aneurin Bevan did not take his defeat without determination to carry on , however, it made him realise the importance of winning over the more Liberal-supporting miners who had been the backbone of the Liberal Party since the 1860s. He had worked hard to convince miners that they should be the standard bearers of the Labour Party, He was forsaking everything for their allegiance, but it wasn't easy to convince the cautious miners. Like their

---
1 Susan E. Demont, 'Tredegar and Aneurin Bevan', 348.
2 *Western Mail*, 4 October 1924.
3 *Merthyr Express*, 25 June, 1927.

early leaders William Abraham (Mabon) and Thomas Richards, they seemed more than ready to support Lloyd George and the Liberals. For Bevan, the challenge was to garner support for a more radical programme. Yet, he had to accept the inevitable vote and realise that, even with his energy, ability and actions, he wasn't going to replace a popular local leader like Sydney Jones a fellow Labour Party member. Yet slowly but surely, Bevan, Sydney Jones and their supporters were changing the social, cultural and political life of Tredegar. The two men were creating a unique Labour-orientated political culture; it was just, for a short time, that Sidney Jones was the more popular guy.

Bevan became a councillor after a hard struggle

Between 1926 and 1929, Aneurin Bevan was demonstrating his ability to lead the men and women who were becoming the backbone of the growing Labour Party. He convinced enough local people who could sing in harmony and tune to join a Labour Party mixed choir. By 1928, Tredegar had a functioning Labour Party orchestra, which was ready to participate at festivals. The choir and the orchestra worked together to put on popular concerts during the summer months.

The town's trade and labour council came forward to sponsor a drama company called Labour Players and plays of note were performed, filling the hall at every performance. This was encouraging to Bevan and his team of helpers and made him hopeful for the future. He also enjoyed the praise which he was receiving regularly from other working-class areas. As far as the Labour Party went, Tredegar was as good an example of a full social and political programme as any town of its size in South Wales. Every aspect of the locals' lives came into contact with the party. Indeed, the local paper, the *Merthyr Express*, praised Tredegar as a Labour town as early as 1924.[1] During the four years that followed, the link was made all the stronger. The efforts of Bevan, Sidney Jones, Reverend J. J. Harrison and other Labour leaders were creating a socialist stronghold with meetings held every Sunday night. During the winter, there were speakers promoting socialism; in the summer, sporting events were held as well as tea parties, carnivals, dances and brass band marches on the streets. Much of this would take place, not on a Sunday evening, but rather on a Saturday afternoon and evening, so that the weekend was full of activities for every age group.

Bevan succeeded in the local elections of 1927 even though Councillor Henry

---

1 The local paper could note the success of Bevan and his compatriots in their campaign. Here is the testimony: ' . . . that in Tredegar they could congratulate themselves upon organising a Labour movement second to none in South Wales, and they add every phase of the movement provided for, even to an orchestra, which was promising to become a very fine one'. See *Merthyr Express*, 22 March 1924.

Bowen attacked him inside as well as outside the council chambers, in the hope he would lose badly at the polling booth. But Bevan had his core staunch supporters, the so-called Quest Club, which by now was making plans for others to be leaders and taking constant action within the Labour Party. Club members were sincere and active comrades, who included some extremely bright young men, such as the future Oxford University graduate Archie Lush, and miners of the calibre of Oliver Powell, Eddie Howells, Len Brain, Oliver Jones and J. B. McPherson.[1]

As a result of all this committed activity, Aneurin Bevan and his co-workers were managing to gain access to key organisations in the town and even to the district council. By 1928, five out of the ten candidates for council seats were members of the Quest Club. Come the following year, Aneurin Bevan was chairman of the Miners' Welfare Committee, the Workers' Club and the Committee for the Unemployed as well as vice-chairman of the Hospital Committee before being promoted to the post of chairman. In time, he would represent Tredegar on a host of other bodies, such as the Monmouthshire Association of the UDC and the Western Valleys Sewerage Board. He was a primary and secondary school governor in Tredegar and a governor of the University College of Wales, Cardiff.[2]

There was, however, one important matter which in his mind, and in the opinion of others, needed attention. The town was not being adequately represented in Parliament. The local representative Evan Davies, who had been the Labour MP for Ebbw Vale for nearly a decade after succeeding Tom Richards in 1920 was completely different to Bevan.[3] The Ebbw Vale constituency had been created back in 1918 and included the three industrial valleys of Ebbw Vale, Tredegar and Rhymney. In 1921, 55.6% of workers over twelve years of age depended upon the coal industry for their living. Like Tom Richards, Davies came from Beaufort and had been since he was a twelve years old when he started at the colliery . Davies landed his first job as a sub-agent in 1904 and, by 1913, he had been made a miners' agent in the Ebbw Vale region. After becoming involved in politics, he won a seat on Ebbw Vale District Council, was chairman of the council in 1914–1915 and was appointed a Justice of the Peace a year later. Davies held a number of important positions and responsibilities, acting as Sunday school superintendent at the Calvinistic Methodist Chapel; he sat on the Temperance Council and was a member of Ebbw Vale Education Committee and the general secretary of the Monmouthshire Association Friendly Society. He and Tom Richards were the best of friends and, after his services to the mining industry, Davies deserved to be considered his successor. He won the nomination and was duly elected without a contest at the General Election of 1920.

---
1 Susan E. Demont, *ibid*, 355.
2 *Ibid*, 356.
3 See J. Graham Jones's valuable study, 'Evan Davies and Ebbw Vale: A Note', *Llafur*, vol. 3, no. 3, 93–99.

Dissatisfaction with the local Labour MP

Unfortunately, Evan Davies didn't possess the passion to represent a constituency where there was so much poverty and injustice. In the 1923 General Election, his seat was contested by a Liberal candidate and many people believed Davies was then in trouble. The Reverend Gordon Lang a very prominent socialist stated in a letter to the fervent Calvinistic Methodist Welshman and anti-establishment supporter, E. T. John on 28 November, that he feared that what was a safe seat would be soon lost to Labour because Evan Davies had been neglectful of the electorate within Westminster.[1] There was no need however for Gordon Lang to worry: Evan Davies retained his seat with a majority of eight thousand. Labour activists and supporters celebrated Davies' victory with a tea party, where delicious food was accompanied by numerous speeches. Evan Davies spoke eloquently enough but was overshadowed by an unemployed miner who had just been elected to Tredegar District Council: the energetic Aneurin Bevan.[2] His mighty words warmed the hearts of families who were struggling to live on next to nothing. As the historian John Davies acknowledged:

> By the beginning of winter 1926, nearly every family was burdened with a load of awful debts; and many valleys children had to go to school barefooted. Invariably, they were transported to school on their fathers' backs while the mothers – who gave of all they had – were fainting through lack of nutrition. The average mortality rate amongst babies was increasing rapidly.[3]

Then, without warning, the constituency was confronted with a serious tragedy. On St David's Day, 1927, an explosion occurred at the Marine Colliery in Cwm, near Ebbw Vale and fifty-two miners lost their lives. When the Prime Minister, Stanley Baldwin, visited Cwm to extend his sympathy to the bereaved families, some of the devastated miners mocked him and called him a murderer. The Federation responded with disgust at the miners who had heckled Stanley Baldwin as he visited the site of the tragedy. The miners' anger erupted and caused the trade union much

---

1 The Reverend Gordon Lang was the founder of the Young Socialists' League and a prominent member of the Independent Labour Party in Tredegar. See National Library of Wales, Papers of E. T. John, 4049, letter of Gordon Lang to E. T. John, dated 28 November, 1923. Here are his words: '*We may lose Ebbw Vale owing to Evan Davies's shameful neglect of duties both at the House and in the constituency. It is a pity as the seat should be unassailable.*'
2 *South Wales Weekly Argus*, 22 March 1924, which is quoted by J. Graham Jones.
3 John Davies, *Hanes Cymru* (London, 1990), 534.

anguish.¹ For Bevan, it was Stanley Baldwin's inhumane government which was ultimately responsible for the dangerous working conditions of the coal mines.

The respectable Evan Davies naturally opposed the cat calls, the boos and the heckling, indeed the whole disturbance. Despite spending his working life in the coal industry and being the local MP during hungry times, he seemed unable to sympathise with the frustration of the rebels in Cwm. What , Evan Davies did was to apologise publicly to the famous Conservative politician who visited the windswept landscape after the disaster. To a socialist like Bevan , the miners' response to the Prime Minister was a perfect example of 'action-taking by some irresponsible lads'.² For Evan Davies, their actions had left a stain on his constituency —he claimed the rest of the world agreed with his condemnation. Aneurin Bevan was bereft. For him, Evan Davies, the people's representative, had aimed his ammunition at the wrong target. Bevan believed he had no option but to speak loudly and clearly on behalf of those 'irresponsible lads' as Evan Davies called his own people. The unofficial miners' leader of north Monmouthshire spoke words which were long remembered within the mining communities:

> I am one of the irresponsible lads who did a little rescuing. We did not know about Baldwin's visit until the police tried to stop us from climbing into a lorry which was going to carry us home because we were caught between Stanley Baldwin and the cameras. We had been overawed by the hypocrisy and could not stop ourselves from voicing our feelings.³

Around that time, as we have seen, a few people were elected as active members of the Bedwellty Board of Guardians by the Tory government. This board cared for the poor inhabitants of six populated parishes, namely Nantyglo and Blaina, Rhymney, Tredegar, Pontllanfraith, Ebbw Vale and Abertillery. This meant a great number of Ebbw Vale's electorate were to be found within the vicinity of the Bedwellty Board of Guardians.⁴

It was Aneurin Bevan who was leading the local campaign for fairer conditions for the poor, the forgotten and the unemployed and not the local Member of Parliament. During 1927 and 1928, the commissioners who were chosen by Neville Chamberlain were seen to be behaving cruelly and bureaucratically, while the local

---

1 Ness Edwards, *History of the South Wales Miners Federation*, Voume 1 (London, 1938), 141. One can understand the sharp words of the Liverpoolbased politician Eric Heffer when he said: 'Labour is nothing without the trade unions, but the trade unions can survive without the Labour Party.' See Eric S. Heffer, *The Class Struggle in Parliament* (London, 1973), 246.
2 Hywel Francis and David Smith, *The South Wales Miners in the Twentieth Century*, (London, 1980), 79–81.
3 *Sunday* Worker, 6 March 1927.
4 Siân Rhiannon Williams, 'The Bedwellty Board of Guardians and the Default Act of 1927', *Llafur*, vol. 11, no. 4, Spring 1979, 65–77.

MP was opting out of the bitter struggle. In Bevan's mind, it should have been Davies who was leading the marchers. It's also true that Davies sent letters to the press expressing concern over the behaviour of those who had voiced their displeasure and charging them with being 'inhumane and bullyish'. Davies went as far as to claim that these grown-up miners acting as vandals had created a 'state of mind which was impossible to come to terms with in a civilised community'.

Failure of Evan Davies, MP to be a hardworking constituency representative

The failure of Evan Davies to take a prominent part in Parliament and not calling on the commissioners to be sacked was a matter of concern to the inhabitants of the communities of the Ebbw Vale constituency. By 1927, Bevan's supporters felt there was a pressing need to replace their local MP. First, Davies' record in Parliament was deplorable. Between February and August 1922, he was one of the quietest of all Labour MPs. Between October 1921 and December 1925 he did not take part in any House of Commons debate. By November 1927, he was regarded as a mute Member of Parliament, having only spoken seven times in seven years.[1] When some of Bevan's supporters challenged him on his atrocious record, he defended himself on the grounds of physical tiredness, claiming he was suffering from neurasthenia, a medical condition characterised by lethargy and tiredness.

A campaign demanding Davies' resignation began. Evan Davies was in deep trouble by now because two key constituency officials seriously opposed him: Aneurin Bevan, chairman of the constituency Labour Party and Archie Lush, its secretary. The people in the terraced houses and farmhouses were at the end of their tether.[2] They wanted and needed working-class leadership and a self-assured defender of their battered communities. The electorate yearned to see Aneurin Bevan, not Evan Davies, as their parliamentary representative. On street corners and in the council chamber, Aneurin continued to highlight the desperate situation. As councillors and Labour leaders, he argued, their duty was to appeal to the commissioners more fervently than ever in order to lessen the pain and worries of those who had so little to live on.

Evan Davies was not only hopeless in his role as representative of the Ebbw Vale

---

1 See *Hansard,* vol. 139, 17 March 1921; vol. 147, 28 October 1921; vol. 189, 16 December 1925; vol. 194, 4 March 1926; vol. 1917, 30 June 1926; vol. 25, 27 April 1927, vol. 211, 20 November 1927

2 Here was the situation in Tredegar in 1928: *'But there was in the town literal starvation. . . They had reached a point – when they had to be grateful for charity in order to keep way hunger from the people.'* The inhabitants of Tredegar received help form the councils of Aberystwyth, Cheltenham, Oxford and Torquay during 1928 and 1929. See *Merthyr Express*, 8 December, 1928.

electorate at Westminster but had completely neglected those communities who were fighting for sustenance, fresh and healthy food, comfort from the cold and cultural provision for their leisure time,[1] He did not answer his constituents' letters nor keep his promise of attending important meetings. Archie Lush, Aneurin Bevan and others heard Davies was worried about debt; however, he kept all this from his officers who might have been able to assist him in his hour of need.

Archie Lush, who was Evan Davies' agent, said in an interview that the responsibility for sorting out the situation of the neglectful Member of Parliament lay on his shoulders, as his friend Aneurin Bevan would never have done anything practical to resolve the situation.[2] As Harold Finch said, there were constant complaints about the MP's indifference and rumours about his behaviour, including flirting with girls and drinking to excess. He was apparently close to bankruptcy at one point. Lush himself felt humiliated and sickened by Davies, who regularly postponed long standing meetings with him and failed to respond to his correspondence. Lush could write to Davies four times on the same issue, without a response, an apology or an offer to reschedule an engagement. Archie Lush couldn't tackle Davies's negligence on his own. He thought of bringing it to the attention of the executive committee of the South Wales Miners' Federation. It was the Fed which sponsored Davies in the Ebbw Vale constituency and not the Labour Party, a situation echoed in many south Wales electorates, such as the Rhondda and Llanelli The Labour Party always needed finances and without the trade unions they were in peril of bankruptcy. Most constituencies with a former miner as an MP depended a great deal on the trade unions. The trade unions could survive without the Labour Party, but the Labour Party could not thrive or win electoral battles without assistance at election times and the levy of trade union members. There was quite a struggle between Lush and the executive committee of the Miners Federation in its Cardiff office because the officials were, for the most part, content with Evan Davies. To them, he was a model parliamentary representative.

An opportunity to replace Davies

After a long discussion, it was agreed accepted that members should be given the opportunity to support Evan Davies or choose a new parliamentary candidate in his place. Davies was, after all, an acceptable and respected politician in the eyes of many of his fellow Labour members who came from a similar mining

---

1 'Occasionally he cancelled meetings in the contituency at the last moment.' See Michael Foot, *Aneurin Bevan 1897–1945,* vol. 1 (London, 1962), 92.
2 Swansea University, Library of the South Wales Miners, tape number 73. Conversation between Sir Archie Lush and Dr Hywel Francis, 11 May 1973, 25.

background. Nominations were submitted on St David's Day 1929, with further ballots held on 16 and 30 March. There were six candidates, including Davies. The results were:

Candidate	First ballot 1 March	Second vote 16 March	Third vote 30 March
Aneurin Bevan	3066	3809	5097
Bryn Roberts	1816	2208	2626
Evan Davies	1533	1859	1710
George Davies	1060	730	–
T. Rowley Jones	328	–	–
W. C. W. Ball	225	–	–

A different kind of Labour candidate for Ebbw Vale

Evan Davies was deselected and Aneurin Bevan was nominated as Labour's parliamentary candidate for the Ebbw Vale constituency; it would be he fighting the 1929 General Election. Archie Lush was convinced his clever, sincere friend was on his way to the House of Commons. There were certain commonalities between Davies' and Bevan's backgrounds. Both came from the same area: Davies came from the small town of Beaufort but now lived in Ebbw Vale, while Bevan had been born and lived all his life in Tredegar. The two had also left school as young lads to work in the mines. But there was also a world of difference between them. Aneurin Bevan took advantage of two years of Marxist-orientated education at the Central Labour College, an experience which had given him a more cosmopolitan outlook. Davies' 'square mile' Westminster approach disappeared with Bevan; who adopted a cosmopolitan approach .Whereas the respectable, self-assured Evan Davies avoided conflict and complicated issues, the younger man was more than happy to stand up for the underprivileged throughout the world. Bevan was fortunate in his friendship with Archie Lush, who had witnessed first-hand Evan Davies' weaknesses during his dedicated voluntary work (for which Davies was most ungrateful).

Evan Davies refuses to accept the decision of the miners

Evan Davies did not accept the verdict of the miners, he even demonstrated his pettiness by writing articles which appeared in the Tory press during the 1929 election campaign. In them, he criticised the Labour Party, launching an attack on its stand on capitalism. He made it clear he didn't swallow the 'socialist utopia' propaganda.[1] He also supported Conservatives policy on war and defence.

Aneurin Bevan campaigning at the 1929 General Election

Bevan's first campaign meeting was held in Beaufort, Evan Davies's home ground, where he and Archie Lush were surprised and anguished at the audience reaction. In fact, Bevan's address was met with deathly silence rather than applause.[2] According to Lush, it was Bevan's speech impediment which was the issue; at least Evan Davies could speak without a stutter. Following the rather depressing meeting, Bevan and Lush headed up Llangynidr mountain for a chat. Aneurin Bevan was in turmoil and wondered if he should have refused the nomination, or pulled out and let Bryn Roberts win? Roberts was from the same mining background and had experienced great poverty after his father's death. The two men had studied together in London and Roberts was now an agent at Rhymney Valley Collieries. In Bevan's view, he would have been the ideal Member of Parliament.

Archie Lush suggested Bevan visit one of the giants of the Labour movement in the constituency, namely Alderman Mike Murphy, and ask him to act as chairman at the meeting in Cwm.[3] Murphy was a strong-minded politician with a prominent moustache, who immediately agreed to chair the proceedings at Cwm village school. Bevan was consumed with anger for the awful situation in which local people found themselves, as a result of Tory government. The colliery disaster in Cwm had given him much to be concerned about and he had many emotional and packed public meetings with miners and their families throughout the election campaign. Aneurin Bevan was at his best in these meetings, where he found himself talking about his vision for Britain. Having overcome his stuttering, he developed into a fiery speaker, full of Welsh 'hwyl'. On these occasions, Bevan would talk for a whole hour, sometimes an hour and a half, without notes. He was just himself, and his strong voice and clear, sincere and relevant material was well-received. Night after night, he

---

1 Evan Davies wrote to the *Western Mail*, 8 May 1929 and 23 May 1929 and to the *Merthyr Express* on 18 May 1929
2 Michael Foot, ibid, 95.
3 *Ibid.*

reminded his audience how the people of Ebbw Vale constituency needed someone to speak up for them. He emphasised his mining background and spoke of how the Monmouthshire valleys had nurtured Chartism in the nineteenth century. They owed a huge debt to his father's generation, he told them. These were the brave people who stood for socialist principles at the beginning of the twentieth century.

Aneurin Bevan knew that his personal manifesto had to expand beyond the confines of Tredegar; he had a sizeable section against him in his own ward. People in the towns of Ebbw Vale and Rhymney had to get to know him, admire his convictions and believe in his burning message. During months of campaigning, Ebbw Vale constituents heard an unfamiliar and very different message from their Labour candidate. At meetings, Bevan focused on the essentials of socialism, democracy and republicanism, believing victory was a matter of political education. He was realising that what he and his comrades had accomplished in Tredegar had borne fruit a hundredfold. When he campaigned for a seat on Monmouthshire County Council in 1928, he had a good team to support him and to distribute pamphlets from door to door. Aneurin Bevan won the seat for Labour and, just a year later, he and his team were ready to dispatch him to Westminster.

Bevan knew there remained important leaders within the constituency who still had a soft spot for Evan Davies. They included representatives of the Miners' Federation of Great Britain and the South Wales Miners' Federation in Cardiff. These officials ignored the blatant truth that Evan Davies was entirely to blame for what had happened. As one of the constituency officials, Lush could not allow him to stay as a representative of a constituency which called out for a candidate who would be ready to support the *status quo*.[1] Davies had been included in the ballot, but failed to gain sufficient votes to win the Labour candidacy.

Aneurin spoke at election meetings in Beaufort, Cwm, Ebbw Vale, Waunlwyd, Victoria, Rhymney, Sirhowy and outside the iron works at Ebbw Vale. He gave a dedicated place to *Labour and the Nation*, the manifesto carefully prepared by the WEA guru R. H. Tawney. The Conservative leader Stanley Baldwin did not manage to inspire the British voters with his slogans or his budget, which bought discomfort to those who needed comfort. For the first time in their history, the British electorate felt the promises made by Labour – and the real sense of political adventure – deserved widespread support. On 1 June 1929, the following results were announced at the Ebbw Vale count:

Aneurin Bevan (Labour)	20,088
William Griffiths (Liberal)	8,924
Mark Brace (Conservative)	4,287
Majority	11,164

---

1 Swansea University, Library of the South Wales Miners, tape Number 48. Harold Finch as interviewed by Dr Hywel Francis, 28 February 1973, 21.

Bevan had won easily – the majority of those who turned out to vote had voted for him. From now on, this would be the pattern, that is for him to consistently win 80% of the vote at every General Election. Evan Davies had lost the nomination because he had forgotten the importance of local activists and maintaining the confidence of his agent and secretary, Archie Lush.[1] Had he demonstrated some dedication, commitment and sensitivity, Davies could have remained as Ebbw Vale's MP for the rest of his life. He was 'a speaker of the highest standard and a clever man, but one who went off the rails', as a friend claimed at the end of the campaign. Loyalty towards a politician used to go a long way and still goes far within the ranks of the Labour Party's safe seats. But the majority of voters in the Ebbw Vale constituency believed Evan Davies had been succeeded by a far more intelligent, charismatic and intellectual personality than him.

The importance of the 1929 General Election

The 1929 General Election was particularly important as it was the first time everybody over twenty-one had been able to vote. Women had had to wait until 1928 to get the vote on the same terms as men. Aneurin Bevan wasn't the only Labour candidate from Wales to have been elected for the first time. W. G. Cove, a politically active teacher from the Rhondda had won the safe seat of Aberavon – a seat which Ramsay MacDonald had represented from 1923 to 1928.[2] Another first was the election of a woman – Megan Lloyd George (Liberal) – in Anglesey. The Reverend Lewis Valentine stood for the National Party of Wales (established in 1925) in the Arfon constituency, but the former soldier and Welsh Baptist minister only managed to gather 609 votes. Labour won 288 constituencies overall, while 261 were snapped up by the Conservatives and 57 by the Liberals. The Labour Party got its second chance of governing with Ramsay MacDonald as Prime Minister. This time, Labour had a greater majority than the Tories had previously had. MacDonald's great weakness, as Bevan soon realised, was that he was too conservative in his approach and attitude. However, according to the interesting correspondent from Germany Egon Wertheimer, he was among the most important leaders of the

---

1 Vincent Brome, *Aneurin Bevan* (London, New York, Toronto, 1953), 72; Andy Missell, 'Wynebau Newydd yn y Tŷ, 1929' ('New Faces in the House, 1929') in *Llyfr y Ganrif* (editors Gwyn Jenkins and Tegwyn Jones) (Talybont, 1999), 127.

2 J. Graham Jones, 'Evan Davies and Ebbw Vale: A Note', *Llafur, ibid,* 99. Ramsay MacDonald was counted as being one of the charismatic Socialists. He was looked upon as 'one of the gods'. See Christopher Howard, 'Expectations born to death: local Labour Party expansion in the 1920s in Jay Winter (ed.), *The Working Class in Modern British History: Essays in Honour of Henry Pelling* (Cambridge, 1983), 73, 273.

nineteen-twenties.¹ The three who stood out on the British stage, according to the German observer, were David Lloyd George, in the Liberal Party, Stanley Baldwin, leader of the Conservative Party, and Ramsay MacDonald of the Labour Party. But Wertheimer went on to comment how it was an awkward situation with the Labour man acting as a Conservative, the Conservative leader being a Liberal and the leader of the Liberals acting in the mould of a socialist.

This is the tribute given by Egon Wertheimer to Ramsay MacDonald in 1929:

> However little else he may resemble Lenin, this he has in common with the great Russian revolutionary – in the slums of the manufacturing towns and in the hovels of the countryside he has become a legendary being – the personification of all that thousands of downtrodden men and women hope and dream and desire.²

Aneurin disagreed wholeheartedly with such praise and was soon attacking the Prime Minister's conservatism as well as his fear of the harm he could inflict upon the Labour Party in the United Kingdom.

Leaving home for London and the kindness of Guy Eden

In the summer of 1929, Aneurin Bevan left his home in Tredegar headed to London for the opening of Parliament. Still a bachelor, he had spent 32 years in his childhood home before venturing into the big wide world. Ten years earlier, when he had gone to London to learn how to become a working-class leader in the coalfield, he had never dreamed that one day he would be travelling to Westminster to become the most forceful and brilliant parliamentarian of his generation.

His friend Harold Finch escorted him down to Newport station and he remembered Bevan saying to him: 'Who are these people? We are just as good, if not better than them.'³ That was a great consolation to him, but he soon realised that the Conservatives' strength lay in the powerful daily press and Sunday papers, in the world of business and commerce and predominantly in the world of agriculture especially the large farms of rural England and the large estates of Scotland.⁴ Aneurin

---

1 Egon Wertheimer's summing up of MacDonald's role in Western European Socialism had this to say: 'Since the deaths of Bebel, the pre-war leader of German Social-Democracy, of Jean Jaurés, the French Leader, of Victor Adler, the Australian Socialist, and the Swedish Hjalmar Branting, he is beyond question the outstanding figure of Internation Socialism'. See Egon Wertheimer, *Portrait of the Labour Party* (London and New York, 1929), 174.
2 *Ibid*, 176.
3 Michael Foot, *ibid*, 96.
4 A. J. Davies, *We, The Nation: The Conservative Party and the Pursuit of Power* (London, 1995), 3.

Bevan arrived at Westminster as a lonely politician; however, he was extremely fortunate to quickly strike up a friendship with the journalist Guy Eden. Bevan actually stayed at Eden's home, where he would talk incessantly. Eden loved his Welsh accent, his socialist ideas and his honest selfcriticism. Bevan was more human and emotional than most of the people Eden came across in Westminster and he soon came under the new MP's influence, the first of many in the world of journalism as well as in the House of Commons. In his conversations with Eden, Bevan expressed his ambition of becoming a Prime Minister one day as Eden recalled:

> I don't want money, Guy, or titles, or rich living. But power – ah that is something different. Yes, I certainly want power. With enough power, you can do things, you can make your mark, you can leave your name in history, you can help those who need it most![1]

This was Aneurin Bevan's personal manifesto at the beginning of his career. He was an ambitious politician who possessed the confidence both to inspire the British working class and work well with world leaders. It will be interesting to see how difficult it would be for him to gain the position of power for which he longed.

---

[1] Guy Eden,' So Near to No 10', *Daily Sketch*, 7 July 1960, 6.

CHAPTER 5

The young MP's vision 1929–1935

Aneurin Bevan had been voted onto Monmouthshire County Council to represent Tredegar Central Division – with a majority of 127 – the year before he was elected as an MP. It was for this reason that he decided to remain a councillor and combine his council and Westminster responsibilities after the General Election. It was a mistake, but Bevan knew how bad things were in South Wales. David Jenkins, the Labour Party candidate in the Neath constituency election, told the 1929 British Labour Party Annual Conference:

> Comrades, I come from South Wales, the place which is today an economic hell. The people there are degraded, demoralised, they have no hope.[1]

After all the unsuccessful strikes of 1921, 1925 and 1926 (the General Strike), Bevan had come to believe salvation would come to the valleys, not as the result of an all-out attack on the political system, but rather through powerful and illuminating debate on the floor of Westminster. From 1910 to 1929, he had been an activist in Tredegar and Monmouthshire, ready to lay down the law to anyone who refused to listen to the Miners' Federation or to his own passionate message. With Labour the largest party in the House of Commons, it was time to debate the dreadful poverty experienced in places like Tredegar and the destitution of disabled men and women, of widowed mothers. For the first time in its history, the Labour Party had the upper hand over the Tories. It had not been easy for Labour to be elected in 1923 and despite being easier in 1929, the party was in a tight spot for the Liberals held the balance of power with 59 seats. Ramsay MacDonald selected cabinet members with wide-ranging experience, however he overlooked Bevan, a passionate

---

1 The Records of the Annual Labour Party Conference, Birmingham (1929), 3 October 1929, 241.

spokesman for the unemployed. In doing so, MacDonald ignored a politician who might have come up with the radical programme of action that was needed. Instead, MacDonald assigned the task of solving unemployment to another Monmouthshire trade unionist. Jimmy Thomas, general secretary of the National Union of Railwaymen (NUR) was appointed Lord Privy Seal.

Aneurin Bevan enters the House with dynamism

Bevan was a comparatively young man when he entered the House of Commons. Many Labour members came from different coalfields but they were years older than he was. These politicians could be depended upon to support their leaders, with the majority were only too ready to support the right-wing attitude within the Labour Party. The new MP for Ebbw Vale was neither middle-aged nor ready to support the right wing. He was one of the unorthodox and hard-working young men of the Miners' Federation, full of anger at the snobbish, misleading, well-heeled Tories and somebody who had retained his involvement in the Monmouthshire County Council. On a political platform, he would use rhetoric, sarcasm and humour to win the argument over his opponents. When Aneurin Bevan arrived at the Commons, he was undoubtedly still unsure of himself and could be extremely emotional, especially when he was in full oratorical flow. He was very lonely in Westminster as his Labour Party colleagues were even unwilling to support him in his criticism of the Tory bogeyman – none other than Winston Churchill.[1] Bevan could not be ignored in terms of his debating skills, his flamboyant personality or his conventional dress. The first time Bevan saw the dark-haired Scottish politician Jennie Lee, one of Parliament's livelier members and the woman who became his lifelong best friend and partner, was on the House of Commons terrace. She was bemused by the appearance of the young MP for Ebbw Vale. It was clear his mother in Tredegar had dressed him like a respectable dark-suited nonconformist minister of religion who hoped to become a stockbroker one day.[2] She had probably bought the suit in Tredegar Co-op! So Jennie Lee got to know Bevan by pure chance and she immediately tried to persuade him to join the Independent Labour Party (where she was one of its stars). The ILP considered her an 'armchair revolutionary'.[3] Aneurin refused, for two reasons. First, he was moved by the oratory of the Independent Labour Party leader James Maxton but was unable to enjoy a discussion with him .. Secondly, he had worked too hard to establish the Labour Party

---

1 Andrew Marr, *The Making of Modern Britain* (London, 2009), 414.
2 Dan O'Neill, 'Great Orator who would have changed our lives.' *South Wales Echo*, 11 November 1997, 23.
3 Clare Beckett and Francis Beckett, *Bevan* (London, 2004), 17.

in Tredegar to forsake it for a small political party which would never form a government.

The Labour government in the hands of a clique of conservative-minded politicians

The 1929 Labour government was literally in the hands of five politicians, all true founders of the Labour Party: Ramsay MacDonald, the Chancellor Philip Snowden, Jimmy Thomas, the Welshman from Newport, Arthur Henderson who had been an anchor in the Asquith/Lloyd George government and the solid trade unionist J. R. Clynes. MacDonald was the most impressive figure and was described as the hero, the illegitimate lad from Scotland who became for a while an icon of the Labour movement. He had great intellectual talent and unusual eloquence. According to one historian: 'As an orator, though no film exists of his great days, he was clearly spellbinding.'[1]

Herbert Morrison

---

[1] Like Fenner Brockway, Jennie Lee was keen on the Independent Labour Party in Parliament in 1929. See: David Howell, 'Traditions, myths and legacies: the ILP and the Labour left' (in) *The ILP on Clydeside 1893–1932: from foundation to disintegration* (eds. Alan McKinlay and R. J. Morris) (Manchester and New York, 1991), 224. Jennie Lee had won the North Lanark by-election in February 1929 and was re-elected with a majority of 6,578 in the General Election. of 1929. See Vincent Brome, *Aneurin Bevan: A Biography* (London, New York, Toronto, 1953), 71. She wrote extensively about her political life and partnership with Aneurin Bevan. On reaching Westminster, Bevan found a place to stay in the flat of Frank Owen, Liberal Party MP for Hereford above a garage in Cromwell Road, Kensington. These details are from the book of Clare Beckett and Francis Beckett, *Bevan* (London, 2004), 17.

Arthur Henderson , an influential member of the
Labour Party in the nineteen – twenties

When Macdonald was Prime Minister and MP for Aberavon many Labour activists regarded him as 'the Messiah'.[1] But, unfortunately, he did not manage to live up to the high expectations. It was unfortunate that Labour was in power in 1929 given the Wall Street Crash in New York and the economic downturn which subsequently overtook the world. The Great Depression caused even more pain and suffering in ordinary homes, like those in Ebbw Vale where most of the workforce earned their living in heavy industries like coal, iron and steel. Wales, Scotland and the North of England, where the heavy industries predominated, were hard hit and there were tales of real adversity on the streets of industrial towns and mining villages. The Great Depression threatened the entire economic structure of large cities like Birmingham, Liverpool, Glasgow and Manchester where working class people were in the majority. Yet, the effects were even more devastating in Wales' industrial valleys. There was nothing left for the Labour activists to do but to organise the soup kitchens which prevented people from starving. Aneurin Bevan was more than

---

1 Andrew Marr, *The Making*, 261; Aneurin Bevan was described by Gwilym Prys Davies as someone who had 'a piercingly sharp creative imagination.' He added that Jim Griffiths and Bevan had 'personal knowledge of the everyday problems and longings of country people'. See Gwilym Prys Davies, *Cynhaeaf Hanner Canrif: Gwleidyddiaeth Gymreig 1945–2005* [The Harvest of Half a Century: Welsh Politics 1945–2005] (Llandysul, 2008), 30– 1. In the biased opinion of Liverpool's Bessie Braddock, the young MP did a lot of harm to the Labour Party in the thirties. *'He made it fashionable to be a dissident.'* See Jack and Bessie Braddock, *The Braddocks* (London, 1963), 203.

ready to speak up for the millions who were suffering. He had made his maiden speech in Parliament on 16 July 1929 in a debate on the Development (Loan Guarantees and Grants) Act. With his slogan 'better dearer coal than cheaper miners', Bevan attacked his fellow Welshman David Lloyd George in both this and another debate on the Coal Mines Bill 1930. The former Prime Minister felt uncomfortable under the lash of the young Welsh politician. Rising to answer him, Lloyd George paid tribute to him as a fellow countryman who had so much to offer and one of the recently elected MPs for whom he already had great deal of admiration. Despite the collective talents of the Labour administration, it deserved Bevan's criticism.[1] For MacDonald deliberately ignored those MPs, like Aneurin Bevan, who represented militant trade unions.[2] One feminist Bevan much admired was the Minister of Labour Margaret Bondfield, who was the first woman to rise to a cabinet position from within the ranks of the Labour Party. There were other gifted Labour politicians in Macdonald's cabinet, such as Herbert Morrison, the Minister of Transport, and Sir Oswald Mosley, Chancellor of the Duchy of Lancaster. Despite the very difficult economic circumstances, some politicians did a marvellous job. One of these was Arthur Henderson, who proved an effective and first-class minister in Lloyd George's coalition government and later served as Foreign Secretary. Aneurin Bevan regretted that there was little socialism to be seen in their speeches or plans; however he welcomed the strengthening of the Widows' Orphans' and Old Age Contributory Pensions Act, the house-building subsidy and the successful placing of a new Unemployment Insurance Act on the government's statute book. As Minister of Health, Arthur Greenwood set up legislation to deal with urban slum clearance and the school-leaving age was raised to fifteen. In the May 1929 election, the Labour Party had clearly identified unemployment as a subject for government action but sadly, Ramsay MacDonald's government was unable to solve that serious problem. Responsibility was placed on J. H. Thomas, George Lansbury and Oswald Mosley to investigate policies for dealing with unemployment and it soon became obvious that they would never agree with each other or be able to solve the calamitous situation. When Labour came to power in June 1929, there were 1,163,000 destitute workers; by December, that number had risen to 2,500,000, a percentage

---

1 Francis William gives a long list of the politicians who belonged to the Labour Party in 1929–3, adding: 'It was in many ways a brilliant team.' See 'Fifty Years' March: The Rise of the Labour Party (London, 1936), 334

2 Remember that Ramsay MacDonald ignored Aneurin Bevan in 1929 just as he had ignored Henderson in the first Labour Government Cabinet in 1924. '*In his first draft Cabinet, for example, he completely ignored Henderson, the prime architect of the new Labour Party, the only member of it with Cabinet experience, and the one man who could if he had wished have successfully challenged MacDonald for the leadership*'. See Francis Williams, *ibid,* 303–4.

rise from 9.6% to 20%.¹ In the face of a dire world economy, it seemed Labour politicians were proving unable to follow through plans to help their own, that is the the working classes. Oswald Mosley put forward ambitious proposals and tried to attract radical Labour MPs like young Aneurin Bevan to support him. Initially, Bevan did support Mosley; however, he withdrew his support because he could not see where the comfortably off aristocrat was going to raise the capital he needed to carry out his ambitious plans.² The friction between J. H. Thomas and Mosley did not help. Mosley managed to secure the discreet support of the Prince of Wales, then William Morris, an Oxford motor-manufacturer, and finally John Reith, the dry, godly Scot and director of the BBC. But Bevan saw further than the three of them. He prophesied accurately that Oswald Mosley would move from serving the Labour Party to become the leader of British Fascists.³ Aneurin Bevan preferred to support the Socialist League which came into being through the efforts of another rich politician Stafford Cripps rather than bolster the fascist ideology of the black shirts. Stafford Cripps thought the world of the young Welsh MP and, as we shall see, they provided each other with mutual support during the thirties. In the summer of 1930, Aneurin joined Jennie Lee and left-wing friends John Strachey and George Strauss on a journey to Russia.⁴ The three knew that Jennie was going to leave them in Moscow so she could spend her time with her secret lover, the married ILP politician Frank Wise, in the foothills of the Caucasus Mountains. Unlike two of the Labour party pioneers Stanley and Beatrice Webb Aneurin did not lose his head over Russia, a trait which was true of him throughout his career. He could not stand totalitarianism anywhere and the complete disregard of the hard-working small farmers of the USSR, as exemplified by the innate cruelty of Joseph Stalin, horrified him. For Bevan, no politician of any party should trample on human rights. His irritation with the Labour government escalated until, on 4 November 1930, he attacked it for its dismal failure to provide more help for the then two million unemployed. Unfortunately, Bevan kept a close association with Mosley and over the 1930/1 New Year parliamentary recess, he spent time producing the official manifesto for Oswald Mosley's New Party along with his friends John Strachey, William Brown and Allen Young. The manifesto was presented to the press and the electorate in February 1931. Bevan was playing with fire by being closely involved with the launch of the New Party. John Strachey, Oswald Mosley and three others

---

1 Emyr Price, *Cymru a'r Byd Modern Ers 1918* (Wales and the Modern World since 1918) (Cardiff, 1979), 32.
2 Bevan had been disappointed when, in 1932, Sir Oswald Mosley set up the British Union of Fascists. See Michael Newman, 'Democracy versus Dictatorship: Labour's role in the struggle against British Fascism 1933–36', in *History Workshop*, No. 5, Spring 1988, 69.
3 Keith Laybourn, *A Century of Labour: A History of the Labour Party* (Stroud, 2001), 65.
4 Michael Foot, *ibid*, 136–45.

were excommunicated by the National Executive Committee (NEC) of the Labour Party. It was MacDonald himself who saved Aneurin Bevan from the same punishment. By 1931, Britain was in a wretched situation economically facing huge financial problems. The truth was that the country was in debt to international bankers and the Labour Party, because of the cowardice and dreadful moral failings primarily of Ramsay MacDonald, Philip Snowden and J. H. Thomas, was in deep water. The United Kingdom was unfortunate in its leaders and, in particular, its Prime Minister was undermining confidence . Contrary to the demands of left-wing politicians, the Labour government decided to obey the diktat of the bankers. MacDonald agreed with the City that the government should lower unemployment benefit and raise taxes.[1] Unsurprisingly, this raised Bevan's hackles. He realised there would be less to spend on goods and the economy would suffer. Montagu Norman, the governor of the Bank of England, arranged loans from the Federal Bank of New York and the Bank of France to raise money to deal with the depression. Loans of £50,000,000 were organised. The amount was insufficient and was used up in a short time. With Snowden's permission, the Bank of France arranged another loan, this time for £80,000,000. Snowden was warned there were no more loans to be had, which destroyed the confidence of the cabinet and caused a rift within it and the Labour Party. Of the twenty-one cabinet members, ten disagreed with the proposed policy seeing it as nothing less than folly.

The bankruptcy of the MacDonald government

The Labour government could not continue. MacDonald asked for the resignations of all cabinet members and requested to see King George V. He returned half an hour to inform his former ministers that there would be a meeting the following morning with the Conservative leader Stanley Baldwin and the Liberal leader Sir Herbert Samuel. At midday, Labour ministers met in Downing Street to hear startling news. Ramsay MacDonald had agreed to stay on as Prime Minister of a national government with Baldwin and Samuel as star members of the new cabinet.

MacDonald gave no reason for the decision and provided no inkling of whether he had any secret talks before the invitation. Clearly, he was pleased to be rid of his Labour brethren even those with whom he had worked closely for decades. Now he was the National Leader and recognised as such by the other two parties. His ex-colleagues were so disappointed that they could not say a word either in praise or criticism. In complete silence, one after another of Ramsey's ministers left the room. MacDonald asked Snowden, Thomas and Lord Sankey to stay behind.

---

1 *Ibid, 125.*

He extended an invitation to the three of them to join him in the new government. All three agreed, but Lord Sankey was the only one who went to that evening's meeting of the Parliamentary Labour Party to explain why he had accepted the invitation. Members admired him for having come to explain but remained upset with their leader's renegade actions. To them, and to the great majority of the Labour Party, MacDonald was, from that point forward, a traitor. The question that should be asked is whether Ramsay MacDonald was, in fact, a traitor to socialism or was he a particularly irresponsible politician, a man whose actions were difficult to fathom. And, if he was irresponsible, how could he have deceived many good people with scrupulous morals like Arthur Henderson, George Lansbury and Clement Attlee? The Labour government concluded in dire straits, but soon there would be worse to face: another General Election.

MacDonald and Snowden were very ready to belittle the Party for which they had worked tirelessly for years. They had accepted support from Attlee and Lansbury, though they did not deserve it in the 1931 election. Philip Snowden called Labour's domestic programme 'bolshevism gone mad' and the Liberal Walter Runciman went as far as to say that the Labour Party had used Post Office funds, that is the 'money of the poor' to pay the unemployed. In the face of such loathsome propaganda, the Labour Party had a high mountain to climb for an electoral victory.[1] When the results were announced, it was clear MacDonald and Snowden, assisted by the Tories and the Liberals, had practically annihilated the Labour Party. It was now as weak as it had been back in 1910. Although only 46 Labour members were elected, Aneurin Bevan was returned unopposed in Ebbw Vale. He lost his seat on Monmouthshire County Council, but was re-elected in February 1932 by a landslide. This pleased him as he loved the ethos of the council, despite having an atrocious attendance record. His council involvement helped him to understand local government. Despite the Labour Party losing 243 MPs in total, the 1931 General Election confirmed Wales was fast becoming a Labour Party stronghold with sixteen Labour MPs. With three exceptions – George Lansbury, Clement Attlee and Stafford Cripps – the party's former leaders such as Arthur Henderson had been defeated. Following the election, the national government had a massive 473-seat majority, a record for the Conservatives. MacDonald's new National Labour Party won 12 seats, the National Liberals gained 35 and the remainder of the

---

1 McNeil Weir, *The Tragedy of Ramsay MacDonald* (London, 1933), 20–80. From the backbenches, Bevan became one of Ramsay MacDonald's foremost critics. So much so, that he enraged Emanuel Shinwell of all people. He said, 'If Bevan or anyone else believes that the party is insipid or lacking courage . . . Then in my judgement they ought to join the Party organisation which they believe has got the attributes that the Labour Party ought to have.' See Harold Finch, *Memoirs of a Bedwellty M.P* (Risca, 1972), 33; Colin Cross, *Philip Snowden* (London, 1966), 302–334. The biographer gave chapter 17 of the book the title: 'Bolshevism Run Mad 1931'.

Liberals won 33 seats. It was a dark day but, for Bevan at least, there would be no let-up in the battle for democratic socialism on British soil.

The spell of Oswald Mosley

Aneurin Bevan had been greatly disappointed in Ramsay MacDonald. At a time of huge disappointment Bevan for a short period came under the spell of Sir Oswald Mosley. The fascist had plenty of tricks up his sleeve and succeeded in pulling 16 Labour MPs together, with the miners' leader Arthur Cook to support him. Their leader published what was called the Mosley-Cook Manifesto. One memorandum after another was published to confuse the authentic socialists. Mosley knew he was going to betray his supporters for he was on the verge of leaving the Labour Party. When he did, Aneurin Bevan refused to follow him, as did the majority of the MPs. In fact, only four MPs joined his New Party and Mosley was tossed into political wilderness, totally powerless. Bevan was greatly pained when Mosley formed the British Union of Fascists (BUF) in 1932, knowing Adolf Hitler had won 12 million votes in his bid for presidency of the Weimar Republic – his opponent was the incumbent Paul Von Hindenburg. The Nazis had again increased their votes and gained 230 seats in the Reichstag that year to become the strongest party in the German parliament. Hitler was on the point of becoming a complete dictator with progressive and ambitious policies, Bevan realised. He was providing work for thousands, building new highways (the *autobahnen*), setting up new armament factories and establishing the huge Krupp's steelworks in Essen.[1] Britain was not in the same league economically as prosperous Germany. The German Social Democratic Party (SDP), which had had a good relationship with the British Labour Party, was determined to destroy the fascists.[2] A shiver of despair went through Bevan when he recognised how fragile the SDP was, perhaps because he knew the Labour Party he served was equally weak. If fascism were to launch a serious attack on the Labour Party, it would disappear like morning mist from the earth. The party had almost perished under the unacceptable leadership of Ramsay MacDonald. Before 1932, the Labour Party had paid little attention to the problem of fascism, much like the other parties. Adolf Hitler's triumph shattered this complacency. Bevan and other

---

1 The classic is Richard J. Evans' book *The Third Reich In History and* Memory (London, 2015), particularly part 3, 'The Nazi Economy', 167–206. I owe a debt to the historian Richard Evans, of Cambridge University, for my knowledge of Germany during Hitler's period and it is from his book that I have taken the details.
2 'Nazi violence was directed not just at the Communists but also at the Social Democrats, who had provided the most solid support for the democratic institutions of the Weimar Republic from the very beginning.' See Richard J. Evans, 185 ; Robert Griffiths, S .O. Davies, *A Socialist Faith* (Llandysul, 1983), 103–6.

prominent Labour members saw the joint dangers of fascism and communism under the memorable heading 'Totalitarian Dictatorship'. It is easy to compare this with the positive characteristics of Democratic Socialism; however, the people of Europe were slow to see this as a worthwhile option. In Germany, the stark choice was between the communists and the Nazis. Walter Citrine, the Secretary of the International Federation of Trade Unions Council and a huge influence on the international attitude of the Labour Party, was very conscious of the development of German and Austrian fascism since the early twenties.

Moderate Labour Party members, such as Clement Attlee, believed Britain had an excellent record on democracy, but even they had to quietly acknowledge that the economic situation and high unemployment rates were helping the fascist cause. But worst of all for Bevan was seeing the national government trying to get out of its mess by lowering wages by 10% and cutting dole payments to the unemployed. This was to be done by means testing. The means test was inhumane and disagreeable, to say the least.[1] Unemployment pay was cut if a son or daughter brought money into a household or if an ordinary family had a little money in the bank. It was a policy designed to create unrest and tears, disappointment and family tension, and the inevitable consequence was yet more unemployment.

Bevan realises the British establishment is anti-Labour

Aneurin Bevan was realising – especially after 1931 – that the Labour Party was unpopular with the British Establishment and so it was essential to campaign continuously on behalf of his loyal supporters, his constituents and the miners. To this end, Bevan took a strong aggressive position as a left-winger, a political stance with which he felt comfortable.[2] For some in politics, both right and left-wing extremism were to be condemned and both communism and fascism opposed. Thus, any flirtation with the Communist Party deserved total condemnation.

This is why Aneurin Bevan had annoyed so many of the moderate trade unionists when he supported his friend Stafford Cripps to form the Socialist League (an organisation with about three thousand members), believing they should work with the communists in the face of the Great Depression and threat of fascism. Harry Pollitt one of the communist leaders in Wales, said: 'The stark reality is that, in 1933, for the mass of the population, Britain is hungry, badly fed, clothed and housed.'[3] Since

---

1 Michael Foot, *Aneurin Bevan*, 127.
2 Michael Newman, *ibid*, 70.
3 Charles Webster, 'Healthy or Hungry Thirties' in *History Workshop: A journal of Socialist and Feminist historians*, No. 13, Spring 1982, 110. The quotation is originally from Harry Pollitt's introduction to Allen Hutt's book, *The Creation of the Working Class in England* (London, 1933,) xii.

the twenties, the authorities had been collecting information about the plight of the British population and an annual report was published under the auspices of the Medical Research Council. The report's main author was Sir George Newman, Britain's Chief Medical Officer to the Ministry of Health from 1919 until 1935. It seems incredible that Newman reported optimism based on the fact that fewer children were dying of the usual childhood diseases. By 1932, not one county in Wales or England recorded more than 100 infant deaths from malnourishment, representing a drop of around half prior to the First World War. This situation had improved hugely thanks to policies like school meals for children. Now, only 1% of schoolchildren needed help because of malnutrition. No medical officer of health in any of the counties would dare to say otherwise[1]. Aneurin Bevan was annoyed by these reports as he knew there were more depressing material which was not being disclosed. He welcomed the research undertaken by friends of his, such as Fenner Brockway in his 1932 book *Hungry England* and the excellent work of the communist Allen Hutt on the British working class. Sir John Orr, one of Bevan's admirers, expressed his opinion on the failure of the civil service to do its work properly. Orr was soon regarded as a political nuisance.[2] The truth was that Sir George Newman was only too ready to ignore the poor state of housing, the poverty and lack of hygiene that was apparent to any sociologist or politician. His reports made no reference to maternal mortality, frequently during childbirth, or to the birth of disabled children – often due to the general health of the mother and poor nutrition. In Wales, many mothers suffered from anaemia, that is a shortage of red blood cells and haemoglobin, and sometimes the life-threatening toxaemia (now known as pre-eclampsia). The pale, ashen-faced women in the Ebbw Vale constituency were perfect examples. Dame Janet Campbell acknowledged that there were many ill and disabled women in every town and city, with their poor medical condition often a consequence of childbirth. She called these 'dull diseases' or chronic diseases which made the lives of so many working class women burdensome.[3] Discreetly, Newman agreed with Campbell but he was unwilling to express his view publicly as he knew that making public the uncomfortable details would lead to more conflict and debate, as well as the need to publish more reports. As far as Newman was concerned, the Ministry of Health was not prepared to undertake further research. Regardless, the dreadful economic situation in the thirties is a factor no historian can ignore as it was responsible for widespread hardship in all communities throughout Britain.

---

1 By 1940, at least two hundred reports of the Medical Research Council had been published. See Charles Webster, *ibid,* 111
2 National Library of Wales. Papers of Gwilym Prys Davies, Box 1.
3 Charles Webster, *ibid,* 123

Bevan's speeches are attracting publicity

In the 1930s, it was evident that Aneurin Bevan's tempestuous personality and passionate speeches were attracting the attention of commentators, newspapers and politicians of all parties. He had a vision of international socialism, managed to analyse a situation convincingly and was praised for his powerful eloquence. Bevan was a brave and independent backbench speaker, who owed no favours except to those who voted for him in the valleys of Gwent. He acknowledged he was the product of cruel and pitiless economic circumstances and took pride in his heritage.[1] For most miners, he was still their comrade and someone who understood the pride that comes from hard manual labouring.

Despite no longer working in the mines himself, Aneurin Bevan remained full of bitterness, hatred and anger towards the mine owners and the support they had from the Tories. He remembered how, in the Blaenau Gwent of his youth, the coal owners loathed workers like him who were ready to challenge their policies and the politicians who spoke up on their behalf.[2] He recalled how he was almost too tired to walk to the train station after eight hours of hard work underground. His time working in the coalfield taught Bevan the importance of cooperation and caring for one another in an environment where there was the constant risk of explosion, fire, flooding and gas leaks. The miner's world was not a selfish one, it was not every man for himself and God for all. When Bevan left the coalfield for the comfortable, highly privileged life of Parliament, he did not forget the importance of the coal workers in Sirhowy, Rhymney and his beloved Tredegar. In London, Aneurin Bevan became a powerful figure who gained the attention of some very rich people. Lord Beaverbrook – Max Aitken – was the owner of a number of popular newspapers and a rebel himself. He took notice of Bevan and invited him to his dinners.[3] There he liked to listen to the MP debating with Winston Churchill and lesser-known Tories, who been deliberately invited to annoy Bevan and enable him to get the upper hand. It became clear Bevan was developing a taste for good and expensive food, the best wines, classical music and poetry that reminded him of the Rhymney poet Idris Davies at his best. He indulged himself greatly on those occasions and we

---

1 *Ibid.*
2 Kenneth O. Morgan, *Labour People: Leaders and Lieutenants, Hardie to Kinnock* (Oxford, 1987), 69. Aneurin Bevan and S. O. Davies kept the socialist flame alive throughout the thirties. These miners were the two who could be most relied upon to raise the temperature of the debates in Parliament.
3 Edward Marjoribanks, a staunch Conservative, was a friend of Bevan and was bold enough to introduce him to Beaverbrook after the MP's attack on Lloyd George in Parliament in 1930. Foot, as well as the Becketts, say that it was at the newspaper owner's luxurious home that Bevan met so many of the people he greatly admired, such as H G Wells. See Foot, *ibid*, 182–4; Clare Beckett and Francis Beckett, *ibid*, 17–18

can understand why Brendan Bracken, one of the most scathing Tories, called him a Bollinger Bolshevik even though the hero of the left would prefer a bottle of red wine on the table to a bottle of champagne.[1]

Constant emphasis of Bevan and his admiration of his fellow Welshmen

Another truth that Aneurin Bevan highlighted in the thirties was that as an individual, his economic status was declining in the face of companies, corporations and people like Beaverbrook. He understood that concentrating so much wealth and capital in private hands enabled those rich people who so wished to buy and rule the lives of people like himself and the working class. He knew the only reason he received invitations into the homes of these capitalists was to create a stir, upset some of them, and make Lord Beaverbrook popular with his friends. Bevan knew, however, that he was like a caged lion who incited pure hatred among them. In the long term, the answer was to educate and organise the workers to recognise their opportunity by joining the trade unions and standing for their rights. The trade unions would defend the workers in the long run on the understanding that they were not led by the left wing. Aneurin Bevan battled hard with trade union leaders as they neglected their responsibility to achieve better living conditions for their members. He regarded the Liberals as pathetic– apart from Lloyd George.[2] Besides, the most radical of them had already joined the ranks of the Labour Party. He admired Lloyd George's standpoint – he wanted to see the national government spending extensively on national road, water and electricity projects. Neither MacDonald or Baldwin listened to him.

What was important to Bevan was to see ordinary people, like himself, his brothers and his sisters, having control over their lives. His truly democratic socialist outlook did not go down well with his family in Tredegar and Bedwellty, whose only choice was whether to work in the ironworks, coal mine, factory or foundry. They could not buy the coal mine but his brother William could work there as a slave. The plight of the working classes convinced Bevan of the need for public ownership and nationalisation. The Socialist League had a long list of industries it believed were ripe for nationalisation for the good of society, but no government was willing to implement such a radical programme.

---

1 This is confirmed in Robert Griffiths' book, *S. O. Davies – A Socialist Faith, ibid,* 80, 132, 136
2 Bevan called Lloyd George 'the most colourful character in British history'. For him, it was a disaster Lloyd George was left out of UK government from 1922 to 1945.

Proud of his socialism

Aneurin Bevan was proud to be called a socialist. He identified with those who had no option but to work in one of the heavy industries in order to earn sufficient money to rent a home, pay the bills and raise a family. In his view, socialist ideology made the most sense when examined in the light of personal workingclass experience. He was a superb campaigner in Westminster and on numerous platforms, campaigning to create a spirit of confrontation against a mean capitalist system which prohibited a better life for millions of people. The Tredegar rebel's view was that principles matter, yet he was not inflexible either as he demonstrated when he was Minister of Health. He was able to adapt, compromise and listen. He did not believe the current parliament, under guidance of the national government, gave any hope to ordinary workers. What Bevan saw in the lives of most MPs was sufficient wealth and respectability. He had a great deal to say about Marxist philosophy and syndicalism since the First World War. He studied aspects of those political theories, how the Irishman James Connelly saw the situation among the dockers of Dublin and Liverpool, the songs that the Industrial Workers of the World (IWW) sang among the Chicago Marxists, the books of Jack London, which kept the reader awake until the very last page, particularly *Iron Heel*. Bevan understood that medium was, in its own way, telling the same socialist story, the essence of which was that successive governments failed dismally and neglected the workers who created the country's wealth.

Bevan the pragmatist

Certainly, the national government was not been keen to help those who bore the burden of poverty and felt unrepresented at Westminster. Aneurin Bevan was convinced the Trade Unions Congress could take decisive action and organise itself for the good of its members. The apathy of the Labour government of 1929–1931 and the national government of 1931–1935 made him angrier and angrier. He was frustrated by the high unemployment in the valleys. In Brynmawr, the Quakers and Pacifists had set up a camp to help the besieged community, while in Merthyr Tydfil unemployment had reached 63% by 1933.[1] Bevan went to Westminster like a boxer ready to fight for socialism against capitalism and was shocked by the hypocrisy of

---

1 .90% of the workers of Brynmawr were unemployed at the beginning of the thirties. A comprehensive study of the problems and plans was made by Elizabeth Jennings: *Brynmawr: 'A study of a Distressed Area'* (London, 1934), 25–78; see also John Burnett, *Idle Hand: The Experience of Unemployment, 1790–1990* (London, 1990;) Roger Smith, 'Utopian

Ramsay MacDonald and Philip Snowden. They on the other hand considered Bevan a traitor. Philip Snowden was ready to accept the annihilation of the Labour Party to which he had contributed greatly during the first two decades of the twentieth century. When Bevan entered Parliament, the proud Baptist from Tredegar felt as if he had entered an Anglican cathedral, with all the valuable paintings of earls and aristocrats hanging around him in splendour. These were not his forebears – there were no images of Keir Hardie, David Bevan, Noah Ablett or Robert Owen – and Aneurin Bevan could not identify with them.[1] It was impossible for him to inherit the kingdoms of the Cecils and the Churchills. Bevan felt uncomfortable with Westminster's traditional proceedings, which demonstrated not an ounce of passion for change. In those early years between 1929 to 1935, visiting Westminster was a tempestuous pilgrimage where he received little support except from three Jewish MPs, Sydney Silverman, George Strauss and Ian Mikardo. The leaders of his party were punished in 1931, with only three important MPs – Clement Attlee, George Lansbury and Sir Stafford Cripps – meekly protesting against the national government still in MacDonald's hands. None of them was as enraged as Aneurin Bevan. He was truly an outsider.

Bevan's frustration with the Labour hierarchy

James Griffiths

To complicate the difficult situation in which Bevan found himself, the National Executive Committee was under the control of leaders of some of the main trade unions and it was they who determined annual conference policies and how to

---

1 For Keir Hardie, see Kenneth O. Morgan, *Keir Hardie, Radical and Socialist* (London, 1975), 3. 'Hardie's achievement remains immense. He is amongst the handful of figures in British history to have forged a new national party, with an abiding mass appeal. Hardie brings the historian close to the enduring base of the Labour Party whose architect he largely was.'

discipline MPs. The majority of these trade union barons had no sympathy with any MP who was unhappy with the social and political situation. With their thousands of members, the trade unions won every vote at the annual conference. As Aneurin challenged the status quo at every opportunity, he was judged harshly by Ernest Bevin, Walter Citrine and lesser-known Labour characters. He could see the Labour Party was ineffectual in the United Kingdom, but was thankful that at least things were different within the South Wales Miners' Federation. In November 1932, Jim Griffiths, Bevan's co-student at the Central College in London, was elected deputy president, one of the youngest to be elected.[1]

Griffiths regretted that, in 1933, Arthur Horner, the communist firebrand from Maerdy, had been elected to his old post as miners' agent in the Gwendraeth Valley in Carmarthenshire. He also heard that his old college friend Aneurin Bevan had linked up with Horner to form a united front among the miners against fascism. The intention was to set up a militaristic movement called the Workers Freedom Group to defend the coalfield communities. In 1933, the Federation arranged a meeting at Cory Hall in Cardiff to protest against fascism. Unfortunately, Aneurin Bevan was ambivalent on that occasion, arguing for a movement which would embrace military action to confront the fascists. At the conference, Jim Griffiths disagreed, for two reasons: firstly, as a pacifist, he could not agree with the proposal to set up a militaristic group in the mining communities and secondly, he believed socialists should not work outside the ranks of the Labour Party and the trade unions.[2] Aneurin, however, had made a thorough study of the careers of the three fascist dictators, Benito Mussolini, the fascist leader in Italy (1922– 1943), Adolf Hitler, leader of the Nazis in Germany (1933– 1945) and General Franco in Spain (1939–1976). The three found acceptability among royalty and large sections of the establishment as they combined three things: they were strong leaders of their respective countries, the Führer in Germany and Il Duce in Italy; secondly, they were determined to check the forces of communism; and thirdly, they were focusing on solving the problem of unemployment. These policies appealed to Labour Party supporters and constant watchfulness was required. The miners were not allowed by their leaders to support Bevan in any planned violent action and army-like preparations. W.H. May, the miners' agent in the Pontypridd district, spoke sobering words at the Cardiff conference when he said: 'Force has never been any remedy.'[3]

---

1 James Griffiths, *Pages from Memory* (London, 1969), 34.
2 D. Ben Rees, *Cofiant Jim Griffiths: Arwr Glew y Werin*, (Talybont, 2014), 103.
3 *Ibid*.

Jim Griffiths disagrees with Bevan and Arthur Horner

Jim Griffiths was not the only leader frustrated with Bevan and Horner's conduct. In a column in the *Western Mail*, Bevan was described as 'the Welsh Hitler', a characteristic exaggeration from the anti-Labour newspaper as far as he was concerned. It appears that the only area which supported Bevan was his home territory Tredegar and nearby villages such as Pontlottyn. Bevan failed to secure the backing of conference mainly due to the strong opposition of Griffiths, the custodian of the Labour Party's conscience in Wales. Griffiths was ready to agree with Bevan and Horner in their constant criticism of the mine owners but he could not agree with the call for a strike or violent action which would paralyse South Wales and represent a failure to heed the lessons learnt by the working class in 1926.

Despite the protests and outcries, the national government dragged its feet. The economic situation improved a little when higher taxes were placed on imports and when the government gave local councils more money for housebuilding with the result that 300,000 houses were built in 1934. In the same year, money was given to a new body, the British Iron and Steel Federation, to modernise the steel industry. Seeing the situation improving, in December 1934, the government decided to enact the Unemployment Act involving a means test. Aneurin Bevan, Jim Griffiths and other Labour MPs were incensed at the likely implications of the decision. The Federation agreed with Griffiths' proposal to lead a public campaign against the means test and, on Sunday 3 February 1935, the southern valleys came alive with an unparalleled protest. It was all recorded by the leading communist novelist Lewis Jones. His novel *We Live*, based on Cwmardy (a fictitious name for Rhondda), is an important book. The novel's main characters believed that the whole world was protesting. Lewis Jones did not exaggerate.[1] In the Rhondda, or Cwmardy, 70,000 people from all strata of the working class walked in groups of twelve to Winton Park in Tonypandy, in the Rhondda Fawr, to protest in no uncertain terms.

An important day and period in history of Wales

The protests in Tonypandy was on a huge scale .. In Aberdare, 50,000 people marched, while 20,000 listened to Ernest Bevin speaking in Pontypool. In nearby Blackwood, a similar number listened to Aneurin Bevan's eloquent speech. There were marches in Merthyr Tydfil, Neath, Briton Ferry and even Barry. The left-wing historian Gwyn Alf Williams, who remembered the protests as a ten- year-old-lad

---

1 Lewis Jones, *We Live in Cwmardy* (London, 1936), 47.

in Dowlais, said the atmosphere was rather like a massive community singing festival or a huge Sunday school rally. At least 300,000 people marched in the Monmouthshire and Glamorganshire valleys on that historic day. One in seven of the whole population of Wales was on the streets and in public parks showing their dissatisfaction. Here are Gwyn Alf Williams' words:

> It was the greatest demonstration Wales had ever known. There had been nothing like it in the history of the Welsh and there has been nothing like it since. A whole community stood up and said No.[1]

They were saying 'no' to the national government and to the Unemployment Assistance Board. Between 1934 and 1945, the Welsh were fed up with seeing young people leave for English towns like Oxford, Luton, Slough and Harrow, or further north for Birmingham, Stoke on Trent, Manchester and Merseyside. The Unemployment Assistance Board made sure that every payment was strictly regulated. Bevan felt there was nothing left but for him to lead the unprecedented protests. Welsh culture suffered hugely, the already basic salary of nonconformist ministers was reduced even more and the Welsh language was weakened because of the huge emigration.

To many like Bevan, the reason behind the Depression was the failure of Ramsay MacDonald's government and the problems with capital. This provided a significant spur to the left wing of the Labour Party and other movements such as the Communist Party. 'Little Moscow' was becoming a reality in the upper reaches of the Rhondda Valley in the village of Maerdy. In fact, the coal mining villages generally were more like Maerdy than Woodstock, near Oxford, Churchill's family home. As the *Welsh Academy's Encyclopaedia of Wales* says: 'As well, prominent members of the Labour Party – most of all Aneurin Bevan – adopted the essential Marxist analysis of the depression.'[2] Aneurin Bevan was a self-proclaimed Marxist when he was at college in London; however, living through the years between 1926 and 1935 forced him to argue for a democratic socialist way of proceeding. His essential philosophy was that socialism was ready to adapt to the circumstances of the time. His belief was immutable, its foundations unshakeable. In his socialism, there was equality of opportunity and democracy at every level, from the coalfield-friendly societies to cabinet ministers with their ability to create, act, defend and civilise brutish human nature. As an MP, Bevan was in the midst of a serious political conflict between

---

1 Dr Gwyn Alf Williams mentions another village in Glamorganshire which was a Little Moscow, namely the village of Bedlinog in the Merthyr area. 'At the height of the battle against non-unionism, Bedlinog, one of those mining villages where you need magnets in your boots to stand upright, at one time elected a Communist Chamber of Commerce, a rather striking anticipation of Eurocommunism'. See Gwyn A. Williams, *When Was Wales? Ibid*, 269

2 *Gwyddoniadur Cymru yr Academi Gymreig, ibid*, 295.

the hopes and aspirations of the Labour Party's right and left wings. He was, after all, a man of vision and he viewed his own experience as what one Welsh hymn writer had described as the pilgrim receiving hope of security in the wilderness.

Bevan sees the importance of a political party

Aneurin Bevan had recognised the importance of political power when he first entered the Tredegar District Council as a young councillor. and later when he stood for Monmouthshire County Council. Without the power of political government, politics was almost a waste of time. That was why he could not understand his wife Jennie Lee remaining in the Independent Labour Party nor his friend Harry Pollitt in the Communist Party, parties which would never gain power in Britain. Socialism must be accepted as the basis of the Labour Party and then win enough support among the electorate in general elections to form a radical, progressive government. The crucial thing was to convince sufficient voters that the only way to have a government which represented the interests of the common people was to return sufficient Labour MPs. This would involve persuasion and determined campaigning. By the thirties, Bevan had realised how difficult it was to convince voters, particularly in England, to vote for the Labour Party. The result of the 1931 election spoke for itself. But he never gave in. Until the end of his remarkable life, he believed the needs of the people and the power of the state could be reconciled. He was steeped in classical Marxism and in the tradition of Victorian socialist thinkers, but he acknowledged that Karl Marx's ideology was insufficient. In his important book *In Place of Fear* he writes:

> From Jack London's 'Iron Heel' to the whole world of Marxist literature was an easy and fascinating step. The relevance of what we were reading [in the Tredegar Workmen's Library] to our own industrial and political experience had all the impact of divine revelation. Everything fell into place. The dark places were lighted up and the difficult ways made easy.[1]

Bevan could never rid himself of the socialist hope in the dismal years for he became determined to spend his energy on the campaign trail. By 1935, he had realised communist countries like the Soviet Union were not adopting the ideology with which he had become familiar in his youth. He could not align himself with a communism which oppressed and inflicted violence on its people. These ordinary

---

1 I was guided in this part of the chapter by Geoffrey Goodman's excellent essay 'The Soul of Socialism' in *The State of the Nation: The Political Legacy of Aneurin Bevan* (ed. Geoffrey Goodman) (London, 1997), 15–35.

folk were sent to the torture cells in primitive prisons or the misery of life in far away gulags in Siberia. In Bevan's view, Stalin was as evil as Hitler and Mussolini. Socialism without freedom of expression or the right to protest and oppose capitalism by striking and debating was not socialism at all. He acknowledged that, in theory, democracy had been assisted in Britain in 1928 when every adult over twenty-one got the vote. He believed however, that 'democracy was not safe anywhere in the world unless it becomes democratic socialism.'

Historians such as John Campbell who never understood Aneurin Bevan

Many biographers failed to understand Aneurin Bevan's political credo. One such writer was John Campbell. As far as Campbell was concerned, Bevan's outstanding talents had been sacrificed to heretical dogma in the form of socialism. His biography was published in 1987 when Margaret Thatcher led the British government. Thatcher's ambition was to bury socialism, the Labour movement and the trade unions, specifically the National Union of Mineworkers. To Campbell, Bevan was a political dinosaur, the last of the foolish dreamers. Throughout the twentieth century, every insult was thrown at socialism and, indeed, it could be argued that by the late eighties, the Welsh, like the English, the Scottish and the Northern Irish, were dancing on the grave of classical socialism.

As Bevan's great friend, the journalist Geoffrey Goodman says: 'Rather, like Christianity, it is probable that socialism will take a long time dying.'[1] In Goodman's view, had Bevan lived beyond 1960, he would have significantly adapted his thinking which had became so fixed during the hungry thirties.

> His concept of the commanding heights would certainly have shifted from a Ben Nevis perspective of the UK economy to an Everest-like vision across the globe.[2]

Bevan, like other intellectuals in the Labour Party, underestimated the great ability of capitalism to overcome straitened circumstances like those experienced in the thirties.

This was Marx's own weakness. One of the few right-wing journalists who saw any goodness in Bevan was Henry Fairlie, who wrote for the *Daily Mail*. Fairlie had little time for Jim Griffiths yet warmed to the rebel from Tredegar, describing

---

1 *Ibid*, 18–19.
2 *Ibid*, 27–28.

him as a man great in stature and in mind, always animated and enlivening debate, his emotions strong and manly, with a deep belief in Britain. Bevan was a unique individual who had faith in ideas and did not want politics to have the last word on the economy and psychology of the masses. Fairlie felt that as Welsh, English, Scots and Northern Irish citizens, we owe him a great debt. And he adds this tribute to be inscribed with care:

> A democracy cannot survive healthily without the example of individual leaders who dare all as individuals and leave, long after their families are forgotten, the imprint of a great human being.[1]

The word which best sums up Bevan as a politician in the early thirties and beyond is imagination. He said many times that imagination was the strongest weapon of the poet, the writer, the preacher and the socialist politician. He used imagination constantly in Parliament and in his addresses, firing up his listeners in Ebbw Vale and everywhere else he was invited to speak. He would thunder on for an hour-and-a-half using colloquial language, humour and always an excess of imagination. A large proportion of his vast audience would leave the hall inspired, believing Bevan's vision could be realised. To ordinary people suffering adversity, he provided confidence and consolation, plus a vision of what Labour could be achieved as a movement and a party. In his view, this was what mattered. It is impossible to exaggerate the essential nature of Bevan's vision in relation to the world of politics and to British socialism. As a young politician, he was convinced that he as well as Stafford Cripps and others could change the situation for millions in the United kingdom if they could win the general election. It is this vision, his unshakeable conviction in the possibility of change, which made him one of the most important political figures of the twentieth century, not only in Wales and Great Britain but throughout the Western world.

The enormous contribution between 1932 and 1935

Between 1932 and 1935, Bevan embraced his role as a parliamentary spokesman for the unemployed. Leaders like him were so few that he and John Strachey could speak on the subject whenever they wanted. The Labour leader was the pacifist George Lansbury, who was supported by Stafford Cripps and Clement Attlee. The three MPs were very ready occasionally to join in Bevan's debate, speaking with equal conviction and authority. Aneurin Bevan would speak about agriculture in

---
1 *Daily Mail,* 7 July 1960 quoted by Goodman, 33.

Parliament . It was he who described Walter Elliot, the Minister of Agriculture who had a huge estates ce in Scotland as 'a man walking backwards with his face to the future'. Another frequent topic was the iron industry as the old Ebbw Vale works continued to be idle. Then Bevan would give his co-politicians a lesson on economics and democracy. He would not forget the problems of continental Europe and tried to persuade Labour Party secretary Arthur Henderson and Walter Citrine of the Trade Union Congress to take up the reins of authority and organise marches. But they were both deaf to him and his hopes were unfulfilled. He travelled to the United States in summer 1934 to collect money on behalf of the those comrades suffering oppressive fascism in Germany. It was Jennie Lee who persuaded him to do this and, although communists were all too evident among the officers of the movement based in America he succeeded by his oratory to raise a considerable amount of money. Bevan returned to London more convinced than ever that the Labour Party, and particularly the NEC, deserved to be condemned for being so lukewarm towards fascism in mainland Europe. These frustrations were shared by many of his fellow socialists in the South Wales valleys.

This internal conflict became obvious at the Labour Party Conference in Southport in 1934, when the Socialist League was threatened with expulsion and Bevan himself was battling once more for his political life. The Labour leaders wanted to expel those party members who belonged to the United Front and the Communist Party from membership of the party.[1] Bevan as a result was bitterly attacked by Ernest Bevin, Emanuel Shinwell and Herbert Morrison. The NEC won the day with an overwhelming majority of 1,820,000 votes to 89,000. But Bevan did not obey the dictum of Ernest Bevin of forgetting the United Front but travelled immediately to Manchester where he shared the stage with another rebel Arthur Greenwood, a member of the NEC, and Willie Gallacher, the Scottish communist leader. A few days later, Bevan marched in Trafalgar Square against one of the government's laws on sedition.[2] He travelled unceasingly and saw the fruits of his labour in the passing of the Special Areas (Development and Improvement) Act in 1934. The Act was essential in helping constituencies like Ebbw Vale. Factories were established on new industrial estates and generous grants were given to attract skilled workers to these corporations. Salvation came to Ebbw Vale with the establishment of the new steelworks, which opened in 1936. This was quite a feather in Aneurin Bevan's cap . He also came to respect Sir William Firth, the captain of the steel industry who provided the finance and bought the steelworks.[3]

---

1 Geoffrey Goodman, *ibid*, 34.
2 Michael Foot, *Aneurin Bevan, ibid*, 165.
3 *Ibid*, 171–2.

The Labour hierarchy has no time for Bevan but he is safe in his Ebbw Vale constituency

Bevan also knew in his heart that Labour had little hope of winning the next General Election.[1] Despite the awful economic conditions, the South Wales constituencies did not receive the attention they deserved. Bevan was not the only pessimist . 292 A. J. Cummings, the political editor of the *News Chronicle*, expressed his regret on the prevailing apathy:

> One must deplore the shameful spirit of political defeatism which has overtaken the Labour Party in this country. One day last week a group of Labour leaders in London were discussing with an air of patient resignation the prospect of returning 170 Labour Representatives to the next Parliament. That was the maximum calculation.[2]

There was scant more enthusiasm at the trade union conference in Margate in September or at the Labour Party conference in Brighton in October. Thus, the outcome of the 1935 General Election came as no surprise.
The Labour Party increased its number of MPs to 154, many fewer than in 1923 despite over 8.5 million voters choosing Labour. Stanley Baldwin's National Government gained 432 seats in the House of Commons. Thus, the reactionaries and appeasers in Tory colours had an invincible majority. In spite of their economic mismanagement, the British people due to their innate conservatism were willing for the right to govern for another five years . The Communist Party had supported the Labour Party everywhere except in Rhondda East and West Fife (where William Gallacher won).[3] Aneurin Bevan himself was re-elected to Parliament. The worthy winner had these results:

Aneurin Bevan (Lab.)	25,007	7.8%
Ethel Scarborough (Con.)[4]	7,145	22.3%
Majority	17,862	56.6%

---

1 *Ibid,* 172.
2 Allen Hutt, *The Post-War History of the British Working Class*, Left Book Club Edition (London, 1937), 272
3 *Ibid,* 274.
4 Francis Ethel Scarborough (1890–1966) was a well-known pianist who was born in Crouch End, London and died in Graffham in Sussex. She was active all her life in the Conservative Party.

To many Labour Party members like Bevan, the most satisfying result was seeing Ramsay MacDonald lose his National Labour seat in County Durham.[1] By now it was clear to most political observers that the Labour Party was unlikely ever to win a sufficient majority to seize power as Aneurin Bevan had optimistically anticipated in the nineteen thirties.

Bevan was dealt a bitter personal blow in North Lanarkshire where his wife Jennie Lee, standing as an Independent Labour Party candidate, lost to the Tory candidate. The Labour Party had deliberately split the working-class vote by putting up their own candidate against Jennie . These childish tactics not only meant Jennie was back to square one , but seemed certain to keep the Labour Party in opposition. For Bevan, there was no other political party in which he could serve, but his precious talents were going to waste, in part due to the jealousy of his fellow MPs. He – and his family – had achieved so much for the Labour Party, and it was a precious part of his own working-class Welsh heritage. Though he suffered one defeat after another, he would never leave the party he cared for . Bevan was an internationalist through and through. From 1934–35, he helped the victims of German and Austrian fascism. He did this despite so many in the Labour Party keeping at arm's length from him because the relief committees were usually in the hands of the Communist Party.

---

1 This gave great pleasure to many left-wing politicians and it is clear that Bevan was one of them. See Allen Hunt, *ibid,* 274, Eden, 'So Near to No 10', *Daily Sketch*, 7 July 1960, 6

CHAPTER 6

The amazing marriage of Aneurin Bevan and Jennie Lee

In 1929, Jennie Lee was just as knowledgeable about the history of the Labour movement as her new-found friend Aneurin Bevan. She had shown her political capabilities in February 1929 by winning a by-election in North Lanarkshire for the Independent Labour Party.

Their shared mining background

Jennie Lee and Aneurin Bevan shared a mining background, although Jennie had better educational opportunities as the only daughter of a miner. She did well academically, went on to university and gained a degree. In contrast, Aneurin left school as a young lad after years of torment at the hands of his headmaster. Aneurin was seven years older than Jennie, but the two became huge friends, so much so that Jennie said to him one evening, when they were both rushing back to the Commons to vote: 'You know Nye, we could be brother and sister.'

The problem was that Jennie had fallen head over heels in love with a politician called Frank Wise, the Independent Labour Party MP for Leicester. He was a married man with two daughters; however, he and Jennie were living together in a luxurious flat in Bloomsbury.[1] When Frank was away with his family or working in his constituency, Aneurin would seize the opportunity to enjoy Jennie's company. The two of them would spend their time walking in London or on the South Downs. Sometimes, Bevan would take her home to Tredegar, but his family did not think

---

1 Michael Foot, *Aneurin Bevan 1897–1945* (London, 1962), 70.

as much of her as he did.[1] Arianwen Bevan, Aneurin's youngest sister, was working as his secretary, dealing with correspondence, typing letters and proofreading his speeches. She was definitely not an admirer of Jennie's. In fact, Arianwen could not utter a good word about the Scottish lass, especially after Bevan used his charm to persuade his sister to help with Jennie's administrative tasks too.

Jennie flirts with a married MP, Frank Wise

Aneurin knew he could not compete with Frank Wise. Up until now, he'd been a self-confirmed bachelor with no interest in finding himself a girlfriend, although he and his friends were known to meet up with young women in Pontypool on Saturday nights, and perhaps sometimes the nurses in Abergavenny.[2]

Bevan's best friend Archie Lush started noticing how the Scotswoman's name often cropped up in conversation. However, Bevan knew that he had no hope of being her lover with Frank Wise around. In fact, the three of them were on good term, being fervent evangelists for the left. Politicians like George Strauss, Barbara Betts (later Castle) and their wealthy benefactor Charles Trevelyan, got to know them both well and realised the two were lovers but that Bevan was more in love with Jennie than she was with him. On a trip to Moscow in the summer of 1931, Jennie left him with his male friends so that she could join Frank Wise in Tbilisi, Georgia, and share the holiday of a lifetime together.[3]

Lee loses her seat in 1931 and seeks new opportunities

Unfortunately, Aneurin Bevan's love letters to Jennie have been lost; however, there is a letter of thanks to Charles Trevelyan, written in November 1931. He had welcomed them to his affluent home at Wallington Hall in Cumberland. In this letter, Bevan praised Jennie to the skies for never losing sight of the important things in life any more than he did.[4] In the 1931 General Election, the Tories in Ebbw Vale constituency decided to allow the new MP to rest on his laurels and were not putting up a candidate to stand against him. This meant Bevan was able to spend the whole campaign period in Scotland supporting an MP who was not on the list of candidates for the Labour Party. However, despite all the hard work, Jennie lost her seat and had to fend for herself. She had no desire to teach, as this

---

1 Patricia Hollis, *Jennie Lee, A Life* (Oxford, 1997), 70.
2 *Ibid*, 72. Michael Foot, *ibid*, 125.
3 Michael Foot, *ibid*, p. 125
4 Hollis, ibid. , 74.

would mean not marrying. Instead, Jennie decided to focus on lecture tours, focusing on the United States of America, a country which had attracted her since she was a child. By 1932, the secret affair between Frank Wise and Jennie Lee was known to many left-wing politicians. Even Frank's wife Dorothy knew of his infidelity. Despite being upset, she did not want a divorce. Neither did Jennie wish to marry a divorced man. Neither was she the first rising female politician to fall in love with a married man. Barbara Castle (née Betts), Ellen Wilkinson and Megan Lloyd George were in the same situation for many years. Tragically, before Frank Wise and Jennie Lee could work out what to do, fate stepped in.

The sudden death of Frank Wise

Frank Wise died suddenly in early November 1932 while spending the weekend at Wallington Hall, near Morpeth with Charles Trevelyan. Wallington was situated in the heart of the Northumberland countryside. Wise died suddenly of a cerebral haemorrhage. His lover Jennie received a phone message from the Liberal MP Frank Owen that evening. Charles Trevelyan was making the necessary arrangements and travelling down to London the following morning to comfort Dorothy Wise and Jennie herself.[1] Charles telephoned Bevan with news of the tragic loss. Bevan promised Charles he would take care of Jennie in her grief. When he shared the sad news with Herbert Griffiths, the drama critic volunteered to be with Jennie whenever she needed him. Jennie would be well looked after in her sorrow.

In a letter read by many, Jennie admitted that Aneurin Bevan was not Frank Wise.[2] He was less dependable than Wise, anxious and short tempered at times. He could be extremely very selfish. But despite recognising his faults, Jennie still felt close to Bevan as if he were her brother, their mining background and socialism creating a close bond between them. By Christmas 1933, Jennie was seriously considering sharing a home with Nye, as she lovingly called him.[3] He was already living in her flat in Guildford Street, despite Jennie continuing to mourn Frank Wise.

---

1 Frank Owen, the former journalist who shared a flat with Aneurin Bevan, phoned Jennie from the office of the *Daily Express*. Charles Trevelyan travelled by train from Newcastle and went straight to Frank's flat to collect Jennie's papers. See: Jennie Lee, *My life with Nye* (London, 1980), 101–2.
2 *Ibid*, 102. Here is part of the revealing letter: 'Frank was solid gold. Ni is quicksilver. He is unreliable as Frank was reliable. He is moody, selfindulgent, but in a curious way he is a brother to me. Our mining backgrounds, outlooks and hopes and despairs are most similar.'
3 *Ibid*.

Jennie and Bevan marry in London

Cohabiting was not commitment enough for Aneurin, with his nonconformist chapel background. He wanted to marry Jennie and so he proposed to her over dinner at his favourite restaurant, the Café Royal. He then spent the summer in the States raising money for German and Austrian refugees, many of them Jewish. On his return, in September, Aneurin and Jennie announced their engagement. Despite their marriage plans, the stubborn Jennie still refused to join the Labour Party.

Neither did she intend to take her new husband's surname and become Jennie Bevan. This was a huge disappointment to Aneurin's mother, who never forgave Jennie for refusing to be proud of his Welsh surname.

On 25 October 1934, the marriage took place at Holborn Register Office in London. It was supposed to be a quiet wedding, without any fuss, a wedding like Jack and Bessie Braddock had enjoyed in Liverpool in 1922, when the only guests were their two witnesses. Aneurin asked his friend Archie Lush to be best man and Marion Balderston to be bridesmaid.[1] Aneurin's oldest brother William, managed to get to London but looked like a fish out of water throughout the short, secular ceremony.[2] Neither Jennie's parents nor Aneurin's mother attended. Despite the couple's wishes for privacy, reporters and photographers flocked to Holborn register office and a crowd of well-wishers gathered outside. Jennie had decided not to buy a new coat for the wedding and refused to wear a hat or gloves. There was no wedding ring to be seen, not because Bevan had forgotten to buy one but because Jennie did not want to have such fetter on her finger. She told the press, 'I'm not fond of rings – that's all.'[3] In fact, the wearing of a wedding ring went against Jennie's feminist beliefs. For Aneurin's mother it was another sign of her new daughter-in-law's indifference to the rules of etiquette. After a meal, Jennie and Aneurin went on to a house party arranged by Marion Balderston, who then disappears completely from the couple's subsequent story. Michael Foot did not even name their bridesmaid in his splendid 1962 biography. George Lansbury and Arthur Henderson presented them with a writing desk and filing cabinets, wedding presents from the Parliamentary Labour Party.[4] The Bevans postponed their Spanish honeymoon until the Christmas holidays.

---

1 *Ibid*, 107–8.
2 *Ibid*, 108. In addition to this he was troublesome, as Jennie mentions: 'Five of us instead of four went off to a private room in the Ivy restaurant, where the proprietor, our friend Abel, had prepared lunch for us. Billy Bevan refused Abel's best champagne and wines and insisted on a special brew of beer that The Ivy did not stock, causing so much fuss and bother that we wanted to strangle him.'
3 Hollis, *ibid*, 83
4 *Ibid*.

Aneurin Bevan's love for his wife

Aneurin had fallen head over heels in love with the dynamic Scotswoman. His Tredegar family and Jennie Lee's closest friends were of the opinion that she had not lost her head to the same extent. Memories of her beloved Frank came constantly to her mind and often brought tears to her eyes. She missed his warm, loving and supportive personality. It is true she had great admiration for Aneurin: he had been patient for years, was a huge supporter of hers and was delightful company. He could make her laugh uncontrollably. They also shared a left-leaning tendency. Both had been mistrustful of authority since their schooldays and were angry at the suffering of the working class and unemployed, the people who continued to be despised by the Tories. Aneurin was interested in the arts and music, books and paintings, and these enriched Jennie's life too. She knew her new husband would take care of her whatever happened and that his family were not expecting too much from her. Bevan would also respect the privacy which meant so much to her. Indeed, both of them craved privacy throughout their political lives.

Moving to live in a delightful cottage

By 1934, Aneurin Bevan's fame and popularity with leftwingers was increasing. The loyal Jennie defended him like a lioness whenever she heard a word of criticism from Tories or and right-wing trade unionists, but she was not familiar with running a household. Her husband dreamt of a house in the country similar to the hillside cottages of south-east Wales. In the window of an estate agent selling unusual properties, he came across an ideal cottage near Reading, some fifty miles from London.[1] Lane End Cottage was a long, low, thatched, whitewashed house. The couple found a fourteen-year-old girl to look after them for their first few months in the cottage, to kindle the fire in the morning, prepare their breakfast, wash the dishes, iron their clothes and clean the rooms. Jennie's brother, something of a wastrel, had the task of looking after the extensive three-acre garden. Jennie acquired a cat to keep the mice at bay.

---

1 Jennie Lee, *My Life with Nye*, ibid, 113.

Jennie's parents move nearby

Jennie Lee was busy with travelling and lecturing overseas and throughout the British Isles; she also planned to stand again for the next general election. This meant she had no time – or inclination – for housework. Jennie's mother had become fond of her son-in-law after seeing him for the first time at the British Labour Party Conference in Edinburgh in 1936. It took longer for her father to warm to the powerful Welshman though they had both been coal miners. Pa Lee suffered very poor health and his daughter did not want to see him return to work in the coalfield and so expedite his death. Her mother longed to leave the village of Lochgelly so Jennie set about arranging their move to the South of England. A two-bedroomed cottage was designed by Jennie and built in a corner of the Bevans' garden. Her grateful parents moved in 1935. Her mother was known as Ma Lee. She was an expert cook. She immediately became indispensable to the two politicians. Aneurin was thrilled to bits. He and his mother-in-law would debate, experiment and have a different menu from the one he'd enjoyed in Tredegar. These arrangements continued until 1945, when they all moved to Cliveden Place, near Sloane Square in London and later to Asheridge Farm in the Chilterns.

Rich and artistic friends

The couple's life was full of excitement and they had many close friends who thought the world of them and welcomed the chance to spend time with them during weekends. Cultured artists, writers, journalists and well-off Jewish celebrities loved the couple's company. Jacob Epstein, the world-famous sculptor and playwright, and Labour MP Benn Levy and his attractive wife Constance Cummings regularly stayed at the cottage. Graham Sutherland, Felix Topolski and Henry Moore, three giants of the fine arts, looked forward to spending weekends with the couple. Another friend was Alfred Hicht, a generous supporter of visual artists.[1] The work of some of these artists was displayed on the walls of their home.

Their best man Archie Lush, an education officer for Monmouthshire and agent for the Ebbw Vale constituency, was also a frequent visitor.[2] . Political colleagues came to stay, including their long standing Jewish friend George Russell Strauss. In 1942, Barbara Castle stayed with them for a week after the burial of her lover William Mellor. Mervyn Stockwood, the clergyman who became a socialist under

---
1 *Ibid*, 161, 229, 250.
2 *Ibid*, 167, 261. He was Aneurin's closest friend throughout the years.

the influence of Sir Stafford Cripps in Bristol, would also spend time with the Bevans discussing Christian socialism, even managing to persuade them to attend the ceremony enthroning him as Bishop of Southwark. From the thirties onwards, Michael Foot and his wife Jill Craigie visited regularly. The four would often spend a weekend in Stratford-on-Avon watching the greats of the theatre namely Peggy Ashcroft, John Gielgud, Ralph Richardson and Laurence Olivier. When they ate out in Stratford restaurants, the eyes of the majority of diners would be on Aneurin Bevan, the famous politician. So many of the diners enjoyed the fact that one of the heroes of Parliament was dining alongside them. Everyone who visited their home agreed there were no more welcoming hosts than Mr Bevan.[1]

Jennie's brother Tommy

Tommy Lee was a difficult man. He had emigrated to Australia, but did not make much of a success of it 'down under' and was unable to keep any job. By the mid-thirties, he was drinking heavily and Jennie and Aneurin was often generous to him . especially when he flew to Australia where he had a family

Friction with the Tredegar family

In his mother's opinion, her talented son Aneurin could have chosen a more conventional and loving woman than Jennie , someone who respected convention like the chapel folk in the Blaenau Gwent coalfield. Jennie could be completely immoral. When Phoebe received an anonymous letter telling her about Jennie's secret affair with the married Frank Wise, she nearly fainted in despair. After that, she could never forget the improper behaviour of her daughter-in-law.

On Phoebe's visit to Lane End Cottage, a domestic quarrel broke out between the two women. Phoebe could not believe the couple were living in a house with a thatched roof, believing her own house in Tredegar was more acceptable than the whitewashed cottage.[2] She worried that Jennie was inept and had no intention of buying suitable furniture. The cottage was devoid of fine furniture, with not one new

---

1 Hollis, *ibid*, 205.
2 This is Jennie Lee's side of the story: 'When she visited us and found we were living under a thatched roof with bare polished wooden or tiled floors and plain white walls, it seemed to her that her impossible son was bent on going backwards just when he ought to have been moving forwards. After a lifetime of selfless hard labour, bringing up a large family and supplementing her husband's wage by running a millinery business in her parlour, she was now living in a solid stone house in the centre of Tredegar. No more ancient cottages for her.' See: Jennie Lee, *My Life with Nye, ibid*, 112.

item to please her. Before long her presence led to an argument between Bevan and Jennie, which was overhead by Phoebe. Jennie was telling Bevan in a loud voice that he had to choose between his mother or her. He was in a hopeless position, as he had also witnessed Jennie being unreasonable with his mother. To him there should be no choice. Without a minute's hesitation, Phoebe packed her bag and returned to her comfortable home. She did not stay away permanently, despite that first confrontation still rankling in her mind. On her second visit, she tried to win over her daughter-in-law by criticising her son for being disrespectful of Ma Lee. Fortunately, Ma Lee and Jennie knew the accusation was untrue, with Ma Lee immediately reminding Phoebe Bevan of the excellent qualities of her outstanding son.[1]

Neither was there a welcome for William Bevan from Jennie, despite Bevan being extremely fond of his brother, who had worked hard for the Labour Party in Tredegar. Jennie considered Billy to be a surly man; she had no patience with him and hoped he would never come to see them. In Arianwen's opinion, Jennie was not worthy of Aneurin or Billy, and was a spoilt daughter who had no passion for cooking, sewing, ironing or caring for the sick. Her mother, a lovely woman, had ruined her. Jennie wanted to pursue her career rather than being Mrs. Aneurin Bevan, a role most single women in Tredegar's chapels would have accepted with pride. The truth was Tredegar meant very little to Jennie. Neither did she have any desire to be a mother and give Phoebe Bevan grandchildren. According to Arianwen, she was a 'frightful woman'.[2] Secretly, the family hoped the marriage would end in divorce and their son and brother could then chose a more worthwhile partner who was worthy of his Welsh background

Lack of cooperation between Arianwen and Jennie

A poisonous relationship developed between Jennie and Arianwen. Aneurin was 36 when he married his only sweetheart and, though fond of women's company, as far as his family were concerned he was an established bachelor. This remained the case until 1934. Arianwen had always been his confidante and his best friend in Tredegar, even more so than Archie Lush or Billy. She would do anything for him, including representing him when there was a difficult problem in the constituency. Arianwen always defended her brother and ensured his good name as a brave and fearless campaigner. She was also extremely capable herself and knew a great deal about the Labour movement. She took great interest in the life of the Monmouthshire coalfield and was appointed the first woman chairperson of Tredegar Labour and

---

1 Hollis, *ibid*, 206.
2 *Ibid*, 207.

Trades Council. Jennie Lee may have taken her place in Aneurin's life, but Arianwen was proud she had always supported her charismatic brother. He came first in her priorities; she had been happy to keep him financially secure during the three years he was unemployed. Now, despite competing with Jennie for Bevan's affection, she put her brother's needs before those of her mother. She continued her duties as his competent secretary and proofread his newspaper articles and speeches. She supervised every aspect of his work, including the administrative duties his own wife had not the time or inclination to perform.[1]

For her part, Jennie had no patience with Arianwen and, when she had drunk too much wine, she could be critical, hurtful and sometimes downright rude to her sister-in-law. One such instance occurred at Asheridge Farm, at the end of the fifties. Arianwen had cooked a delicious meal and done the washing-up. Jennie came into the kitchen and told her sharply to put the plates away in the nearby cupboard. Arianwen was incensed by Jennie's dictatorial attitude and shook her head. Jennie responded with:

> 'If you don't, I'll throw the whole lot on the floor.'

Arianwen knew this was no idle threat and, not wishing to see the plates wilfully destroyed, she did as Jennie demanded. Arianwen was not blameless. She was constantly looking for Jennie's faults and delighted in being over-critical.

Jennie, in turn, was purposely arrogant. Arianwen never forgot the disrespect that was shown towards her. When Patricia Hollis came to interview her for her biography of Jennie years later, Arianwen provided her with a very detailed picture of the tension and relationship between the two sides of the dysfunctional family.

Jennie evidently had her own way most of the time at home. Aneurin Bevan was a politician who regularly gave in to his partner. When he wanted a huge dog, for company and friendship as he relaxed from his responsibilities, he was told immediately that would not be possible. Such a dog – a Labrador or a bulldog – would make her parents nervous. On that occasion, Jennie did have a point: dogs require constant attention and he had no time to walk it. Neither would Jennie allow Aneurin to have a dedicated secretary to reduce Arianwen's responsibilities back in Wales. Rather, she wanted to combine the secretarial role with a companion for her mother after her father's death. It was unrealistic and none of the secretaries stayed for long. Thus, when Aneurin Bevan entered Attlee's cabinet in 1945, he found himself with more to do than anyone else. Jennie Lee had again entered Westminster after winning the Cannock constituency. Fortunately, Bevan allowed marital disagreements to go over his head.

---
1 *Ibid.*

When Bevan had spells of illness, Jennie found it hard to deal with his condition, believing Arianwen would be her usual critical self whatever she did. In Arianwen's opinion, Jennie would keep well away from the sickroom. This became much easier when she became the Cannock MP. To political pundits, her behaviour was understandable as she had also responsibility to her own electors. In truth, she was often more focused on her own issues: her incessant longing for Frank Wise, bodily pain and growing anxiety, the latter brought on by excessive drinking of wine. Arianwen said her sister-in-law left the responsibility of looking after her ill husband to others. She was certainly not the only person who was critical of how Jennie acted over the years.

Disagreement over the house in Queen's Square Tredegar

Arianwen Bevan-Norris, as she became known after her marriage, and Jennie Lee also crossed swords over the grand, stone-faced house in Tredegar which Aneurin Bevan had bought in the first place for his mother in 1938. Aneurin contributed generously towards this house so that his mother could have the abode she longed for. A century earlier, the building had been the town workhouse. Before the house was bought, Jennie had suggested, reasonably enough, that it would be much better for her mother-in-law to rent a modern and convenient council house rather than spending so much money on a huge Victorian house. The Bevan family was incensed. Like most of their contemporaries, Bevan's brothers and sisters wanted to better themselves and turn their backs on the poverty which had played a significant part in their early lives in Charles Street. Jennie had never experienced true poverty. After Phoebe Bevan died the house was handed over to Arianwen and her family who came to live in it with her husband and son. Bevan used the house on his visits to the constituency to meet with the electorate. Having sold their thatched cottage near Reading and moved to a comfortable house in London, the Bevans had rather hoped to use the house in Queens Square, Tredegar as their 'country cottage'. They saw no point in buying another house when they had a comfortable, luxurious house in Tredegar where they could stay for a night or two in peace, privacy and comfort. It also meant Jennie avoided doing anything domestic as the responsibility for housework would fall on Arianwen.

Bevan and Jennie used three of the four bedrooms on their visits, which meant Arianwen's son Robert had to give up his bedroom and sleep in the living room. Jennie Lee had bought expensive furniture and carpets from the large store in Tottenham Court Road in London. Unfortunately, on their first visit, some wine was spilt on the carpet. When the couple next visited Tredegar, Jennie reprimanded her sister-in-law for failing to clean up the stain. She grabbed a pillow case and tried to clean the stain herself without noticing it was one of the best in the house.

Being out of the public eye

By now, the Bevans were well-known political celebrities and Tredegar offered them some peace from the spotlight. After a morning surgery was over, they both would escape to the uplands around Tredegar and walk the mountain paths where they saw only sheep and the occasional rambler. They enjoyed stopping for a drink and a snack in one of Blaenau Gwent's interesting and remote inns. One Saturday afternoon, the couple attempted to visit the popular Tintern Abbey, as the poet William Wordsworth had once done. Unfortunately, Bevan was immediately recognised by visitors as he arrived in the car park. They left at once, their visit having been ruined by the curiosity and sincere admiration of those who had heard him speak. Bevan would have preferred to remain anonymous. On another occasion, they were getting ready to leave London when Arianwen phoned to say Bevan's niece would be staying the same weekend. If that was the case, he told her, then they would be postponing their own visit because his niece would most certainly intrude upon their visit. Arianwen was hurt and voices were raised but neither sibling was prepared to give in. Instead of heading to Tredegar, he and Jennie went to Buscot Park, the home of their bachelor friend and sympathiser Lord Faringdon. The couple had a great time at Buscot and Jennie was glad her husband had decided not to travel to Tredegar. It was generally she who was blamed if they cancelled because Arianwen had invited someone else, but they both hated visiting Queens Square and being unable to relax.

Bevan's family attitude to Aneurin and Jennie

Bevan's family could not understand the couple's reluctance to opt out from the constant publicity. They needed the tranquillity that Tredegar offered. In London, they had no choice but to accept the attention of journalists and photographers. Jennie Lee wrote letters to Arianwen where she tried to explain why she and Bevan valued and needed the refuge provided by Tredegar. They were both constantly approached wherever they went for their autographs and to sign this pamphlet or this photograph in whichever hotel they stayed. It was almost worse when they stayed at their rich Jewish friends' luxurious houses. Here, they would feel obliged to 'pay' for their lavish welcome by providing scintillating and non-stop conversation on the issues of the day. Here are Jennie's words to Arianwen:

> But again you have to pay for that hospitality in the nervous wear and tear
> of endlessly going over political issues till you scream and screech inside

yourself like a blunt gramophone needle playing over and over again the same old records.¹

Both felt that Arianwen's chief contribution to her brother's political career would be to offer them occasional peace and refuge from Friday night to Sunday mid-afternoon. occasionally. In doing so, she and her husband could free them from the pressures to socialise and converse. She explains their raw feelings:

> It is not a matter of disliking the people we must sometimes run away from. We leave behind good friends and relatives in London. It is simply that there are times when we simply must have room to breathe freely without too many hands clutching at us. We need a tranquil, trusting and trusted atmosphere.²

Jennie's words illuminate the strain and tension of the famous couple often experienced due to the mounting expectations of their friends, admirers and family. By the outbreak of the Second World War, Tredegar had become their Avalon in a way the family did not fully understand. In her correspondence, Jennie stressed that she and Aneurin did not expect too much: ten visits a year at the most, perhaps less, and with ample notice.³ When the Bevans were not there — at least 40 weekends a year —they were free to invite whoever they wished. But when she and Bevan were at Tredegar, the only company they wanted was Arianwen's immediate family.⁴ Of course, there was fault on both sides. The Bevan-Norris couple thought Bevan and Jennie were being unreasonable and thoughtless, and there are many examples which would justify that accusation. But there one problem simmered throughout Aneurin Bevan's marriage, the words of his mother Phoebe: 'Jennie is not a suitable wife for our Aneurin'. Most of the conventions that existed in Tredegar had been forgotten or discarded by the free spirit Jennie. In Tredegar, it was expected that a married man and woman would sleep in the same bed. Phoebe Bevan could see that this was not happening in the thatched cottage, at Asheridge Farm or Cliveden Place. Bevan had his own bedroom and Jennie had hers. The only time they were certain to sleep in the same bed was in Tredegar! Jennie's explanation for their sleeping arrangements was that she liked to get up early and Aneurin came to bed in the early hours of the morning. By having a separate bedroom, he could come

---

1 *Ibid*, 209.
2 *Ibid*.
3 Jennie Lee's letter to Mrs Bevan-Norris, letters dated 16 and 21 August 1950, which can be seen in the biography of Hollis, Jennie Lee: *A Life, ibid*, 209.
4 Here is part of a letter explaining why the niece's presence alarmed them: 'As it was a youngster with good home, father, mother, all the prospects and opportunities in the world before her, she had to be humoured even at our psychological expense . . . So I repeat again, our need to run away from people sometimes is not a mark of dislike or indifference. It is the reverse.' See Hollis, *ibid*, 210

to bed without waking her. The truth was that their marriage was far from conventional. Aneurin Bevan was after all a Welsh Puritan from a proud nonconformist background, although he might forget that at times in the Café Royal. His upbringing meant he would never expect illicit sex before marriage. She was completely different, compared by one friend as a queen bee who was tempted to go from one flower to another. There were no fetters in her relationship with other politicians such as Frank Wise, whom she continued to long for until her own death. Jennie wrote of their strange marriage, but she had not understood his views:

> To Nye, I was friend and mistress – never wife. The word offended me as ugly. Nye would not have wanted or been content to accept a 'wife' in the conventional sense.[1]

She saw him as a socialist friend, a companion, the word she was fond of was the Marxist term *comrade*. She thought the world of him but she did not love him physically as she loved Frank. She had but one lover. He died young. It was Aneurin Bevan who had wanted them to get married – so he could keep in his mother's good books. Jennie would have preferred they had lived together without having to go through any ceremony. She wanted freedom from the shackles of married life. When she lived in the Guildford Street flat, she would worry Bevan by going out at night alone, obviously missing the huge garden and space for dreaming she'd enjoyed at Lane End Cottage. Their contentment came from their ceaseless campaigning for worthy causes and the leadership Bevan gave in Parliament in the thirties and during the Second World War. The Labour Government of 1945–51 provided an excellent opportunity for the world to see his potential. They had no children, although Bevan was always up for a game of cricket with the children of friends, once bowling for an hour with two sons of neighbours. Arianwen believed Jennie did not want to be a mother; however, she not know that, early in her marriage, her sister-in-law had failed to get pregnant and, according to her mother, was told she would not be able to have children. Jennie was apparently ready to consider pregnancy at 40 but was advised by Dr (later Sir) Dan Davies from Pontycymer, who was a physician to the royal family, that at her age she should stop thinking about childbirth.[2] In old age, Jennie regretted her choice to remain childless; however, in the rare photographs that exist of the couple with children, it is Bevan who is embracing them and never her.

---

1 Hollis, *ibid*, 211.
2 *Ibid*, 217.

Their stay in 23 Cliveden Place

Towards the end of the Second World War, the Bevans decided to move to London to be nearer Westminster and the cottage was sold for £3,000 to their friend Israel Sieff. The house at Cliveden Place was five-storey and large enough for everyone, including Jennie's parents; unfortunately, two days before they moved, a German bomb landed nearby. The front of the house was destroyed, all the windows were blown out and the cellar was flooded. It took some time for the house to be restored to its previous condition. By August 1945, it was ready and the *Daily Mirror* came to take pictures of the Bevans; new London home. Aneurin is lying on the sofa with Jennie sheltering in his strong arms. The *Daily Mirror* praised Cliveden Place, stressing that every square inch of it was a real home.[1] There was a long newspaper report about the couple and their hopes, and we learn a great deal from the interview, including that their Siamese cat was called Smoky and Bevan would regularly sing Welsh hymns and popular songs in the garden. Scores of gramophone records were on view in the living room as well as two expensive typewriters. On the library wall there were maps of countries and settlements which they knew well and when Jennie was asked what her hobby was outside politics, she replied, 'My husband is my hobby.' It was a reply which would not have pleased some of the family in Blaenau Gwent. Cliveden Place was an exceptionally comfortable home for them at a time when they were so busy with their parliamentary duties. But after Labour's failure to win the 1951 General Election, it was not so imperative for the couple and their inlaws to live in London, so they began to dream of returning to the countryside.

There was no back door to Cliveden Place, so it was impossible to escape from photographers, who were determined to record Bevan and Jennie's every last movement. In 1952, when her father was on his deathbed, the Tory-supporting *Daily Express* placed a camera in the attic window of the house opposite so they could chronicle every movement of left-wing Labour leaders who came to show their solidarity.[2] When returning home from Parliament one evening, they discovered someone had pushed a firework through the letterbox and set the hall carpet on fire. The house could have burnt to ashes. They had just about had enough of living under such tension and siege.

---

1 *Daily Mirror*, 14 August 1945.
2 But remember that the *Daily Express* invited Jennie Lee to travel to Russia in winter 1936 to write a number of articles on the situation of people in that huge country. See Jennie Lee, *My Life with Nye*, ibid, 119–20.

Friendship with a Scottish farmer who shared the same idealism

Aneurin Bevan had the idea to move back to the English or Welsh countryside, to the landscape inhabited by his ancestors before they moved to the coalfield. During the 1951 election, he met and befriended a socialist farmer John Mackie. The men became great friends, sharing walking holidays in Scotland's rugged Highlands. Mackie was a proud Scot who owned two thousand acres in Scotland as well as a thousand acres in Lincolnshire. Bevan talked to him about his longing for a farm where he could live for the rest of his days and Mackie supported the idea.[1] He began searching the papers for a farm. To his delight, he spotted an advertisement for a farmhouse three miles from Chesham Station and only thirty miles from London. His dream was about to come true.

Buying a farm near Chesham

The farmhouse came with 52 acres of land, two stone cottages and a number of brick and wood outbuildings. There was also a large barn with impressive timber work. Within five minutes of arriving, Aneurin Bevan had fallen in love with Asheridge Farm. In July 1954 – with a £6000 mortgage and the support of John Mackie – he bought the whole estate from the retiring owner Mr Dugdale for a bargain £9000.[2]

Jennie, Bevan and Ma Lee moved into the farm but, within a few weeks, Jennie's mother was misdiagnosed with cancer[3] Ultimately, it turned out to be an abscess; Ma Lee lived another eight years and outlived Bevan himself. Ma Lee loved the lively, busy man she called Nye, telling Jennie daily how lucky she was to have a life-partner like him to care and look after her.

Bevan travelled to the 'Far East' on a parliamentary mission soon after moving into the new home. While he was gone, Jennie and her mother set about transforming and modernising the farmhouse, installing central heating, extending some rooms, and decorating and furnishing it. Over the years, they would buy antique objects and furniture, with the fine works of his friends Henry Moore, Graham Sutherland and John Piper on the walls of their rooms.

---

1 *Ibid*, 208–9. 'John Mackie said he would see to things for us. Without his encouragement and help it would have been madness for us to embark on this kind of venture.'
2 *Ibid*, 208.
3 *Ibid*, 210.

Asheridge Farmhouse was the ideal home: an extensive, light house with a front door opening onto a grand living room and fireplace where they could burn wood from their land during the winter months. The dining room was ample size to sit eight; and there was smaller sitting room (where milk was kept cool), plus a kitchen. The oak staircase led to four bedrooms, the dressing rooms and bathrooms, then, up on the next floor, there was an attic room where Bevan could prepare his speeches and meditate on the ways of the world with no-one to disturb him.[1] The barn was transformed into a splendid eye-catching house for guests. One close friend who stayed there was Pierre Mendès France, who was accompanied by the celebrated photographer Henri Cartier-Bresson. Cartier-Bresson took several famous photographs of the two icons of the left.[2] The Bevans chose not to sell or rent any of their farmland or outbuildings. They were now enjoying what was most important to them in life: privacy from prying eyes of Tredegar and London, or wherever else they appeared in public. By this time, Aneurin Bevan was one of the most familiar faces in Britain, up there with the Prime Minister, the King or, later in 1953, his daughter Queen Elizabeth.

Aneurin Bevan as a farmer

Bevan rather fancied himself as a farmer as did James Callaghan in his later years. He employed a bailiff on the farm to keep an eye on everything and loved the fifteen Guernsey cattle and sixty hens they had inherited from the previous owner. He hoped the farm could pay its way but, unfortunately, it saw an inevitable annual loss. John Mackie told him, time after time, the farm was far too small to make a profit. There was no end to the spending the Bevans had to face: fencing and new machinery were needed, the cattle shed required improvements, buildings needed to be restored and a pigsty prepared. Aneurin was known to the famous cartoonists as a politician who was very fond of pigs. As time passed, he noticed the cattle were paying their way rather than the pigs and hens, so within three years, he had increased the number of Guernsey cattle from fifteen to sixty. In the meantime, he bought hundreds of hens and two hundred and fifty sows and piglets.

---

1 Hollis, *ibid*, 22
2 *Ibid*.

Aneurin Bevan becomes part of the local community

The farm was a strange experience for the famous politician.[1] He had plenty of disagreements with his disgruntled farm workers. The first two lads left within a few months of arriving. Their successor was kicked by a pig and injured his back. He was off work for a long time and, when he returned, he brought a legal case against his employer. Bevan consulted the National Farmers Union and the advice he received somewhat relieved his anxiety. However, the truth of the matter was that the couple could not keep staff. One after another left. Jennie believed they were taking advantage of her husband as he was much too kindhearted and was better at attacking employers than being an employer himself. They took advantage of him knowing that he, of all people, would never want press publicity accusing him of being a miserly, bad tempered and hopeless boss. Fortunately, he befriended a local farmer Tony Harman (a Labour supporter) and his family. They became good friends and Bevan would often visit the Harmans at Grove Farm, between Orchard Leigh and Whelpley Hill, for advice.

The enjoyment and frustration of farming

Bevan was astounded by the farm expenses, and he had no option but to consult a first-class accountant to fill in his tax return. He was expected, when his accountant completed the task, to list all the money that was spent on wages, improvements and payments on the farm buildings, cattle feed and vets' bills. There were also the maids' wages to pay. The farm expenditure just piled up and shocked Bevan. After paying staff, insurance, taxes, mortgage, bills for heating, cleaning and for improvements, he needed a rather deep pocket. One year, a new bathroom was installed in the house and the following year, a new car was bought. These were the expenses of a working farm as the income tax authorities knew very well.[2]

The couple's income flow was complex. They received MP salaries, and made a great deal of money from journalism, investments and radio programmes. From 1954 onwards, there was the income from the farm. The Bevans could not fill their income tax returns in themselves. Like Cledwyn Hughes, Labour MP for Anglesey, they depended on an accountant and an accountancy firm. When Aneurin Bevan received a tax demand, he immediately presented it to his loyal friend, the

---

1 *Ibid*, 222. 'The farm gave Nye especially, huge pleasure. He immersed himself in it' John Buchan saw him standing upright all night, nursing a sick cow, its head on his lap. See: John Buchan, 'Portrait of Aneurin Bevan', *BBC Programme*, 21 August 1961.
2 Patrick Hollis saw a draft of the 1957–8 and 1958–9 accounts. See Hollis, *ibid*, 422.

well-known lawyer Arthur Goodman who was notable for dealing with the financial complexities of many high-level politicians.

Jennie had an altogether different approach to paying bills and would delay payment for as long as possible, sometimes months after the work had been completed. The staff of the company that laid a new floor in the cowshed let cattle walk on it before the cement had set (with Bevan's permission), leaving hoof marks. Jennie refused to pay on the grounds the floor was uneven, despite being partly responsible for the mistake. She was often useless as a farm treasurer.[1]

The years on the farm gave immeasurable pleasure to Bevan and he spent hours looking after the animals he loved. For example, he would often stay overnight to care for a sick cow. The couple mixed with their farming neighbours and liked to spend time in the local pub The Blue Bell, where they were well-liked by the landlord Ted Sheax and his wife, who was a Labour supporter. The couple bought food in two Chesham shops, sometimes surprising the local Conservatives with their bottles of Spanish Roja. Bevan would prefer to buy a cow at market than purchase a new overcoat. Shortly before his death, he was even discussing the possibility of buying a field adjacent to their land so that they could enlarge his favourite place.

Despite all their efforts for privacy, the national media refused to leave the couple alone used every trick in the book to waylay them, including hiding behind garden hedges or in ditches, and eavesdropping on conversations between Aneurin and visiting friends. The Bevans' world was a comfortable one. Bevan worked mid-week on his parliamentary duties, catching the morning train from Chesham Station to Euston. Rhondda-born Denzil 'Taffy' Walter would get up at 4.30 a.m. each day to run a newspaper stall at Chesham Station. and Bevan would buy his newspapers from his fellow Welshman every morning. They greeted each other in Welsh and chatted about their longing for the home country. MP salaries had risen steadily over the past decade, from £1000 in 1946 to £1250 in 1954 and £1750 in 1957; however, they could earn double that amount from journalism. By 1955–56, an MP could expect an income of around £5000, ten times more than a religious minister.[2] On the downside, the farm continued to make a loss, despite reducing their income tax slightly. On the other hand, the eggs, milk and garden produce did have a positive impact on their living costs.

---

1 *Ibid*, 222.
2 *Ibid*, 223.

Generosity of admirers to them both

Fortunately, Aneurin Bevan's admirers were extremely generous, particularly Sir Charles Trevelyan who paid the couple's election expenses, bought them a car, paid for their holidays and covered their personal insurance. Another Bevan benefactor was the Jewish publisher Howard Samuel, the owner of McGibbon and Kee Press which published the first volume of Michael Foot's excellent biography of Aneurin Bevan in 1962.[1] Samuel paid a great deal of Bevan's travel and accommodation costs when he was campaigning the length and breadth of Britain. He also looked after most of the weekly bills associated with the weekly T*ribune*, established in 1937. During the Second World War, the couple belonged to the Pheasantry Club in King's Road, Chelsea, where their Italian friend Rene de Meo was very generous towards them. Bevan would enjoy a tasty meal two or three times a week at the owner's flat. Jennie would often accompany him and, on the Sundays they spent in London, they would dine at the club. Afterwards, de Meo would accompany them back to Cliveden Place with a bag of bottles and expensive food. On Saturdays, Jennie's mother would call into the kitchen and be provided with a bag of nourishing food, including a bird to cook. In August 1948, Bevan and Jennie stayed with de Meo in his home in Formia near Naples.[2] The family appreciated the Italian's kindness and the unlimited generosity of another supporter Howard Samuel. In 1956, after a successful evening's gambling, Samuel presented Bevan with an envelope containing his £1,000 winnings. With the money, Jennie opened a bank account to cover the cost of special continental holidays when they really needed them. Samuel would regularly give Bevan envelopes full of notes, advising him how to invest in order to make more profit. The famous band leader Jack Hylton was another rich friend. In 1959, he presented the MP with £2,500, a considerable amount of which was used to help Bevan's left-wing friends to help them with general election expenses.

---

1 *Ibid*.

2 All the information about the friendship between Bevan and Rene de Meo comes from an article in the *Western Mail,* 26 September 2006 under the title 'The incriminating statement of Miss Joan Parsons'. She was Rene de Meo's mistress. (Thanks to the Revd. Ivor Thomas Rees, Sketty, Swansea for sending the material to me) .

The care of the medical fraternity for the creator of the National Health Service

Aneurin Bevan was on good terms with Dr Tom Wise, the family doctor, although himself was under the care of his friend Sir Daniel Thomas Davies[1] He had so many generous friends who felt that they should give them gifts, sometime money. But he would never accept a brass farthing from newspaper owners like Lord Beaverbrook. In fact, Bevan was delighted to be welcomed into Lord Beaverbrook's circle where he met some of the people he had admired greatly since he was a young man. One such person was H. G. Wells.[2] Through Beaverbrook's kindness, Bevan found himself socialising with the author who shared his vision for the new Jerusalem. Aneurin Bevan enjoyed his life in Tredegar and in his homes in England; however, it was only at Asheridge Farm that he experienced hours and hours of intense happiness. He took an interest in local Labour politics and joined Tony Harman on 29 April 1955 at a public meeting for Labour in Chesham's Cooperative Hall. He spoke again at Billingdon Village Hall on 24 June 1955, when he met members of the District Labour Party. In February 1956, Bevan was delighted to accept an the invitation from the Chesham and District Cricket League to become their Vice-President. Essentially, Aneurin Bevan was a man of the soil and it is unsurprising his favourite lines of verse were words of the Welsh poet from Porthmadog Eliseus Williams, better known by his bardic name Eifion Wyn:

> *Pam gwnaethost Arglwydd Cwm Pennant mor dlws*
> *A bywyd hen fugail mor fyr*

The lines can be translated as:

> Why Lord did you make Cwm Pennant so beautiful
> And the life of the old shepherd so short.[3]

---

1 Jones, Sir Daniel Thomas Davies (1899–1966) [in] *Y Bywgraffiadur Cymreig 1951–1970 (The Welsh Biography 1951–1970* (eds. E. D. Jones and Brynley F. Roberts) (London, 1997), 23.
2 'But there Bevan met in the flesh some of the heroes of his youth, H. G. Wells, Arnold Bennett, and even more men of letters, for Beaverbrook's company was the most catholic in the kingdom. Wells and Bevan got on like a house on fire; they were fellow crusaders in that foreign land, ever ready to lay their sacrilegious hands on Beaverbrook's sacred cause of splendid isolation or more agreeably for their host, to sound the trumpet of Covenanting Republicanism to the consternation of cavalier guests.' See: Michael Foot, *ibid*, 183.
3 The poem 'Cwm Pennant' was written by Eliseus Williams (1867–1926) (Eifion Wyn. He wrote delightful lyrics and hymns which can be seen in *Caneuon Ffydd* (Aberystwyth, 2001), numbers 164, 197, 213, 240, 503, 681 and 844

He would recite these words with conviction to the architect William Clough Ellis as they walked together in Gwynedd and especially when they were spending an afternoon together in the tranquillity of Cwm Pennant.[1]

---

[1] Jonah Jones, *Clough Williams-Ellis: The Architect of Portmeirion* (Bridgend, 1998), 197.

CHAPTER 7

Bevan continues to oppose the political establishment (1935–1945)

During the nineteen thirties, Aneurin Bevan mixed with leftwing intellectuals such as Professor Harold Laski, the clever barrister D. N. Pritt, the socialist thinker and Old Etonian John Strachey, and Stafford Cripps, another wealthy socialist and hugely successful barrister.[1] Despite this, Bevan did not neglect the working-class voters in his Ebbw Vale constituency and he would travel back to South Wales every month if possible. His forte was understanding ordinary people – the miners and steel workers – and their fears and prejudices. He was himself an ordinary Welshman who had been enriched by natural talent but he never forgot his humble roots.

Bevan as the icon of the left in Parliament

By the time of the 1935 General Election, Bevan and Stafford Cripps had become seen as representatives of the left. Elwyn Jones, one of the young socialists of Llanelli, was spellbound by Bevan's eloquence and sincerity when he addressed over 4,000

---

1 Dingle Foot goes a step further, saying that Bevan was a Parliamentarian from the moment he arrived and delivered his maiden speech. According to Dingle Foot, he belonged to the finest tradition of Parliament and could be compared to great figures such as Chatham, Charles Fox, William Pitt, W. E. Gladstone, Benjamin Diraeli, H. H. Asquith, David Lloyd George and Winston Churchill, each truly excellent from the moment they arrived at Westminster. See Dingle Foot, 'The Constant Rebel', *Observer*, July 10, 1960, 10

people in the market hall on the eve of the 1935 Election.[1] To a newspaper mogul like Lord Beaverbrook, Aneurin Bevan was the greatest and most able orator of them all; be it right wing or left wing. He delighted in dining at home in the company of two political bulldogs: Winston Churchill and Aneurin Bevan.[2] Beaverbrook could not stand Stafford Cripps nor Harold Laski. Bevan and Cripps were calling for a grown up attitude towards the communists and for a different way of looking at foreign affairs in the face of the dangers from fascism. Instead of placing too much faith in the United Nations, they argued, it would be much wiser for the Labour Government, if it were in power, to breach the gap and come to some sort of understanding with the Soviet Union on the international front. But such ideas were anathema to the leaders of trade unionism like Ernest Bevin and Charles Dukes. Bevan was criticised at the 1934 Southport conference for flirting with communistic movements which constantly attacked the Labour Party. The Tories, under Stanley Baldwin, won easily the 1935 General Election but to some extent, Baldwin won it through deceit. The government managed to get the support of middle-of-the-road Labour Party leaders as they were in favour of the United Nations. It was soon revealed that they had been led on a wild goose chase. The real policy the Conservative government had in mind was rearmament. In 1934–1935, pacifism was more important than ever to a large number of the electorate as the United Nations was strongly supported across the United Kingdom. The Welsh Council of the League of Nations was set up in 1922 under the sponsorship of Lord David Davies of Llandinam was led by Welsh Baptist minister the Revd. Gwilym Davies.[3] He was an honorary director of the League of Nations in Wales from 1923 to 1945. In 1935, under his leadership, the Welsh Council persuaded 62,000 people to sign the petition for peace. Bevan was extremely proud of his nation and the Peace Pledge Union was formed in 1936. Regrettably, at the same time, the government decided to spend £300 million on an arms programme and in February 1937 that sum was increased to the incredible amount of £1,500m.[4]

---

1 Many Christian socialists like Stafford Cripps had eternal admiration for Aneurin Bevan. They included Bishop Mervyn Stockwood, Dr Donald Soper, Tom Driberg, George Thomas, Hugh Delargy, Cledwyn Hughes and Tudor Watkins. There is a reference to an address in a memorable meeting at Llanelli in Lord Elwyn-Jones' book, *In My Time: An Autobiography* (London, 1983), 48. The religious people of the town were impressed by Bevan's knowledge of scripture, a tribute to his Sunday school days.

2 In the thirties, at a time when Churchill was in trouble in the Conservative Party for criticising their arms policy and Bevan was about to be expelled from the Labour Party, the two dined together. Churchill suggested to Bevan that they should unite to form an opposition to the government. According to the story, Bevan turned and said: 'What use would I have for a lieutenant who has turned on so many of his party leaders?' See Vincent Brome, 'Bevan and Churchill', *New York Times Magazine*, 21 November 1948, 78.

3 National Library of Wales: Papers of Gwilym Davies. See United Nations V/2/40;V/2/42;V/2/43;V/2/44 'Why the United Nations Failed, 24 October 1944.

4 Gwilym Davies, *Y Natsiaid a'r Cenhedloedd Bychain yn Ewrop* (The Nazis and the Small Nations of Europe), (Wrexham, 1941), 25–29.

The fear of fascism

Oswald Mosley's fascists had been walking boldly and confidently through the streets of England's main cities. Industrial unrest was increasing. Railway workers, civil servants, Post Office workers and bus drivers were equally unsettled and unhappy about how they were being treated by their employers and politicians. There were many unofficial strikes. The communists were blamed but that was only partly true in South Wales. Remember that the popular communist Arthur Horner, a good friend to Bevan, had succeeded Jim Griffiths as the President of the South Wales Union of Mineworkers. There was strife in the pits in Merthyr Taff Vale, Bedwas, Nine Mile Point and Cwmfelinfach in Monmouthshire.[1] There a skirmish between the police and miners were witnessed. Sixty-nine miners and six women were arrested, with 33 of them receiving prison sentences from three to fifteen months. Bevan argued against these harsh sentences. The protests in the mining communities continued. Throughout 1935 and 1936 many, including Aneurin Bevan, campaigned against the Tory government and highlighted the plight of the unemployed. He was strongly opposed to means-testing and supported the hunger marches from Aberdeen in Scotland, from Carmarthen in West Wales, from Jarrow in the North East of England and from Glamorganshire and Monmouthshire in South Wales. It was estimated that between 150, 000 and 200, 000 marchers as well as the Home Counties and London's Labour Party supporters gathered in the capital city at Hyde Park on Sunday 8 November 1936, under the banners of the Labour Party, the trade unions, the Independent Labour Party, the Co-operative Movement, the Communist Party, the peace movement as well as the young people's movements and students' groups . Such unity raised the spirits of left-wingers. The huge crowd saw and heard Clement Attlee, the leader of the opposition, as well as the communist Wal Hannington the organiser of the marches, addressing the marchers.[2] However the star of that historic day was the finest speaker in the Labour movement, the one and only Aneurin Bevan. As a great walker himself, he praised the marchers. They had achieved a huge feat of physical stamina. For the first time ever in the Labour movement, they had succeeded in bringing together a galaxy of speakers of all shades, but completely united against the greedy and merciless capitalists. His message to them was:

> We have held joined hands and we shall not let those hands disappear. This protest says to the country that the Labour movement needs a united leadership.[3]

---

1 D. Ben Rees, *Cofiant Jim Griffiths: Arwr Glew y Werin*, (Talybont, 2014), 105.
2 Allen Hutt, *The Post-war History of the British Working Class* (London, 1937), 282.
3 *Ibid*.

At first, the unrepentant, hard-headed Conservative government refused to meet a delegation of the protesters. Eventually, after a heated debate in the House of Commons, Stanley Baldwin had no option but to relent. The delegation of socialists were welcomed to the offices of the Baldwin. Another important blow had been struck on behalf of the unemployed. Bevan believed the Labour Party should be less indifferent to the suffering experienced and much more aggressive and willing to support those leading the battle for fairness and employment. Labour needed to renew itself and no longer be apathetic as in the current crisis. Through the efforts of Harry Pollitt, the Communist Party expressed its sincere hope of forming a strong bond with the Labour Party; however, with Ernest Bevin and Walter Citrine dominating the Labour hierarchy, there was very unrealistic chance of this happening. Neither was Bevan in favour of the Pollitt inspired application, despite the fact that 1200 socialist-inspired societies were ready to support,[1]. This number included 765 trade union branches and 360 branches of the Labour Party.[2]

Aneurin supports the unemployment marches

Aneurin Bevan had endeared himself to the unemployed marchers from all over Britain .He travelled a few miles outside London to lead his friend Ellen Wilkinson representing the devastated town of Jarrow into the city centre . He also took care of the march organiser Wal Hannington, Arthur Horner and half a dozen of his Welsh mates. They all made their way to Bevan's flat for a shower and a delicious meal of eggs, bacon and tomatoes, prepared by the Bevan family maid. [3] The impromptu meal was enjoyed for all, despite the maid having had no advance warning.[4] But Bevan's kindness and friendship with well-known at all times. Unfortunately the leading communists caused him some unneeded grief; the right wing of the Labour party was determined to rid itself of every politician with sympathy or any links with Soviet Russia.[5]

The Annual Meeting of the Socialist Council was to be held in London on 31 October 1936 to condemn fascism and discuss the best way to deal with Sir Oswald Mosley and members of the British Union of Fascists. Representing the Labour Party were Bevan, being the main speaker, with Sir Stafford Cripps and William

---

1 *Ibid,* 283.
2 *Ibid,* 288.
3 Jennie Lee, *My Life With Nye,* (London, 1980), 115.
4 *Ibid.*
5 *Ibid,* 116. 'Life would have been easy for Nye if he had joined the hunger marchers with the support of the official trade union movement. Instead, he had to face the bitter hostility then shown towards any activity such as this that meant joining forces with Communists. The National Unemployed Workers Movement was Communist led.'

Mellor with him. Harry Pollitt and Palme Dutt represented the Communist Party, while James Maxton and Fenner Brockway were the delegates from the Independent Labour Party. All seven men abhorred capitalism, the political philosophy which they blamed for the suffering and deprivation of the unemployed throughout the industrial areas of England, Scotland and Wales.

The appearance of the weekly *Tribune*

By 1937, Aneurin Bevan had identified the need for a weekly newspaper to promote the left-wing vision of the Labour Party. The publication was needed to discuss the worsening situation in Europe, the failure of the government of the day in Westminster to respond and the excuses they made for their blunders. At the 1937 Annual Conference in Edinburgh, Bevan, Cripps, Laski, Mellor, Strauss and a number of other left-wing leaders agreed to move immediately to publish the aptly named *Tribune* on a weekly basis.[1] The situation in Spain was dire and by now Mussolini had colonised Abyssinia in Africa for himself while Hitler had retaken the Saar and the Rhineland. Commentators on the left saw that there was strong support already for the Left Book Club and that their dream of seeing *Tribune* in the shops was a distinct possibility.[2] George Strauss and Cripps provided the capital needed to establish a highquality paper, generously giving £20,000 apiece, and it was hoped *Tribune* would quickly reach a circulation of 50,000. In January 1938, the first edition of *Tribune* came out, with copies sold in the shops and on street corners in London for twopence. The experienced journalist William Mellor was appointed editor with a management board to help him. The board itself comprised six effective politicians, namely George Strauss, Ellen Wilkinson, Stafford Cripps, Harold Laski, Noel Brailsford and Bevan. He was the strongest voice among them, he also attended the editorial board and spoke often within the executive team. William Mellor (who had an extramarital affair with a married left-winger Barbara Castle) was a difficult man to deal with. As Michael Foot expressed it , working with William Mellor was like 'living on the foothills of Vesuvius'.[3] Yet despite being a difficult comrade, Mellor had no option but to toe the line when Bevan was in attendance. Mellor soon

---

1 Michael Foot, *Aneurin Bevan, 1897–1960*, Vol. 1 (London, 1962), 235.
2 *Ibid*, 241. From the first edition, Bevan's work is seen in the weekly magazine. John Campbell paid tribute to him, saying: 'Bevan is not normally thought of as much of a writer; but these weekly articles reveal a surprisingly good journalist. Though strictly political, their variety expresses the richness of his mind, always able to focus a general argument on a telling detail or extrapolate an historical theory from a trivial episode. As well as major polemics there are a host of throwaway epigrams, satirical squibs, some very accomplished, sketch writing and – undoubtedly most irritating to the leaders and loyalists of the Parliamentary Labour Party.
3 *Michael Foot, Aneurin Bevan 1897–1960*, 245.

realised that he had to be careful for he could not dislodge Bevan from his power base. Bevan always got the upper hand in a political discussion as many of the editorial board have testified. The leaders of the Labour Party as we knew were totally opposed to the existence of the United Front, but *Tribune* proved an extremely effective weapon in promoting the meetings, particularly at those held outside London. Bevan wrote himself a delightful weekly column under the title 'Inside Westminster'. Attlee and Herbert Morrison believed that co-operating with the Communist Party would wreck any chance of the Labour Party winning the next election in 1939 or 1940. They knew the Tories, under the leadership of Neville Chamberlain, would make a huge song and dance of the supposed relationship, scaring the middle classes from voting Labour . Labour needed the middle class to win a general election.[1] The NEC saw an inextricable link between communism and fascism; it was therefore adamant that there should be no affiliation to a political party that believed in totalitarianism rather than democracy. In March 1937, the NEC banned any members of the United Front or Socialist League from being Labour Party members. Cripps and Bevan had little choice but to dissolve the United Front and thus continue as full members of the Labour Party. Unfortunately for the two rebels, that wasn't the end of the matter and meetings of dissent continued. The Left Book Club, by now enjoying huge success in its book sales, threw itself into the campaign for British socialism.

Working in harmony with Sir Stafford Cripps

Aneurin Bevan and Stafford Cripps had opened the eyes of enthusiastic members of the left, and convinced them feeling that the trade unions were much too domineering in Labour affairs. They had the largest share of the vote at the Labour Party Conference and this allowed right-wing leaders to gain the key positions . For many, the Labour Party was in the hands of a small clique of four right wingers ,namely Clement Attlee, then Herbert Morrison supported by the trade unionists such as Walter Citrine and Ernest Bevin. Both Cripps and Bevan longed for a change of leadership. Their own support came mainly from the constituencies and not from the trade unions.

Cripps regarded the leadership of the Labour Party as weak and aimless. Bevan agreed with him. The bitter conflict between these two opposing factions meant the Labour Party was in constant turmoil. Cripps's application to organise a large meeting of the United Front in the Albert Hall was immediately turned down. A

---

1 *Ibid,* 257. A characteristic remark of Bevan when Chamberlain took up the reins: 'In the funeral service of capitalism the honeyed and soothing platitudes of the clergymen are finished, and the cortege is now under the sombre and impressive guidance of the undertaker.'

letter was sent to the trustees disputing the decision and asking for the application to be re-considered.

Churchill a trustee replied on behalf of the Albert Hall trustees:

> You are working in political association with the Communists at the present time. And it has always been the rule whenever they have the power, they forcibly suppress all opinions but their own.[1]

Cripps replied in his usual effective way, accusing Churchill of prejudice against the communists and consequently destroying the principle of free speech. Right wingers in every party saw danger in the United Front's campaign. The time had come to act. On 12 January 1937, the Labour Party NEC published an appeal to the Labour movement condemning the United Front and reminding its own members that two annual conferences had voted overwhelmingly against allowing the Communist Party to join them and condemning the Popular Front propaganda. The NEC emphasised that members should show loyalty to the Labour Party as their first priority. Less than a week later, on 17 January, the Popular Front responded publicly by publishing its manifesto.[2] This called for unity among industrial workers and all members of the working class against fascism and war. The Conservative government was condemned as a medium of capitalism and imperialism. The Popular Front believed the only way of rescuing people worldwide from their predicament was to work for peace, to work with the Soviet Union and to implement schemes geared for better conditions. For historians like myself, it is absolutely clear that the manifesto came from the hands of Harry Pollitt and William Gallacher rather than from the brain of Stafford Cripps and Aneurin Bevan. Cripps was a constant opponent of the United Nations but Bevan was not. He firmly believed that it was necessary to act against Hitler and Mussolini and Franco. But he knew as well as anyone that Britain and France were not at all ready to withstand Hitler or Mussolini on the battlefield. At the 1937 Labour Party Conference, there was a long discussion about the Popular Front and the National Executive Committee carried the day. Every Labour Party member would be dismissed from its ranks if he or she were seen sharing a political platform with members who belonged to the British Communist Party.[3] It was agreed that constituencies would have the right to vote

---

1 Mark M. Krug, *Aneurin Bevan: Cautious Rebels* (New York and London, 1961), 51.
2 *Ibid*, 50.
3 There was a lot of discontent in the Labour Party strongholds in South Wales, especially the Rhondda constituencies. The United Front was seen as a crafty way for the communists to undermine the strength of the Labour Party. It could be argued that setting up the South Wales Regional Labour Party Council in 1937 was done to confront the influence of the communists and bring Labour activities together. Chris Williams, *Democratic Rhondda* (Cardiff, 2003), 200–2.

for a small number of leaders to join the NEC.[1] This is how Stafford Cripps and Harold Laski became members in 1938, with Bevan' hoping soon to join them. At least their constant call to see more democracy within the Labour Party was gradually becoming a reality.

Bevan was scathing in the House of Commons

In the House of Commons, Bevan was scathing in his attack on the Chamberlain government's foreign policy and especially on Britain's unwillingness to help in the Spanish Civil War. In the Monmouthshire coalfield, there was a small militant section of socialists who were great admirers of Bevan. Three of them, Bob Jones, Bob Cox of Tredegar and Jim Brewer of Abertyswg (who boasted that his great-great- grandfather was a Chartist), went to Spain to join the International Brigade.[2] Aneurin Bevan was highly supportive of the International Brigade and told Brewer he would have loved to have gone himself to Spain but neither the authorities nor Parliament would allow it. The truth was that the long involvement with the United Front had left Bevan and Cripps completely isolated politically. Bevan criticised Chamberlain's appeasement but he himself had, in the manifesto, opposed the National Government's programme to arm for war.

How did Bevan expect Chamberlain to confront Hitler without weapons? It is not easy to explain this dilemma. One has to see the Popular Front's campaign as being somewhat inconsistent. One example after another reveals just how inconsistent Bevan could be in his involvement with the United Front Appeasement, that is the effort to come to an understanding with Hitler, is now viewed as a villainous and totally shameful policy. But at times, it was the policy of many a capable British politician.

The ineffective Prime Minister

It was in the month of September 1938, that Neville Chamberlain returned from Munich to London waving a piece of paper which, in his political naiveté, he called the Munich Agreement.[3] Chamberlain was willing for Hitler to annexe Sudetenland, land which belonged to a neighbouring country despite its majority German popu-

---

1 But the NEC, under the Welshman Morgan Phillips, kept a close eye on the elections. The Labour Party in Newport was banned from even
2 The story is told in full in Hywel Francis, *Miners Against Fascism: Wales and the Spanish Civil War* (London, 1984).
3 Emyr Price, *Cymru a'r Byd Modern Ers 1918* (Cardiff, 1979), 35.

lation, on the understanding he would not claim any more territory in Europe. (The West repeated the same mistake with Russia's invasion of Ukraine in 2014 and 2022.) Hitler promised to accept the British Prime Minister's condition and Chamberlain believed him, famously saying:

> 'I believe in peace for our time.'

Soon after, Hitler attacked Czechoslovakia, taking Memel and Danzig before attacking Poland in 1939. On 9 January 1939, Cripps prepared a memorandum calling on the Labour Party to oppose the National Government's policy and adopt a policy of peace with France, Russia and the United States.[1] The memorandum argued for a united front between the opposition parties, naming the Labour Party, the Liberal Party and the Communist Party as a strong possibility . The memorandum was sent to the press and to every constituency. The Labour Party NEC naturally rejected the memorandum by ten votes to three, warning that anyone who campaigned or supported it would be expelled from the Labour Party. Stafford Cripps was stubborn and refused and so he was expelled on 31 March. Aneurin Bevan and his parliamentary friend George Strauss blindly and foolishly followed suit . They published their full support for Sir Stafford Cripps and were expelled along with Robert Bruce, the generous Charles Trevelyan and E. P. Young.[2]

Dissatisfaction at how Cripps and Bevan were treated

Stafford Cripps and Aneurin Bevan's supporters were infuriated and regarded those who had been expelled as martyrs of the dictatorial National Executive Committee. The *New Statesman and Nation* who was nearer the Labour Party thinking predictably expressed its opposition to left-wing papers including the *Tribune*.[3] The expulsion highlighted just how much the political profiles of both men had increased in the past decade. Morrison feared the United Front would destroy the Labour Party and he was an uncompromising enemy of Aneurin Bevan throughout the thirties. There followed in British politics a constant conflict between the trade unionists within the Labour Party and the nonconformist, socialist tradition which Bevan upheld throughout his life. But there were exceptions. All except Cripps were allowed back into the Labour Party eight months later (in November), after promising not to take part in any campaigns that undermined Labour Party policy. Only Cripps held out for a few years, and one could argue that he had been a bad

---
1 Eric Estorick, *Stafford Cripps* (New York, 1949,) 143.
2 Mark M. Krug, *Aneurin Bevan: Cautious Rebel, ibid*, 55.
3 Editorial, *New Statesman and Nation,* 18 March 1933, 412.

influence on Nye Bevan. Some trade unions, such as the National Union of Mineworkers, were very much in favour of the aggressive nonconformist tradition with which Bevan was associated. In South Wales, there was a strong tradition of communism in the mining industry, particularly as a large proportion of the population had been raised in militant homes.

The Civil War in Spain

To a large extent, this left-wing tradition explains the obvious support given by Wales to the Republicans in the Spanish Civil War. Politically aware left-wingers from all over Europe were flocking to Spain to fight against Franco. Writers of every sort ventured there, such as George Orwell (who became an admirer of Bevan), Ernest Hemingway and the poet W.H. Auden. A host of miners joined up, including Will Paynter from the Rhondda and Tom Jones (or Tom Sbaen as he was called) from Rhosllannerchrugog in North East Wales, who was soon captured and held as prisoner. Other left-leaning miners, like Dai Francis of Onllwyn, helped the cause by collecting money in the collieries of west Wales for the International Brigade. Francis and others, including Aneurin Bevan, Jim Griffiths and his wife Winifred, also raised money for the Spanish children sent to Wales for protection.[1]

Franco was destined for triumph from the outset. His opponents in the International Brigade were an amateurish and inexperienced army and not totally united against Franco, even on the battlefield. Franco had the establishment behind him; the whole Catholic Church in its pomp was very supportive as was the army in its barbarity and the rich men in their castles. Above all, there was the practical help flooding into the country from those two cruel dictators Hitler and Mussolini, neither of whom was willing to allow a socialist-communist government to rule Spain in the age of fascism. In many ways, the Spanish Civil War was seen as a rehearsal for a greater war. The capitalists in Spain had too much to lose and, when Franco crossed the Mediterranean with his army from Morocco to Spain, everyone knew that a bloody war was on the horizon. It was not easy for Franco who depended on Hitler and Mussolini for the extra soldiers to fight, for arms and for planes. In fact, Madrid and Barcelona proved a real stumbling block for Franco.

The Spanish government also received help from another brutal dictator Josef Stalin, who sent arms, food and men from Russia. It was only when it was certain Franco would win, that Stalin withdraw his support for the Republic. In contrast, the UK's National Government refused to provide any support, to the great distress

---
1 D. Ben Rees, *Cofiant Jim Griffiths: Arwr Glew y Werin*, ibid, 121.

of Aneurin Bevan and his left wing supporters. When Barcelona surrendered in January 1939 and Madrid in March of the same year, Franco was on his way to his throne and Hitler and Mussolini were dancing in Berlin and Rome to their fascist followers' delight.

As Bevan argued, the wicked men and their evil powers were on the verge of an inevitable victory. Franco was victorious because those countries which claimed to be democratic had refused to defend the democratic government elected by the people of Spain. The communists were still viewed as the threat, feared as much by the Conservatives as the Labour Party. The spineless conduct of the British government in relation to the Spanish Civil War gave significant encouragement to Hitler, Franco and Mussolini, who saw it as evidence that democratic countries could do hardly anything on the battlefield. 'Pathetic' is likely to have been the word Hitler used when describing Chamberlain to his Reich comrades Himmler, Goering and Hess.

Analysing the philosophy of Bevan in 1939

Aneurin Bevan's clear stance as an intellectual leader of the left wingers of the Labour Party is on record in the speech he delivered at the Rhondda East by-election in April 1939.[1] The speech was preserved in the papers of William H. Mainwaring MP at the National Library of Wales, and as such documents are scarce, I shall make use of the presentation which was delivered by Bevan in the Tylorstown Welfare Hall.

Mainwaring is one of the forgotten characters of Welsh politics . Very little has been written on him.[2]

Aneurin had a long relationship with the Popular Front through his friendship with Stafford Cripps.[3] They respected each other but Bevan disagreed with Cripps refusing to come back immediately to the ranks of Labour. He asked the NEC as soon as he could to be taken back into the fold of the Labour Party before the end of 1939. In April 1939, Aneurin recognised the threat of a world war which could destroy civilisation and how it would y affect ordinary people. He could see the working classes of the Rhondda and Ebbw Vale in danger of being degraded and belittled. We haven't got anything that Hitler wants. You the working classes of Great Britain are in no danger directly because we possess nothing that the governing

---

1 National Library of Wales: Papers of W. H. Mainwaring. Aneurin Bevan's speech in April 1939, 'The Popular Front', pp. 1–20
2 See D. Ben Rees, *Cofiant Jim Griffiths*, (A Biography of Jim Griffiths) 59, 61, 75, 108, 114, 148–9, 156.
3 *Ibid*, 2.

classes of Germany and Italy wants.[1] Aneurin Bevan argued that Hitler and Mussolini desired to conquer Britain, France, the Netherlands and Belgium as they all had empires and colonies. He believed that the working class had benefited from the bravery of the Chartists, South Wales miners, the Tolpuddle Martyrs and everyone who stood up for human rights and a better life. It was not the uniformed classes who had become activists for development and democracy but the ordinary people who battled and campaigned for a more democratic world[2]. Wherever Hitler triumphed, democracy had been killed stone dead. Here is one of Bevan's very characteristic quotations:

> We the ordinary people are ready to help the governing class and to defend their capital if they are ready to help us defend our freedom.[3]

Bevan recalled how he had opposed rearmament at the Labour Party Conference in Bournemouth. At that time, he was opposed to it for the simple reason that he did not want to place devilish weapons into the hands of our enemies.[4] Subsequently, he changed his approach and aligned himself with fellow Labour members who believed it was necessary to have arms to defend democracy, particularly after what had happened in Spain. Bevan believed the politician who best understood the difference between wealth and poverty was Oliver Cromwell, one of his heroes[5]. According to Cromwell as well as Bevan, for the rich man wealth was freedom, whereas freedom for a poor man is the right to attack that wealth. Health, poverty and democracy coexist. When poverty and democracy coexist, then wealth will come under siege. When reconciliation between nations is impossible, fascism is at hand. The task of the governing class is to compromise in the inevitable conflict for the time being. Often poor people are told to vote for a better world and for wealth. At other times, they are persuaded to vote for democracy. It is hard for people who do not see the link between the three elements to see and understand the problem and the differences springing from it. When fascism wins the day as it did in Spain, democracy is pushed far into oblivion. In the opinion of Bevan the capitalist is often geared to consider , wealth as the sole purpose in life. He is not thinking about the votes of the plebs: indeed, he does not give a fig about them only that his capital is safe.[6] But democratic institutions are beneficial and valuable.

---

1 *Ibid*, 3.
2 *Ibid*.
3 *Ibid*.
4 *Ibid*.
5 Blair Worden, *God's Instruments: Political conduct in the England of Oliver Cromwell* (Oxford, 2012), 71–5
6 National Library of Wales, Papers of W. H. Mainwaring, Aneurin Bevan's Speech, *ibid*, 5.

They are what we have to stand against the tyrannical state.[1] The destruction of a democracy is a distressingly dark day for its people. The Soviet Union in the days of Lenin and Stalin was to Bevan a glorious example of the destruction of a system that had some democratic elements. Bevan's argument in the British Labour Party conference at Bournemouth was that it was necessary to defend Sudetenland. That was how it was in 1938.[2] Then, in 1939, the UK government continued to support an arms programme in order to defend other countries from the fascist bullies. In his speech at Tylorstown (which happens to be the birthplace of Jimmy Wilde, a miner who became one of the world's best flyweight boxers), Aneurin Bevan praised the Labour movement in the decade following the Great Strike of 1926, when its leaders were well-supported by the miners and activists in the Popular Front and the United Front. The miners were, in fact, the aristocrats of the trade union movement as the brilliant actor Richard Burton, a proud miner's son from Pontrhydyfen and a big fan of Aneurin Bevan, reminded his American audiences. Bevan will be remembered for his unsuccessful plea to the Labour Party to back protests and demonstrations like the 1936 hunger marches, which were supported by the miners. Bevan acted as one of two national treasurers for the marches and by the end of March at least £600 had been donated.

Bevan acknowledged there was a powerful working class in Wales, less so in Scotland, and extremely weak in Ulster outside the shipyards of Belfast. In England, however, the working class had been battered by the Tories and had only survived by sticking together as comrades in arms in their communities. Aneurin Bevan believed the working class needed the strong, uncompromising leadership he provided them with throughout the nineteen thirties. Unfortunately, many of those he so desperately wished to help were reluctant to allow him to take his rightful place among the leaders of the Labour Party.

In the House of Commons, he would hear some of the best political speeches in the democratic world, delivered by David Lloyd George, Winston Churchill, Harold Macmillan and Ramsay MacDonald.[3] Most would add Bevan himself to that list for he became one of the foremost debaters during his first decade in Westminster. In his opinion, what made a good speech was 'tears from the heart of a man who is full of sympathy' with the lower classes. That said, he felt that speaking well was not enough and what was needed was the passion to mobilise the government to take action. Far from representing true democracy, the MPs representing those parties forming the National Government would back it obediently on every issue. Bevan wanted them to remember 'the blood of our comrades

---

1 *Ibid*, 5.
2 *Ibid*, 6.
3 *Ibid*, 7.

from Spain is on our hands'.[1] Neville Chamberlain, who had hailed from a dynasty of Birmingham politicians, was proving the worst national leader the UK had seen in the twentieth century. For a year, he had had the backing of Parliament in his appeasement policy towards Hitler. The Labour Party lacked Bevan's courage in attacking him at every opportunity, a big mistake on their part.[2] Following the German working class, Chamberlain had simply gone along with Hitler's dictates. Aneurin Bevan believed the National Government and Liberals again needed a leader of the calibre of David Lloyd George. Bevan realised how fortunate Welsh workers were to have the strong socialist leadership and ideology provided by the miners leaders from 1919 to 1939.[3] He became one of the fiercest critics of the coalition government of Attlee and Churchill and, throughout the war, continued to remind MPs of their responsibilities.

Aneurin Bevan's friendship with Michael Foot

Bevan had a faithful disciple in Michael Foot, another left-wing socialist and a man who eventually succeeded him as the MP for Ebbw Vale constituency. Both men were part of the *Tribune* team. As Kenneth O. Morgan says about the relationship between Foot and Bevan:

> He would be his Boswell, his Engels, his John the Baptist and of course his parliamentary heir.[4]

Bevan was very fond of the friendship he had with Michael Foot because of his intellectual pursuits , his love of literature – for both of them would love to quote from the poetry of John Keats and William Wordsworth –and his continued support to Tribune from the middle 1930s. The evening before Michael Foot stood in the 1935 Monmouth by-election, there was a revivalist-like meeting where Bevan and Jim Griffiths got carried away. They were like two preachers in the political meetings.[5] Despite viewing each other as comrades in arms, Bevan and Foot came from very different backgrounds: Bevan was a working class intellectual while Foot hailed from a well-off middle- class Liberal family. He was part of the English establishment, despite kicking against the traces. Politically, Foot stood in the tradition of the Quakers (he was educated at one of their independent schools) and he kept

---

1 *Ibid*, 9.
2 *Ibid*, 15
3 *Ibid*, 16.
4 Kenneth O. Morgan, *Michael Foot*, London, 2007, 96
5 *Ibid*, 54.

alive the flame of Keir Hardie and George Lansbury. In contrast, Bevan was convinced that protest in opposition was futile. Labour needed to be in power before it could act on behalf of the poor and the unemployed.[1] For him, the ultimate aim of a politician was to win elections, even though his rather raw, insulting and aggressive attacks on the Tories ended up alienating many people who might otherwise have voted Labour.

A critic during the Second World War

Bevan maintained his role as a critical MP throughout the Second World War. He was in a very different position from his friend Jim Griffiths. Within three years of entering the House of Commons, Griffiths was regarded in Labour Party ranks as a safe pair of hand; the same was not true of Bevan. Ten years as an MP and he was still regarded as a dangerous ally, hard to handle and impossible to silence. In fact, he was viewed as one of the most dangerous Labour backbenchers since the Labour Party's formation in 1906. But, at the outset of the Second World War, Griffiths and Bevan were of one mind: both believed the Labour Party should shun the coalition government. When Neville Chamberlain invited the party leader Clement Attlee to join the National Government the invitation was refused. The situation suddenly changed in May 1940, when the British Labour Party came together for its annual conference in Bournemouth. At an NEC meeting the night before the conference started, Attlee reported that Chamberlain had again invited Labour to join the National Government under his leadership. For his part, Attlee had made it perfectly clear to Chamberlain how Labour felt about the issue. He would not work as Chamberlain's deputy or with Lord Halifax, who was predicted to be another possible successor.

Bevan's disagreement with Labour leaders

Bevan and Cripps believed that the Labour leaders like Attlee and Bevin should insert firm conditions before joining in the new coalition under Winston Churchill.[2] They saw no place in a future cabinet for the foot soldiers of the Munich Agreement: in particular the Conservative leader Neville Chamberlain and the Liberal leader Sir John Simon in the new war time coalition government .The Labour Party leaders had no patience with this stance. Now was not the time for a far reaching

---
1 *Ibid,* 154. Prof. K. O. Morgan called Foot an 'agitator of protest' and Bevan a 'politician of power'.
2 Estorick, *Stafford Cripps, ibid,* 212.

debate – the defence of Britain called for national unity. Attlee, ever the diplomat, accepted the position of Deputy Prime Minister and Ernest Bevin, Herbert Morrison, Arthur Greenwood and Hugh Dalton all agreed to act in the new coalition cabinet.

For MPs like Aneurin Bevan the decision to support the new coalition government was far from an easy one. Like all backbenchers he would be expected to support the new cabinet, while simultaneously holding together the Labour Party identity and unity. When the Parliamentary Labour Party met after the annual conference, two things were agreed: first, that Attlee would allow MPs who were not members of the government to sit on the opposition benches and secondly, an administrative committee would be set up with those elected onto it occupying the 'opposition' front bench.

No place for Bevan on the opposition front bench

At a time when he should have been leading the opposition with Jim Griffiths, Aneurin Bevan once again found himself on the back benches.[1] The agenda for the House was determined by the Prime Minister, the Deputy Prime Minister and the Whips. In the face of this difficult situation, Aneurin had three options.

He could stay quiet, spend the majority of his time at the offices of *Tribune* or continue to challenge government leadership.[2] Bevan chose the latter two pursuits, becoming a strong critic for the opposition side. In Parliament, his oratorical skills were unsurpassed and he always had the last word on *Tribune*'s editorial board. Nobody could get the better of him. With Attlee, Bevin and Morrison now in government there was an unprecedented opportunity for left-wing leaders, in particular Aneurin Bevan and Emanuel Shinwell, to be gadflies.

In 1941, a movement called Radical Action was established by Liberal businessman Lancelot Spicer and Megan Lloyd George, the Liberal MP for Anglesey. She had huge charm and numerous political insights, and she immediately became a prominent member of the group. Megan Lloyd George was greatly admired by Aneurin.[3] A movement called *Forward March* was formed by the Liberal MP Richard Acland and then in the same year a movement called Commitee 1941 was established by

---

1 D. Ben Rees, *Cofiant Jim Griffiths*, (Biography of Jim Griffiths) *ibid,* 125– 139.
2 Unwillingly, Bevan took over the editorship during the war though he had neither the time as an MP nor the professional knowledge of how to produce a weekly paper. He left Jon Kimche to move to the office as the effective editor under Aneurin's supervision. As Bevan and Strauss were so busy, their wives Jennie Lee and Patricia Strauss, along with Michael Foot, were persuaded to become members of the editorial board. But *Tribune*'s opinion of people like Bevin and Attlee reflected what Aneurin would say's to Foot at the dining table in a restaurant or on one of his walking trips. See Mervyn Jones, *Michael Foot*, (London, 1994), 103 and 141.
3 Mervyn Jones, *A Radical Life: The Biography of Megan Lloyd George* (London, 1991) 170.

the Bradford born socialist and author J B Priestley.[1] Bevan was forbidden to take part in a BBC radio programme by Churchill, after which the BBC did not dare to give him a voice. The discovery that, during the Second World War, BBC chiefs were more ready to hear prominent communists than the lovable socialist from Tredegar came as a huge shock to George Orwell.[2] Richard Acland's Forward March movement and Committee 1941 came together to form a party – the Common Wealth Party –which was successful in by-elections during the war.

It was during the war years, that Aneurin Bevan gained a reputation for being the best speaker in the Commons.

Politicians of all parties flocked into to the Chamber to listen to him debating. He was one of the few Labour politicians who refused the Prime Minister any leeway at the dispatch box. Churchill and Bevan were constantly cited as two of the House of Common's most outstanding speakers of the twentieth century. Winston Churchill was usually able to respond to Aneurin's attacks with eloquence, but on one occasion he lost his temper. Bevan responded in a pitying tone:

> The Prime Minister has lost his temper not because of one of his ministers but with a poor, simple backbench MP.[3]

No MP of any party was safe from attack by Bevan. When he was interrupted in mid-flow by an MP who was relatively new to the House, Bevan struck back:

Once, while Aneurin Bevan was addressing the House, he noticed Winston Churchill was whispering to one of his Whips. Bevan threw the Prime Minister a smile and advised him he would learn much more from listening to him than he would learn from the lips of one of his officials. Bevan was not afraid of making fun of Churchill and especially of his habit of dressing in military uniform. He frequently belittled Attlee too and was very sharp-tongued when Herbert Morrison decided to ban the Communist Party paper the *Daily Worker,* as a result of its propaganda over many months, leading to the subsequent protest. The communists were a small minority: Bevan did not support them but he believed they should have the right to publish their propaganda. Freedom of the press was essential even during wartime.

Bevan condemned the unacceptable propaganda of the *Daily Mail* and the Home

---

1 *Ibid*, 171.
2 This is what was said about Aneurin Bevan and the BBC at the time of the Second World War. 'Bevan was a director of *Tribune* and one of Orwell's keen supporters there both at the time of the People's Convention and later. Politically he was a controversial figure but without the slightest suggestion that he was a communist. It is therefore particularly interesting that whereas Orwell succeeded with J. S. B. Haldane, he failed with Bevan. Although the subject is still shrouded in mystery, it is clear that Bevan was one of those who in the words of the controller, 'would be better left alone – without any mention of a blacklist of course'. See W. J. West, *The Larger Evils* (Edinburgh 1992), 73.
3 *Hansard*, vol. CCCLXXIV (1944), column 1980.

Office's foolish actions. Herbert Morrison believed Bevan had gone too far and struck out at him:

> My Hon Friend and I have had great experience of Labour Party democracy. If I wanted to find one distinguished member of the party, who more than any other, has set aside the democratic decisions of the majority of his colleagues, I think I should choose my Hon Friend the Member of Ebbw Vale. Therefore, his democracy is rather skin-deep. He speaks of democracy for himself and not so much for the other fellow.[1]

Only six people supported Bevan on that occasion and two of those were Communist Party MPs. Aneurin's position on the *Daily Worker* issue was completely unacceptable to most MPs and 323 voted against the proposal to keep the *Daily Worker* in circulation. Even the most gifted politician can go too far, and this was one time Aneurin Bevan stood almost alone in his convictions. And there were similar examples throughout the years. Bevan had unusual moral strength but, during the war, he was often the whipping boy because he dared to question and challenge Churchill and the Labour leaders within the coalition. If Bevan were asked his opinion of Attlee, he would be sure to talk of his 'suburban middle-class values.'[2] He would readily refer to William Hazlitt's essay on the politician William Pitt written after his death in 1806.[3] Like Pitt, Attlee had no strong feelings or indeed a penetrating vision. After quoting Hazlitt, Bevan would add:

> Only the bovine English could have brought forth such a Mirabeau to guide the beginnings of their Revolution. Here was no Lenin leading the masses but rather Labour's Lord Liverpool, the Arch-Mediocrity.[4]

In January 1940, Bevan wrote to *Tribune* stating that the Labour Party leaders had failed to emphasise the very obvious weakness of Chamberlain's government. He even criticised the Labour-supporting *Daily Herald* for not being sufficiently courageous in its stance and for failing to rise above the standard of a parish magazine.[5] Attlee reacted at once but this was not enough. The *Tribune* headline on 19 January 1940 was *Speak Up Mr Attlee*.[6] *Tribune* became the tool with which Bevan could thrash the speeches of Attlee and others every week. He believed Churchill was deceiving the

---

1 *Hansard*, Vol. CCCLXVIII (1941), column 516.
2 John Bew, *Citizen Clem: A Biography of Attlee*, (London 2016), 19.
3 Ibid.
4 Michael Foot, *Aneurin Bevan, ibid*, 30
5 John Bew, *Citizen Clem, ibid*, 235–6
6 *Ibid.*

population. Labour members supported this deceit, even 'putting petrol in the national car', but it was the Tories who were in charge of the driving. Throughout the war, *Tribune* bore down heavily on Attlee, Herbert Morrison and Ernest Bevin for being so docile. This continual criticism abated for a while when Ellen Wilkinson became a member of the coalition government (she was a former a contributor to the newspaper).[1] Later, Stafford Cripps, the barrister politician, generously subsidised *Tribune* before he too joined the coalition government.[2] Despite these appointments, Bevan remained an outspoken critic of the Coalition Government. He criticised it –and principally Churchill – for inviting Lord Beaverbrook to be the Minister of Aircraft Production. For Bevan, Beaverbrook was minister in name only; it was Churchill who retained the power. In Parliament, Bevan asked for assurance that Beaverbrook would spend more time in Britain instead of forever travelling to Washington.[3] By 1942, Bevan feared that Winston Churchill would not be able to lead Britain to the victory that the country – and the entire Labour movement yearned for .[4]

Supports the miners and publishes his book, *Why Trust the Tories?*

Aneurin Bevan constantly emphasized the importance of the coal industry to Britain's economy and the huge debt owed to the miners, without whom the country would not survive. For him, the solution for an ailing industry was to nationalise it.[5]. He would often talk about the Soviet Union. There was no problem of the Soviet miner being absent from the coalfield for he had a personal stake in the mines which belonged to him and his fellow workers. Bevan's Labour Party comrade Ness Edwards was praised for his stand for the working class as was Georgie Buchanan, who defended the old, the sick and the unemployed. Despite this, Bevan was often overlooked by those who knew of his courage and recognised the relevance of his remarks .[6]

Aneurin Bevan argued the Labour movement should be more confrontational towards the Tories. In 1944, his new book *Why Not Trust the Tories?* gained huge circulation.[7] Its success – and the results of wartime by-elections – gave him reason

---

1 *Ibid*, 236.
2 *Ibid*, 254.
3 Aneurin Bevan, 'Labour Has Been Tricked', *Tribune,* February 13 (268), 1940, 1–2.
4 Aneurin Bevan, 'What Churchill Must Do', *Tribune,* February 20 (269), 1942, 2.
5 Aneurin Bevan, 'Consider Coal', *Tribune,* March 20 (273), 1942, 2.
6 Jack Wilkes, 'In Parliament', *Tribune,* March 20 (273) 242,1.
7 The book *Why Not Trust The Tories?* was very important when it came out in 1944 and was a bestseller according to Victor Collancz. It was published under a pseudonym rather than under the author's name. The first volume *Guilty Men* was a success but W.H. Smith refused to sell it.

to be optimistic that, come the end of the war, the country would be ripe for a change of government. Rhys Davies, MP for Westhoughton and a pioneer of the Labour movement in Wales, believed Bevan was right to continue attacking the Labour leaders.[1] Davies was originally from Llanelli and had done a great deal for Welsh people in Manchester. He believed the Labour Party was often out of touch with the ordinary people and seemed to be moving to the right while workers and members of the armed forces were marching metaphorically to the left.[2] By May 1942, there had been 86 strikes in the coalfields with 58,000 miners staying off work.[3] In October 1942, Parliament discussed the coal industry. Four Welsh politicians took part: the Liberals D. O. Evans (Cardigan) and David Lloyd George, and the two Labour giants, Jim Griffiths and Aneurin Bevan. Bevan condemned Churchill as primarily responsible for the coal industry's problems; he had the miners fighting in the armed forces when they were needed in the pits.[4] Bevan frightened many politicians, which was the main reason he was overlooked for promotion in the House of Commons. In character, he was very different from Jim Griffiths, who was appointed as one of Labour's representatives in the reconstruction conferences. Jim Griffiths addressed these conferences with a spirit of hope and resolve. Like the majority of Labour MPs, though not Bevan, Griffiths thought, by the end of 1942, that the end of the war was in sight. The combined forces of Great Britain, the Commonwealth, the United States and the Soviet Union must certainly have the upper hand over Hitler and the German army. There were better days to come.

The Beveridge Report is accepted

The publication of William Beveridge's report in 1942 was like 'manna falling from heaven' to left-wing politicians and Labour Party leaders. The report was warmly received and all 600,000 printed copies were sold within two days. The Conservative party was not at all enthusiastic on the reforms proposed in the report, while the Churchill-supporting press was equally lukewarm. Bevan and a number of other Labour rebels expressed their dismay that the government had handed out copies

---

1 Rhys John Davies was an uncompromising pacifist. He was a Westminster politician holding fast to his Welsh nonconformist heritage. Davies' brother – known as Cenech – was a Welsh language poet. Davies published *Y Seneddwyr ar Dramp* (Parliamentarians on the March) and *Y Cristion a Rhyfel* (The Christian and War) in 1937. Both books are extremely entertaining.
2 Aneurin Bevan, 'Labour Must Lead Now', *Tribune*, May 22, 1942 (282), 6–7. He refers to the criticism of Rhys J. Davies, MP
3 Leading article in *Tribune*, June 5, 1942 (284), 1–2.
4 The coal industry was regularly discussed in *Tribune*; see the October 1942 editions.

of the report to a number of newspaper editors before sharing them with MPs.[1] The *Daily Mail, Daily Express* and *Daily Sketch* immediately condemned the report, while the *Tablet,* the mouthpiece of the Catholic Church, attacked its totalitarian principles. It was only the *Daily Herald, New Chronicle, Daily Mirror, Times* and *Manchester Guardian* who welcomed the findings of Beveridge.[2]

For Bevan, William Beveridge had prepared a document which presented the needs and challenges of the most vulnerable members in society: the old, the widowed, the unemployed, the sick and the growing number of deprived children. The report recognised human need as a priority: the plight of worker who had an accident, the miner with scoliosis or the industrial worker with health problems. The difficulties experienced by women whose husbands had died and those without work was also highlighted. These people needed government help. Bevan could still remember the twenties, when parents in his Ebbw Vale constituency were unable to pay for a doctor to come out to a sick child. A cataclysmic battle lay ahead; however, Bevan and *Tribune* were grateful for the Beveridge Report in presenting the reality of many people's lives to the government of the day. In February 1943, three days were set aside by the Speaker of the House of Commons to discuss William Beveridge's plan. On the second day of debate, the opposition parties led by Labour offered complete support for the report and pressed for a vote on the issue. There was no realistic hope of winning the vote but Jim Griffith's contribution in making the offer is long remembered. When the proposal was defeated by 325 votes to 119, the country at large realised the Conservative Party had no intention of implementing the recommendations of the Beveridge Report when the war was over.[3] The outcome of the debate resulted in the Fabian Society inviting six people to give lectures on the future of Britain after the Second World War. These lectures featured exciting ideas about how the welfare state might look like in the near future, presented by its prospective architects, that is Aneurin Bevan and Jim Griffiths plus four academics, William Beveridge, G. H. D. Cole, R. H. Tawney and Harold Laski.[4] Bevan did not believe Winston Churchill should have the last word on something as important as the Beveridge Report. The Prime Minister's authoritarian manner dominated his cabinet and Tory politicians were reduced to listening to his reasoning like small children. Bevan's description of Churchill at the end of 1942 were close to the mark: 'He is like a huge tree, nothing grows in its shadow.'[5]

---

1 See the Beveridge Manifesto, *Tribune*, Dec. 4, 1942, (310), 1–2 and Vernon Bartlett in the same edition on the response of the press p.5
2 *Ibid.*
3 D. Ben Rees, *Cofiant Jim Griffiths*, (Biography of Jim Griffiths); *Tribune*, 11 December 1942 (311), 7
4 *Ibid.*
5 Aneurin Bevan 'Labour and the Coalition', *Tribune*,11 December 1942, (311),7.

The Beveridge Report provides an opportunity to build a better world.

Aneurin Bevan believed the country should be indebted to the Beveridge Report and the debates it had prompted. Which leader would implement its recommendations? Since the early 1920s, he had struggled to recognise any socialist ideals in those important Labour figures who were now in the coalition government. In his heart of hearts, Bevan believed that a new order was imminent. The all-important discussions would likely come at the end of the tragic war, when the country would need to rebuild and reconstruct a new world order in the aftermath of destruction. For Bevan, it was time to act but, as always, the Conservatives' approach was to delay all important and essential changes.[1]

Bevan was determined that the basic essentials he had envisaged should be put in place and saw an excellent opportunity to establish a welfare state at the end of the war. At last even England's prevailing conservative society would have to take notice of Labour. Bevan carefully read Hugh Ferguson's important article in *Tribune* about doctors and the needs of patients in the health service.[2] In his analysis, Ferguson showed that a high percentage of doctors came from well-off families as scholarships were scarce and medical training long and costly. Bevan could not believe that, in 1944, only 7% of medical students in Wales and England were of working-class origin.[3] Like the author of the article, he came to the conclusion that the health of the country would become a huge concern when the war ended. Attlee was fiercely criticised in *Tribune* at the beginning of March 1945 and, in the same month, Bevan was so angry with the leaders that he challenged the Speaker of the House of Commons.[4]

Tribune welcomes articles from Welsh authors

In the *Tribune* office, Bevan was extremely keen on getting contributions from Welsh writers and, principally, from Alun Lewis, the soldier-poet from the Cynon Valley, Rhys Davies from the Rhondda Valley and Keidrych Rhys from the Tywi Valley. Keidrych Rhys wrote notes from the battlefield in April 1945, referring to the fact

---

1 *Ibid.*
2 Hugh Ferguson, 'Doctors and the People', Tribune, 5 January, 1945 (419), 7.
3 *Ibid.*
4 Anon. 'Attlee's Crowning Blunder', *Tribune*, 2 March 1945, 1–2.

that the Welsh poet Alun Llywelyn-Williams had been injured.[1] Keidrych's observation was: 'That this is the price his generation had to pay.'[2]

Keidrych Rhys did not think there would be huge support for the Tories if a General Election was called in 1945. The soldiers on the frontline were not pro-conservative and the Celts fighting alongside their English comrades wanted to see a better world once the guns were silenced. Rhys was dismayed with the reticence of the English soldiers and officers, who rarely spoke of the need for change. This is his conclusion, parodying Kipling:

> And while the Celt is talking from Llanberis to Kirkwall, / the English, ah the English, don't say anything at all.

Keidrych Rhys's notes attracted a great deal of attention from *Tribune*'s readers, including a letter from a Jewish Welshman Leo Abse of Cardiff, himself a soldier. The letter was sent to Bevan.[1] In it, Abse wrote that creative people should "work for a better world". A year earlier, Aneurin had earlier turned down an article from Leo Abse when he was in Skegness camp for reasons of space.[4] He had returned the article to Abse on 30 November 1944 with his apologies.[5] That same Leo Abse became Aneurin Bevan's political neighbour when he was elected MP for Pontypool in 1955. Bevan warmed greatly towards the Welsh nation during the war years. On 17 October 1944, his inspirational words in the House of Commons, recorded in Hansard, endeared him immensely to his admirers, including North Walians Huw T Edwards and Cledwyn Hughes:

> Wales has a special individuality, a special culture and special claims. There may be arguments – I think there is an argument – for considerable devolution of government"

He could not have uttered more appropriate words. After all, Bevan had spent the previous decade fearlessly fighting dragons and despair. One thing which can be said is that Aneurin Bevan was sincere in every battle he fought, the reason he was so admired by working-class people.

---

1 See Alan Llwyd, 'Barddoniaeth Alun Llywelyn-Williams', (The Poetry of Alun Llywelyn-Williams) *Barn*, 206 (1980), 73–6, and Gwyn Thomas, 'Bardd y byd sydd ohoni: Alun Llywelyn-Williams, *Barn*, 253 (1984), 19– 21.
2 Keidrych, Rhys, 'A War Correspondent's Notes, *Tribune*, 13 April, 1945, 9–10
1 Leo Abse's letter in *Tribune,* 20 April 1945, 13.
4 National Library of Wales: Papers of Leo Abse, C/9-/-. Aneurin Bevan's letter dated 30 November 1944 to 1094858 ACL Abse, Skegness.
5 *Ibid.*

The Labour Party Conference in Blackpool and the coming General Election

At the Annual Conference of the British Labour Party in Blackpool in May 1945, Bevan showed a great deal of wisdom in his dealings with the trade unions. While he considered that the Labour manifesto *Let Us Face the Future* was a middle of the road document, he knew party unity was necessary for the Labour Party to win the General Election with a sizeable majority. He was enthusiastic, confident and demonstrated his willingness to cooperate with Labour leaders. He also made sure that *Tribune* took the same editorial line.[1]

Bevan was duly elected to the NEC, gaining the support of a large number of constituencies, despite winning nearly as many votes as Herbert Morrison or Harold Laski. That summer, Parliamentary candidates were expected to work hard and an orator like Aneurin Bevan was in constant demand. His campaigning paid off, on election day.[2] 82.6% of his constituents turned out to vote and he won with an impressive 80.1% share of the vote.

Aneurin Bevan (L)	27,209
Charles Stanley Parker (C)	6,758
Majority	20,451

In Wales, the campaigning work of Aneurin Bevan, Jim Griffiths and others was bearing fruit such as was not seen again until Tony Blair's victory in 1997. Wales was, without doubt, turning red. Labour won seven new seats and saw their strongest support coming from Wales. There were majorities of over 20,000 in mining constituencies like Caerphilly, Neath, Ogmore, Pontypridd, Aberdare, Abertillery, Bedwellty and Ebbw Vale. In Llanelli, the majority was an incredible 34,117. Overall, 58.5% of Welsh electors voted for Labour candidates while, in the rest of the United Kingdom, the figure was 48%.[3]

Secret police follow Aneurin Bevan

Though there was quite a competitive spirit between Jim Griffiths and Aneurin Bevan, Jim acknowledged the sharpness, eloquence and charisma of the Tredegar

---

1 Mark M. Krug, *Aneurin Bevan, ibid,* 76.
2 Beti Jones, *Etholiadau'r Ganrif 1900–1975* (Talybont, 1977), 192.
3 D. Ben Rees, *Cofiant Jim Griffiths, ibid,* (Biography of Jim Griffiths), 148–9.

giant. There is no evidence of the secret police having followed Jim Griffiths but that was Bevan's fate during the Second World War. An MI5 agent was following him and managed to gain entry to his home. Bevan made friends with this man not knowing he was an M15 agent. Then he learned the truth but he kept the friendship intact . Then Bevan learnt that the spy he knew as an M15 agent was betraying him and circulating serious information as well as lies about him in the press. It was hurting him . Having become suspicious, Bevan followed his 'friend' into the bathroom one evening at his home before he could lock the door. Bevan put his strong hands around the spy's neck and forced him to confess who he really was. Bevan did not have anything like the trouble Harold Wilson experienced during the sixties and seventies but at least he learned that the secret police were suspicious of him.[1] Bevan also maintained a good relationship with politicians from his college days. He and Jim Griffiths were the two most prominent politicians of the Welsh Parliamentary Party, especially after the death of David Lloyd George earlier in the year. In 1945, there were gifted men among Labour's MPs, yet no women. Eirene L. Jones had failed to win the Flint seat despite coming fairly close. She had to wait until 1950 to win her Flintshire East seat.

Ben Rees at Westminster with Greg Rosen and Lord John Morris.

Cledwyn Hughes

---

1 A. J .Davies, *We, the Nation: The Conservative Party and the Pursuit of Power* (London, 1995), 241.

Ben Rees and Nick
Thomas-Symonds

Morgan Phillips, Dennis Healey and Len Williams

Clement Attlee

Harold Wilson

Ramsay McDonald

CHAPTER 8

Political obstacles stand in the way of the proposed National Health Service

It could be argued that the Welsh nonconformist ethos, the Welsh way of life and its radical conscience inspired three politicians who were prominent in establishing the welfare state: David Lloyd George, prior to 1914 and Jim Griffiths and Aneurin Bevan between 1945 and 1950. The three believed that there was a place for the welfare state in the United Kingdom. They supported old age pensions, the building of council houses, the establishment of a Ministry of Health, and the enactment of the National Insurance Act. Their collective legacy is priceless and Bevan's legacy, in particular, is a very precious one, as every biographer recognises.

It took Aneurin Bevan a long time to achieve his goal. After David Lloyd George lost power in 1922, politicians routinely ignored what Bevan believed were the pressing issues for ordinary people. It wasn't until the end of the Second World War, and the publication of William Beveridge's Report, that the country was ready for the revolutionary programme of change, including nationalisation, that was about to take place under the first Labour Government.

The atrocious aftermath of the Second World War

The 1945 General Election saw the political parties launching more radical manifestos than previously. Capitalism remained under a cloud for many and even the Conservative Party manifesto favoured an improved health service.[1] Labour Party had long realised change was essential but were divided over the way to implement far reaching changes.[2] Now, after their decisive victory of 1945, the Labour Party had an excellent opportunity to introduce progressive policies. The House of Commons opened its doors to a new Labour government on 1 August 1945. Old and new members filled the corridors and the main hall. In the King's Speech, there was the promise to complete a massive programme of reform, to include nationalising the coal industry and the Bank of England, improving the existing scheme of social insurance and establishing a comprehensive national health service.

Bevan chosen to key departments in the new Government

On 3 August 1945, the new Prime Minister Clement Attlee set about appointing his cabinet. Before the end of the day, he travelled to Buckingham Palace to present King George V1 with the names of nineteen MPs who were willing to serve alongside him.[3] Seven were ex-miners.[4] One of Attlee's most inspired appointments was Aneurin Bevan as Minister for Health, Housing and Local Government.[5] A devout Anglican, Attlee was clearly divinely inspired (though senior members of his team like Dalton may have also had a role to play). Despite Bevan's rebellious nature, Attlee recognised the Welshman's potential and his ability to be an excellent minister. This was Bevan's opportunity to make up for his understanding of the health issue in the thirties.

When the Labour MPs came to Westminster to take the oath, Attlee spoke briefly with each one of them. He was not a natural orator and had no talent for small talk; however, he had a gentlemanly manner, neither deafening people with rebuke or soft-soaping them with empty words.[6] Bevan was eagerly awaiting the challenge being placed upon his broad shoulders, but when Attlee told him what he was expected to do he was briefly lost for words. It was an almost impossible burden,

---

1 Donald Sassoon, *One Hundred Years of Socialism: The West European Left in the Twentieth Century* (London, 1996), 140.
2 Ibid, 139. The electorate looked forward to receiving health care and security in their employment though they did not want nationalisation to interfere too much in their private lives.
3 John Bew, *Citizen Clem: A Biography of Attlee* (London, 2016), 355.
4 *Ibid*, 350. Of the 26 ministers of the Crown, 15 had been to state schools and only 10 to university. Only two had been to Eton and Bevan called one of them, Frederick W. Pethick-Lawrence, the Secretary of State for India a 'crusted old Tory'. A. J. P. Taylor, *English History 1914–1945* (Harmondsworth, 1970), 724
5 Lord Attlee, 'Bevan as Hero', *Observer*, 21 October 1962.
6 Attlee said to them, 'I am a very diffident man. I find it very hard to carry on conversation. But if any of you come to see me, I will welcome you'. See Francis Williams, 'The Prime Ministers', *Spectator*, 10 August 1945.

starting immediately with a house-building programme of epic proportions to meet a desperate need. Next, he was expected to transform the public health system. Thirdly, he must encourage local authorities to fulfil their statutory obligations.

Looking back, it is clear Bevan surpassed all Attlee's expectations to become, as Marvin Rintala and David Widgery have argued, the architect of the National Health Service, an excellent Minister for Housing and a much-admired Minister for Local Government.[1]

The Conservatives and the welfare state

From the beginning, the Conservative Party opposed Bevan's vision for an embryonic welfare state. In fact, there was no political consensus at all, even on the third reading of the Health Bill. Winston Churchill, the leader of the opposition, urged his own MPs to oppose the plans for the NHS at every step. Bevan met fierce resistance in the House of Commons but the opposition coming from the Tory-dominated House of Lords was even fiercer. Despite this, Churchill had great admiration for Bevan's ability as a debater since he had made his maiden speech in 1929, telling him: 'It is so seldom that we hear a real debating speech nowadays'.[2] Some years later he presented Bevan with a copy of his book on Marlborough, with the greeting:

To Aneurin Bevan with every good wish for a lifetime's happiness.[3]

Aneurin Bevan was the only MP who could stand up to Churchill and, at the same time, associate with him outside Parliament.[4] Not only was he often able to get the better of Churchill, but no-one else could even compete. Most viewed Bevan as the best debater in the House of Commons, though his fellow Welshman Goronwy Roberts, the new MP for Caernarfon, believed Emanuel Shinwell deserved that honour.[5]

In relation to the proposed new public health service, Churchill did not speak in favour of the proposal other than making sure Bevan's idea to prohibit private medicine did not form part of the Act. Hugely disappointed to have lost the 1945 General Election, Churchill had even less interest in sick people than he had in medicine. The Coalition Minister of Health was Henry Willink, a barrister who

---

1 David Widgery, *Health in Danger: The Crisis in the National Health Service* (London, 1979), 25.
2 Michael Foot, *Aneurin Bevan 1897–1945*, Vol 1 (London, 1962), 108.
3 *Ibid*, 242.
4 C. King, *With Malice Towards None: A War Diary* (London, 1970), 306.
5 Patricia Hollis, *Jennie Lee: A Life*, (Oxford, 1977), 111. 'Yet Nye ended the war as one of the few men who had the measure of Churchill and the mastery of Parliament'; Michael Foot, 'Bevan's Message to the World', in *The State of the Nation: The Political Legacy of Aneurin Bevan* (ed. Geoffrey Goodman), 189; Marvin Rintala, 10; Lord Hill of Luton, *Both Sides of the Hill* (London, 1964), 92.

saw himself as an caring Conservative with an international outlook. The 1944 White Paper, *A National Health Service,* was written by civil servant John Hawton but published in his name. Willink was not at all keen on the plan and his hypocrisy in opposing Bevan on the basis of not following the White Paper was the greatest surprise. Bevan took the Willink-Hawton White Paper home with him one weekend and returned on Monday morning saying it was of no value to him as he prepared for his entirely new Bill.[1] He then tossed it into his waste paper basket. We do not know whether Bevan read Ernest Brown's 1941 paper proposing a free hospital service to be run by local authorities, but, it is unlikely due to Bevan's animosity towards the former Minister of Health. While protesting firmly against Brown's reactionary policies in 1937, Bevan was temporarily deprived of Parliamentary privileges.[2]

In the Coalition Government of the Second World War, it was Arthur Greenwood and Ernest Bevin, rather than the Tories, who were primarily responsible for choosing William Beveridge as chair of the Social Insurance and Other Services Committee. The civil servants on the committee were already in place prior to Beveridge becoming chairman. In fact, the tough trade unionist Ernest Bevin could recall Beveridge's contribution to the Board of Trade in 1908 under Lloyd George and he wanted to get rid of him as his economics advisor. Beveridge was not to everyone's liking as he had an unfortunate, aggressive way of speaking and tended to be extremely snobbish.[3] Beveridge could not stand Churchill, his description of him in January 1945 of being 'a tiresome old man', but neither did he like Labour's Clement Attlee, Ernest Bevin or Hugh Dalton.[4] He did not have a good word for Aneurin Bevan despite the fact that he and Jim Griffiths were the main supporters of his 1942 report.[5] The truth was that neither Attlee nor Churchill was keen on Beveridge's famous report and they were unwilling to either praise him or suffer the agony of listening to the snobbish, clever civil servant and Liberal Party guru.[6]

Bevan, on the other hand, had complimented Beveridge as 'a social evangelist of the old Liberal school'. He gave his support to the Beveridge Report because it described excellently 'where it was possible to take the tears out of capitalism'.[7] Bevan saw the report as a judgment on the weaknesses and sins of capitalism in Britain. The author was a Liberal to the marrow and, after the death of Lloyd George, he was the most prominent of the small remaining crew who had waved

---

1 N. Goodman, *Wilson Jameson: Architect of National Health,* (London, 1970), 122.
2 Foot, Aneurin Bevan, Vol 1, (London, 1962), 241, 256–7, 284.
3 R. Lowe, *The Welfare State in Britain Since 1945,* second impression, (London, 1999), 134.
4 C. King, *With Malice Towards None: A War Diary* London, 1970), 287.
5 Marvin Rintala, 16.
6 T. Burridge, *Clement Attlee: A Political Biography* (London, 1985), 150; Francis Williams, *A Prime Minister Remembers: The War and Post-War Memoirs of Rt. Hon. Earl Attlee,* (London, 1961), 57.
7 D. Hill (ed.), *Tribune 40: The First Forty Years of a Socialist Newspaper* (London, 1977), 4 and 46.

the Liberal Party flag in its glory days. The essence of Lloyd George's policies was to tax the rich more so that the poor could receive more help, to tax the landowner to pay for old age pensions; that was how things were done in the twenties and thirties. Beveridge was not in complete agreement with Lloyd George. He believed the worker who received good wages should also help those less fortunate, including the unemployed. He did not wish to be known as the founder of the health service; it was not his child. The 1911 system of health insurance set up by Lloyd George was an important step forward and continued for 35 years, but it was no more than that. It still existed in 1948 when the National Health Service Act came into being and the National Insurance Act was repealed. In 1911, only one politician was able to steer a National Health Act through cabinet and Parliament in 1911.[1] Lloyd George was that magician.[2] Lloyd George was lucky that Christopher Addison, MP, a very able physician, ensured that sufficient doctors backed the scheme. Addison's support was vital to Lloyd George in his confrontation with the British Medical Association.[3] In 1919, the Prime Minister made Addison the first Minister of Health and it proved a blatant mistake. As Addison was moving from his role as President of the Board of Local Government to Minister of Health, Lloyd George merged responsibility for health with house-building and public health, viewing all three areas as social services.[4] In time, Addison crossed the floor of the House, turning his back on the Liberal Party and joining the Labour Party. It was by then the party closest to his radical political beliefs.[5]

The need to build houses had consumed the attention of the combined housing and health ministers during the interwar years. The extensive bombing of cities during the Second World War meant one in three homes had been destroyed and there was a dire shortage of new housing.[6] New family homes were desperately needed everywhere from London to Liverpool to Swansea and Southampton. Clement Attlee made a serious mistake in overburdening Aneurin Bevan and expecting the impossible from him. Amazingly, Bevan proved successful across the board, excelling in his health remit. Despite his admiration for Bevan as a speaker, Churchill felt he did not deserve to wear the mantle of fellow Welshman Lloyd George. For Churchill, there was no-one like the Earl of Dwyfor, the 'greatest Welshman of all times'.

---

1 F. Honigsbaum, *The Division of British Medicine: A History of the Separation of General Practice from Hospital Care 1911–1968* (London, 1979), 132.
2 It is not surprising for Wilmot Herringham, doctor and scholar, to say in 1919 'What has been accomplished we owe to the insight of a single individual'. See W. Herringham, *A Physician in France* (London 1919), 149.
3 J. Grigg, *Lloyd George from Peace to War 1912–1916*, (Berkeley, California, 1985), 258.
4 Alan Taylor (ed.) *Lloyd George: Twelve Essays* (New York, 1971), 240.
5 Clement Attlee, *As It Happened* (New York, 1954), 215, 297–8.
6 Henry Pelling, 'The 1945 General Election Reconsidered', *Historical Journal*, 23 (2 1980), 413.

Comrades in cabinet

Aneurin Bevan was an exceptionally gifted and outstanding socialist, an individual who surprised everyone with his diplomacy, charm, determination and charisma. From 1929 to 1945, he was the rebel of the Labour Party, the conscience of the left wing. Despite being expelled in 1939, he returned to the ranks as he could not live without his beloved Labour Party. He was savage in his criticism of Ernest Bevin, by now Secretary of State for Foreign Affairs, which did not endear him to the man or the huge Transport and General Workers' Union (TGWU) Bevin had founded. So strong was Bevan's opposition to Bevin it very almost had him dismissed from the Labour Party again. Bevin was not the only important leader in the Labour ranks to be at the receiving end of Bevan's sharp tongue.[1] The Home Secretary Herbert Morrison was the personification of Labour's 'right wing' and had no respect for the words of the MP for Ebbw Vale.[2] In his criticism of Morrison, Bevan went so far as to call him the 'witch-finder of the Labour Party, the smeller-out of evil spirits'.[3] In a debate on nationalising industries, he called one of the greats of his party 'a fifth-rate Tammany Hall boss' in a reference to the corrupt government in Chicago and New York. He suggested that Morrison loved interfering with the work of politicians backstage.[4]

Bevan had been completely disrespectful: Morrison did not belong to the fifth-class politicians but to the first. He was one of the most successful London leaders in the history of the British Labour Party. Morrison was the big personality of London County Council (LCC), comparable to Joseph Chamberlain ruling in Birmingham and Sir Archibald Salvidge in Liverpool. If anything, Morrison was more powerful in London than the other politicians were in their cities. In 1940, London County Council owned about forty thousand hospital beds and about 35,000 mental hospital beds, making it the biggest authority in the world in terms of public health provision. It was not just big but also extremely successful.[5] Morrison had ensured there was work for many people at a time of heart-breaking unemployment and, in 1939, he longed for the opportunity to take the city's voluntary hospitals under his wing.[6] Labour councillors up and down the country were

---

1 Alan Bullock, *Ernest Bevin: Foreign Secretary* (New York, 1993), 77; Roy Jenkins, *Nine Men of Power* (London, 1974), 92; K. O. Morgan, *The Red Dragon and the Red Flag: The Cases of James Griffiths and Aneurin Bevan* (Aberystwyth, 1989), 6.
2 King, *With Malice Towards None*, 211–13.
3 Foot, *ibid*, Vol 1, 355.
4 *Ibid*, 356; Vera Brittain, *Great War Diary 1913–1917* (London, 1945), 140.
5 S. Inwood, *A History of London* (London, 1998), 308.
6 C. Webster, 'Conflict and Consensus: Explaining the British Health Service', *Twentieth Century Political History*, 8, (3), 1990, 144.

managing to get admission for themselves and their families to the most famous local authority hospitals through the offices of Morrison. The situation weighed on the conscience of the medic-novelist A. J. Cronin, who was a doctor in Tredegar, and he writes about it in his books.[1] One can understand therefore why Bevan's fierce wish to nationalise all hospitals raised Morrison's hackles. The contest between the two was a nasty encounter and Harold Wilson accurately likened it to a 'classical confrontation'.[2]

As a cabinet newcomer, Bevan was not the most important nor the wisest politician and he had no experience of preparing Labour Party documents or memorable articles on the topic of health.[3] It was the greatest surprise to himself and everyone else that Attlee asked him to become Minister for Health, Housing and Local Government. Some, like Hugh Dalton, were totally stunned and wondered if Attlee was suffering short-term memory loss as a result of dementia![4] If Attlee wanted a compliant cabinet, then why appoint a rebel to such an important ministerial position? It had never happened before and is unlikely to happen again.[5]

Aneurin Bevan shone in the Labour cabinet of 1945–1950, one of the most experienced cabinets in the history of parliament. As well as Bevin, Bevan and Morrison, other ministers included the intellectuals Stafford Cripps and Hugh Dalton, each easily able to step into Attlee's shoes. Morrison was the Lord President of the Council, then Deputy Prime Minister, and always sat next to Attlee. He was the first to speak and he was Bevan's principal enemy, day after day.[6] Morrison said this about Bevan:

> Power, that is all he wants, power for himself and he does not care what happens to the Party as long as he has power.[7]

Bevan would agree with Morrison. It *was* power he strived for. He had realised very early on in Tredegar that power is the essence of politics. That is why it is always better to be in government and have power than to be in opposition without it. But Morrison saw that Bevan was naturally annoyed with him:

---

1 Marvin Rintala, *Creating the National Health Service*, 38.
2 Harold Wilson, *A Personal Record, The Labour Government 1964–1970* (London, 1971), 765.
3 C. Forsyth, *Doctors and State Medicine: A Study of the British Health Service* London, 1966), 119; J. Campbell, *Aneurin Bevan and the Mirage of British Socialism* (London, 1987), 169; Hollis, *Jennie Lee*, 112; K. O. Morgan, *Labour in Power 1945–1951* (Oxford, 1958), 151; W. Rodgers a B. Donoghue, *The People into Parliament: A Concise History of the Labour Movement of Britain* (London, 1966), 145.
4 Hugh Dalton, *The Fateful Years: Memoirs 1931–1945* (London, 1957), 470; Morgan, *Labour in Power*, 151.
5 Burridge, *Clement Attlee*, 1987; Lowe, *Welfare State*, 183 and 376.
6 R. Rhodes James, Anthony Eden (London, 1987), 336; R. Pearce, *Attlee* (London, 1997), 154.
7 B. Donoghue and C. Jones, *Herbert Morrison: Portrait of a Politician* (London, 1973), 46. The best study of Morrison.

'A feeling of hatred for me' is how he describes it in his autobiography.[1]

However, other prominent politicians had taken note of Morrison's failings. Conservative politician Harold Macmillan stated that he was a 'mean man', one of the worst he had come across, 'utterly incapable of magnanimity'.[2] When, at the end of 1945, Morrison began to disparage Bevan's aims in relation to nationalisation, Bevan was in deep water.[3] Nobody in cabinet was inclined to save him from his sharp accuser; they remembered all too well his disparaging attitude to nearly every one of them.

Ernest Bevin did not forget the criticism he received from the mouthy Ebbw Vale politician throughout the period of the coalition government. Bevin was very thin-skinned man, despite being a physically strong with such a sharp tongue he had forced George Lansbury to resign as Labour leader. Bevin had no respect at all for his co-politicians, he never ever bothered about them.[4] He boasted that he was not keen on reading books and he reckoned that Aneurin Bevan, despite his working-class mining background, was one of the most intellectual members of Parliament.[5] For Bevin, intellectuals such as Bevan could not be depended upon and were completely irresponsible. Bevin suffered the wrath of the intellectuals during the thirties and could not forget the insult he had felt. Bevan was lucky that he was not the only politician who was anathema to Ernest Bevin. The politician who most annoyed him was Herbert Morrison. The two hated each other with a perfect hatred. Uttering the word Herbert or Morrison was enough to drive Bevin completely berserk. From 1931 onwards, the two were like a couple of tigers baring their teeth at one another at every opportunity[6].

Bevin made sure he would not support Morrison at any time; however, Bevin and Bevan slowly came to tolerate each other. They were far from being bosom friends but could at least drive a bargain and do business together. On his death bed in 1951, Bevin's wish was to see Bevan as his successor in the Foreign Office. He said: 'I'd sooner have had Nye than 'Erbert.'[7] Bevan would have done a great deal better than Morrison, who was a failure as Foreign Secretary. Consequently, the Labour Party were again at each other's throats. Harold Wilson called these

---

1 Herbert Morrison, *Herbert Morrison: An Autobiography* (London, 1960), 263.
2 Horner, *Macmillan* (London,1974), 339: 'Bevan and the Architecture of the National Health Service' in *The State of the Nation, ibid,* 106–127. A penetrating and valuable essay.
3 Alan Bullock, *The Life and Times of Ernest Bevin,* Vol 1, (London, 1960), 571; Hollis, *Jennie Lee,* 79; R. Jenkins, *Nine Men of Power,* 72.
4 M. Cole, *The Life of C. D. H. Cole* (London, 1971), 193; Bullock, *ibid,* Vol 1, 531 and 553.
5 K. O. Morgan, *Labour People: Leaders and Lieutenants, Hardie to Kinnock* (Oxford, 1987), 152, 177; K. Harris, *Attlee,* 228.
6 Bullock, *Ernest Bevin,* 834.
7 Harold Wilson, *A Prime Minister on Prime Ministers* (London, 1977), 291.

giants – Bevan, Bevin, Cripps, Dalton and Morrison – 'five head-strong horses'[1]. Bevan and Cripps had been solid comrades but Bevan did not have the support he deserved from him either.[2] Sir Stafford Cripps was a wealthy man related to Beatrice Webb and it was Morrison who persuaded him to represent the LCC.[3] When Cripps had to leave his post as chancellor due to ill health, he ordered Attlee not to be tempted to give the responsibility to Bevan. It seemed Bevan was without a single friend in the cabinet, although he was occasionally supported by a fiery politician from the North East of England . She was none other than Ellen Wilkinson. She and Jennie Lee had been on good terms with each other until Ellen became great friends with Morrison – to be precise she became his mistress – after which the women's relationship cooled. Ellen worked unstintingly to get rid of Attlee so that Morrison could become Prime Minister. It is surprising Attlee invited her into his cabinet, for she was canvassing on that platform prior to the 1945 General Election. Red Ellen, as she was became known, was resolute. Bevan was surprised to see her in the cabinet, knowing as he did of her schemes, her relationship with Morrison and her depression, which caused her sadly to take her own life early in 1947.[4] Another of Aneurin Bevan's supporters was the oldest member the cabinet, Lord Christopher Addison, who gave Bevan priceless assistance.[5] With Lloyd George dead, Churchill silent and Beveridge failing to offer practical advice, Addison was the historical link between the decades. His unwavering support ensured that Bevan's vision of universal medical care – not just for those who were insured – became a reality. Addison encouraged those who sat on the fence to take a positive stance.

He was Attlee's confidant in cabinet, his only true friend.[6] Aneurin Bevan and Herbert Morrison were complex characters who were ready to throw their long relationships, as well as their Labour Party brotherhood, over a cliff. It called upon Clement Attlee to act as centrist and mediator. The Prime Minister did not have strong views on the National Health Service and it is understandable why Burridge and Harris's biographies make no mention of Attlee and the National Health Service. The oversight is understandable as Attlee was not prominent in the creation of the NHS and the Prime Minister felt his responsibility was to keep the plate spinning in cabinet. He did not see that there was much difference in the long run between the various viewpoints. The cost would necessarily fall on the Treasury.[7] Dalton, the Chancellor of the Exchequer, did not want to be a stumbling block as he now had

---

1 C. Cooke, *The Life of Richard Stafford Cripps* (London, 1957), 189–93, 236–7.
2 P. Strauss, *Cripps Advocate Extraordinary* (New York, 1942), 59.
3 P. Brooks, *Women at Westminster: An Account of Women in the British Parliament 1918–1966*, (London, 1967), 118–19; Morgan, *Labour People*, 179.
4 O. Morgan, *The People's Peace*, 38; K. O. Morgan (*Labour People*), 191.
5 Morgan, *Labour People,* 138, 146–7, 191; Harris, *Attlee*, 87.
6 Burridge, *Clement Attlee*, 189.
7 *Ibid,* 355, note 89.

huge admiration for Bevan. He had changed his own mind since the thirties and now, in 1947, he believed Morrison's stubbornness was the stumbling block to the success of the Labour Government. Attlee understood where both Morrison and Bevan were coming from, though he always gave the impression he did not favour one over the other. His impartiality is perhaps the secret of how he succeeded in remaining leader of the Labour Party for twenty years. Before 1945, Attlee had not had much to do with Bevan though he remembered the arrival of the young MP in Parliament after the 1929 election. Indeed, Attlee and Herbert Morrison had voted to expel him from the Labour Party in 1939. As was his style, Bevan attacked him emotionally in Labour Party circles and especially in the pages of *Tribune*. Morrison would have been delighted to throw Bevan out of the cabinet and the Parliamentary Party but there was no hope of that any longer as the Prime Minister had set the seal of his blessing on him and brought him into the inner circle. Attlee says, in his autobiography:

> For Health, I chose Aneurin Bevan whose abilities had up to now been displayed only in opposition, but I felt that he had it in him to do good service.[1]

It is interesting to analyse that sentence as it suggests many things. In the first reading, there is the implication that Bevan's huge talents had not been used creatively from 1929 to 1945. Ramsay MacDonald was at fault as was his successor Lansbury and Bevan himself. Attlee gave Jim Griffiths an opportunity during the war, but Bevan was ignored.[2] One could also interpret Attlee's words as meaning that Bevan's contribution to Labour Party politics had been completely negative and that the Prime Minister was giving him another chance to use his abilities. Both analyses quite properly emphasise the significance of Attlee's choice. As the American scholar, Marvin Rintala, says:

> Without Attlee's initiative, Bevan would not have been appointed minister of health, let alone with Cabinet rank.[3]

Certainly, neither Herbert Morrison nor almost anyone else would have given Bevan this opportunity, the greatest of his life. Attlee's choice of health minister was one of the most inspired in Britain's history of Britain. As he said: 'I chose Aneurin Bevan.' Another way of looking at things is to remind ourselves of the words of the fiery Anglesey preacher John Elias when some of the leaders of Pall Mall Welsh Calvinistic Methodist Chapel, Liverpool asked him what they should do with one

---

[1] Attlee, *As It Happened*, 215.
[2] D. Ben Rees, *Cofiant Jim Griffiths*,(Biography of Jim Griffiths), 128.
[3] Marvin Rintala, *Creating the Health* Service, 45.

of the members who was continually criticising, disagreeing and laying down the law. The answer was 'Make him an Elder. Give him the authority of leadership.' That is what was done, and the man changed for the better overnight. Bevan reacted in a similar manner after taking up his cabinet position.

We can only wonder at Morrison's ambition and his record of plotting and trying to get rid of even Attlee on more than one occasion. Fortunately, Attlee was too clever for him and continued in office long enough to ensure Morrison would not succeed him. In important cabinet meetings, Attlee summarised the debate in favour of Aneurin's plans, thus helping him win over fellow ministers.[1] It was a pivotal moment in the creation of the National Health Service. All the hospitals in Britain were to be nationalised.[2] And Attlee was in complete agreement. An unyielding politician who was used to getting his own way with the Labour Party, Herbert Morrison continued to oppose Aneurin Bevan's plans. He set about persuading his supporters to send letters to the press, especially to *The Times,* to arrange delegations to city hospitals to support those health officials who were protesting against the plan to nationalise them.[3] Aneurin was not willing to let Morison's supporters win that easily. He addressed the Labour Party NEC in London and got the majority of them over to his side. Soon afterwards, he won vital backing from the London County Council despite the opposition of Morrison and some of its leaders.[4] Morrison continued to find fault with Bevan's National Health Service scheme. In his useful publication *Government and Parliament,* which came out in the sixties; Morrison admitted he was not initially happy with the idea of an NHS. He thought local authorities should be responsible for administering the hospitals. Bevan summed up his own opinion in *In Place of Fear.*

> Local authorities are notoriously unwilling to delegate any of their functions or responsibilities to others.[5]

Morrison did not lose his argument completely because local authorities was given the right to enact a host of public health measures.[6] The LCC employed five thousand people to administer the new health service, but they lost 32,000 workers across 98 institutions. through the creation of NHS by Bevan.[7] Quite simply, the

---

1 K. O. Morgan, *Labour People,* 208.
2 P. Addison, *Now the War is Over: A Social History of Britain 1945–51,* (London, 1985), 99; G. Codber, *The Health Service: Past, Present and Future* (London, 1975), 16
3 Honigsbaum, *Division in British Medicine,* 212, 290.
4 John Parker, *Father of the House: Fifty Years in Politics* (London, 1982), 84.
5 Aneurin Bevan, *In Place of Fear* (London, 1952), 199.
6 R. Brain, *Medicine and Government* (London, 1967), 4.
7 D. Fox, *Health Policies, Health Politics: The British and American Experience (*Princeton, 1986), 139.

nationalisation of all hospitals was one of the most forward-looking decisions ever taken by a European country in the twentieth century.[1]

In cabinet, Morrison continued to argue that nationalising the hospitals had not been mentioned in the Labour Party's 1945 General Election manifesto. For Aneurin, his achievements were very much within the spirit of the manifesto. In fact, when the manifesto is re-read today, one can see that there are openended promises with an emphasis on unfulfilled aims such as health centres. The major promise was to care for mothers and children, the family unit, though there is no mention of fathers! But clearly, this is the key sentence:

> Money must no longer be the passport to the best treatment.[2]

The Labour manifesto emphasised how nutritious food and warm damp-free houses were one way of preventing ill-health among the inhabitants and that more research was needed in order to overcome every illness. Despite this, it is clear that, in 1945, the Labour Party did not have any plan for a comprehensive health service for everyone without expecting a single penny for the provision.[3] Bevan is the author of such a provision. In the British Labour Party Conference in 1945, the Socialist Medical Association argued that hospital doctors should be salaried but that everything should, as Morrison wanted, to be administered by local authorities. Bevan laughed when he heard the proposal:

> You can't do that to me. Go away and put your minds to work again.

Bevan was not in favour of a medical service under the control of local authorities. A number of socialist-leaning doctors, both within Parliament and the country as a whole, were disillusioned with his proposals. We must remember that, during the thirties, the Labour Party had not been progressive in its approach to a universal health service. It was not identified as a priority in the 1935 General Election nor in Labour publications booklets. The intellectual minded Fabians, who wrote so extensively about Britain and the New World, did not consider the need for a health service for everyone. Sidney and Beatrice Webb made no mention of the idea in their 1910 book *The State and the Doctor*. As far as leading Fabians were concerned, only poor people should receive free medical treatment. This should be provided by medical practitioners, who were not necessarily noted for their compassion or capabilities. George Bernard Shaw, a leading Fabian, had no more to say on

---

1 P. Porter, *The Greatest Benefit to Mankind: A Medical History of Humanity* (New York, 1998), 653
2 See the section "The Health of the Nation and its Children" in F. Craig (ed), *British General Election Manifesto 1900—1974* (London, 1975), 129.
3 J. Jewkes and S. Jewkes, *The Genesis of British National Service,* second impression (Oxford, 1962), 2.

the matter.[1] The person whose views on health provision came closest to Bevan's own was C.D.H. Cole, an influential man of letters.[2] Cole maintained that medical treatment should be free of charge for everyone. He listed institutions which should be nationalised but even Cole did not include hospitals. Yet, Jim Griffiths had presented a motion calling for a national health service at the 1942 British Labour Party Annual Conference. Consequently, a 1943 report was published called *National Service for Health*. Unlike the Beveridge Report, this report discussed health policies seriously, emphasising the need to focus on preventative services and look for cures for health conditions.[3] The report was the strongest declaration on health the Labour Party made prior to 1945. Sadly, it was all but ignored even by Aneurin Bevan himself as it lacked the necessary changes.

Labour tacticians believed Bevan's proposals needed further detailed discussion. As they stood, there was nothing mentioned on preventing ill-health or what role local authorities would play. Politicians of every creed, especially those belonging to the Labour Party, were rather taken back that Bevan was in favour of nationalising the hospitals.[4] The British Medical Association (BMA), the powerful body representing doctors, controlled the existing and highly profitable British medical system, under which doctors sold their services and competed for customers were up in arms. Bevan believed this was not at all consonant with a civilised society and felt it belittled both patients and doctors as human beings. For him, any national health service of worth should confront 'the structure of capitalist society'.[5] It seems to me that Bevan was the only one of the Labour elite who could not stand the thought of buying and selling of medicine as though sick people were in a cattle auction in Abergavenny.

Furthermore, there was no question of bright young people from poor community going into medicine as a vocation without a radical exciting programme. Medical students were anyway expected to pay for their training, meaning most of them came from well-heeled homes. Bevan became more and more incensed at how the BMA was defending its elite practices, especially when members voted 229 to 13 to keep the health service in a strait jacket. He refused to concede an inch to what he rightly regarded as greedy medical practitioners who wanted to retain their profitable business. As a result, the 1946 National Health Act stated that no medical practitioner could sell his good-will within his private practice or any

---

1 George Bernard Shaw, *The Doctor's Dilemma: A Tragedy* (London, 1987), 86.
2 See C. D. H. Cole, *Great Britain in the Post World War* (London, 1942), 82–91 and 141.
3 *Labour Party National Service for Health* (London, 1943), 13.
4 S. Grimes, *British National Health Service: State Intervention in the Medical Market Place, 1911–1948* (London, 1991), 136.
5 Bevan, *In Place of Fear*, 86.

part of his good-will to anyone else in the medical profession.[1] This was Bevan at his best. The practice of buying and selling family doctors' private practices did not disappear completely until 1976.[2] Despite this, Bevan wanted, as Peter Hennessy says, to have his personal values set out clearly in the future plan.[3]

The contribution of the minister

Aneurin Bevan's contribution to the Labour Government of 1945–1950 was huge.[4] It is impossible to imagine a Conservative government Minister of Health daring to nationalise voluntary or local authority hospitals. Even within the Labour Party, Bevan was unique. It's true that Christopher Addison, who was Minister for Health under Lloyd George, placed some exciting groundwork in place, but he completely lacked Bevan's persuasive skills. Bevan was the ultimate architect, the brilliant theoriser and the doer. For him, establishing a free national health service was the greatest priority of the Attlee administration and was even more important than building houses and restoring bombed cities. Between 1945 and 1950, Bevan was at his peak of his ministerial prowess, being exceptionally thorough and hardworking day after day. During these years, he was by far the most charismatic post-war parliamentary orator, a superstar among his parliamentary colleagues. Above everything else he was determined to achieve his grand plan.

There is no doubt Attlee had placed an incredibly heavy load on Aneurin Bevan's shoulders. He headed up three vast ministries – housing, health and local government – employing thousands of civil servants. After the horrors of the Second World War, the public understandably prioritised housing; for Bevan, health and hospitals were what was needed.[5] The reserved but compassionate Attlee gave a free hand to his ministers (as H. H. Asquith gave to Lloyd George), which enabled the Welshman to publicise his plans. A combination of careful administrator and spirited encourager, Bevan amazed his opponents as well as his friends. He succeeded in mastering each field he had to take care of , that is every document produced by civil servants and every Act, despite never having held any high-level position in any government previously. Prior to 1945, his role had been to deliver savage criticism, to lay down the law without apology. Now he himself was subject to unfair crit-

---

1 Gemmill, *Britain's Search for Health*, 117.
2 *Ibid*.
3 Peter Hennessy, *Never Again: Britain 1945–1951* (London, 1993), 132.
4 B. Griffith, S. Iliffe and C. Rayner, *Banking on Sickness: Commercial Medicine in Britain and the USA* (London, 1987), 26.
5 . Martin Pugh, *State and Society: British Political and Social History 1870–1992*, (London, 1994), 240; Morgan, *Red Dragon*, 9.

icism, something he accepted as inevitable if he was to see his vision through. With graciousness and detailed reasoning, Bevan persuaded the Chancellor Hugh Dalton to provide generous and unlimited funding for his health scheme, thus setting in motion the 'bottomless pit' that continues to this day. Bevan presented his plan for a publicly funded healthcare system to the cabinet, the trade unions and other socialist movements, and health societies. Journalists who had harassed him daily, were amazed to see Bevan's exceptional success as a busy and committed minister juggling three portfolios. Now, he was being viewed as a potential Labour Party leader, a politician who might one day become Prime Minister. Despite his vociferous enemies and opponents, Aneurin Bevan always had the last word. By 1948, an opinion poll revealed that the Tories in the country at large were ready to back his health scheme by a substantial majority.[1]

The hardest challenge for Bevan was to persuade the BMA to step down from its entrenched position and agree to a compromise. He had answered doctors' questions knowledgeably, without seeking advice from civil servants or advisers. In 1945, Dr Charles Hill opposed Bevan one hundred per centre and wrote articles in the *British Medical Journal* making his stance clearly in the opposition camp .[2] Nearly thirty years later, in 1973, Hill was of a different opinion entirely, writing with style of the Welsh politician's greatness and genius.[3] Bevan's triumphs meant the Ministers of Health who followed him had public support for standing up to powerful groups.[4] The period between 1945 and 1950 saw him revealing to the world at large his undoubted ability .He reached his political greatness, after years of battling hard against the opposition and his own party from the backbenches. From 1951 until his death in 1960, Bevan continued to confront when needed other politicians, with the result that he lost some friendly comrades and to create life long hatred with words which should have never been spoken. They should have remained unspoken. But, during the five years between 1945 and 1950, his battles were in the main creative and his ability to compromise, build bridges and make friends among doctors came to the fore. He changed tack to create a precious national service free of charge for everyone. Always an ambitious and radical personality, Aneurin Bevan was now a popular politician among the working and middle classes who supported the Attlee Government. His vision for free healthcare for all is universally acknowledged by historians as a determined achievement and the name

---

1 Grimes, *British National Health Service*, 192.
2 The magazine's words in 1960 on Bevan's death were: 'The medical profession may hope to find in future Ministers of Health, men with the imagination and flexibility of mind of Aneurin Bevan.' See *British Medical Journal*, 26 July 1960, 204.
3 Lord Hill of Luton, 'Aneurin Bevan Among the Doctors', *British Medical Journal*, 24 November 1973, 469.
4 H. Dalder, 'Cabinet Reform since 1914' in V. Herman and J. Alt (eds.), *Cabinet Studies: A Reader* (London, 1975), 258.

Aneurin Bevan will be forever linked to National Health Service.[1] When the Conservatives seized power again in 1951, there was no political will to change his plan significantly.[2] Bevan acknowledged his surprise at this about-turn in *In Place of Fear.* [3] In the 1980s, when the Tory Prime Minister Margaret Thatcher was threatening the National Health Service, one of its principal defenders was the BMA while, in a 1990 opinion poll, 85% of GPs voted against the idea of being severed from the NHS.[4] Yet, despite worldwide admiration for the UK's health service, many countries still seem unwilling or unable to adopt Bevan's model. In the US, President Barack Obama was unable to do what Bevan had achieved. Marvin Rintala said:

> Perhaps no other nation has replicated the National Health Service because no other nation has had Aneurin Bevan making health policy decisions.[5]

Bevan's life achievement is undoubtedly the creation of the National Health Service in all its glory. Perhaps now is the time to acknowledge how his Welshness, his mining background and his experiences in Blaenau Gwent inspired him all the way. The opposition he experienced for years was the result of ingrained friction between an establishment full of conservative, middle and upper class, Anglo-Saxon people and the so-called uneducated socialists, many of whom were cultured working people. In her inimitable way, Jan Morris expressed the conflict as a struggle between neighbours:

> To Englishmen he was in many ways everything they most detested about the Welsh – the high insistent voice infuriated them, his lordly style bewildered them, his loyalty to Britain seemed to them dubious – was it not Bevan that Churchill himself, in the middle of the Second World War, called a squalid nuisance.[6]

Aneurin Bevan kept going with the certainty of a Welshman who knew his own mind – a mind which reflected the neighbourly spirit of the valleys and mutual aid at the time of the Depression. The South Wales miners in the Glamorgan and Monmouthshire valleys and in Carmarthenshire were the backbone of his political

---

1 K. Layburn, *The Rise of Labour: The British Labour Party 1890–1979*, (London, 1988), 116; Burridge, *Clement Attlee*, 190; Hollis, *Jennie Lee*, 123.
2 K. Robbins, *Churchill* (London, 1992), 161.
3 Bevan, *In Place of Fear*, 87.
4 *The Guardian*, 10 October 1990, 2.
5 Marvin Rintala, *Creating the Health Service* , ibid, 61.
6 Jan Morris, *Wales: Epic Views of a Small Country* (London, 1998), first impression from Oxford University Press 1984, 441.

party and Bevan was steeped in that militant tradition. He was born to a mining family and appreciated the delightful Welsh language poem 'Ode to the Miner' which won the Reverend Gwilym R. Tilsley the chair at the National Eisteddfod of Wales held in Caerphilly in 1950.[1]

Aneurin represented one of the poorest constituencies in the United Kingdom and took an active part in his constituents' lives for over forty years. They were his people and he shared their values. As their MP, he spoke on their behalf at every opportunity, fighting battles he could not hope to win. A book by the German economist Joseph Dietzen had become popular with miners during the 1920s. In *The Positive Outcome of Philosophy*, Dietzen argued: 'A new religion is needed – the religion of social democracy.'[2]

In essence, social democracy was the ideology those well-read miners pursued. Social democracy combined with brotherliness, socialism, co-operation and shared goals. Bevan's own personal and political convictions were formed in Tredegar, where he spent the first thirty-two years of his life. According to Michael Foot, Bevan embraced the ideas of the philosopher José Enrique Rodo, who influenced him even more than Karl Marx and Friedrich Engels. Rodo's social democracy combined planning with politics, the exact strategy Bevan applied to creating the National Health Service.[3] He followed Rodo's call to 'consecrate part of the soul to an unknown future'. He ventured eagerly on a faith in socialism which embraced creative, artistic life and combined all the aspects of his colourful personality; this provided him with constant joy as his wife testifies. Bevan had no patience with dry and unadorned provision for society. If he was alive, he would find the 'age of austerity' which has come about through the governments of David Cameron, George Osborne, Nick Clegg, Theresa May and Boris Johnson – and still continues in 2023 – abhorrent. He would have detested how successive Conservative governments have imposed severe cuts on the devolved governments of Northern Ireland, Scotland and Wales, and on local authorities of all political shades. He would recognise the monumental failure of governments. If Bevan was the present-day Leader of the Opposition, he would have been out there campaigning and addressing a hundred rallies to persuade the Conservative Government to reconsider its cruel and destructive policies.

But it was the death of his father in his arms, from a condition common to miners, which stayed with Aneurin Bevan for the rest of his life, the decisive event which

---

1 '*Awdl y Glöwr*' ('The Ode of the Miner') from the work of Gwilym R. Tilsley, a Wesleyan Methodist minister based in Aberdare Valley.
2 Cyril E. Gwyther 'Sidelights on Religion and Politics in the Rhondda Valley 1906–26', *Llafur*, vol. 3, no. 1, Spring 1980, 42
3 Michael Foot was entertaining on the philosophy of José Enrique Rodo, M. Foot, *Aneurin Bevan*, vol. 1, 47–8, 179–181, 192–4, 466–7.

directed every action he took as a progressive politician and as Minister of Health. David Bevan, had taught the basics to his son.[1] He was also one of the founders of the Tredegar Working Men's Medical Aid Society. When he took his seat on the Committee of Tredegar Council Hospital, Aneurin Bevan eyes were opened to the medical care that was being provided over and above the care provided by family doctors. He realised there was an abysmal lack of hospitals with modern equipment in the Blaenau Gwent area. When he became health minister, he remembered the need he saw at that time to provide every sick person with the highest quality medical treatment.

Aneurin Bevan's great achievement was to reach his intended goal. Despite recognising the weaknesses of the 1911 Act, his admiration for Lloyd George – whom he had criticised for not showing enough respect for the miners when he first entered Parliament –increased. Bevan could see there was no political party, including his own, with any revolutionary idea or ambition to realise his vision of a National Health Service. The Beveridge Report had failed to explain how every individual could access medical care when they needed it, while civil servants seemed unprepared to ask searching, important questions. The BMA had opposed every move to improve the situation, since Lloyd George's days. But Bevan was a more independent politician and had served his constituents on the back benches faithfully since 1929. He saw early on that he needed medical specialists to advise him. There was not an extensive choice. Lord Addison was one such person, but there is no evidence of Bevan having pursued him. Lord Bertrand Dawson, who was extremely influential, had died some months before Bevan was appointed to the post of Minister. Fortunately, there were two other renowned doctors from whom he could get valuable advice for his NHS plans.[2] Charles Wilson, namely Lord Moran, was President of the Royal College of Physicians .There was no hope of persuading Lord Thomas Horder to support him. Horder was a favourite of everyone in the medical world who was against the scheme and had led family doctors' opposition to it.He was a huge celebrity and the more well-known of the two.[3] In essence, the disagreement between Horder and Moran over creating a national health service was a battle between two of the most distinguished doctors in Britain. Neither was it a battle, rather a war which lasted for 35 years. Horder was the older of the two and his was the stronger and more influential voice for a long period.[4] He was

---

1 Bevan, *In Place of Fear*, 26; Foot, Vol.1, 48.
2 H. Morris-Jones, *Doctor in the Whip's Room* (London, 1955), 160.
3 See Lord Horder, *Fifty Years of Medicine* (London, 1953), 72.
4 B. Watkin, *The National Service: The First Phase 1948–1974 and After*, (London, 1978), 3; L. Witts, 'Thomas Jeeves Horder', in E. Williams and H. Palmer (eds.) *The Dictionary of National Biography 1951–1960* (London, 1971), 502; Earl of Woolton, *The Memoirs of the Rt. Hon. The Earl of Woolton* (London, 1959), 279.

physician to the most prominent members of the establishment, the royal family and former Prime Ministers such as Bonar Law, Ramsay MacDonald and Neville Chamberlain. The Welshman David Thomas, Lord Rhondda, thought so much of him he left Horder ten thousand pounds in his will.[1] Neither was Moran without influential patients; he was Winston Churchill's personal doctor. But, in the end, it was Moran and Bevan who were triumphant. In October 1945, Bevan called the medical élite together at the Café Royal for an informal discussion of his plan. Dr. Charles Hill, Secretary of the BMA, was responsible for inviting important figures such as Dr. Guy Dain, a Birmingham family doctor and BMA Chair, Sir Henry Soutar, the BMA President, Sir Alfred Webb-Johnson and Lord Moran to this important gathering . There were only men present. Bevan, in the opinion of many of us, did not give a place in his plans to women such as Dr Edith Sumerskill. He believed in equality for women was always careful to say anything to denigrate feminism within earshot of Jennie Lee. There are however few examples of Bevan failing dismally in his relations with assertive female politicians such as Jean Mann and Bessie Braddock. Jennie Lee was herself careful on these controversial questions to do with feminism.[2]

It is unfortunate that no women doctors or nurses were invited to join in these key important debates. The Royal College of Nursing, the College of Midwives and the Royal British Nurses Association had no representation in the debate. The important Negotiating Committee had no woman present to speak with authority or put forward the opinion of nurses'. Bevan should have invited some senior nursing officers to be involved in the discussions, but the BMA feared the presence of the President of the Royal College of Nursing or anyone else of the same stature, in case they held their own contrary views.[3] Of those who attended that first meeting in the Café Royal, some became very prominent in the creation of the NHS, while others receded into the shadows. Sir Henry Soutar lost his post as President of the BMA for supporting Aneurin Bevan and Dr. Guy Dain and Dr. Charles Hill came to the forefront of the scheme. Lord Moran could not stand seeing or hearing Sir Alfred Webb-Johnson. He called him an ass and warned Aneurin to say nothing confidential to Webb-Johnson as he would be sure to reveal it all to the officers of the BMA.[4] Lord Moran also detested Dr. Charles Hill and the two men refused to compromise with one other.[5] Bevan acknowledged there

---

1 Peter Stead wrote entertainingly about D. A. Thomas. See Peter Stead, 'The Language of Edwardian Politics' in *A People and a Proletariat: Essays in the History of Wales 1780–1980* (ed. David Smith) (London, 1980), 148– 165. As one miner says about the owner of the colliery and the MP: 'we all know that all through his career D. A. Thomas's chief delight has been to put cats among pigeons', p. 159.
2 Hollis, *Jennie Lee*, 140, 149–50, 158.
3 Grey-Turner and F. Sutherland, *History of the British Medical Association*, Vol. 2 (London, 1982), 54.
4 Lovell, *Churchill's Doctor*, 255, 299, 301.
5 *Ibid*, 291.

was no respect between the two. The only thing they had in common was wanting to keep Lord Horder, who had wished to be involved, out of the discussions. Lord Moran, at St. Bartholomew's Hospital, and Lord Horder, at St Mary's, had been on unfriendly terms since their early days in the twenties, something Bevan was all too aware of. Moran and Bevan became close friends and co-workers and he depended greatly on the renowned doctor in his creation of the National Health Service. Bevan believed he owed a responsibility to the House of Commons rather than to the medical profession; he told the doctors he wanted no further debate with them but promised to consult them from time to time. But even so, he was not as open as expected. MPs of his own party complained of his unreadiness before hand to discuss the details of the legislation which was to be brought before Parliament.

Despite this, Bevan placed Lord Moran on a pedestal and the two would regularly dine together in upmarket restaurants.[1] It was true that Bevan enjoyed the best wines and good cuisine, of frequenting the most expensive restaurants in Soho and the surrounding area. Some of his chapel-going friends believe the so-called puritan nonconformist socialist who represented the South Wales coalfield in Westminster was denying his background especially when he got friendly with Lord Beaverbrook. For his part, Bevan always claimed it was Lord Beaverbrook who was responsible for inviting him in the first place to the home where he enjoyed a cuisine that was not available in Charles Street .

Bevan's ambition was to introduce a standardised national service; however, he did not know how to bring this about within one term of government. He was keen to learn as much as he could about medicine and Lord Moran stepped in to educate him. He also made certain the politician fully understood the status and importance of doctors. Moran later said Bevan deserved the highest marks as a pupil:

He would come to the heart of my case almost before I had put it to him.[2]

Ernest Bevin too had described Aneurin Bevan as a natural intellectual.[3] Moran came to appreciate Bevan's vision of life as well as his intellectual prowess. The first thing the two friends discussed in detail was the number of hospitals that existed and the proposal to nationalise them. Bevan had not yet discussed nationalisation in much detail with Attlee or his fellow Labour ministers. In fact, those who knew Bevan well, wondered if the suggestion originated from Moran himself.[4] Or maybe

---
1 Honigsbaum, *Health*, 174, 216.
2 *British Medical Journal*, 16 July 1960, 236.
3 H. Nicholson, *Diaries and Letters 1939–1945* (London, 1967), 192.
4 Michael Foot, *Aneurin Bevan*, Vol. 2 (London, 1973), 132; Hennessy, *Never Again*, 137.

Bevan, with Moran's backing, may have gradually come to the conclusion that the hospitals should be nationalised.[1] Moran saw nationalisation as the perfect way to overcome the vast regional differences in hospital standards across the country.[2]

Under the Bevan scheme, surgeons and physicians would receive generous salaries. Lord Moran knew it would be necessary to give them enough freedom to receive extra pay for treating well-off private patients. In *In Place of Fear*, Bevan acknowledged that allowing this private practice was a glaring mistake on his behalf. He should have 'seen from the beginning' the consequences and that he of all people on this issue did not have enough backbone to say 'No!'[3] It is clear he was influenced by Lord Moran when he made what was, in the view of a number of medical socialists, an obvious mistake, indeed a huge blunder.

It was primarily Moran's personal knowledge of important Harley Street surgeons and physicians which persuaded Bevan to compromise. Moran viewed family doctors as second-class inexperienced professionals, individuals who had not received a thorough enough training so that they could never be surgeons or physicians. In his view, these doctors should not be allowed to work on hospital wards and receive the same handsome salaries as the brilliant surgeons who spend hours operating on extremely sick folk.

Bevan has been criticised by some historians, with reason, for going out of his way to please the medical elite who had very little empathy with the Labour Party. The truth was he had no choice. In his own colourful but accurate words:

> 'I had to stuff their mouths with gold.'[4]

Gold was not his only gift to the medical profession : soon these well-known medical giants were praised by patients who received free treatment and were applauded by the hospital administrators for the treatments they implemented. They were to govern the hospitals.[5] The result was the creation of an obvious split between specialists and family doctors. At that time, the idea of a group general practices had not taken hold, partly because Bevan did not want them to compete with each other for patients. Inevitably, within the hospitals, some doctors would be more important than others, principally those in training hospitals of which there were only thirty centres in the United Kingdom. Other than in Scotland, these hospitals had a large measure of independence from the Regional Hospital Boards. Moran's ideal was to create three classes of doctor. General practitioners would make up the

---

1 Grimes, *British National Health Service*, 136.
2 J. Peter, *The Making of the National Health Service* (London, 1981), 175
3 Bevan, *In Place of Fear*, 96; Campbell, *Aneurin Bevan*, 169.
4 Campbell, *Aneurin Bevan*, 168.
5 Hollis, *Jennie Lee*, 130.

third class, while the second would comprise the majority of hospital surgeons and physicians. At the top of the ladder, there would be a small number of elite doctors, mostly created professors by the Universities , who would be based in medical schools linked to universities.

Moran believed in the system of giving honours to those of ability and paying a decent salary to the most dedicated well educated doctors. They should have the same salaries as any civil servant who were employed as permanent secretaries to government departments. These talented and capable doctors deserved pay as good as that of the judiciary and even cabinet ministers.[1] Moran was looking after his own interests too. He suggested to Bevan that he should be appointed chair of the Standing Awards Committee, meaning he would decide who was recognised for their specialism. Moran remained in the post until 1962, the most powerful medical star in Britain. He understood how to succeed through being Aneurin Bevan's confidant.

A hard battle to create the National Health Service

Despite Moran's support, a fierce battle raged between Aneurin Bevan and his many opponents from the summer 1945 to the summer of 1948. When he talked about his nationalisation plan in March 1946, Sir Bernard Docker, Chair of the British Hospitals Association (BHA), commented that Bevan was committing a terrible atrocity for his plans meant obvious danger to many people.[2] Lord Horder came to defend Bevans vision .Aneurin's words on the subject were that Lord Horder 'had a heart of gold but a mind of steel and, unfortunately it was with the steel that the Government had to deal'.[3] Lord Horder's opinion of Aneurin Bevan was that he was the cleverest politician, firm minded, with a fanatical faith in dogma. He had compassion in his heart and his conscience moved him to action. He saw Bevan as a powerful politician who was leading the common people towards the fruits of the National Health Service .[4] But, worst of all in Horder's opinion, was the close relationship between the Minister of Health and Lord Moran, who he viewed as a traitor. But for Moran's support – by now the two were working hand in glove – Bevan would never have dared to criticise Horder. Bevan provided every time he spoke in the House of Commons on the NHS a copy of his speech to his friend so that Lord Moran would naturally sing from the same hymn sheet in the House of Lords .Horder did not give up his opposition and, after the NHS was established , he criticised the leaders of the BMA and continued to represent

---

1 A. Clegg and T. Chester, *Wage Policy and the Health Service* (Oxford, 1957), 60–1
2 Grimes, *British National Health Service*, 135.
3 M. Horder, *The Little Genius: A Memoir of the First Lord Horder* (London, 1966), 98.
4 Lord Horder, *Fifty Years of Medicine*, 43.

the doctors who were unhappy with the changes. Over seven hundred doctors attended one meeting, he organised resulting in the formation of the Fellowship for Freedom in Medicine (FFM). Horder was chief spokesperson for the FFM and remained its chair until his death in 1955. He opposed a National Health Service chiefly because Moran was in favour of it. The last years of his life were tedious and busy. He left his childhood denomination, the Congregationalists, took up Humanism and was involved with the Crematoria Committee from 1947 to 1951. One thing he and Bevan were in agreement about was that more crematoriums should be built. In 1951, Ernest Bevin's funeral was held at a crematorium and was attended by Bevan.

The vision of the politician from his Tredegar background

Bevan's Tredegar background was key to his political ambition and drive. He was not afraid of debating with his fellow cabinet ministers, as he knew that most of them were from similar backgrounds, dissenters by nature and by religion. He also recognised the background which had enriched him and so many others was fast crumbling. The Baptists, Independents, Wesleyans and Presbyterians were losing the immense influence they had enjoyed in his childhood days.[1] By the thirties, Nonconformity had reared a generation of famous MPs from Wales, England and Scotland. Jim Griffiths, the Minister for National Insurance was a firm nonconformist and responsible for the Family Allowance Act which was passed on 15 June 1945. It was first paid on 6 August 1946. This was paid then to 2.5 million families. Griffiths worked long hours to promote the National Insurance Act and the Industrial Injuries Act, which came into force in 1948 and greatly pleased Aneurin Bevan. Ellen Wilkinson was a Methodist and Ernest Bevin im his youth a Baptist Sunday school teacher. In those days , Bevin had been an open-air evangelist and, like Jim Griffiths, had considered a career as an evangelist or minister of religion. Bevan could not totally cast off his religious roots and it was he who gave the inaugural speech at the inception of the Christian socialist movement in 1960.[2] Despite ill-health, he could not refuse the request of his socialist friend the Revd. Dr. Donald

---

1 A glimpse into the influence of the chapel is reflected by the second generation Spaniards working in Abercrave coalfield in the upper reaches of the Swansea Valley who would express themselves: 'The Sermon on the Mount, can you beat it? He used to tell me . . . it was pure socialism. But organised religion was quite a different thing altogether. So what he said was this, "If you don't learn anything bad by going to Sunday School or going to Church or to Chapel, all right, fair enough, you can go."' See Hywel Francis, 'The Secret World of the South Wales Miner: The Relevance of Oral History' in *A People and a Proletariat*, 166–186. The quotation is on pages 172–3.

2 The story of Christian socialist witness is told by Chris Bryant, *Possible Dreams: A Personal History of the British Christian Socialists* (London, 1996), 1–351.

Soper of Kingsway Hall, Holborn to come and inspire an important tradition within the Labour movement. Indeed, he insisted that bringing health provision under the welfare state reflected the Christian ethic. His admirer George Orwell expressed it well when he said :

> If only I could become Nye's eminence grise we'd soon have this country on its feet.[1]

Aneurin Bevan's great contribution was overcoming the obstacles, fears and political opposition and putting strong Christian fundamentals beneath the National Health Service. He faced an enormous task but succeeded amazingly, as the Welsh historian John Davies, said in his autobiography:

> Establishing the Health Service was the greatest feat, a daring undertaking remembering that Britain's debts as a percentage of its income was much higher in 1948 than today (in 2014).[2]

Huw T. Edwards, the Welsh trade unionist leader on Deeside and a good friend of the politician, was not far from the truth when he said Aneurin Bevan's National Health Service was Christianity at work and definitely incorporated 'the kingdom of God on earth'.[3]

---

1 George Orwell, *A Patriot After All, 1940–1941*, Peter Davison (ed.), (London, 2000), 189.
2 John Davies, *Hunangofiant John Davies, Fy Hanes I* (An Autobiography of John Davies: My Story) (Talybont, 2014), 46.
3 Gwyn Jenkins, *Cofiant Huw T. Edwards: Prif Weinidog Answyddogol Cymru* (Talybont 2007), 22.

CHAPTER 9

Achieving the goal: creating a National Health Service

The most surprising thing about the 1945–1950 Labour Government was when the new Prime Minister Clement Attlee extended the right hand of fellowship to his main critic, Aneurin Bevan. John Bew, the most recent of Attlee's biographers, explains the situation memorably and fairly:

> The underlying reality was that Attlee's political instincts were far subtler and more attuned to the mood of the Country, than those of the main critics, Bevan and Laski. Bevan was a hero for a portion of the Labour Party, but was widely regarded as hysterical, disloyal and unpatriotic by those outside it.[1]

Throughout the Second World War, Bevan frequently failed to be loyal, fair and supportive. Bevan would have chosen to lead Labour out of the Coalition Government on a number of occasions and was always calling for Winston Churchill's resignation.[2] It was Attlee, the wise man, who would calm the wars of words, refusing to consider the unrealistic demands of Bevan and Laski for a moment. Attlee could not believe these two clever men were so out of touch with ordinary people. Laski, who was a Professor of Politics at the London School of Economics, and Bevan, who was considered one of the most intelligent left wingers of his generation, could easily have been more reasonable in their attitude. Attlee used a memorable line in a letter to Bevan at the end of the war, 'In serving the country, you are also serving the Labour movement.'[3]

---
1 John Bew, *Citizen Clem: A Biography of Attlee* (London, 2016), 361.
2 Paul Addison, *The Road to 1945* (London, 1996), 261 and 272.
3 Bew, *ibid,* 362.

The huge challenge before Aneurin Bevan-

But there was a particular challenge facing Bevan in his new role. All over Britain, hospitals were calling out for a progressive government and a perceptive health minister. The Labour politician Bessie Braddock had a particular interest in Liverpool's hospitals. In her memoirs, she gives a vivid depiction of conditions at Sefton Hospital in Wavertree where an ant infestation and steam flies in the boiler room were causing daily problems. The sound of the crickets was deafening to the extent that the patients were unable to sleep at night.[1] Braddock visited the kitchens at the 950-bed local government hospital of Alder Hey Children's Hospital and asked Sir Thomas White, chair of Liverpool's Hospitals Committee, to accompany her.[2] He was apprehensive, knowing very little about the hospital, but he saw, with his own eyes, children who had remained on the wards for twenty years. Every now and again, there were attempts to improve things – the Midwifery Act of 1936 was an important step forward – though the voluntary hospitals were under constant threat of closure more than local authorities hospitals. . This perilous situation was the reason the Penny in the Pound Fund was set up in Sheffield and other cities like Liverpool back in the 1870s. People in good jobs were persuaded to contribute a penny for every pound earned during the week to a fund which subsidised the voluntary hospitals.[3] Liverpool continued with this scheme after the inception of the National Health Service because the city was responsible for four convalescent homes: one on Lake Windermere, one in Birkdale near Southport, one in Colwyn Bay and the other in Rhos on Sea. After a period in the state hospital in Liverpool, patients would convalesce for a short time in the Penny in the Pound homes before returning home.[4]

It was extremely hard for sick people to be cured before the National Health Service became a reality. Childbirth was difficult and there were frequent examples of mothers dying during labour. Many people died of tuberculosis (TB) and even the common cold turned to pneumonia in 50% of patients (some who then went on to die). Pain, coughs and spitting up blood was part of everyday life for ordinary people. The working class did not expect much in terms of comfort and, in wanting the best for them, Aneurin Bevan was very different from most of his political contemporaries in the Conservative Party . Family doctors worked long hours and were regarded as heroes. Many people would not trouble their doctor unless they were desperate because over half the population had to pay for a doctor's visit and

---

1 Jack and Bessie Braddock, *The Braddocks* (London, 1963), 130.
2 *Ibid*, 133.
3 *Ibid*, 143.
4 *Ibid*.

for any medicine prescribed. In middleclass homes in the areas where Lloyd George's insurance scheme was not operating, there was sure to be five shillings on the table ready for the doctor's visit. In poorer homes, that amount was reduced to three shillings and six pence.[1]

The serious state of health provision before 1945–1950

The health service in Britain was given a new lease of life by the creator of the National Health Service.[2,3] By 1945, after six years of unremitting battle, the majority of Britain's family doctors were weary. Many younger doctors had enlisted in the Armed Forces, leaving the burden of medical care during the war to fall to middle-aged and older doctors, including female doctors who had done their training during the First World War. The 1944 Education Act established a Schools Health Service, with special attention given to children's teeth. The responsibility for hospitals remained with local authorities and voluntary bodies, with councils responsible for TB hospitals. In total, there were 32,600 beds across England and Wales. In 1947, 23,000 people died of TB and there were 52,000 new cases identified. Half a million children suffered from diphtheria during that hard winter and there were 7000 cases of polio with 500 deaths. Another problem facing Aneurin Bevan was the devastation to the country's infrastructure caused by the Second World War. Not one hospital in London escaped German bombing.[4] Two out of three hospitals had been built before 1891 and a good number of those before 1861. The old buildings were short of operating theatres for surgery, pathology and radiology and nurses were overworked, though advances in medication –particularly penicillin and digoxin – undoubtedly helped survival rates. Rheumatic heart disease was a huge killer. There were three reasons for its high mortality rates. First, the majority of people only sought hospital help when they were in a very poor physical condition and it was too late. Secondly, modern-day technology and drugs were not yet available, for instance, anaesthesia for operations was not always effective. Thirdly, there were few specialists working in most hospitals. Young medics returning from the battle-fields or finishing their training would serve their apprenticeship under a specialist – the chief. They had to remain single and were expected to live in the hospital

---

1 Based on the experience of a child in rural Cardiganshire 1945–1948.
2 Andy Missell, 'Iechyd Da' (Good Health) 1948' in *Llyfr y Ganrif* (The Book of the Century) (eds. Gwyn Jenkins and Tegwyn Jones) (Talybont, 1999), 201. 'The health service of a miner's son from Charles Street, Tredegar. He devised the scheme which was the jewel in the crown of the Welfare State. And the National Health Service remains a memorial to the multi-talented Aneurin.'
3 *Michael* Foot, *Aneurin Bevan 1897–1945, Vol 1* (London, 1962), 108.
4 Keith William Lowe, *The State and Medical Care in Britain: Political Processes and the Structuring of the National Health Service*. PhD Dissertation Wolfson College, University of Oxford, 1981

precincts, and to be on duty day and night.[1] The voluntary hospitals claimed to be independent; however, they depended on the generosity of wealthy individuals and the charity of organisations, societies, companies, chapels and churches for sustenance. There were also training hospitals – twelve in London for instance – as well as small cottage hospitals, located mainly in market towns and on the outskirts of rural villages. Local family doctors generally kept an eye on cottage hospitals but their day-to-day management was down to the matron. The Local Government Act 1929 saw counties and county boroughs assuming responsibility for the former Board of Guardians hospitals, otherwise known as the workhouse hospitals. Since 1830, these hospitals had been providing for poor and elderly people, tramps, sick or discarded prostitutes and people who were disabled or physically weak with chronic conditions. Funding came from taxation and a 40% grant from central government but there was little co-operation between hospitals.[2] During the thirties and even the Second World War, there were some huge improvements in many city hospitals. First-class surgeons became high profile and gave hospitals such as Birmingham Accident Hospital, the Royal Marsden Hospital, London and the Royal Infirmary, Liverpool a reputation to be proud of.[3]

Mental hospitals

We must not forget mental hospitals, or asylums as they were called back then. Denbigh Mental Hospital in North Wales was immortalised in Welsh literature by a sub-editor on the *Daily Telegraph*. Caradog Prichard described what happened to his mother in the slate quarrying town of Bethesda in Snowdonia. Mrs Pritchard became so depressed after her husband's death in an accident that, in the end, she was unable to live alone and was admitted to a mental hospital for care. She spent the rest of her life in the vast institution. Despite ample hospital provision for people suffering mental illness, before 1948 no-one but Aneurin Bevan had considered mental hospitals would become part of the National Health Service. The hospital buildings were mostly old and badly resourced, with some having over two thousand beds. They were usually located in out-of-the-way places where they could be forgotten about by everyone except the patients' loved ones. With patients spending ten or more years in these asylums with no hope of discharge, they would lose hope, decline into extreme dementia or even commit suicide.

---

1 *Ibid*, 5.
2 *Ibid*, 6.
3 *Ibid*, 8.

Improvement within the health service

By the time of the Second World War, specialist units within hospitals were attracting well-deserved attention. Of particular note were the Archibald McIndoe Burns and Plastic Surgery Unit in East Grinstead, the Ludwig Guttman Spinal Injuries Unit at Stoke Mandeville and the Wylie McKissock Neurological Unit in Atkinson Morley Hospital, Wimbledon. There were orthopaedic and ear, nose and throat specialists at Oswestry and Liverpool. Successful physicians expected to serve a long apprenticeship. Alongside hospital doctors, the work of county and urban medical officers of health was important and an Emergency Public Health Laboratory Service was established under the auspices of the Medical Research Council. All these constituent parts were brought together under Aneurin Bevan's Health Service Act.[1] While his vision was for a National Health Service, once it was up and running, Bevan ensured that a regional service was established in 1946 to look after it.

Another effect of the Second World War was to promote scientific research in hospital laboratories. Britain was a long way behind in medical research in comparison with European countries like West Germany and the well-resourced U.S.A. The Haldane Commission (1907–1913) called for an extensive research programme but there was the inevitable dragging of feet. In 1939, only three of London's medical schools had a clinical professor in any subject or discipline. In the thirties, the British Postgraduate Medical School in Hammersmith Hospital was the only one of its kind.[2]

By 1942, medical education was a topic of study and a committee was set up to discuss the basic needs. It was chaired by William Goodenough, a director and chairman of Barclays Bank. One of the committee's most vociferous members was none other than Janet Vaughan, the principal of Somerville College, Oxford, who had strong views about the need for women to become doctors. A 1944 report emphasised the need to extend existing medical training provision, adding that there should be a medical school in Wales. Unfortunately, Bevan did not follow this practical suggestion, although he did appreciate the importance of linking medical schools to universities. Unfortunately, in the National Health Service Act Bevan had to refuse the input of academics, to the disappointment of many. But the Act ensured that there was a responsibility on the Government to make sure that there was clinical provision for those who were trained and a chance to undertake medical research.

---

1 There are many names which could be mentioned such as Thomas Kilner in Oxford, Frances Avery Jones, appointed in 1940 to Central Middlesex Hospital, Henry Cohen and the Welsh surgeons in the city of Liverpool. William R. Williams, Edgar Parry and John Howell Hughes gave outstanding service. Dr Emyr Wyn Jones played an important part in the work of establishing the cardiac services in Liverpool and we know about the orthopaedic surgeons Dr. Goronwy Thomas and Prof. Robert Owen

2 Lowe, *ibid*, 15

The welfare and training of nurses

Bevan was also concerned about the welfare and training of hospital nurses. He appreciated that the vocation had changed greatly since the twenties when he was dealing with Tredegar Hospital. He realised that, as Minister for Health, he had a great deal of material to master such as the Wood Report on the Recruitment and Training of Nurses and the Horder Committee of the Royal College of Nursing from 1942 to 1952. The 1943 Nurses Act granted a status to assistant nurses for the first time, establishing a hierarchy of all those in nursing roles and arranging examinations for them. By 1948, over 20,000 assistant nurses had registered as State Enrolled Nurses (SENs).[1]

Aneurin Bevan knew the success of the National Health Service would depend not only on doctors but also on nurses. In 1945, he set up a group of specialists including nurses, sociologists and doctors under the chairmanship of Sir Robert Wood. Their initial remit was to assess the need for nurses and determine exactly what work they should be performing. They would work out how to recruit and retain more nurses in hospitals. Their report, published in 1947, made it clear that too many nurses were leaving the profession because they were too heavily disciplined and otherwise restricted in their leisure time. Bevan invited the public and health specialists to respond. There was criticism of the Royal College of Nursing's definition of the nursing role and its expectations of nurses generally. These committed and caring women were expected to live in nurses' hostels and accept discipline redolent of another age. Like the soldier, the nurse had to wear a uniform and polished shoes, with her hair in place under a little cap and no make-up. The hospital matron was all-powerful. Bevan welcomed the developments that were taking place when he became health minister. A new union –the Confederation of Health Service Employees (COHSE) –was now representing mental hospital nurses (nurses who had never been accepted by the Royal College of Nursing) and unqualified nurses. Another important union – the National Union of Public Employees (NUPE) – was formed with one of Bevan's friends at the helm.[2] The importance of the work of midwives was recognised by the Midwives Act of 1936. Half the babies in Britain were born at home and midwives could be looking after between 50 and 100 mothers a year. Theirs was specialist, hard, lonely and amazingly important work.

---

1 *Ibid*, 16.
2 *Ibid*, 17–18.

The failure to reform the health service for two decades

From 1920, up to Bevan's time as Minister of Health, there were discussions about the future of the health service but reports were quickly buried. Bertrand Dawson chaired an Advisory Committee offering a system of teaching hospitals and regional centres with training hospitals working with universities. The idea of regionalisation was highlighted in the Sankey Report and, during the Second World War, ten studies were published focusing on various cities. George Goodber made a thorough study of Sheffield, which became the basis for other studies by the government. There was talk of bed shortages, old and defective buildings, a lack of suitable equipment, insufficient specialists at hand because of a lack of flexibility and a lethal conservatism. Medical staff themselves tended to sit on the fence. The shortage of specialists was a constant concern. There was only one gynaecologist for the whole of Lincolnshire and no full-time radiologist in the county. The city of Nottingham was in a similar situation.[1]

Radical intellectuals were most concerned

There were people in the Labour Party who worried about the extent of the problem. One was Janet Vaughan, the Principal of Somerville College. In the Second World War period, she had come across a very able student from Grantham called Margaret Roberts, who later married and became Margaret Thatcher. Vaughan did not share Thatcher's politics and believed no-one could become a doctor unless they were a socialist, an opinion shared by Julian Tudor Hart, a Glyncorrwg doctor in Glamorganshire. There were others like them in the south Wales valleys. To Janet Vaughan and Dr. Hart, Bevan was a hero and they expected a new dawn to break when he took over. Bevan spoke of having an 'atmosphere of safety and serenity throughout the whole country for families in distress and troubled by ill-health.'

The cost of treatment in a TB hospital was enormous. If someone needed long drawn out treatment, for example for two years, their hospital stay could cost thousands. Some university teaching staff complained the system enabled wealthy people

---

1 Bryn Roberts, a college friend of Aneurin, built up NUPE, the main Labour union for health workers. When he was appointed secretary, the union was weak and almost finished. Roberts performed miracles. He understood that the health service was dependent on those working in hospitals, on the wages they received and the freedom and opportunities they would have. He ensured there was a mechanism for discussing and determining issues around wages and job descriptions. Thus, the Whitley Council came into existence. See W. W. Craik, *Bryn Roberts and the National Union of Public Employees* (London, 1955), 23–8.

to live comfortably thanks to the generosity of successive Chancellors of the Exchequer. When Bevan came along, to borrow a simile from Scripture, he choose 'a strong man to run a race' with a mission to transform the status quo. He realised every suggestion on offer had been rubbished by those who were tasked with providing health services: leaders of local authorities, hospital personnel and doctors. He had no choice but to take the most unpopular step of nationalising the hospitals and providing free health services to every individual from the cradle to the grave.[1] Despite spending years as a councillor himself, he understood it was vital to release hospitals from the grip of local authorities and the charity of chapels, churches and generous benefactors.

It is not surprising that so many historians write: 'this is the work of a genius'.[2] For Bevan, nationalisation was the key to his plans, for without it there was no way of changing things within the voluntary or urban hospitals. Both wanted to keep their grip on their situation and were unwilling to yield an inch.

Despite the challenges ahead, Bevan's stance was a breath of fresh air to the civil servants in the health department, particularly Sir Wilson Jameson, George Godber, John Horton and John Patiez. Each man recognised that the new minister was a clever operator and a politician from head to toe. Bevan did not bother to discuss the details, even after the first reading of his Bill. Nurses were one hundred per cent in favour of his plans as were the young doctors. The strident opposition came from the conservatively minded, the 'old stagers' who were involved with the charitable societies and local authorities. These were used to lording it over the voluntary hospitals. Fortunately, the war had made many rank and file doctors recognise the need for change, encouraging them to support plans to improve community health as a whole rather than pursue purely selfish ends. Aneurin's philosophy was always to create a better world. He wanted to demonstrate how a proud socialist such as himself could achieve better public health than his Tory predecessors with their constant emphasis on control of the situation and wealth. For him, the proposed new health service summed up socialism in its purist form. And it was the doctors, nurses and patients who were at forefront of the revolution.

The post-war era was the Labour Party's golden age; however, the change to the health service did not happen without a hard, hard fight from Aneurin Bevan in particular. Many distinguished doctors viewed the birth of the National Health Service with dismay, seeing it an the enemy and damning it with faint praise at every opportunity. Every week there was a selection of letters in the British Medical Journal prophesying that the National Health Service would be a complete failure. If the service were miraculously to come into existence, it would be a complete

---

1 Lowe, *ibid*, 28.

2 Bryn Roberts' verdict on the scheme was: 'It was certainly the most humane measure of all time – and the most socialistic'. See W. W. Craik, *ibid*, 149.

disaster. One of the fiercest critics was none other Dr. Ffrangcon Roberts of Cambridge . It should be noted that the health ministers, of all political colours, who came after Bevan, were equally denigrated by the BMA: that happened to Enoch Powell, Barbara Castle, Kenneth Robinson, Richard Crossman and Kenneth Clark. It was natural to blame the Minister for Health for everything, although all politicians naturally had to depend on specialist advisers. Bevan outlined what he saw as his own role, that was to establish a public health service which could be trusted and admired. Within that health service, the medical professionals would remain responsible for treating the sick person, analysing their need and doing whatever was needed to help them recover. There was a world of difference between the Minister who set up the framework and the doctor and surgeons who followed his vocation within that framework, dealing with the patients who were sick . Bevan's only wish was medical care should be carried out as professionally as possible. He succeeded in creating a system of safe, professional healthcare which transformed countless lives in the decades to come .

Huge task of the Minister of Health

The task facing Aneurin Bevan was enormous from the very beginning and involved bringing together the myriad of medical professionals and advisers needed to meet his goal of creating a first-class health service.[1] The National Health Service would be financed by central government. The owners of the right-wing English press continued to attack Bevan's argument that the scheme was 'socialism in action'. He, on the other hand, talked of hope and inspiration for the future, speaking of himself as a Welshman under attack like all those Ministers of Health who had preceded him:

> A Socialist, representing a Welsh constituency, and they find me even more impossible.[2]

Within the medical and hospital structures and all the organisations involved in the setting up of the NHS, there were four important areas of contention. First, the existing health establishment, as it might be called, could not accept Bevan's intention to get rid of the customary action of buying and selling general medical practices. Family doctors had invested capital in their practices and the arrangement was important to their personal finances. Secondly, the doctors did not agree with the proposal to set up a specified salary as part of their conditions of employment.

---

1 Rivett, 28.
2 Nicklaus Thomas-Symonds, *Nye: The Political Life of Aneurin Bevan* (London, 2015), 136.

The Coalition Government had been first to propose a full-time salary for doctors in 1943. Aneurin was therefore able to argue that the salary idea not come originally from him, the socialist Minister of Health, but from a government containing Liberals, Conservatives and leading Labour politicians. Bevan had rejected the original coalition plan because he believed medics under 30 would be forced to carry a financial burden. Now he thought a salary of £300 plus a per capita allowance would be more acceptable. Another argument was that agreeing to a partnership in a medical practice would be problematic. In response, Bevan asked the Lord Chancellor and the Attorney General to appoint a legal commission to look at the issue and come up with acceptable agreement.[1]

A fierce debate with militant medics

The more militant medics argued the new proposals removed doctors' legal rights. Bevan disputed this and addressed all the misunderstandings presented to him. For example, it was blatantly untrue that doctors would lose their right to appeal to the courts against unfair dismissal – they would have the same rights as every other citizen. Bevan did, however, regret that some doctors were asking for the right to appeal to the courts even if they were dismissed on the grounds of misconduct and neglect. For him, this demand verged on the impossible from both a legal and governmental position; however, he was prepared to ensure that any doctor in this position was treated fairly. Before Bevan's time, the system put in place by the Insurance Act meant any doctor facing dismissal could appeal to the Minister of Health. A committee would report the doctor to the Minister, who would then investigate the circumstances of the case. The medic was allowed to remain in post until an outcome was reached, then either kept in post or asked to resign . The loss of a doctor's position under the new system carried a heavier penalty than under the National Insurance Act. Bevan set up a system to sort out future disagreements between patient and doctor to the satisfaction of the local executive council, which held contracts with the doctors, and the NHS. The initial committee would comprise seven representatives, elected by doctors, who would discuss each case in detail and present their findings to the Minister of Health. If they believed there was a case for the doctor to be de-registered, the committee would express this to the Minister, who would then hand over the case to the tribunal. The chair of the tribunal was appointed by the Lord Chancellor and was joined by a doctor and a lawyer.[2] If the tribunal decided that the doctor should remain in practice in the

---

1 Hansard HCB (series 5), vol. 499, 7 April 1948, col. 166.
2 Nicklaus Thomas-Symonds, *Nye,* 147.

health service, the Minister of Health must accept that verdict. If the verdict was dismissal, the doctor could ask the Minister to reconsider the tribunal's decision. The Minister could subsequently arrange another investigation, either public or private and with witnesses if required, setting the tribunal to work for a second time. When Bevan spoke about this system in Parliament, one of the most colourful backbench Labour MPs Reginald Paget (Northampton) rose to his feet to say that the Minister was giving more security to doctors than to any other profession in society. Bevan had to agree saying:

> In fact, the doctor can go to the courts, as I understand it . . . on the ground that this tribunal, or the Minister has carried out the statute, or has prejudiced the case by the way in which it has been handled by the tribunal, or otherwise. There is adequate protection at every stage.[1]

The doctors had no better friend than Aneurin Bevan and he was always ready to compromise. The militancy of the thirties had subsided and spirit of amity existed. For example, although voluntary hospitals were being nationalised, there were no plans to nationalise old people's homes where there was ample nursing care.

The Minister's fairness to those in the health service

Bevan did not want all doctors to have the same salary; it was possible, of course, to earn more cash through private work. He introduced four types of hospital care: wards which were totally free, wards where patients would pay for extra comforts, wards where surgeons, pathologists, radiologists could ask for a reasonable payment and wards where there were no restrictions on payment. In terms of salary, the sum of £300 was proposed, plus a per capita allowance, the total amount paid depending on the number of people on the doctor's register. Thus, a doctor caring for a thousand people would receive £300 plus £758, making a total of £1058; if there were another thousand patients an additional £788 would be paid. Travel allowances would also be available. Bevan was willing to reconsider these salaries and payments in two years. Bevan appealed strongly to the British Medical Association to give the proposals a least a chance to work. Unfortunately, they had a completely different agenda to pursue.

Bevan feared the BMA more than any other pressure group within the health service. He realised they did not want to cooperate and enjoyed putting all sorts of obstacles in the way of the new National Health Service. They were always ready to

---

1 *Ibid*, 147.

feed the hostile press with unhelpful material, insisting that Bevan was the obdurate one, the beastly villain. By the beginning of 1948, the situation was looking pretty bleak for him. On 8 January 1948, the BMA expressed its overwhelming unhappiness with the outcome of discussions with Bevan, emphasizing his lack of understanding of the profession's arguments. The organisation also expressed its lack of confidence in the Minister of Health's performance. Bevan was aware of two things, however. First, the BMA did not represent all doctors and, secondly, that many of its leaders were well aware that there were progressive doctors who were warming to the plan as explained by the Minister.[1] In the face of such hostile prejudice and propaganda, the Prime Minister asked Bevan to prepare a report on the situation for the cabinet.

Bevan presents his plans to the Prime Minister and cabinet

In his report, Aneurin Bevan dealt with three difficult issues: the situation relating to GP partnerships, the right of doctors to appeal to the courts for a tribunal verdict on dismissals and the question of salaries. He explained that the issue of GP partnerships was being discussed by a committee of legal specialists, but he was not willing to compromise on the other two issues. After two and a half years, Bevan realised that the doctors were certain to vote as the BMA instructed them, that is. against the NHS Bill. If that happened, he would reluctantly accept the situation but, in his opinion, it would not mean the majority of doctors were unwilling to become part of his national health scheme. Bevan was ready to take a chance as he did not believe that the BMA's antagonist attitude echoed the views of every doctor in the country. On 22 January 1948, the cabinet agreed with Bevan. No further compromise would be forthcoming and Britain's National Health Service would come into existence on 5 July 1948.[2]

Further confrontation with the BMA

On 29 January 1948, in the House of Commons, Bevan attacked the BMA eloquently for their negative vote. It was not a secret vote, he pointed out, but they should remember his day of victory was near. He called on Attlee to speak on the issue, but the Prime Minister was fearful. For Bevan, the BMA was full of 'poisonous, political people'. It was the medical chiefs who were the problem, he argued, and not the doctors working hard in hospitals and GP practices around the country.

---
1 *Ibid*, 146.
2 Webster, Charles, *The National Health Service: A Political History* (Oxford, 1983)), 148.

The BMA's antagonism was not directly at Bevan personally – no Minister of Health since 1911 had received its full backing. As far as Bevan was concerned, these people had no compassion for the sick and those awaiting operations. The medical professional needed better leaders, not meddling politicians hiding under the cloak of medicine.[1]

Failure of Bevan to get the support he needed

The crucial vote was held on 17 March 1948 when 84% of doctors turned out. Of the 45,540 votes cast, only 4,735 supported the National Health Service with 17,037 family doctors voting against the scheme.[2] Bevan spoke again with the principals of the Royal Colleges and made an important announcement on 7 April 1948. In cabinet. he had said there would be no further compromise, but by April he was ready to acknowledge certain flaws in his scheme, despite his firm belief in his overall vision. Another vote would take place in May 1948. There was a good turnout of 74% and this time 24,842 were against the National Health Service with 14,620 in favour. Despite the increase in support, it was still a poor result. Bevan acknowledged that family doctors and full-time voluntary hospital staff, plus many of the specialists – at least 13,981 of them – remained stubbornly opposed to the proposed changes. The truth was the majority of doctors were antipathetic to the idea of creating a National Health Service. The only chink of light was Bevan estimated he had enough doctors on his side to reach his proposed target to launch the National Health Service on 5 July. By June 1948, 26% of the family doctors in England had joined the NHS, with 36% in Scotland and 37% in his beloved Wales.[3] By failing to take part in the important debates in February 1948, Attlee had stalled Bevan's campaign.[4]. The Welshman was fortunate in possessing a strong clear-minded personality with the confidence to stand up for his scheme at cabinet. Even then it, was a great disappointment to him that he had to compromise so much and allow private beds into hospitals to appease the specialists. Another compromise was allowing hospital surgeons to carry out private work, separate to their NHS contract. But, on the whole, great deal of progress had happened in a period of two years . The NHS measure had passed its second reading as far back as May 1946 which was a time for rejoicing to the Labour Party in Westminster.[5] Bevan expressed his view:

---

1 Nicklaus Thomas-Symonds, *Nye,* 148
2 *Ibid*, 146.
3 *Ibid.*
4 *Ibid,* 147.
5 *Ibid.*

> In the conflict between the doctors and the public, the public will win every time if they are led bravely. The (alleged) rights of doctors as a special group in society raise the hackles of the majority of the population.[1]

Aneurin Bevan was a first-class communicator, whether it be in Cabinet, Parliament or when talking to the press. It was easy for him to smite blow after blow against the doctors' leaders. He called them 'a small band of speakers who have constantly misled the great profession to which they belong'. He consistently praised the doctors who were working hard and keeping out of the debates and away from 'that little worthless silent coterie who believe they represent the whole profession'.

Days of celebration as the NHS is born

Aneurin Bevan regarded the BMA as a politically hostile organisation, which delighted in poisoning relations between the medical profession and politicians. Fairness and the need for medical care overrode all other considerations for Bevan and he was overjoyed when 93.1% of the UK population registered for his new National Health Service. Bevan travelled to Manchester for the launch and attended a large meeting on 4 July when he spoke about the effect Conservative Party policies had had on him and his generation. He recalled how he had to live on the earnings of his sister Arianwen and the advice he was given by a friend to move away from his beloved Tredegar.

Here are his controversial and shocking words:

> No amount of persuasion can erase from my heart the deep, fierce hatred towards the Conservative Party for forcing those experiences upon me. As far as I am concerned, they are lower than vermin. They condemned millions of fine people to (a life of) semi-starvation.[2]

It was a speech which caused excitement on the one hand and disappointment on the other.[3] For Attlee, Bevan had gone too far in his oratory, but Archie Lush believed his lifelong friend had spoken the truth as in his book *Why Not Trust the Tories?* The Conservatives turned the speech to their advantage, in particular the word *vermin*.

---

1 *Ibid*, 338
2 *Times*, 5 July 1948, 1.
3 On 4 July 1948, thousands flocked to listen to the finest speaker of his time giving an address in Manchester. It was hugely successful but went amiss because of one word. For Harold Laski, a left-wing intellectual, the creator of the NHS should have avoided the word vermin for the Conservatives.

The Tories began to establish 'vermin clubs' to throw cold water over the following day's celebrations. Churchill called for an apology. He accused Bevan of creating unpleasantness. He turned his rhetoric on Attlee saying that he should get rid of his troublesome, vexatious minister.[1] Privately, Attlee had rebuked Bevan for losing control of his tongue. Bevan answered with his usual confidence: 'I love being the bugbear of the Tories.' But Attlee had responded: 'You can't be the bugbear of the Tories and be regarded as a statesman.' Attlee went on to teach his Minister of Health a basic lesson.

It had been agreed that we wished to give the new social security scheme as good a send-off as possible and to this end I made a non-polemical broadcast. Your speech cut across this . . .. You had won a victory . . . but these unfortunate remarks enable the doctors to stage a come-back and have given the general public the impression that there was more in their case than they had supposed.[2] Vermin became a word that was uttered on the streets and towns and cities in England in the summer of 1948, especially in the Conservative held constituencies.

Attlee was personally hurt by Bevan's foolish words but could not, for a moment, listen to Churchill or anyone else. Though Bevan once mentioned he had asked to be Minister of Health in 1945, it is certain he would not have had the post were it not for Attlee. Overall, the Prime Minister was a great admirer of Aneurin Bevan and could not think of any other Cabinet member who would have succeeded as he had. Bevan had championed, his gift of compromising with his opponents highlighting his political talents. Throughout his life, Attlee continued to praise Bevan, the Minister, even after reading the first volume of Michael Foot's splendid biography which underlines a great deal of Bevan's contempt for Attlee. Attlee's verdict in his posthumous article was:

> I admired him greatly, to the extent that I believed he could be the natural leader of the Labour Party if one could be sure he could learn to keep his temper.[3]

But, as Attlee noted, Bevan's strengths and weaknesses were both equally evident.

---

1 Winston Churchill, *Observer*, 11 July 1948.
2 Lord Attlee, 'Bevan as Hero', *Observer*, 21 October 1962.
3 Kenneth Harris, *Attlee* (London, 1982), 425.

Strengths and weaknesses of the outstanding Minister of Health

Aneurin Bevan was an incredible visionary and idealist, but he lacked patience. He believed, erroneously, that people were not ready to fight in any war except a class war, failing to realise the Tories loved England above other UK countries and were determined to safeguard the privileges of their own affluent class and the establishment, including royalty and the House of Lords (and the pomp and ceremony that accompanied both).[1] Bevan's other weakness was his tendency to talk disparagingly of the founders of the Labour movement. Labour members who had been active and effective for generations, speaking on city street corners and taking leadership roles in the heavy industries long before Bevan ever joined the Labour Party were often dismissed by him. He was critical of pioneers like Clement Attlee, Ernest Bevin, Arthur Greenwood and Herbert Morrison, each of whom was treated unmercifully in Bevan's oratory. He forgot each politician had served the Labour Party week after week, day and night. as conscientiously as he himself had done. They had consecrated their time, energy and their ability to the Labour Party until it became their way of life. Aneurin Bevan's anger towards them was, at times, very extreme, unfair and sometimes shameful.

Bevan had always emphasised the value of introducing a UKwide National Health Service. He wanted to help people see better by providing spectacles to those with impaired sight, he wanted hearing aids for those who were hard of hearing and false teeth for people who had lost their own. All these was to be provided free of charge to anyone who needed help. In Parliament, Bevan said the condition of the teeth of ordinary British people dismayed him.[2]

A day to remember in British history

Bevan would never forget 5 July 1948 – the greatest day in the history of Britain for him. One man's vision and leadership had sparked a revolution. Over half a million people were working in the new National Health Service, both directly and as contractors. Only the British Coal Board and the Transport Commission had more employees. Of the workers, 360,000 were hospital staff, including 150,000 nurses and midwives. Another 200,000 people worked for the mental health service. In a short period of time, Aneurin Bevan had succeeded in preparing 3,100 hospitals

---

1 Lord Attlee, 'Bevan as Hero', *ibid, Observer,* 21 October 1962.
2 468.

with more than 550,000 beds. The National Health Service was a tribute to the millions who had lost their lives in two world wars. The British people had needed and deserved a better health service. Now they had one which brought together specialists, advisers, physicians, cardiac, orthopaedic and thoracic surgeons and a host of other medical professionals.[1] The verdict of historian Charles Webster in 2002 was:

> Indeed it is arguable the early NHS succeeded better than any of market-oriented models introduced under later governments in meeting basic health care objectives.[2]

By 1949, Aneurin Bevan and Jim Griffiths — more than any among their contemporaries — had succeeded in creating the most developed welfare state in the world.[3] These two exceptional Welshmen, ex-miners and students together in London, had performed a feat that will never be forgotten. The Swedish socialists followed Bevan's scheme. In April 1951, when the Prime Minister was ill in St. Mary's Hospital, Twickenham, Bevan and Gaitskell failed to show any discipline or respect for one another at a cabinet meeting.[4] Bevan remained on his well-known socialist territory, scoffing at the fact that financial considerations were going to betray the principle behind the NHS. Morrison reminded ministers that Attlee wanted them to try to compromise but, if that was not possible, the Chancellor would have the last word. Furthermore, if the Labour administration continued to be at loggerheads, the great danger would be a Tory victory. In such circumstances, neither Aneurin Bevan nor Hugh Gaitskell would have any influence at all. Bevan spoke saying that he was not at all surprised to hear the Prime Minister's attitude. Anyway, he was beginning to think that he would have more influence outside the Cabinet than inside it.[5] His intention now was to leave the Government within a few days after the Prime Minister came out of hospital. It was a big mistake. In the middle of this unpleasant row there came the news, on 14 April 1951, that Ernest Bevin had died.[6] On the 20 April Hugh Dalton went to see Attlee and who did he find around his bed but Herbert Morrison, Hugh Gaitskell and James Chuter Ede discussing Bevin's death and the probable resignation of the flamboyant Aneurin Bevan.

---

1 Parliamentary Debate in the House of Commons, 30 April 1948, *Hansard*, Vol 422, cc. 43–142.
2 Charles Webster, *The National Health Service: A Political History*, Oxford (second impression, 2002), 96, 148, 208, 214, 253, 258.
3 *Ibid*, 214.
4 *Ibid*, 142.
5 Cabinet Conclusions, 9th April 1951, Prem 8/1480.
6 *Ibid*.

Bevan resigns with Harold Wilson and John Freeman

After the three had left, the Prime Minister turned to Hugh Dalton and said that he had sent Bevan a final message and given him the choice either to accept the budget or tender his resignation. Attlee called Bevan a 'green-eyed monster' not words characteristic of the Labour leader, a well-known mediator.[1] Clearly, he had lost his patience with Bevan. He now expected him to resign, quite forgetting the force of the Welshman's charismatic nature. The resignation came on 22 April. Bevan published his resignation with two others, Harold Wilson, then a minister on the Board of Trade and John Freeman, the MP for Watford.[2] Wilson resigned so that he could feature on the national media's front pages alongside the mighty Bevan and thus build his reputation as a left winger. By the time he became a Prime Minister in 1964, Wilson was a centrist rather than a left winger. Attlee was weary and dismayed at the resignations, but managed to phone Alfred Robbins from his sickbed to ask him to take responsibility for the Department of Labour and National Service as Bevan's successor.[3]

A warm welcome in Blaenau Gwent for the conquering hero

In the wake of his election in Ebbw Vale, Aneurin Bevan had been given a hero's welcome. They knew that he had resigned on a principle, he was welcomed home to the glorious words of the Welsh hymn 'Guide Me, O Thou Great Jehovah' by William Williams, an indication that Welsh Nonconformity had not been entirely extinguished in Blaenau Gwent. Bevan's confidence was strengthened by his welcome and the voices of his fellow countrymen. He did not expect Attlee to accept his resignation in the same light as those who supported him back home .Bevan began running down his Labour critics. Bevan blamed Attlee, accusing him of a lack of faith and of revealing the contents of the Cabinet debate to the press. Though he had not previously brought the issue up in Cabinet, Bevan now accused Attlee of promising to spend profligately on rearmament after his meeting with Harry Truman, President of the United States. Attlee reminded his Cabinet, that Bevan was trying to retaliate for being out of the inner circle .

---

1 500.
2 *Ibid.*
3 Frances Williams, *A Prime Minister Remembers: The War and PostWar Memoirs of the Rt. Hon Earl Attlee* (London, 1961), 248. Attlee sent Bevan a letter on 21 April 1951.

Bevan upsets Attlee who is recovering from an illness

Unfortunately, at this time Aneurin Bevan did not have sufficient supporters among Labour MPs to challenge Attlee for the leadership. In Parliament, his resignation speech was ordinary enough. It lacked the characteristic flair of oratory that one would have expected. The faces of his fellow Labour members on 23 April 1950 tell the story in full. Bevan's resignation would have far-reaching implications and Attlee felt no relief about regaining his strength .He complained to his brother Tom at the end of April that 'the Bevan business is turning out to be the greatest nuisance. It's a miracle that we in the Cabinet have kept him on the straight and narrow so long.' He had hoped to have a chance to relax and rest in Chequers over Easter but the 'Bevan business' sapped him of all his energy. While Attlee gave his ministers the impression he was recovering, he confessed to his brother that his stomach was troubling him day and night. With Bevan's followers rushing about like predatory wolves, Attlee's government was unable to achieve much. Attlee tried to pacify Bevan, stressing that the cuts in the National Health Service would be for only two years, after which everything could be reviewed. The situation after the 1950 General Election had looked bleak; however, the Labour Government was able to remain in power with a small majority. There were difficult problems abroad, particularly in the Middle East. There, the nationalist government in Egypt was threatening to nationalise the Suez Canal and the government of Iran had actually nationalised the Anglo-Iran Oil Company. The loss of Ernest Bevin at the helm of the Foreign Office was keenly felt, particularly as his successor Herbert Morrison was so ineffective. Bevan could be compared to a roaring lion, awaiting his chance from the outset. Stafford Cripps was deteriorating with cancer and thus helpless to advise Attlee. Bevan was annoyed with his old friend and was glad that he had ensured it was Gaitskell who succeeded him in 1950 and not his Welsh colleague of almost twenty years.

Attlee fails to reconcile with Bevan

By the end of April 1951, the Labour Government was without its two important heroes. Ernest Bevin was dead and Aneurin Bevan was restless and rebelling. Attlee was the only one left of the top three and he struck a lonely political figure. He could not believe that anyone thought him a hero but in July, Attlee had a princely welcome from 30,000 Durham miners and their families.[1] However, by September,

---

1 *Ibid*, 502.

he was feeling depressed again, with his back extremely painful on top of all his other physical problems. According to his most recent biographer: He was still sulking at Bevan and refused to be the one to initiate a reconciliation.[1] As he said to Hugh Dalton:

> He walked out on me; it's up to him to come and see me if he wants to.[2]

The wise man was new in danger of behaving like a sulky child himself. His political predicament perhaps explains why he made the unwise choice to announce another General election in October 1951. Attlee was tired of politics and of being Prime Minister, but he was too stubborn to give up the leadership to someone younger like Aneurin Bevan. The truth was he favoured Bevan over Gaitskell. But as he said of Bevan:

> Nye had the leadership on a plate. I always wanted him to have the leadership. But, as you know, he wants to have two things at once, to be a rebel and a leader at the same time and you cannot do both.[3]

Attlee lost the 1951 General Election but had enough confidence to continue as Labour leader until 1955, despite colleagues like Hugh Dalton urging him to stand down in favour of the right wing protege Hugh Gaitskell Aneurin Bevan was the undoubted favourite of Labour activists, though the powerful trade union bosses were not so supportive of him.[4] Ultimately, Bevan was not sufficiently ambitious or meek spirited to praise and foster good relationships with the 'great ones of the movement'. Attlee concluded that Bevan, like a horse, worked better in harness. A leader of a political party has to suffer fools gladly. That is one thing that Bevan could not do.[5] Attlee read Bevan's character carefully and came to the conclusion that his early years under the Tory administration had damaged him emotionally to such an extent that he could not help himself hitting out at his own comrades constantly. Aneurin Bevan was never able to develop 'the sense of responsibility' which is essential for a successful political leader. Clement Attlee gave him an excellent opportunity in 1945 and Bevan responded by establishing a jewel in the crown of British government with the establishment of the National Health Service. Yet, despite his ambition to lead the Labour Party, Bevan ultimately squandered his

---

1 *Ibid*, 502–3.
2 *Ibid*, 505–6.
3 Ben Pimlott (ed.), *ibid*, entry for 4 September 1951, 533
4 Kenneth Harris, *Attlee*, 543.
5 Bevan showed more grace than he usually did in his tribute to Clement Attlee on his retirement as leader. See Aneurin Bevan, 'Clement Attlee', *Tribune*, 16 December 1955.

chances. But as Minister of Health he did achieve and perform brilliantly for four years despite the opposition he received from all sides. His critics were fierce and many, not because of his failures but because of his incredible success. Bevan succeeded in creating a social and medical revolution and in building civilised communities in cities which had been wrecked by German planes. He built adequate, solid family homes which are still standing and his National Health Service has been for over seventy years a source of national pride. Bevan's challenge was to transform a conservative society to accept a brilliant scheme . The United Kingdom was always unprepared to react to the most impressive visions .[1] He was ready to offer solutions to problems which continue today across the world, including rich countries. Bevan stood as a reformer, a visionary of socialism and a politician who could not be silenced or corrupted. He waited patiently for his opportunity and when it came, he did not waste the excellent opportunity to revolutionise society for the benefit of the whole population. His concern extended to everyone; old and young, rich and poor. Despite the Tories' intentions at times to privatise the NHS , Aneurin Bevan created the best universal health service possible which has stood the test of time.Some Labour MPs with medical backgrounds, like the surgeon Somerville Hastings, were disappointed that Aneurin Bevan had given in to the demands of the BMA. Others understood his need to compromise, recognising him as a supreme realist faced with a difficult situation.[2] The vast majority of doctors were not socialists and did not support the utopian scheme called the National Health Service. Bevan well understood the criticism but, as a compassionate and fair-minded man who stood firmly on the side of the poor and sick, he had no option. Bevan was constantly resented by the British Establishment and attacked mercilessly by populist newspapers like the *Daily Mail* and *Daily Express*,by radio commentators and right-wing politicians. Cledwyn Hughes, the Labour MP for Anglesey, knew Bevan well and spoke often to me of how he managed to overcome the unfair criticism.He did so by his healthy sense of humour.[3] Reverend Donald Soper, a socialist who regularly took the soapbox to Hyde Park , told the congregation in his London Methodist Church, Kingsway Hall, that the establishment of the National Health Service was the finest Christian political event of his age and indeed one of the most powerful Christian acts in British history.[4].

---

1 Lord Elwyn-Jones said of Bevan 'There he was a determined champion of Parliament as an institution and as the means by which democratic socialism could be achieved. The Health Service will remain his finest and lasting achievement.' See Lord Elwyn – Jones, *In My Time: An Autobiography* (London, 1983), 152.
2 Somerville Hastings, *Aneurin Bevan: an appreciation of his services to the Health of the People* (London, 1960).
3 Conversations when I met regularly with Cledwyn Hughes in Menai Bridge in 1974.
4 Address to the executive committee of the Christian socialist movement in Kingsway Chapel, Holborn, some time in 1963. I was a member of the executive committee.

Bevan and Jennie Lee

CHAPTER 10

Minister of Housing

Aneurin Bevan will be forever remembered for his radical, ambitious and popular feat of creating a massive ,new National Health Service. However, from 1945, his ministerial role meant he was also responsible for housing and local government. In fact, following the wide scale destruction of many towns and cities during the war, Bevan embarked upon a huge rebuilding programme to provide affordable houses for families.[1]

The need for houses

Roughly 280,000 houses were destroyed during the war and 250,000 were made uninhabitable by enemy bombs. Another 2.5 million were seriously damaged and required renovation. In 1945, there were 700,000 fewer houses than when war broke out. During a radio broadcast in March 1944, Churchill had spoken of plans, under the Ministry of Works, to build prefabricated homes called 'Portal houses' (named after Wyndham Portal, a Minister of Works). The original plan was to build these new homes with steel but this had to be abandoned as steel was needed elsewhere after the war.

---

1 The journalist Hanen Swaffer, who came to every National Eisteddfod of Wales when I was young, spoke these words after Bevan's speech on 17 October 1945: 'If he now builds the houses he is in direct line for the Premiership. If he does not, he is for the high jump.' See Michael Foot, *Aneurin Bevan, 1897–1960* (ed. Brian Brivati) (London, 1999), 259.

The influence of John Wheatley

Bevan wished to be remembered for building housing fit for the working classes. John Wheatley had been one of David Bevan's heroes in the first Labour Party Government.

Wheatley's Housing Act had greatly benefited the first MacDonald government. In the interwar years, despite high unemployment and the effects of the Depression, some enlightened local authorities like Liverpool and, in Wales, Newport and Wrexham, had embarked on large-scale housebuilding projects. Regrettably, the same thing did not happen in rural Wales, despite the fact that tuberculosis was spreading at an alarming rate because of the poor state of housing in the Welsh countryside. In 1939, an important report was issued under the chairmanship of Clement Davies, the Liberal MP for Montgomeryshire. The report was highly critical of local authorities, both for the condition of their housing and the pervasive mindset that nothing could be done to tackle tuberculosis. Bevan understood this approach and that is why he desired to build good quality, decent-sized homes as one of his priorities. In 1945, Richard Titmuss, the celebrated sociologist, prepared an important report for Luton.[1] In it, he called for the nationalisation of land and for local authorities in co-operation with central government to build extensively. For Titmuss, the plan would be called 'council housing'. These were houses built principally by local authorities for ordinary people who could not afford to buy their own houses. The family in the council house would pay a weekly rent to the local authority. The ideal was to have the same facilities in council housing as in private housing; in some towns, council housing went back to John Wheatley's vision in the 1920's. Aneurin Bevan's policy was to support and greatly increase the number of council houses being built by local authorities rather than to focus on private housebuilding. He was so successful that by the 1960s, one in three houses in Britain was in the hands of a local authority.

---

1 This is the conclusion of Titmuss's report: 'There is evidence that the country is moving towards a wide acceptance of the principle that services provided by the people for themselves through the medium of central and local government shall compare in standard with those provided by private enterprise. As it is with hospitals and clinics, so should it be with schools and houses. The council house should in the future provide the amenities, space and surroundings which hitherto have often been the monopoly of private building.' See David Kynaston, *Austerity Britain 1945–1951*

Determination against the odds

The main criticism of Bevan's scheme comes from Alison Ravetz, who regretted that local government had become such large-scale housing providers.[1] In her view, the massive and rapid increase in post-war council housing had given local authorities a great deal of power, creating unchallengeable landlords who could often be indifferent to their tenants' complaints. She regretted that Bevan and the Labour Party had not considered establishing agencies, as for example . housing associations and cooperative groups, to oversee the schemes. For Bevan, the most important ingredient was that the houses should be well constructed and of a high overall standard. He viewed prefabs with disdain dimly, referring to them as 'rabbit hutches'.[2] His vision was to provide families with solid twostorey houses with a toilet on each floor so they wouldn't have to go downstairs at night (or upstairs during the day).[3] He encouraged builders to enlarge the living area of the new houses from 750 to 900 square feet. Aneurin Bevan realised his success, or otherwise, would be assessed by the number of houses that were built during the first two years of his time as a minister . Thereafter, it would be the quality of construction and type of house that people would judge.

Importance of the communities

Living in Tredegar had taught Bevan the importance of diverse communities, where people with the working-class occupations lived alongside the middle-classes, where different income groups mixed freely. He feared the massive post-war rebuilding programme was creating 'colonies' whereby low-income people were living in well-constructed council houses and, a mile or two away, those on higher incomes occupied private housing. This was not what Bevan wanted at all. As he said:

> This is a wholly evil thing, from a civilised point of view . . . It is a monstrous infliction upon the essential psychological and biological oneness of the community.[4]

---

1 *Ibid.* 155, See Alison Ravetz, 'Housing the People', in Fyrth (ed.), *Labour's Promised Land* (London, 1995), 160–165.
2 *Ibid.*
3 *Ibid.* He said, 'We shall be judged for a year or two by the *number* of houses we build. We shall be judged in ten years' time by the *type* of houses we build.'
4 *Ibid.*

Bevan's ideal reflected the reality of Tredegar, where people from different income groups lived in the same street and mixed with each other like brothers and sisters. This was true of mining and quarrying villages in Wales and in England, where a row of labourers' cottages might be next to the butcher's shop, and the village doctor lived among his patients.[1]

Difficult to reach the target

I must admit that it can be difficult to understand exactly what Aneurin Bevan's vision was when it came to establishing new communities. Did he want the family doctor to move into a council house or did he want to restrict the number of council houses being built in those areas with a higher level of home ownership. Whatever he intended, he had a mammoth task ahead of him as not all local authorities took house building seriously. It is hard to believe it was the city of Hull that built most houses during Bevan's first ministerial term, 79 properties compared to just 35 in Birmingham. It was a sad situation, highlighting the dire situation the housebuilding industry found itself in. The war had a huge impact on the country's finances and the UK now found itself in a difficult economic situation.[2] All Bevan wanted was for a decent home to be available to rent for every family that wanted one, something which had never previously been the case. Despite the post-war downturn, Bevan was never one to back away from a challenge. By 1950, his housing record was praise-worthy: 623,347 houses had been built, 157,145 of them temporary abodes, while 420,000 properties had been rebuilt after being destroyed in the Blitz.[3] At the end of October 1945, Bevan spoke strong words to the Council of the Building Congress.[4] He viewed the building industry as a sick man without the means of recovery. The industry, which had often been in trouble, was now without the financial resources to fulfil the great task of rebuilding Britain. Bevan spoke of his wish to see rural properties brought up to the standards of houses in towns.[5] He faced an enormous task, not least because there was no-one available to build them. There was a real

---

1 Brian Lund, *Housing Problems and Housing Policy* (Harlow, 1996) 41; Nicholas Timmins, *Five Giants* (London, 2001), 145; Kynaston, *ibid*, 165; Steven Fielding, *England Arise!* (Manchester, 1995), 103–104
2 Aneurin Bevan, 'Cinemas or Houses?', *Coventry Evening Telegraph,* 10 February 1950, 6.
3 *Ibid.* See Nicklaus Thomas-Symonds, *Nye: the Political Life of Aneurin Bevan* (London and New York, 2015), 158–159.
4 'Aneurin Bevan Won't be Orthodox', *Gloucester Citizen,* 1 November 1949, 8.
5 'Aneurin Bevan, Housing Need for 100,000 Extra Farm Workers', *Coventry Evening Telegraph,* 3 March 1946, 1. He was critical of the English middle class: 'The middle class in England had always been the source of social ugliness, inflicting on us appalling architecture so that many of our housing estates looked like railway sidings. In future they must try to arrange their homes in groups of 4, 6 or 10, where they suited each other.'

need for local authorities to employ enough dependable and capable workers. The estimates coming in from many of the house-building companies were far too high, in part because they had no way of calculating the exact cost of materials and the wages of the tradesmen and labourers. Bevan realised that building the number of houses required by government's long-term commitment was a huge requirement. By 1948 onal Health Service a resounding success, he was able to announce that the Department of Housing had succeeded in providing 750,000 additional houses since the end of the Second World War. About half of them were permanent homes, while others were temporary, including the prefabricated houses Bevan hated. Large housing estates sprang up in cities like Liverpool and redundant properties, including factories, were adapted to provide flats. Yet, despite all the building going on, there were still insufficient housing for the British people.

The need for houses was disturbing Bevan

By the mid-forties, the housing shortfall had reached millions and the large-scale clearance of slums in cities like Glasgow, Liverpool and London had yet to begin. In the London borough of Willesden, social surveys held in 1946 and 1947 revealed that at least 61% of residents were unhappy with their rapidly deteriorating and often over-crowded terraced housing.[1] The primitive conditions and significant lack of privacy people were suffering bothered politicians, Aneurin Bevan in particular. Many of those interviewed were very keen to leave London or to move to better housing on the outskirts of the city.[2]

Immigrants needed housing

Aneurin Bevan was unable to build anything like the three hundred thousand houses a year he wanted. Resources were scarce and he was not prepared to lower building standards or build tiny matchbox-sized houses. There was additional pressure on housing from the many immigrant workers who were persuaded to move to the UK from India, the Caribbean and other Commonwealth countries to meet post-war need. One such family was that of seven-year-old Harry Webb (later to find success as the singer Cliff Richard) who left India with his parents and three sisters for Carshalton, England in 1948. The Webb family lived in one room where they prepared their food, lived and slept. After a year, things became so intolerable they

---

1 Bertram Hutchinson, *Willesden and the New Towns* (1947), Parts III and VII; *The Times*, 7 March 1946; Patrick Dunleavy, *The Politics of Mass Housing in Britain*, 1945–1975 (Oxford, 1981), 229.
2 Kynaston, *ibid,* 157.

moved in with one of Cliff's aunts, before eventually being offered a council house in Cheshunt.[1] Though they were invited to come to the UK, the number of immigrants arriving put additional pressure on housing. Then there was the issue of the slums. During the war, many people had moved out of their atrocious city-centre homes, another reason for Bevan to increase his ambitious programme of public housing. His solution to the distinct problem of London's slums was to build fourteen new towns, more than half of which were within reach of London, i.e. Stevenage, Crawley, Hemel Hempstead, Harlow, Hatfield, Welwyn Garden City, Basildon and Bracknell. Farther afield were Corby in Northamptonshire and Newton Aycliffe and Peterlee in the north-east of England.[2] Peterlee primarily provided housing for the miners from the Durham coalfield and was named after Peter Lee, one of the colourful miners' leaders. Two new towns were planned for Scotland: East Kilbride and Glenrothes.[3] There was only one new town proposed for Wales: Cwmbrân, in Monmouthshire, not too far from Tredegar. A Department of Town and Country Planning was set up, with Lewis Silkin appointed as the minister who would work alongside Bevan on his ambitious plans.

Bevan tours the country

The need for better and more housing preoccupied Aneurin Bevan and he made it his business to travel the breadth of the country visiting the new housing estates which were meeting a dire need in the lives of so many people. On one occasion, he returned home grief-stricken: his faithful chauffeur had suffered a heart attack and died within days. Jennie Lee was wise when she asked her husband, 'was he working too hard?' One of Bevan's chief officers in the Housing Department had a nervous breakdown and Bevan himself became seriously ill from the constant travel and heavy workload. His bout of flu turned into pneumonia and he was treated by Sir Daniel Davies and John Buchan.[4] Jennie's mother looked after him by day and Jennie by night. His wife worried constantly about him, particularly his distressed breathing in the early hours of the morning. But Bevan pulled through and took up his duties again, making sure he arrived at his desk each morning by nine o'clock at the latest.[5]

---

1 *Ibid*, 330–1.
2 See Gary Phillipson, *Aycliffe and Peterlee New Town* (Cambridge, 1988).
3 Meryl Aldridge, *The British New Towns* (London, 1979).
4 *Western Daily Press,* 4 March 1947, 4. This paper says he is cancelling every commitment for a time. The Derby town newspaper speaks of his illness in March 1949. He was in bed with a dangerously high temperature but got up on 19 March. See *Derby Daily Telegraph*, 10 March 1949, 5.
5 Jennie Lee, *ibid,* 158–9.

Ministerial responsibilities

As a government minister, Aneurin Bevan had wide-ranging responsibilities which took a physical and emotional toll on his health. As well as health services, he had to keep an eye on the Department of Town and Country Planning, the Board of Trade and local government administration, not to mention his huge housing remit.

In *Why Not Trust the Tories*, Bevan devotes the fifth chapter to housing. The issues discussed in 'Will you get that house?' featured heavily in his 1945 General Election campaign.[1] The chapter references what had been achieved by governments in the interwar period and raised his concerns that private builders had created a dire housing situation. He writes:Between the two wars, private enterprise produced a shocking state of affairs. The population was distributed in a most lop-sided fashion.[2]For Tories, private development always took priority over the needs of the community. And when the local authorities started to push for action, the Coalition Government's tactic was to establish a Royal Commission and more committees to deal with the crisis. After having published these reports, the Tories then conveniently forgot all the recommendations. When the Uthwatt Committee's report was published, many an MP, like Ronw Moelwyn-Hughes, the Labour MP for Carmarthen, asked searching questions about its contents.[3] Indeed, on 21 October 1943, thirteen leaders of bombed cities wrote a letter to *The Times* calling for the publication of the plans and expressing concern that the local authorities were failing to make decisions because of the tardiness of the coalition government.[4] The Uthwatt Committee favoured the nationalisation of land, some sort of tax, but the matter was ignored by Churchill's coalition government. The report served as first-class propaganda for Labour, highlighting as it did the Conservatives' obsession with making profits. Bevan warned the British public: If you vote for the Tories in the next election, you are actually voting against your hope of getting a house in the place where you want it and at a reasonable price. Remember this next time you and your family are talking about your ideal house.[5]Bevan knew exactly the kind housebuilding programme he wanted, but legislation was required if he were to succeed. Arthur Greenwood leant on him to do as much as he could before Christmas 1945. But, as with the National Health Service, Bevan had to stand up

---

1 *Celticus* (Aneurin Bevan, MP), *Why Not Trust the Tories* (London, 1944), 1–89.
2 *Ibid*, 66.
3 *Ibid*, 68.
4 *Ibid*, 69. The towns which experienced widespread destruction in Wales were Swansea and Cardiff, while in England, Plymouth, Sheffield, Norwich, Southampton, Portsmouth, Birkenhead, Bootle, Liverpool, Wallasey, Exeter, Coventry, Salford, Bristol and London experienced the worst German bombing.
5 *Ibid*, 78.

to Herbert Morrison on the issue of the freedom of local authorities to build. There were other pressures too, including financial ones. Still more troublesome, the wood ordered from Sweden or Germany was not coming to the builders.[1] The subject was thoroughly discussed and especially the need to persuade a Scandinavian country such as Sweden to sell Britain the timber needed for building new houses. This was the message of Bevan to the Cabinet on 23 January 1946. Despite frequent discussion, the shortage of timber remained an issue. Stafford Cripps had prepared an important memorandum stressing the need for timber with the possibility of getting it from Germany.[2] Bevan suggested to Cripps, the President of the Board of Trade, that they should link up with Edvard Kardell, the Deputy Prime Minister of Yugoslavia, as there was the possibility of setting up a sawmill there. There was even talk of obtaining timber from Romania, Finland or Russia. But the wheels turned slowly as Bevan lamented in Cabinet on 6 May 1946. The local authorities had only provided 741 new houses , had repaired another 2,570 while 790 had been built by the licence provided by his department .Thousands of new houses were to be built being built while 78,224 properties damaged during wartime needed urgent attention . were rebuilt.[3] It transpired that Stafford Cripps had misled them in the Cabinet with his talk of getting suitable timber from Germany. The British-ruled region of the country was itself very short of timber. Angry at having been misled, Bevan prepared his own memorandum for the Cabinet sitting on 17 July 1946. He regretted that prices had risen and that timber was so scarce. It was impossible to build houses without timber but they should not depend upon Germany. It would have to be Russia. Bevan's words added fuel to the flame. Two Cabinet members prepared their own documents. Cripps was vociferous and spoke of perhaps buying timber from Canada or Russia, or maybe even Germany, Sweden or Finland, although it was clear he had not spoken with timber merchants in those countries. John Hynd, a high-ranking officer of the National Union of Railwaymen, was pessimistic but more realistic. He thought it just as unlikely for Britain to be able to buy timber from Austria as it was from Germany.[4] .Bevan continued to raise serious matters at Cabinet, speaking forcefully on 25 July 1946 and again on 8 November. He knew he had no control over the lack of timber in the building world and looked for a temporary solution. In Cabinet on 10 December, he vowed to reach his target of building 240,000 houses in 1947. Unfortunately, the lack of timber kept his programme in abeyance.

---

1 Nicklaus Thomas-Symonds, *Nye, ibid*, 154.
2 *Ibid*, 154–5.
3 *Ibid*, 155. Based on Prem 8/226, CP (46), 417, *Timber for Housing: Memorandum by the Minister of Health*, 8 November 1946.
4 '*Ibid,* 156. John Hynd, Chancellor of the Duchy of Lancaster, pointed out that the British zone was the least forested of the German occupation zones.

Bevan and the establishment of the new State of Israel

Despite all his domestic responsibilities, Bevan took a natural interest in the fate of the Jewish people who had escaped the Holocaust and fled to Palestine. Along with his Cabinet colleagues Stafford Cripps, Herbert Morrison, Hugh Dalton, and Hugh Gaitskell, Bevan was extremely sympathetic to the idea of establishing the State of Israel in 1947. The five MPs divided into two groups. The first, under the leadership of Herbert Morrison, supported the State of Israel, with Jews and Palestinians living alongside one another and a peacekeeper role for the United Nations. The second group, under the leadership of Aneurin Bevan, argued for dividing Palestine into two separate countries.[1] Bevan believed there was no hope of the Jews and Palestinians living in harmony. David BenGurion, the leader of the Jewish community in Palestine, knew as well as anyone that Aneurin Bevan was one of his main supporters in the British government. Foreign Secretary Ernest Bevin was not particularly sensitive to the issue and believed the United States should give leadership instead of sitting on the fence. Clement Attlee was much of the same view. After discussion, the US President, Harry Truman, agreed that permits should be issued to a hundred thousand European Jews enabling them to emigrate to Palestine, the first step towards the creation of a state for the Jewish people. It was a most delicate issue In March 1946 a number of Americans and British politicians visited Palestine. They published a report which encouraged refuges from warn torn Europe to emigrate at once .Bevan kept quiet while his friend Ben -Gurion called for violent action immediately.[2] The Jewish flag would be seen in Negev, then Galilee and to the north of Haifa down to Gaza. Palestine would be able to fly its flag over the west bank of the River Jordan, the Gaza Strip and the border area between Egypt and Sinai. But, as we know, the plan Bevan approved did not come to pass and we still await peace between the Jews and Palestinians.

Aneurin Bevan's relationship with top civil servants

Aneurin had an excellent relationship with the Permanent Secretary Sir William Douglas and the Deputy Secretary Sir John Wrigley, the man who was in charge of the house-building programme under Bevan's guidance.[3] They backed his plans completely and were delighted that by 1947 284,230 permanent houses had been built. They believed it would be possible to reach the 300,000 figure demanded by

---
1 Joseph Corney, *The British Labour Movement and Zionism, 1917–1948* (London, 1983), 214–221.
2 Dan Kurzman, *Ben-Gurion, Prophet of Fire*, New York, 1983), 264.
3 .*Ibid*, 265. This book gives a particularly memorable account of the tension and conflict.

the Tories by 1948. But unfortunately because of shortage of material, in particular timber as well as land , they would have to settle for the building of 200, 000 instead of the initial 300,000 .The Treasury and the Prime Minister intervened [1] Bevan was extremely angry at the goal of two hundred thousand new housed in Britain in a year and threatened to resign from the Cabinet. Since his ministerial appointment, he had battled over almost everything and faced constraints the public was unaware of. Sir John Wrigley told him:

> Minister, if we build more than 200,000 houses, I'll be sacked by the Chancellor, and if we build less [sic] I'll be sacked by you.[2]

Bevan understood the country's poor economic situation meant he would need to make cuts in various departments, but maintained the priorities of his coministers were shameful.

Bevan and local government

It should be remembered that Bevan was also responsible for local authorities. In fact, he had a lot of admiration for the councillors and leaders of district, county and metropolitan councils. In 1945, the coalition government appointed a well-known barrister, Sir Malcolm Eve, to chair a commission to look at local government structure.[3] Two years later, the report of the Local Government Boundary Commission was published. The commission argued that the government should create new county councils with 200,000 people within each.[4] Bevan did not agree with the recommendation, believing the unit size was too big. To him, local authorities needed to be close to communities to know what was happening within them. In spring 1949, Bevan sought ministerial backing to establish a Royal Commission on local authority reform. In his inimitable way, Morrison ensured Bevan did not get his way and the proposal was buried without ceremony. The original commission was dissolved by special legislation in 1949 and Bevan set about preparing his own plan for local authorities. Remembering the 1947 report, he suggested establishing 300 local authorities which would vary greatly in size: some would cover just 50,000 residents while another might serve a million. This time his plan was

---

1 . Jennie Lee, *ibid,* 158.
2 *Ibid.*
3 *Ibid,* 159–60.
4 Nicklaus Thomas-Symonds, *Nye, ibid,* 160.

opposed by James Chuter Ede.[1] Ede was not ready to turn his back on the existing structure, which had been so effective, with parish councils at the most local level, town councils covering towns and districts, and the larger county councils and boroughs overseeing much bigger populations.[2] Most people, in England and Wales anyway, liked this system of local government and would vote for it if asked. Ede recognised there was no need to act on Bevan's plan as the Labour Party would have to fight an election soon.

A word on the 'vermin clubs'

By the time of the 1950 General Election, Aneurin Bevan was one of the Labour Party's main attractions, a speaker to rival Winston Churchill. However, it was his address when he launched the National Health Service that remained in the memories of Conservative Party candidates and leaders. By now, scores of 'vermin clubs' existed and their vociferous members came to public meetings and shouted 'vermin, vermin' during Bevan's speeches. Michael Foot devotes plenty of material in his biography to the attacks on Bevan; excrement was posted in envelopes to his home in Cliveden Place.[3] In the run up to the 3 February election, Bevan travelled countrywide, speaking at as many meetings as possible. He addressed voters in his wife's constituency in Cannock and spoke in Devonport where Michael Foot was standing. Towards the end of the campaign, he addressed a meeting at Waun Pound, on the mountain between Ebbw Vale and Tredegar, safe in the knowledge he could speak his mind about the Labour government without risk of losing support. For a long time, Bevan had had only one political opponent: Graeme Finlay, a native of Monmouthshire and a barrister who had represented the Tory Party since 1946. The UK electorate delivered a swinging blow to the Labour Party, which saw its majority fall from 152 to 6. In Bevan's opinion, his party deserved a fifty-seat majority for creating such a unique National Health Service. The energetic Bevan was close to achieving his targets for the service, despite continued opposition from others in the Labour Cabinet.

---

1 Nirmala Rao and Ken Young, *Local Government Since 1945, Making Contemporary Britain* (Oxford, 1997), 91.
2 Nicklaus Thomas-Symonds, *ibid,* 160; Rao and Young, *Local Government Since 1945*, 96–101.
3 Foot has a whole chapter under the title "Vermin" See Michael Foot, *Aneurin Bevan* (London, 1999), 362–376.

Congratulating Bevan as Minister of Housing and Health

At the 1950 Annual British Labour Party Conference, Aneurin Bevan was congratulated on his pioneering achievements in housing and health. Britain had built more houses in five years than any other country in mainland Europe. Yet, despite the success of local authority house-building departments compared to private developers – who only built 27,863 houses between 1945 and 1947 – Bevan continued to oppose the idea of nationalising the building industry. He also praised local authority housing departments – including those run by Conservative administrations – for rebuilding bombed properties and creating comfortable homes for families.

The 1950 General Election

The results of the Ebbw Vale constituency brought huge satisfaction to Bevan, his agent and his canvassers considering the dismal results throughout Britain 656:

Aneurin Bevan (Labour)	28,245 (80.7%) +0.6
Graeme Finlay (Conservative)	6,745 (19.3) –0.6
Majority	21,500 (61.4%) +12

The turnout in Ebbw Vale was 34,990, representing 86.7% of the population (4.1% greater than in 1945). At least 80.7% of the electorate supported Aneurin Bevan. The results demonstrated that Bevan's work as a Minister of the Crown was much appreciated by his own people in Blaenau Gwent.

CHAPTER 11

A brave stand and socialist ideas

Aneurin Bevan was very satisfied with what the Labour Government had achieved between 1945 and 1950 but he and his co-ministers were under huge strain. As Bevan himself noted, the Labour government was not comfortable carrying on the vision that Bevan propagated [1] At the Blackpool Conference on 6 June 1949, Morrison and Bevan were in conflict, primarily because Bevan wished to push forward with more nationalisation. Eight months later, Bevan missed the first cabinet meeting after the election due to ill health on 25 February. In his absence, ministers agreed not to enact any previously agreed legislation if there was any danger of angering the opposition. When Bevan returned, he argued strongly that they were losing a golden opportunity to effect change and persuaded ministers to at least consider the nationalisation of the steel industry, something which was very important to his electorate in Ebbw Vale. His plea went unheard and the King's Speech was unambitious, leaving Bevan very discomfited. John Campbell, editor of the Communist daily paper, the *Daily Worker*, described him as 'rumbling like a volcano'.[2]

---

1 David Marquand described Bevan thus: 'If we want to understand Bevan we should see him, not as a philosophical Marxist but a wonderfully articulate, though distinctly opportunistic, dissenting radical dressed sporadically and unconvincingly in Marxist clothes.' See David Marquand, *The Progressive Dilemma: From Lloyd George to Kinnock* (London, 1991), 121.
2 John Ross Campbell (1894–1969) was prominent as the editor of the *Daily Worker* in 1939 and again from 1949 to 1959. He stood for the Communist Party in the Ogmore constituency in Wales in the 1929 and 1931 General Elections as well as in the 1931 by-election.

Bevan has no time for the 'hard left' and has his doubts with the 'soft left '

Aneurin Bevan was fed up with the conservatism of some of his Cabinet colleagues, yet he was also critical of members of those on the hard left, chiefly Konni Zilliacus (MP for Gateshead), J. F. Platts Mills (MP for Finsbury), Leslie Solley (MP for Thurnock), Leslie Hutchinson (MP for Rusholme, Manchester) and Geoffrey Bing (MP for Hornchurch).[1] With Bevan's blessing, most of them were expelled from the Labour Party in 1949, creating outside the Labour Party the Independent Labour Group. A number of other socialist groups came into existence within the Labour Party at the time, one of which was called Keep Left. The members were mainly Bevan's friends, fifteen hard working MPs who enjoyed promoting the viewpoint of the traditional left and regarded Bevan as the most interesting intellectual of all Labour intellectuals . He was like no other. Richard Crossman was a keen member of Keep Left, while Anthony Crossman, who discussed socialist ideas for the fifties was in favour of revisionism. So was Evan Durbin and Hugh Gaitskell, a pair of socialist eggheads who had shone at Oxford University. Bevan's support from these men was down to his charisma and mesmeric personality. Despite this, Richard Crossman quietly believed Bevan got into unnecessary political brawls due to his political naiveté. The côterie of Labour intellectuals around Bevan provided constant support and became known as Bevanites. Like him, they had no time towards the right wing of the Labour Party. Neither Bevan nor his supporters gave way to the right's opinions. Andrew Thorpe explains it thus:

> Bevan was not anti-intellectual: far from it. In the sense of having a questioning and open mind, looking for new solutions and being receptive to new ideas, he was more of an intellectual than Gaitskell himself.[2]

So why were those followers of Aneurin Bevan known as Bevanites? They were just MPs who admired the man, believed in socialism and had nationalisation at the heart of their philosophy. Bevan believed nationalisation was not only a tool 'to create a more egalitarian society but a necessity'. He argued that the socialist realised that parliamentary strength can be used to increase the extent that all economic resources

---

1 Martin Shipton, *Political Chameleon: In Search of George Thomas* (Cardiff, 2017), 40–43. It is clear that George Thomas had been on the edges of the hard left linked to Konni Zilliacus. In the papers of Huw T Edwards, deposited in the National Library of Wales, one has a file A1/18 which deals with correspondence between Konni Zilliacus and Aneurin Bevan.

2 Andrew Thorpe, *A History of the British Labour Party* (Basingstoke, 200), 122.

come under public regulation.[1] Evan Durbin was for the most part in agreement with Bevan; however, Anthony Crosland opposed nationalising all industry.[2] One of the most prominent Bevanites was another Oxford graduate, Harold Wilson. He had nowhere near such a magnetic personality as Bevan but enjoyed his position as a scholarly follower and a rebel. Richard Crossman's biographer believed that Wilson turned out a far better leader than Bevan would have ever been and was able to deal effectively with difficult Cabinet members like George Brown and Willie Ross.[3]

Attlee has second doubts about Bevan's ministerial career.

Attlee did not think of moving Aneurin Bevan from his unique ministerial post until February 1950. The original intention was to offer Bevan the post of Secretary of State for the Colonies, a position Jim Griffiths came to enjoy.[4] But the Prime Minister changed his mind, fearing Bevan would be too much of a risk. He was likely to side with local leaders in the Colonies who were demanding independence – he knew many of them personally and they admired him. For example, Attlee knew Bevan had more to say about political nationalism in Kenya than in Wales itself. As previously acknowledged, Attlee had been inspired when he asked Bevan to be his Minister of Health and Housing in 1945; however, by 1950, the political situation had changed. Bevan was hoping to move to the Foreign Office – he knew as much about foreign affairs as anyone else in government – but Attlee did not offer him that opportunity. Instead, he invited Bevan to become the Minister of Labour and National Service. Bevan- always the sincere socialist – was sorely disappointed and could not understand Attlee's decision. He remained the Labour Party hero in the constituencies, which viewed the weekly magazine *Tribune* as the voice of conscience. Attlee could have been resentful of the Welsh voice from Tredegar that was heard in every conference, mass meetings and within the Cabinet. Furthermore he severley criticised the Labour government on their attitude to the Cold War and the issue of the Middle East. He became an opponent of the Soviet Union and confided to many his disappointment at the establishment of the North Atlantic Treaty Organisation (NATO) to protect the West from the threats of Russia and the forces of Communism.[5] The founding members were America, Britain,

---

1 Aneurin Bevan, *In Place of Fear* (London, 1952), 31.
2 Victoria Honeyman, *ibid*, 50.
3 *Ibid*, 42.
4 D. Ben Rees, *Arwr Glew y Werin* (Talybont, 2014), 162–174, as well as in the English biography. See D Ben Rees, *Jim: The life and work of the RT Hon. James Griffiths: A hero of the Welsh nation and architect of the welfare state* (Liverpool 2020), 167–180.
5 Emyr Price, *Cymru a'r Byd Modern ers 1918* (Wales and the Modern World since 1918) (Cardiff, 1979), 85.

France, the Netherlands, Belgium, Luxembourg, Norway, Denmark, Iceland, Italy, Portugal and Canada. Turkey and Greece became members in 1952 and, in 1955, West Germany joined the military body.

Bevan has his doubts about Joseph Stalin

By 1955, Bevan had strong views on the need to safeguard Britain militarily in the context of Stalin and his determination in pursuing Soviet domination .He was quite ready to see British tanks moving through the Russian sector to liberate West Berlin and teach a lesson to its Communist administration. On 24 June 1948, Joseph Stalin had broken transport links between his sector of Berlin and the sectors held by the Western Allies by closing every road and railway into the city. His actions meant essential goods could not be transported to the residents of West Berlin. Neither could Russian families living in West Berlin travel to the Russian sector of the city.

The situation nearly turned into another nasty armed dispute. Bevan agreed with the immediate decision of America and the Western Allies to fly food into Berlin. The freight planes were CD-3 Dakotas and for nine months the pilots flew by day and night.[1] The Berlin Airlift succeeded and Stalin was forced to yield. The Attlee government was determined to co-operate with France and America to safeguard Germany from Stalin's madness. In 1949, the Western Allies united their sectors to create the state of West Germany. It was given the name of the Federal Republic of Germany, namely West Germany by the Chancellor Dr. Konrad Adenauer. As expected, Stalin reacted by establishing the German Democratic Republic and appointing Walter Ulbricht – a 'yes man' with hard-line communist credentials - as the new leader of East Germany. In his foreword to Denis Healey's book *The Curtain Falls*, published in 1951, Bevan attacked Russia for destroying what was left of democracy in Eastern Europe.[2] That is why many historians have maintained that, had Attlee chosen him as Foreign Secretary (a post he deserved), Aneurin Bevan would have astonished everyone. Certainly, he would have stood with courage as an anti-communist leader and he would have pleased the right wing in the Tory press and in Parliament.[3] While this can be difficult to believe this in the light of Bevan's many stances during the 1950s, I can see the validity of this observation. Bevan more or less took the same position as the American stratgeist George Kennan did on Russia.

---

1 *Ibid*, 84.
2 There is an important study of Healey in Williams and Bruce Reed, *Denis Healey and the Policies of Power* (London, 1971).
3 Kenneth O. Morgan, *Labour People: Leaders and Lieutenants, Hardie to Kinnock* (Oxford, 1987), 212

A fiery colleague

Aneurin Bevan remained a fiery colleague throughout 1949, 1950 and 1951. He continued to argue for the nationalisation of the steel industry –a sign of his socialist zeal – and was surprised to win the support of Hugh Dalton. He protested louder than anyone about the cuts in the house-building programme and, on more than one occasion, warned Cabinet colleagues he was ready to resign as a minister on a matter of principle if there was any unfavourable interference with the National Health Service. Despite his personal disappointment, Bevan supported Labour policy that was decided upon at a meeting in Dorking in May 1950. Under increasing pressure from the Treasury, he propagated the Butler- Gaitskell approach of the mixed economy and focused on improving the image of those industries which had been nationalised. Bevan was proud of the nationalisation of the coal industry in 1946 when the National Coal Board was formed.[1] In the same year, there was further nationalisation of the passenger aircraft industry and the transport industry. British Railways, the waterways and heavy goods lorries were then nationalised. The National Health Service was launched in 1948 and the electricity industry was eventually nationalised a decade later . But then on 24 November 1949 the steel industry was nationalised but then to Bevan's regret denationalised by the Tories in 1951

The Welshman is disillusioned with Hugh Gaitskell

Bevan was unable at most times to compromise with Hugh Gaitskell. Bevan was extremely disappointed that Attlee, his deputy Herbert Morrison and the majority of the Cabinet were all in favour of Gaitskell. They were all in favour of his appointment as Chancellor of the Exchequer following Cripps' resignation. One can understand Bevan's deep disappointment at being ignored for promotion after creating an unmatched National Health Service as Minister for Health and Housing. In Bevan's opinion, Gaitskell did not deserve the post of Chancellor for he was, in

---

1 There was acceptance of nationalising the coal industry in South Wales as is seen in the reaction of Emlyn Williams (1921–1995) of Aberdare. He said, 'In 1947 the coal industry was nationalised. Williams was sceptical from the beginning about the extent to which the mines really were now "owned by the people", remaining so all his life.' He later commented that 'I would rather have seen socialisation than nationalisation . . . But if you ask me truthfully if I regretted nationalisation – no, never did nationalisation bring the miners together and the betterment of the mines was a result of the pressure within the unions within the nationalised industry.' See Ben Curtis, 'Emlyn Williams (1921–1995), Miners' Leader' [in] *Dictionary of Labour Biography,* Vol XIV (eds. Keith Gildart and David Howell) (London, 2018), 289–296; see the quotation on page 290.

his own words, 'nothing, nothing, nothing.'[1] By the winter of 1950–51, the Labour Party was experiencing the internal discord which would ultimately result in a decade of political wilderness.

Not Minister for Foreign Affairs but Minister of Labour for Bevan

The Minister of Labour post proved a bed of nails for Bevan; within his first three months he had crossed swords with several trade union leaders. As early as 1 August 1950, he had made it clear he was against a £350m defence programme which was expected by the Americans. The Korean War (1950–1951) was underway, with fierce fighting between North Korea, backed by Russia and China, and South Korea, defended by America, Britain and its allies. There was no victor in the conflict and an armistice agreement was finally signed in 1953. Bevan was right in saying the Labour government should have had second thoughts in entering the conflict on the insistence of the White House . Bevan's constant antagonism towards Labour government decisions is undoubtedly why Attlee, Morrison and Gaitskell would be glad to see him returning to the political wilderness. Emanuel Shinwell, Patrick Gordon Walker, Hugh Dalton and a few other well known politicians who were ready to misunderstand the Titan of British politics. Ernest Bevin, whose health was rapidly failing, and the ageing Christopher Addison realised that the Labour cabinet was on the point of losing its most charismatic politician.[2] They were right, Bevan resigned on 22 April 1951, his talent once more lost to the Labour executive. The final straw for Bevan was when Hugh Gaitskell wanted to reduce the National Health Service budget – forcing people to pay for their false teeth and glasses –in order to buy more arms for the to Korean conflict . Bevan resisted fiercely within the Cabinet but Gaitskell would not give an inch.[3] The cabinet could have rejected this proposal but it did not. Bevan's resignation was also accepted without argument.

Jim Griffiths agreed with Bevan's standpoint but did not feel anyone should resign over the Chancellor's policy. To the contrary, Harold Wilson (Chairman of the Board of Trade) and John Freeman (Minister for the Administration) agreed that the introduction of NHS charges was a resigning issue. Both of them stood down from their cabinet posts. Bevan's was afraid that the UK and USA arms programme would undermine the British economy, create massive unemployment and lower the

---

1 Kenneth O. Morgan, *Labour People, ibid.* 213.
2 *Ibid,* 214
3 Ralph Miliband says in *Parliamentary Socialism* (London, 1964), 296 that this action was the catalyst which led to organised groups of left-wing politicians: before that they were 'a fairly loose group of MPs without any hard centre' going under the banner of Keep Left.

standard of living for working-class people. He attacked with gusto Gaitskell, saying that the Chancellor had more interest in arming Britain than in upholding a high-class National Health Service

Conflict with A. P. Wadsworth, editor of *The Guardian*

Bevan became also involved in a bitter conflict with A. P. Wadsworth, the influential editor of the *Manchester Guardian* from 1944. This disagreement continued to the year 1956. Wadsworth could not forgive Bevan for having dared to attack him personally and regularly. While he was an old fashioned Liberal rather than a Tory diehard , he did at all appreciate Bevan referring to the Tories as vermin.[1] Bevan knew from first class experience thsat there was a great deal of bitterness stll towards the Tories in the mining communities. This bitterness had arisen, as Bevan tried to explain, from the years when the Tories had treated miners like Bevan himself as if they were no more than vermin. Wadsworth could not forgive Bevan for his colourful language and thereafter began to attack the Bevanites. He wrote :

> And behind their facade of unity there is Mr. Bevan and the hate gospellers of his entourage.[2]

For Wadsworth, 'Bevan and the hate-gospellers' were the main reason for the electorate's growing disillusionment with the Labour Party in the fifties. As he saw it, these left-wingers were willing to tear a political party to shreds, leading to the Labour Party losing the 1951 General Election.[3] They should have won it .To Wadsworth, the Bevanites failed dismally to convince the electorate because they were too much under the influence of the Welsh politician .. This able editor felt most of the time emotionally alien to the Welsh socialist. There was to be no easy reconciliation between the influential *Manchester Guardian* and Aneurin Bevan.

Resignation of Bevan and two colleagues

Following their resignation from the Labour hierarchy, Wilson and Bevan set out their ideas in a pamphlet entitled *One Way Only*. By the time of the Scarborough Labour Party Conference in the first week of October 1951, Bevan was the idol of a large swathe of the British Labour Party. All three ministers who resigned had

---

1 *Manchester Guardian*, 18 May 1955.
2 David Ayerst, *Guardian: Biography of a Newspaper* (London, 1974,) 606.
3 *Manchester Guardian,* 18 May 1955.

joined Keep Left within three days and called on others to follow them. By 1951, at least 57 Labour Party politicians belonged to the pressure group and it was clear a General Election was imminent. Throughout 1951, the Keep Left politicians formed a close bond and devised a plan by which MPs in safe seats like Ebbw Vale were expected to help members who were fighting marginal seats. Attlee announced the election for October 1951. The trade unions were concerned and increasingly angry that the cost of the Korean War was increasing steadily while their wages were being held down. The resignations of Bevan, Wilson and Freeman had weakened the Labour government and a well-known observer, Sir Norman Angell, like Wadsworth blamed Aneurin Bevan for the fact that Labour lost the 1951 General Election. The blame was placed firmly on Aneurin Bevan's shoulders:

> It is no secret that a great many of the Labour Party, especially on the trade union side, regard Mr. Aneurin Bevan a far greater menace than Mr. Churchill in the world of the British workers' desires.[1]

Despite the Labour Party securing 48.8% of the vote compared with the Conservative Party's 48%, Attlee only won 295 seats while the Conservatives now had 302 MPs. Attlee's time as Prime Minister should have ended there and then. Aneurin Bevan won in Ebbw Vale with a large majority as did Jim Griffiths in Llanelli. Then disaster struck, Morgan Phillips the influential Secretary of the British Labour Party turned fiercely against his former friend. In terms of background, personality and thinking, Phillips was more like Bevan than Gaitskell. Born in Aberdare in 1902 to a Welsh-speaking mining family, he had worked in the Rhymney Valley collieries before becoming active in the Independent Labour Party and later the Labour Party. Like Bevan, Morgan Phillips revelled in his Welshness, which was characteristic of the mining communities: the male voice choirs, the singing of hymns on the rugby field and in nonconformist chapels, the working men's clubs, the enthusiasm for sport, namely football, rugby union and boxing, plus the activities of the Miners' Union. Unlike Bevan, Morgan Phillips was a fluent Welsh speaker who always conversed with Jim Griffiths in Welsh. Phillips would much have preferred to see Bevan leading the Labour Party than Gaitskell and, in May 1960, said these words of Gaitskell: 'What an impossible man he is.'[2] Alas, the same thing could have been said of Aneurin Bevan in 1951. The friendship between him and Harold Wilson was shortlived. While Wilson was Bevan's chief supporter in the wake of the resignation, four years later he canvassed on behalf of Hugh Gaitskell in the leadership

---

[1] Martin Ceadel, 'Sir Ralph Norman Angell (1872–1967)', *Oxford Dictionary of National Biography* (Oxford, 2004), 150–153.
[2] *Ibid.* 236.

election.[1] Wilson voted for Gaitskell, to the astonishment of solid Bevanites like Stephen Swingler, a politician who loved the Cardiganshire coast, the villages of Llanon and Llanddewi Aberarth. .Unfortunately, in 1951, the leadership of Keep Left was not in Swingler's hands but in the hands of Richard Crossman, Ian Mikardo and Harold Wilson.

The results of another General Election

The Labour government was facing a host of problems as it faced a General Election by the beginning of the fifties.[2] Despite being the administration responsible for building the welfare state and creating the National Health Service, the 1950 General Election was a sad milestone for the Labour Party.

Aneurin Bevan had believed these huge steps forward would guarantee the party support for the next quarter of a century.[3] In the period between the two elections, Attlee continued to steer and preside over one of the most effective and lively governments in terms of introducing and passing important measures to improve the quality of life for the entire population, from cradle to grave. The truth was that Attlee, Morrison and others did not want to upset the upper classes. They wanted to retain the established church, the royal family and public schools (after all, Attlee was the product of one). They had no issue with the various archaic ceremonies and honours which existed, including the House of Lords. Just like the Liberals (Lloyd George came closest to changing the order of things but ultimately preserved the status quo) and the Conservatives, Attlee's Labour administration did not want to change anything which might annoy the establishment. As a historian said in the latest biography of Clement Attlee: The serious point is that Attlee never intended a cultural revolution nor a purging of the establishment.[4] It was this, more than anything else, that enraged Bevan and meant he was constantly in the minority in the 1945–1951 Labour governments. Aneurin's political stance was democratic socialism. Vincent Brome, a researcher in the Labour Party Research Unit, had the opportunity to have a long talk with Bevan about government and Labour Party aims. For Bevan, democratic socialism was an excellent means of translating social conscience into action. He saw social

---

1 *Ibid.* 250.
2 The trade unions were famous for keeping things as they were. The trade union leaders were short of political ideas with only a minority ready to accept Marxist ideology. Remember Paul Johnson's daring words: 'The British Trade Union movement does not have sinister ideas. The trouble is that it has no ideas at all.' See Paul Johnson, 'A Brotherhood of National Misery', *New Statesman*, 16 May 1975, 655.
3 Keith Laybourn, *A Century of Labour: A History of the Labour Party* (Stroud, 2001), 10.
4 John Bew, *Citizen Clem: A Biography of Attlee* (London, 2016), 389.

conscience expressing, as well as manifesting, itself in thousands of families where children, both in the home and at school, were taught the virtues of pity, kindness and thoughtfulness for others. This credo was strengthened by Christian teaching tying everything together in a tradition of service and making the individual proud of his working-class upbringing. But when the young man or woman leaves the family circle, he or she soon realises that the material world around them behaves in totally uncaring manner with regard to those aspects taught to children in a cultured British home. Economic demands soon become an obvious obstacle to their standards and moral yearnings.

Bevan recognised there were aspects of the Labour Party programme which clearly followed the lines of the 'nonconformist conscience', for which he was grateful. He gave examples of the dilemma facing a socialist who cleaves to his or her ideals. Many people sympathise sincerely with someone who is sick and everyone is in favour of the poor woman who is on a waiting list to get a house suitable for her as well as her children. But unfortunately, these good people who are sympathetic can still believe the way to overcome difficulties lies in the hands of individuals. Under capitalism, the thinking is that the poor cause their own troubles and should therefore overcome them through their own efforts. Bevan believed in reasoning and debating the important issues, as he had been taught in his childhood at Sunday school and later in the Tredegar Query Club. He had done this throughout his life. He was proud that Labour government had been able to transform the circumstances of tens of thousands of individuals by stepping in with help at a national level. For Bevan, socialist preaching without action or with insufficient action from political leaders, achieved nothing and lead to moral disability. Vincent Brome, then a young man, was completely convinced by Bevan's argument; indeed, his interview led him to write one of the earliest biographies of Bevan. For forty minutes, the ideas poured from the politician's lips. He used rich, meaningful phrases, barely stopping for breath, then suddenly rose from his chair, listing his commitments for the rest of the day and ushering Brome to the door.[1] Thus, another astute journalist came to appreciate what Aneurin Bevan believed in – and what he had accomplished. Richard Crossman pointed out that, although he did not fulfil his potential, Bevan performed well as a Minister of the Crown.[2] He was an excellent Minister of Health and Housing and an inspirational left-wing leader throughout the years.[3] He had a

---

1 *Ibid*, 3–4 , 'I had witnessed one of Aneurin Bevan's "performances", which quite possibly was turned out for my benefit. The Bevan interested in philosophy, man of ideas, fascinated by "intellectual" explorations, had broken out into what one close friend describes as "his turgid period" and another as "eloquence". There was no doubting a brilliant gift for words.'
2 Victoria Honeyman, *Richard Crossman, ibid*, 7.
3 Kenneth O. Morgan, *Labour's People*, 218. In 1987, the historian's verdict was this: 'He remains, perhaps, the most attractive figure that the British socialist movement has produced in its eighty-odd years of fitful life.'

comprehensive vision and sufficient tenacity and intellectual determination to fulfil his dream of creating a National Health Service and embark on a massive post-war housebuilding project. Bevan had made his own words come true: 'No society can legitimately call itself civilised if a sick person is denied medical aid because of lack of means.'[1]

---

1 Aneurin Bevan, *In Place of Fear*, 100

CHAPTER 12

Aneurin Bevan and Wales

The role Aneurin Bevan's Welsh background played in his political beliefs should not be under-emphasised. In the most recent biography of him, Nicklaus Thomas-Symonds, MP for Torfaen, sums it up in one short sentence: 'For Bevan was a proud Welshman.'[1]

The Welsh background of Aneurin in Monmouthshire

The research of Kenneth O. Morgan and Dai Smith provides firmer ground for discussing Bevan the Welshman. He had a Welsh forename and he witnessed 'Welshness' in the life of his father and in the societies around him in Tredegar. Emyr Humphries compares Bevan to another talented boy, Idris Davies of Rhymney, who was born across the mountain from Tredegar.[2] Like Aneurin, Davies worked underground in the coalfield but his academic ability provided him with an early escape and he trained as a teacher in Loughborough Training College. He could speak for Aneurin when he says:

I lost my native language for the one the Saxon spoke by going to school by order for education's sake.

The first half of the twentieth century was the period of betrayal of the Welsh language, chiefly by school teachers and religious and social leaders. The unconventional cleric the Revd. Kilsby Jones (1813–1889) spoke words with which ninety percent of his fellow Nonconformist ministers would agree:

---
1 Nicklaus Thomas-Symonds, *Nye: The Political Life of Aneurin Bevan* (London, 2015), 50.
2 Emyr Humphreys, *The Taliesin Tradition: A Quest for the Welsh Identity* (London, 1983), 211–212

Stick to Welsh on a Sunday, but when Monday morning business and the language of the most adventurous nation on earth.[1] comes, I advise you to speak English as that is the language of

Idris Davies the poet

By the time Aneurin was born, Tredegar had welcomed a large number of immigrants. There was a synagogue in the town suggesting a sizeable Jewish community resided in the area. There were occasional confrontations between the Welsh, the Irish and the Jews, with English immigrants backing the Welsh. The Anglo-Welsh writer Gwyn Thomas (1913–1991) from Rhondda blamed the Welsh language for most of the problems of the valleys. His observation is even more inflammatory than that of chapel preacher Kilsby Jones, for Thomas maintains in his essay:

The Welsh Language stood in the way of our fuller union and we made ruthless haste to destroy it. We nearly did.[2]

Gwyn Thomas would have been ready to see the language disappear from every hearth in the land of song but Aneurin had a different view. Like Thomas, he had been raised in the tradition of the Welsh chapel and communal singing, of eisteddfods and the Cymmrodorion society. Unlike Thomas, Bevan cherished these symbols

---

1 *Gwyddoniadur Cymru yr Academi Cymreig* (The Welsh Academy Encyclopaedia of Wales), 231.
2 *Ibid.*

of Welshness throughout his life. Like Idris Davies, Bevan read avidly and extensively. As a local leader he supported the Carnegie Trust to put wireless sets in fourteen locations in the coalfield where people could listen to the news, sport and discussion. We can see why, in 1928, Bevan gave the nonconformists some concern when , he suggested it would be a treat for many if the local cinema opened on a Sunday evening. He was criticised harshly by the local Free Church Council for suggesting the county council might 'sully the Welsh Sabbath.'[1]

The Labour Party provides an important answer to him

By the twenties, Bevan realised that the 'respectable' Liberals were stifling his vision of a better world, based on socialist principles. The Labour Party was the focus of all his social, political and cultural activity and he recognised the need to extend the party's reach. Not every miner in Sirhowy or Rhondda or steelworker in Ebbw Vale wanted to spend their free time reading books on socialist themes or debating from morning to night as he did. Many of them liked to dance or play in (and listen to) brass and jazz bands. Some preferred to take part in sporting competitions or to sing in male voice or mixed choirs. By involving the Labour Party in a range of community activities, Bevan hoped they could widen its appeal to voters and support the campaigns of those standing for council or parliament in Labour colours. Labour could sponsor the local cinema and hold card evenings, as well as supporting the brass bands and eisteddfods which were an integral part of the community. By winter 1924–1925, Bevan had organised a full Sunday evening programme of lectures on socialist culture.:

> In Tredegar they could congratulate themselves upon organizing a Labour movement second to none in South Wales and that had every phase of the movement provided for, even to an orchestra, which was promising to become a very fine one.[2]

The Labour Party was no longer on the fringes of Welsh society but in its midst and winning over many scores of active members who, like Bevan and his family, were ready to live for the Labour movement and follow his example. By 1929, Bevan was chairman of the Miners' Welfare Committee and the Working Men's Library, the County Omnibus Committee, the Committee for the Unemployed, and vice-chair of the Hospital Committee (before becoming chairman). He represented

---

1 See Dai Smith, 'Bevan and Wales' in *The State of the Nation: The Political Legacy of Aneurin Bevan* (ed. Geoffrey Goodman) (London, 1997), 68–69.
2 *Ibid.* 70–71.

Tredegar on a host of organisations such as the Western Valleys Sewerage Board, the Monmouthshire Association of Urban District Councils and the Board of Governors of University College, Cardiff. He chaired not only the political meetings but also would deliver an address as president of the many concerts and cultural events. When a series of contemporary plays was staged, Bevan was at the helm and when a talented Russian violinist came to give a performance, he was again on stage to present him to the audience and afterwards thank him for his performance. There was no end to Aneurin Bevan's activities. He enjoyed talking to the children of unemployed people in Tredegar after he and his team organised a tea party for them. He was ready to judge various Sirhowy miners' competitions and spoke eloquently at the opening of the Miners' Institute in Dukestown.

Defending the unemployed and cooperating with the Communists

Bevan attended all these events with the purpose of representing the Labour Party. His major political concern was the plight of the unemployed in and around Tredegar in the 1920s. In the South Wales coalfield, a staggering 30% of people were without work. The Unemployed Workers Movement emerged from left and Communist Party discussions on the future of the coalfield. At that time, the Welsh Communists were leading the way by publishing the powerful novel of Marxist writer and miner Lewis Jones and the writing of coalfield leaders Arthur Horner and Will Paynter. Emyr Humphreys memorably crystallised the situation, suggesting that the good relationship between Bevan and people like Horner had prevented him taking more responsibility as a politician. He goes on to say:

> Like Lloyd George and Churchill, he was deeply distrusted by the apparatchiks of his own party. As an individualist and a Welshman, he was built on a heroic scale. Indeed, Bevan's state of open rebellion and unstinting honesty made him a more sympathetic product of the Welsh Non-conformist conscience than Lloyd George. He was not so narrowly concerned with the pursuit of power for its own sake. His generosity of spirit and the manner of his giving are sufficient in themselves to ensure his Arthurian status among his own people.[1]

Emyr Humphreys put his finger on the fundamental truth: that Aneurin Bevan combined classical nonconformity and social conscience at its best.

---

1 *Ibid*, 81.

Bevan inherits the work of a few nonconformist ministers

Bevan was heir to the scores of nonconformist ministers in Gwent – from the Reverend Evan Jones (Ieuan Gwynedd) to the unorthodox Leo Atkin of Bargoed (and later Swansea) – who had prepared the way for socialist agitators like him.[1] He never lost sight of that radical nonconformity; it spurred him on and was at the root of his amazing ability to bring people around to his point of view. One of the pioneers of Welsh socialism whose writings were familiar on David Bevan's hearth was Robert Jones Derfel (1824–1905).[2] In his articles, Derfel reconciles Christianity, socialism and nationalism within a Welsh context.[3] Aneurin Bevan was not a nationalistic socialist but he was a proud patriot.

Problems with devolution and the granting of a Welsh Day

The consistent failure of the British Labour Party to outline a vision for socialist idealism in the context of the rights of the Welsh nation was a source of frustration to many Welsh Labour supporters. Bevan himself changed his view about devolution a year before he died, when he allowed Jim Griffiths and Cledwyn Hughes to place a commitment to Welsh devolution in the 1959 General Election manifesto.

During the Second World War, Aneurin Bevan's name is seen among those prominent Welsh who were officers in the Welsh Parliamentary Party. He was co-vice chair with Megan Lloyd George, both elected to Parliament in the 1929 election. Jim Griffiths was the secretary of the parliamentary party from 1938 and remained in office until the 1945 General Election. In July 1943, Winston Churchill was notified by letter that a subcommittee had been formed to discuss the problems of government in Wales and particularly the priority of establishing a Welsh Office and a Secretary of State for Wales. Jim Griffiths and others knew Bevan was lukewarm on administrative decentralisation but his involvement in the parliamentary party – and some of his letters I have seen – suggest his views did not differ hugely from Griffiths' own. In fact, Bevan agreed with the measure of decentralisation already in place, in terms of the existing Department for Education in Wales and the Welsh Board of Health. It is interesting to note Bevan's reaction to Parliament's

---

1 Emyr Humphreys, *ibid*, 213.
2 One of the best essays in the Welsh language on him is Arthur Meirion Roberts' article: 'R. J. Derfel (1824–1903)', *Y Traethodydd*, clxv, January 2010/6, 458–476.
3 David Bevan would have read R. J. Derfel's articles and also T. E Nicholas's seminal article 'R. J. Derfel: Y Gwrthryfelwr Cymreig', *Y Genhinen*, xxxii (Gŵyl Ddewi), 59–62.

first Welsh Day on 17 October 1944.[1] Megan Lloyd George was beside herself with delight; this was the first occasion in four hundred years when Welsh Members of Parliament were provided with an opportunity to discuss important matters which were specific to Wales. Sir Arthur Evans, the Conservative member for Cardiff South, rejoiced as did Jim Griffiths. Aneurin Bevan threw cold water on the project. As far as he was concerned, it would be much better to focus on a sector like the coal industry or agriculture on an allocated day but to include non-Welsh parliamentarians with an interest too. Let us, he argued, set aside a day to look at a specific industry throughout the length and breadth of the UK rather than cramming a discussion about the Welsh coalfield into one day. As he had been pointing out for decades, Welsh sheep were not a jot different from those grazing the hills of England, Northern Ireland and Scotland.[2]

Bevan's support for Welsh patriot and pacifist Iorwerth Cyfeiliog Peate

One of Aneurin Bevan's most admirable actions during the Second World War was his unstinting support for the socialist and pacifist, Iorwerth Cyfeiliog Peate. Peate, a poet, was a friend of Jim Griffiths and a keen reader of *Tribune*. Local authorities like Cardiff and Swansea councils instructed their employees to be whole-hearted in their support for the war.[3] Peate was caught in the net. He appeared before a tribunal as a onscientious objector and, as a result, was dismissed from his post as a curator with the National Museum of Wales where his vision for folk culture was so essential. Peate's many friends considered this to be complete lunacy and that he should be reinstated to his key post. A meeting of the members of the National Museum of Wales was organised for 24 October 1941.[4] On the platform

---

1 Andy Missel, 'Dydd Cymru 1944' in *Llyfr y Ganrif* (eds. Gwyn Jenkins and Tegwyn Jones) (Talybont, 1999), 188.
2 *Hansard*, H.C./5, Vol. 403, columns 2311–2312, 17 October 1944; Nicklaus Thomas-Symonds, *Nye, ibid*, 49, 'There are sheep on the Welsh mountains, and there are sheep on the mountains of Westmorland and in Scotland, but I do not know the difference between a Welsh sheep, a Westmorland sheep and a Scottish sheep'. The First Minister for Wales, in the Assembly, Carwyn Jones, was not at all happy with the comparison. See Carwyn Jones, *The Future of Welsh Labour* Cardiff, 2004, 8, 'He (Aneurin Bevan) failed to see the difference between English sheep and Welsh sheep.'
3 Jim Griffiths said he had received more letters on the issue of the dismissal of Dr. Iorwerth C. Peate than on any other subject for some time. See *Y Cymro,* 1 November 1941, 1 and 12. Iorwerth C. Peate was strongly supported in his case (24 October 1941) in Cardiff by the MPs Sir William Jenkins, D. O. Evans, R. Moelwyn Hughes, Evan Evans, S. O. Davies, Aneurin Bevan, Jim Griffiths, Will John and Robert Richards.
4 D. Ben Rees, *Jim: The life and work of Rt Hon. James Griffiths: A hero of the Welsh nation and architect of the welfare state* (Liverpool 2020), 124.

were the museum's chairman Lord Plymouth (the Earl of Plymouth), its director Cyril Fox and the secretary Archie Lee. There were also several MPs in attendance, including three Labour MPs who were great admirers of Peate, despite knowing he was a member of the Welsh Nationalist Party. The Welsh scholar Dr. Thomas Parry's evidence of the contribution made by Aneurin Bevan and his comrades, Jim Griffiths and Ronw Moelwyn Hughes, has been translated:

> And they had an incomparable chance to perform in their own particular way. They attacked the men on the platform mercilessly and I never saw anyone blasted so scathingly.[1]

At the end of the debate, the museum's court of governors voted, with a large majority, for Peate to be reinstated to his post as curator of the Department of Welsh Folk Culture. Aneurin Bevan had spoken with authority to right the wrong to one of the great cultural figures of the Welsh nation.

The voice of Wales in Atlee's cabinet of 1945–1951

Aneurin Bevan was the principal voice of Wales in Clement Attlee's cabinet between 1945 and 1951. He was more outspoken than anyone else and Jim Griffiths was not in the cabinet between 1945 and 1950 because the Minister of national Insurance had no place in the Cabinet in that government .. Bevan argued in the war years that there was no point creating the post of Secretary of State for Wales as that would not solve the country's 'economic problems'. His opinion was supported by one of his best friends, the north Wales trade unionist Huw T. Edwards, as can be seen in his memorandum The Problems of Wales, drawn up in 1946 and sent to Morgan Phillips, the general secretary of the Labour Party.[2] Edwards thought it

---
1 Thomas Parry, *Amryw Bethau* (Denbigh, 1996), 321–324.
2 Gwyn Jenkins, *Cofiant Huw T. Edwards: Prif Weinidog Answyddogol Cymru* (Talybont, 2007, 110. A copy of The Problems of Wales is to be found in the archive of Huw T. Edwards, Welsh National Library, A4/1.

would be much better to appoint a Commissioner for Wales with an advisory committee at his service. The commissioner would be able to go directly to the cabinet secretary without having to consult with the civil service. Edwards was incensed when he heard of the plan to set up a committee of chief civil servants of government departments in Wales. He thought a committee of civil servants was not remotely acceptable and it would be much better to have politicians dealing with education and health in Wales.[1] One of the greatest tragedies of twentieth century Welsh politics was Aneurin Bevan's failure to recognises himself as the most important Welsh politician of his generation. In the view of a large section of the Welsh people, he was the greatest Welshman of all times. Bevan knew England – under Conservative and Liberal governments –was guilty of treating Wales badly for centuries. He understood the radicalism of the Chartists and knew about the dreadful betrayal of the 'Blue Books' in 1847, as well as the view of English intellectuals, like Matthew Arnold in 1852, that the Welsh language was a hindrance that should be removed An admirer of Aneurin Bevan Professor William J. Gruffydd defeated the nationalist candidate Saunders Lewis to become the Liberal MP for the University of Wales constituency from 1943 to 1950. Gruffydd expressed a viewpoint that a fair number of Welsh Labour Party members could agree with.[2] Discussing R. A. Butler's Education Act on 3 July 1944, Gruffydd made his position very clear and unambiguous:

> It is as much the duty of this house to safeguard the nationhood of Wales as it is to safeguard the nationhood of England or of Scotland. We are not a subject nation, to be dragooned into assimilation; we regard ourselves as a full partner with Britain.[3]

For a long time, Bevan saw his contribution in the House of Commons strictly in terms of class rather than nationhood. He overlooked the fact people belong to both, to a nation as well as a class. Gruffydd had a great deal to say about the devolution position:

> Self-government cannot be given by one stroke of the pen. We must grow to be worthy of it, to learn it; we must grow into self-government.'[4]

---

1 *Y Cymro*, 27 December 1946.
2 W.J. Gruffydd fostered the belief that England had mistreated Wales. He tried to make Wales comprehensible to the English and Scots in Parliament. See T. Robin Chapman, *Dawn Dweud: W. J. Gruffydd* (Cardiff, 1993), 191.
3 *Ibid*, 189.
4 *Ibid*, 8.

Bevan agreed with this sentiment; however, it took him a long time to understand the implications of decentralisation. He took no interest at all in the 1950s campaign for a Welsh Parliament, apart from opposing the dismissal of rebel Labour party colleagues for their part in the campaign. He and Cledwyn Hughes admired and respected one another greatly as politicians but on the question of Stephen Owen Davies's Private Measure Bill for Welsh self government, Bevan was noncommittal. He had no enthusiasm for what was, in his opinion, a rather futile project.

Lost opportunity with regard to the drowning of Tryweryn

On the issue of the drowning of the valley of Tryweryn, Bevan was, for once, rather non-committal. Ever since the flooding of Capel Celyn village between Bala and Trawsfynydd in Merionethshire by Liverpool Corporation in the mid-fifties, Welsh politics had become a battlefield between the socialists who scorned Plaid Cymru and the nationalists in the name of Plaid Cymru who were hoping for a breakthrough in Westminster (they had to wait till 1966). The shadow of Tryweryn loomed over Welsh politics for decades to come. Even the continuation of the Welsh nation came under question. No politician of the stature of Aneurin Bevan or Jim Griffiths seems to have realised that brave and decisive leadership was needed. Both men cast aside the opportunity to show their true patriotism, despite speaking to Hugh Gaitskell about the issue. The fact that the depth of feeling throughout Wales was being ignored by Welsh politicians spurred much debate, including an important discussion between Gaitskell and Griffiths. After visiting a number of Welsh constituencies, Gaitskell realised that the Tryweyn controversy deserved more serious consideration and less prejudiced comments.[1] In a comprehensive letter to the British Labour Party headquarters and its secretary Morgan Phillips, Gaitskell said it was necessary to consider a policy that would be fair to the whole of Wales and there should be immediate consultation within a cross section of the Labour movement. As a result, a Parliamentary sub-committee was established within the Labour Party in cooperation with the Welsh Regional Council to consider giving leadership on the difficult constitutional question raised by Gaitskell himself. Jim Griffiths became chairman while Bevan became a member of the committee. But before the committee came to its conclusion, Bevan was welcoming the biggest Welsh-language cultural festival to his constituency.

---

1 D. Ben Rees, *Jim: The life and work of Rt. Hon. James Griffiths* (Liverpool 2020), 200–202.

Bevan welcomes the National Eisteddfod of Wales and Paul Robeson to Ebbw Vale

In 1958, the National Eisteddfod of Wales came to Ebbw Vale. Aneurin Bevan's command of the Welsh language was not good enough for him to address the thousands of native speakers gathered in the main pavilion.[1] The only way for the audience to hear his voice was in the *Cymanfa Ganu* (community hymn singing festival), which was held on the Sunday night before the official opening on Monday morning The Welsh-only rule prevented Bevan speaking from the eisteddfod stage . Fortunately, for Bevan —and the Eisteddfod officials — Paul Robeson, his friend and an icon throughout the mining valleys, was also invited to the Sunday night singing event.[2] There had been a special and affectionate relationship between the charismatic singer and Welsh miners after he had met unemployed miners singing and seeking sustenance in London's Oxford Street during the Depression. Welsh miners' leaders and politicians, like Bevan, felt empathy for Robeson when he was persecuted by the US government under McCarthyism for expressing his genuine sympathy for people in the Soviet Union. Accused of being a communist, Robeson's passport was taken away from him for eight years. Thus, hearing his rich bass-baritone voice was a great joy for the many Welsh people who filled the pavilion on the eve of the 1958 National Eisteddfod.[3]

Monmouthshire had been treated as an appendage to Wales since the time of Henry VIII and the 1536 Act of Union between England and Wales. There was always reference in documents to Wales and Monmouthshire.[4] The county comprised both industrial valleys and attractive towns like Monmouth, Caerleon, Abergavenny and Raglan. Since the First World War, the majority of the population spoke only English. Despite this, the people of Monmouthshire knew their county was in Wales and identified as Welsh. Bevan had understood this since he was a child,

Bevan changes his mind on the setting up of a Secretary of State for Wales

Bevan was one of the most vociferous and articulate opponents of a Secretary of State for Wales; however, there were other Labour MPs who shared his views. Some,

---

1 Huw T. Edwards, 'A pen-portrait of the late Aneurin Bevan', *Aneurin* (A Welsh student socialist magazine), vol. 1, no. 2.
2 Paul Robeson (1898–1976), *Gwyddoniadur Cymru yr Academi Gymreig*, 787–788.
3 *Ibid*.
4 Fred J. Hando, *The Pleasant Hand of Gwent* (Newport, 1949), which summarises the background.

like Ness Edwards (MP for Caerphilly) and Iorwerth Thomas (MP for Rhondda West) had very little empathy with the language and culture of Wales and voiced even more outlandish views on Plaid Cymru.[1] The Labour Party organiser, Cliff Prothero, a member of the committee chaired by James Griffiths gives a vivid picture of what happened in the emotional deliberations. It was so emotional that Hugh Gaitskell had to take over from the experienced James Griffiths:

> After several meetings of protracted and heated discussion and now what turned out to be the final meeting and right in the middle of a very heated debate to everyone's surprise, Mr. Aneurin Bevan proposed 'That we include in our policy statement that a Secretary of State for Wales will be appointed'.[2]

With no further debate, the chairman called the committee to an end. As he left the room, Cliff Prothero turned to Ness Edwards and said:

> I cannot understand the complete change of attitude by Aneurin.

Ness replied:

> If you were a member of this house Cliff, you would not be surprised at what has taken place this afternoon.[3]

The momentous decision of the Labour Party to create a Welsh Office and the position of Secretary of State for Wales in the cabinet was not announced until the 1959 election manifesto. Bevan had once again gained a Labour Party commitment for the Welsh socialists. He had been was one of devolution's loudest opponents at the outset, but he had listened to the debates and had eventually come to support the long held beliefs of his friend Jim Griffiths.[4] Bevan also suggested to his Welsh Labour MP colleagues that a parliament or assembly should be created for Wales and Scotland. He would have liked a Royal Commission to consider the best course of action; sadly, he did not live long enough to see the establishment of a Secretary of State for Wales in 1964.

---

1 Gwilym Prys Davies, *Cynhaeaf Hanner Canrif: Gwleidyddieth Gymreig 1945–2005* (Llandysul, 2008), 45. 'They wanted to kill off the argument and kill it stone dead in the sub-committee.'
2 National Library of Wales: Papers of Cliff Prothero, Biographical Notes, 137.
3 *Ibid*.
4 R. Griffiths, 'The Other Aneurin Bevan', *Planet*, 41, 1978, 26–28. So many prominent Welsh people saw Aneurin Bevan's ultimate strength as a politician of devolution.

Tension between Ness Edwards and Aneurin Bevan

The political giant continued to make himself popular to many in the Welsh Labour Party by arguing in favour of a Parliament or an Assembly for Wales and Scotland and suggesting establishing a Royal Commission. This appeared in his article in the Empire News a Sunday newspaper, on 1 February 1959.[1] Bevan's proposal was not welcomed by Ness Edwards and a huge gulf grew between the two men who had been friends in their younger days. Edwards believed also that Bevan had made a mistake in resigning over the issue of prescription charges; believed Bevan should have respected the cabinet's verdict. Therefore, Edwards felt uncomfortable in the company of intellectuals like Michael Foot, Richard Crossman and Ian Mikardo who had supported Bevan. Thereafter, Edwards worked hard in opposition to Bevan's supporters in his constituency.[2] He condemned *Tribune* as a 'party within a party'. Edwards faced fierce opposition in the South Caerphilly constituency where 89% of Labour members were on Bevan's side. By the end of the fifties, the two men had overcome their differences and become closer again At the suggestion of Edwards, the Rhymney Valley Conference was held in 1958 under the auspices of the Gelligaer Town Council; its purpose was to discuss the future of the area. The three local MPs, all ex-miners, were invited to speak: Aneurin Bevan, Harold Finch and Ness Edwards. The conference concluded conclusion that there was a need to attract new industries to the Rhymney Valley and to start arranging themselves locally rather than expect salvation from London. Any initiative must come from the local authority and it was suggested that they set up three industrial estates, one in the south, another in the middle of the valley and one in the north.[3] Caerphilly succeeded wonderfully with Tir-y-Berth and Pontygwindy estates but there was very little relief for Blaenau Gwent. Bevan himself was gradually becoming disillusioned and, in 1960, the charismatic Welshman's career came to an end at a comparatively early age. Thankfully, before he left politics, Bevan joined hands with Welsh-speaking Labour MPs Jim Griffiths, Cledwyn Hughes, Goronwy Roberts, Tudor Watkins and Megan Lloyd George on the issue of devolution. Sadly, the peace between them lasted for just a short time. It should be remembered, however, that Bevan once wrote an article for Keidrych Rhys, editor of the periodical *Wales* in 1947, in which he confirms his great pride in his native country. In my opinion, that article deserves to be regarded as Bevan's personal manifesto on the land of his forefathers.[4]

---

1 Aneurin Bevan, *Empire News*, 1 February 1959. See Gwyn Jenkins, 'Keep up with the Macs: The Devolution Debate of 1957–1959', *Planet*, 821990, 84–89. Huw T. Edwards welcomed his opinion, *Liverpool Daily Post*, 11 December 1958.
2 Wayne David, *Remaining True: A Biography of Ness Edwards* (Caerphilly, 2006), 66.
3 *Ibid*.
4 Aneurin Bevan, 'The Claim of Wales: a statement', *Wales*, 25, Spring 1947, 13.

Ebbw Vale town centre c. 1938

Nye Bevan unveiling the William Firth Gates at Eugene Cross Park, 1959, watched by Sir Eugene Cross

Nye Bevan and and Jennie Lee attending the
visit of the Duke of Edinburgh, 1958

Nye Bevan opening Bevan's Crescent in Ebbw Vale in 1951

Nye Bevan listening to a speech made by County Councillor Harry Phillips

CHAPTER 13

Aneurin and the Bevanites (1951–1955)

The days of the Bevanites were tiresome and distressing for Aneurin Bevan despite him being the main inspiration behind the movement which grew within the British Labour Party between 1951 and 1955. After all, he was the brightest star in the Labour government of 1945 to 1951 and had created the National Health Service. Bevan wanted a society where individuals were more important than capital.[1] Despite being wounded by the Chancellor of the Exchequer and his subsequent resignation, Bevan still had much to contribute to the Labour Party. He always loved to discuss politics in the light of his socialist ideology. Bevan had charisma and revelled in taking the platform, at conferences as well as in Westminster. His speeches were imaginative and demonstrated his knowledge and conviction; however, he was not completely comfortable to find himself the inspiration for the Bevanites. As Ian Mikardo, one of his admirers, said:

> To anyone who knew him and worked with him, the idea of Bevan as a power-hungry conspirator was a belly-laugh.[2]

The Bevanites had, in fact, started off as Keep Left, but the group changed its name to the Bevanites when its heroes Aneurin Bevan, Harold Wilson and John Freeman resigned in 1951.

---

1 Nicklaus Thomas-Symonds, *Nye: The Political Life of Aneurin Bevan* (London, 2015), 205: 'He had a vision of society – to be given expression in his book *In Place of Fear* – in which the human spirit meant more than material wealth.'
2 Ian Mikardo, *Back-bencher* (London, 1988), 169.

Analysing the significance of the pressure group

The Bevanites comprised 32 Labour MPs when the left-wing grouping formed in 1951. Over the years, it expanded to 47 individuals, including two peers from the House of Lords.[1] The small but powerful group contained five ex-ministers, two who later became leaders of the British Labour Party, fourteen who went on to become ministers in the sixties, nine who served their terms on the National Executive Committee and nine who became peers.[2] Six of the Bevanites became serious authors and nine others were among the finest debaters in the House of Commons. Yet none of them approached Aneurin's brilliance as a thinker, doer or speaker. The Bevanites were tasked with carrying out careful research, preparing memoranda for debate, providing articles (mainly for *Tribune*) and writing discussion papers for the whole group.[3]

Fenner Brockway was among the early heroes of the Independent Labour Party. This Bevanite became an authority on the colonies, writing well about Sudan and Uganda, two African countries he knew well. Richard Crossman was an intellectual and an often inspiring Bevanite who was willing to discuss the problems he recognised related to arming Germany. Richard Acland had established a political party called Commonwealth during the Second World War and was happy to look at life in Britain without the help of the Marshall Plan and American dollars. Barbara Castle was vivacious, lively in conversation and very talented as the electorate of Blackburn were aware. She was a huge admirer of Bevans and one of the original Bevanite.

Following his resignation, Aneurin Bevan knew he needed to produce a document for the Labour left. *One Way Only* was the first pamphlet published under the auspices of *Tribune* and as there were two well-known names responsible for its contents – Bevan and Harold Wilson – it was likely to sell well. A hundred thousand copies of *One Way Only* were printed and it was relatively well received.[4] The pamphlet argued that the problems of Britain and the world could be faced within the framework of socialist principles. There was further useful discussion about the rumour that the Soviet Union was eagerly awaiting the moment when it would attack the West. The only reason they delayed was because Britain, France and the United States had destructive weapons and bombs which the enemy feared. The Russians, and especially Joseph Stalin, knew as well as anyone that there was no basis to this irresponsible claim and the Soviet Union did

---

1 *Ibid,* 120.
2 *Ibid.*
3 Nationalisation was one of the priorities.
4 Mikardo, *ibid,* 121.

not have sufficient resources to mount a successful attack on the capitalist West. The pamphlet *One Way Only* was followed by another called *Going Our Way?* Geoffrey Bing's pamphlet *John Bull's Other Ireland* had an even wider circulation than *One Way Only*, which was extraordinary. There was considerable interest, obviously, in the situation of the Emerald Isle. Woodrow Wyatt wrote a study of Israel, *The Jews at Home*.[1] The trade unions and their leaders were extremely suspicious of the Bevanites. Their natural tendency was to argue for the status quo, with the exception of the British Union of Miners who were often spurred on by communists to be more pro-Soviet than any other union. Arthur Deakin, who had close links to Wales, could not, for the most part, agree with Aneurin Bevan.[2] The card-carrying communists infuriated him, even a left-wing proponent like his co-officer Huw T. Edwards irritated him when they worked together on Deeside as officers of the Transport and General Workers Union. The concern about the threats to the British Labour Party leadership was highlighted mainly in trade union newsletters and magazines. Thomas Williamson, the leader of the National Union of General and Municipal Workers (NUGMW) was another general secretary highly critical of the Bevanites.[3] As was Sir William Lowther, the miners' leader who had supported Bevan and the left for years in the 1930s but was now a leading proponent of the right wing. In the opinion of these trade union barons, Hugh Gaitskell was the leader who deserved support.[4] They had the unfailing support of the hard-line Tory press which relentlessly attacked Aneurin Bevan and his followers. Certain daily newspapers, like the *Daily Mail*, would have been delighted to see the Labour Party and the Bevanites eradicated from the face of the earth. Unfortunately, there were committed Labour MPs who felt the same hatred and impatience.

---

1 *Ibid*.
2 See the study of him by left-wing historian V. L. Allen, *Trade Union Leadership, Based on a Study of Arthur Deakin* (London, 1957). Deakin
3 See T. Williamson, 'Disloyalty Within the Labour Party' in *NUGMW Journal* Vol. 15, No.11, November 1952, 336. The British Labour Party manifesto was prepared for the 1951 General Election by Aneurin Bevan, Hugh Dalton, Sam Watson, the Secretary of Durham Miners' Union and Morgan Phillips.
4 During the Annual Labour Party Conference in Scarborough in October 1951, the most important trade union leaders decided to prevent Aneurin Bevan becoming Labour Party leader. Will Lowther, the President of the National Union of Mineworkers, Tom Williamson, General Secretary of the General and Municipal Workers Union and Arthur Deakin, Bevin's successor in 1945 as TGWU Secretary, met together in the St. Nicholas Hotel to discuss and discard as soon as possible the suggestion of having Aneurin Bevan as a successor to Attlee. Gaitskell was the choice that day and for the years to come. See Nicklaus Thomas-Symonds, *Nye, ibid*, 199.

The critical views of Bessie Braddock on Aneurin Bevan

One of these was Bessie Braddock, the Labour MP for Liverpool Exchange constituency. For a long periiod in the nineteen thirtees they had been loyal friends , when Bessie was a parliamentary character and Bevan a left wing MP. But then she under the influence of the trade unionists Arthur Deakin turned against Bevan and became a severe critic of him. She believed that Aneurin Bevan was the politician who had done most damage to the image of the Labour Party especially during the Second World War and in the early fifties.[1] The trouble, with Bevan, said Bessie Braddock, was that he had a Jekyll and Hyde personality. First, his urge to express himself to the public had led to the Tredegar MP becoming the best speaker in the House of Commons. Secondly, he was an extreme character in his views at times who found it hard to compromise. After 1945, Braddock found Bevan and his Westminster colleagues difficult to work with. Thirdly, Bevan uttered some shameful words when he was addressing public meetings. In 1941, he said 'the Labour Party is dying and will soon be dead.'[2] It was a statement both unfounded and incorrect. Finally, Bevan criticised his fellow Labour activists and leaders mercilessly. He criticised Sir Walter Citrine, the general secretary of the Trade Unions Congress who had so much to offer the Labour Party. Bevan unfairly called him an 'illiterate politician'.[3] Citrine's influence on the Labour Party was immense in the thirties as a number of people, including the author of this book, have emphasised in articles and books.[4] Ernest Bevin was another who was unfairly criticised. Braddock understood Bevin to be a jealous man but not as wild as Bevan's utterances suggested. On 20 July 1946, during the miners gala celebrations in Durham, Bevan told the miners and Labour Party stalwarts that, by the next General Election, his government would have built enough houses to meet the need in Britain. There would be no shortage of housing in Britain and the majority of the working classes would have homes. He failed to reach the target and realised this when he made his promises. Herbert Morrison claimed Bevan's empty talk had cost the Labour Party at least thirty seats in the 1950 General Election.[5] After all, Bevan had been

---

1 Jack and Bessie Braddock, *The Braddocks* (London, 1963), 203.
2 *Ibid*, 204.
3 *Ibid*, 205.
4 See Neil Riddell, 'Walter Citrine and the British Labour Movement 1925– 1935', *History*, 85/278 (2000), 285–306. For a study of what was written about Citrine.
5 Jack and Bessie Braddock, *The Braddocks*, 207; Bernard Donaghue and G.W, Jones, *Herbert Morrison* A Portrait of a Politician (London, 1973).

attacking the trade unions for over twenty years, ultimately creating unpleasantness in the upper ranks. Bessie Braddock called him 'Wild Aneurin' and 'Thoughtless Aneurin.[1]

The activities of the Bevanites

Bevan could no nothing right with her, even when when he created the NHS.

The Bevanites introduced local discussion groups called 'brains trusts' which were organised along the lines of a popular wartime BBC radio programme. Each brains trust comprised a panel of four or five interesting and popular speakers. People were invited to ask them questions under the chairmanship of a well-known politician, usually Ian Mikardo. The brains trusts moved around the country, visiting one constituency after another. Jennie Lee and Barbara Castle were among the popular panelists as were Julius Silverman and Konni Zilliacus, who was exceptionally knowledgeable about foreign affairs. However, the star panelist was, without doubt, Welshman Harold Davies, the MP for Leek in the North Staffordshire coalfield but originally from Pontypridd.[2] Davies' healthy laugh and Welsh accent earned him a lot of devoted listeners. The weekly meetings were advertised in *Tribune*, the *New Statesman and Nation* and were packed to the rafters. The Labour Party faithful came to listen, collect signatures and shake hands with the chairman and his panelists. In 1952 and 1953, Labour Party membership increased to a high point of over a million members, even more than Jeremy Corbyn managed when he was leader of the Labour Party between 2016 and 2019.[3] Yet besides the brains trusts, Bevanites had no exciting and different political programme to be shared with the electorate. Nicklaus Thomas-Symonds argued, fairly, that the two camps, the Bevanites on one hand and the Gaitskellites on the other, were extremely close to each other in terms of ideology and political stance.

There is, in fact, a deeper explanation that neither Gaitskellites nor Bevanites would care to admit. Gaitskell and Bevan were not that far apart on domestic policy. Both identified themselves as socialists . While their adherence to the main political actors, Bevan and Gaitskell, divided their followers, beyond that it was not so easy to identify Bevanites as 'left' and Gaitskellites as 'right'.[4]

It was not Britain's social issues which divided the MPs and others but their views on foreign affairs. Until summer of 1950, throughout the years of government

---

1 Jack and Bessie Braddock, *The Braddocks*, 206.
2 Mikardo, *ibid,* 124.
3 David Butler and Gareth Butler, *Twentieth Century British Political Facts 1900–2000* (London, 2000), 158–159; Kenneth O . Morgan, *Michael Foot* (London, 2007), 160.
4 Nicklaus Thomas-Symonds, *Nye, ibid*, 206–207.

and especially since 1945, Bevan had supported Attlee's and Bevin's policies regarding the United States. In 1950, the war in Korea meant the United States moved from providing economic assistance to Korea to financing weapons of war. The Labour government accepted the need to use resources for arms but the left wing was unhappy and that became more obvious after Bevan's resignation. The gap between the Bevanites and the Labour Party widened and was one of the key reasons Labour failed to return to government in 1955.

Criticism of the Bevanites on a number of issues

The Bevanites were critical of America's foreign policy on all important issues: on co-operating with the fascist General Franco in Spain, on the re-arming of Germany and, primarily, the US support for South Korea over North Korea. The US also failed to acknowledge China's emergence on the world stage.[1] The Bevanites had no goodwill towards the 1952 Republican administration, and abhorred Jack McCarthy's 1953–1954 crusade against left-wing thinking, which hounded people like Paul Robeson.[2] By the mid-fifties, the left's support for the United States had more or less disappeared. Jennie Lee had regularly crossed the Atlantic in the thirties and she was not the only one: many left-wing politicians did the same. Now Bevan and his supporters were not in government, they felt free to attack US policy. Bevan could see no sense in America's attitude towards China and believed there should be some consensus on Britain's future relationship with the communist world. The situation – and the failure to build bridges with other countries – was endangering Britain's position in Europe as well as in the Middle East, in his view. By failing to reach any agreement with communist countries, Britain was simply leaving the door open for Communist influence to spread. Aneurin Bevan had his critics within the Bevanites, two of whom surprised and disappointed him. The Oxford educated Harold Wilson and Richard Crossman felt Bevan frequently decided to speak or act without any consultation with them or anyone else and then demanded unwavering support. Ian Mikardo expresses this character weakness extremely well:

> The trouble with Nye was that he wasn't a team player: that was a defect which often worried me and occasionally irritated me though sometimes I wondered whether it was too much to expect a man of this incomparable political genius, of his stature head and shoulders above the rest of us and

---

1 Henry Pelling, *America and The British Left: From Bright to Bevan* (London, 1956), 152.
2 Henry Pelling says, "Just as in the period of the Marshall Plan, the Labour Left had found ideological reasons for its friendship with America

of everyone around him, to have the patience, the restraint, the self-obligation that team working demands.[1].

Everyone realised Bevan was more or less indispensable to the political left. There were very capable politicians in the Labour movement: people capable of political bargaining who could speak and write eloquently. They did not, however, possess Bevan's powerful personality. Richard Crossman revelled in spreading gossip, plotting and telling stories at the dining table.[2] Harold Wilson was very different. His sole aim was to become leader of the Labour Party and, if possible, Prime Minister. When he was eight, Wilson's father had taken him to the door of No. 10 Downing Street and ever since he had wanted to walk through it. Aneurin Bevan had no such an egocentric ambition. As he said:

> I started my political life with no clearly formed personal ambition as to what I wanted to be, or where I wanted to go. I leave that nonsense to the writers of romantic biographies. A young miner in a South Wales colliery, my concern was with the one practical question: where does power lie in this particular state of Great Britain and how can it be attained by the workers?[3]

Jennie Lee was another outstanding left-wing politician with a strong character and unshakeable convictions. As Mikardo and Tom Driberg said, she had sacrificed her political career to support her 'dear Nye', backing him even when he was wrong. After Bevan's death, she was finally rewarded: Wilson invited her to be Minister for the Arts.[4] One of Jennie Lee's great achievements was establishing the Open University, an institution with a long record of achievement and an apt memorial to Lee's undoubted talents. Michael Foot had been an admirer of Aneurin Bevan from their first meeting, as had the Oxford-educated journalist J. P. W (William) Mallalieu who became the Labour MP for Huddersfield and, after boundary changes, Huddersfield East.[5] Lee, Foot and Mallalieu were members of the *Tribune* editorial board. Tom Driberg, often unstable and focused on his homosexuality, was another Bevan fan. Driberg delighted in his particular brand of Christianity and wrote an entertaining column on Sunday in *Reynold's News*. In April 1954, President Dwight Eisenhower decided to organise a military blockade in Southeast Asia. Anthony Eden when he became Prime Minister on 6 April 1955 gave him complete support.

---

1 Ian Mikardo, *ibid*, 151.
2 *Ibid*, 152.
3 Aneurin Bevan, *In Place of Fear* (London, 1997), 21.
4 Read her book *My Life with Nye* (London, 1980), which is extremely entertaining about the partnership.
5 Nicklaus Thomas-Symonds, *Nye, ibid*, 206.

Attlee wanted to support the US from a distance but anticipated a fierce attack from Aneurin Bevan. He was right. Bevan walked to the despatch box in the House of Commons and announced that he could not support Clement Attlee.

Bevan keeps an eye on some of his most able supporters

The following day, without consulting any of the Bevanites, Bevan resigned from his role in the Labour Party. Under party rules, his resignation created an immediate vacancy in the Shadow Cabinet. The leadership position was offered to a politician who had the biggest vote in the most recent NEC election; Harold Wilson. Despite supporting Bevan's stance on Southeast Asia, and, much to the surprise of his friend Mikardo, Wilson leapt at the chance.[1] . Bevan realised that some of the politicians close to him, especially Wilson and Crossman, were ready to betray him to improve their own political chances. Bevan also knew the trade union leaders wanted to keep him and the Bevanites as quiet as possible in the annual conferences. This had happened in October 1952 at the particularly contentious Labour Party Conference in Morecambe. Ian Mikardo and Barbara Castle were kept off the stage completely and Aneurin Bevan was only able to take part in one debate.[2] Hugh Gaitskell and his followers, on the other hand, were given plenty of opportunity to argue their case.[3] The election of members to Labour's National Executive Committee was the high point of the conference. From them, Labour Party leader would then choose his shadow cabinet .The Bevanites were lobbying hard for the constituency representatives to vote left-wing politicians onto the NEC. Bevan was victorious, gaining more votes than any of his socalled followers. Barbara Castle came second with Ian Mikardo and Tom Driberg winning places on the NEC for the first time. Harold Wilson and Richard Crossman were elected while middle-of-the-road politicians like Herbert Morrison and Hugh Dalton lost their places.[4] The only non-Bevanite who kept his place was Jim Griffiths, who was at the peak of his popularity between 1951 and 1955.[5] When Attlee retired as leader, Bevan paid tribute to him in *Tribune*, a clear sign of the fiery Welshman's magnanimity.[6] In writing the tribute, Bevan hoped Labour Party members would see him as a safe successor to Attlee. The outgoing leader had never been a politician of enormous talent; however, what

---

1 Mikardo, *ibid,* 153
2 Lisa Martineau, *Politics and Power: Barbara Castle, A Biography* (London, 2000), 117. Ralph Miliband calls Bevan one of the 'old guard'. See Ralph Miliband, *Parliamentary Socialism: A Study in the Politics of Labour* (London, 1979, 2nd Impression), 326.
3 Stephen Haseler, *Gaitskellites* (London, 1969), 62–63
4 .Lisa Martineau, *ibid*, 118. James Griffiths, *Pages from Memory* (London, 1969,) 133.
5 James Griffiths, *Pages from Memory* (London, 1969), 133.
6 Aneurin Bevan, 'Clement Attlee', *Tribune*, 16 December 1955. 102d.

Attlee did have was what Bevan called a 'unique gift of intuition'.102 Bevan felt that it had been a privilege despite frequent disagreements to have served under Clement Attlee. Clearly, had Jim Griffiths been ten years younger, he would have easily succeeded Clement Attlee as the leader of the Labour Party. Bevan decided to stand, as did Herbert Morrison, who had been eyeing up the position for twenty years! But on 14 December 1955, Hugh Gaitskell emerged as the clear winner, securing 157 votes compared to Bevan's 70 and Morrison's 40 votes.[1] At hearing the result, Morrison left the room with his head lowered and without a word. George Wigg, a Midlands MP with his fingers in every Labour pie and Mikardo tried their best to console him.[2] His own resounding defeat at the hands of his fellow Labour MPs made Bevan realise the best thing he could under the circumstances was to co-operate with Gaitskell for the benefit of the Labour Party. Aneurin Bevan and Hugh Gaitskell were very passionate politicians with plenty of opinions to convey. The leadership vote, at the Labour conference in Margate, announced to the UK population, as well as the Labour movement, that Bevan and his followers had no place in any future Labour government.[3] There were 188 politicians who wanted the Bevanites removed from the Labour Party. In November 1952, Bevan stood again against Herbert Morrison, this time for the post of being deputy leader. He was again humiliated, with Morrison winning 194 votes and Bevan only 82. The following month, to the relief of Attlee, Morrison and Dalton, the Bevanites agreed to 'shut up shop' with a consequent threat to *Tribune* and the brains trusts. Fortunately, both were saved from the scrap heap. A few sane leaders argued that the weekly newsletter and the discussion panels both created a great deal of interest in the constituencies.

Relationship of Bevan with a number of world leaders

Aneurin Bevan was realising that his radical, rebellious mood was causing him needless trouble. He did not have many dependable disciples even within the Bevanites. To him, the publicity seeking Tony Benn symbolised the young middleclass politicians who had no time for him. He decided to raise his sights and enter the world stage, accepting invitations to India, Pakistan, Burma and Israel. On 28 February 1953, in a

---

1 Haseler, *The Gaitskellites*, 41, 'The new leader (Hugh Gaitskell) gave revisionism and the revisionists the important and decisive role which they had hitherto lacked.' Jim Griffiths was a great admirer of Gaitskell and believed that Bevan's tactic of withdrawing his name if Gaitskell did this had upset some of his supporters. Jim says, 'It was altogether too Machiavellian and created cynicism and finally decided many to turn and vote for Hugh Gaitskell, who won easily with 157 votes to Bevan's 70 and Herbert's 40. See *Pages from Memory*, 145.
2 Mikardo, *ibid*, 155.
3 Nicklaus Thomas-Symonds, *ibid*, 219.

speech to the Council for World Affairs in Delhi, Bevan outlined his specific vision on the subjects of the day. He was in favour of the 'third stream' and reminded India to avoid aligning itself with the great powers, the US as well as Russia. In August that year, he and his wife travelled to Yugoslavia and, in December, he was entertained in Egypt. Bevan was much admired in these countries, his popularity greater abroad than among his own Labour MPs. Over the years, he had become firm friends with statesmen of the non- aligned countries: Pandit Nehru, Marshall Tito, Pierre Mendès France, Pietro Nenni, Ben- Gurion and Figal Allon. In Britain, the Jewish people were more generous in their view of him than any other ethnic group .

A visit to Israel

In Israel, Bevan met with the parliamentary delegation, which included Ian Mikardo, Elwyn Jones from Llanelli (and MP for West Ham), and another Welshman, the Cardiff MP George Thomas.[1] Three Welshman and a Jew befriending each other in the Promised Land. The four met in the British Embassy in Tel Aviv. Bevan knew about the Parliamentary representatives' presence in the Israeli city through his wife. The Welshmen were very amused that Morrison, of all people, had been vanquished by George Thomas.[2] Bevan gave the others a detailed report on his visits and particularly on the situation in the Indian sub-continent. India was increasing its influence on the world stage. Burma, after a bloody civil war, was looking towards the Soviet Union and Pakistan, an Islamic country, which as usual had problems with the world of human rights.[3] Each Labour politician learnt a great deal from Bevan. Imparting knowledge was, after all, one of his huge political strengths.

Farming at Asheridge gives the Bevans a new lease of life

The purchase of Asheridge Farm in summer 1954 marked a big change in the lives of Aneurin Bevan and Jennie Lee. At Asheridge, Bevan could escape the scrutiny of journalists and his fellow politicians. By 1955, a clique of people led and supported by Herbert Morrison – Arthur Deakin (the trade union leader from Deeside), Hugh Gaitskell and Tom Williamson – were liaising to oust him from the Labour Party

---

1 E. H. Robertson, *George: A Biography of Viscount Tonypandy* (London, 1993), 138; Marcia Falkender, *Downing Street in Perspective* (London, 1983), 176. She mentions that Wilson, as well as Bevan, was on excellent terms with the well-known Jewish politicians like Golda Meir, Yitzhak Rabin. Abba Eban, Shimon Peres and the diplomats Gideon Rafael and Eppie Evron.
2 *Ibid,* 139
3 *Ibid.*

once and for all. On 7 March 1955, the parliamentary committee of the Labour Party met to discuss the troublemaker Aneurin Bevan.[1] The plan was to deprive him of the Whip and all the benefits of being a party member. Only four people from the Labour hierarchy were on his side: his faithful friend Jim Griffiths, Harold Wilson, Hugh Dalton and Alf Robens.[2] Bevan was spared their cross-examination only because he was unwell. At a meeting on 16 March, the veteran trade unionist Fred Lee (MP for Newton) tried to ease the situation by offering an amendment. Unfortunately, the majority of the Labour members did not want to spare Bevan the ultimate punishment and they voted 141 to 112 to remove the Whip from him.[3] The drama then moved to the NEC, which discussed the question of dismissing him from the Labour Party completely. Several constituency executive committees sent letters to Transport House pleading for the NEC to show mercy but, as we have seen, Bevan had made enemies within the large trade unions. One such enemy was Sir Vincent Tewson, the general secretary of the Trade Union Congress, who sent a hateful letter to Gaitskell in which he said:

> Somewhere along the road Nye ceased to be of use to democratic socialism and became a rogue elephant – a menace to the movement.[4]

Tewson's words could not have been more devastating to the founder of the NHS. For Bevan, the purpose of politics was to promote democratic socialism. He did not wish to be a burden and a danger to the movement he had loved so passionately since his youth.

Attlee cares about Bevan's future in the Labour Party

Clement Attlee must be admired for his defence of the prodigal son. At the fateful meeting of 23 March 1955, he told Bevan to prepare a statement for the NEC and to be prepared to be thoroughly cross-examined by the sub-committee, which was answerable in the end to the full committee.[5] This approach was agreed by a hair's breadth with the voting 14 to 13. Attlee then took matters into his own hands and met with Aneurin Bevan, suggesting he should, as soon as possible, apologise in

---

1 Nicklaus Thomas-Symonds, *ibid*, 219.
2 *Ibid*.
3 *Ibid*.
4 Letter to Hugh Gaitskell, 20 March 1955. It can be seen among the papers of the Trade Union Congress, Modern Records Centre, University of Warwick (MSS 292/752/2). As the letter is among the papers of Sir Vincent Tewson, scholars maintain that he must be the author of the letter condemning Aneurin Bevan.
5 Kenneth Harris, *Attlee* (London, 1984), 530–531.

sackcloth and ashes. By the time the sub-committee met on 29 March and the NEC on the following day, Attlee had managed to calm the storm. Bevan's apology was accepted by a vote of twenty to six. Clearly it was Attlee who had the last word, though there were obvious reasons for keeping Bevan within the ranks at a time when they were certain to be facing a General Election soon.[1] Attlee knew that had Tewson, Williamson and the rest of the powerful trade union barons succeeded in expelling Aneurin Bevan, the Labour Party would have been severely damaged for ever. Anthony Eden took advantage of the Labour Party's distraction and, on 15 April, he called for a General Election to take place on 26 May. Bevan tried hard to appear contrite, but, even in his weakest moments, his language remained as colourful as ever. Referring to a parable of Jesus, he compared the Tories to the swine rushing over the cliffs to be drowned in the sea. The Tories created a huge fuss about the comparison, which was meaningful to a generation who still attended nonconformist chapels in large numbers — the chapels in the anthracite coalfield of South Wales were still comfortably full. The astute TV pundit and academic David Butler memorably said:

> It was only an innocent biblical metaphor but it was eagerly seized on by Conservative speakers and journalists as evidence that the man who had once called them vermin was now calling them swine.[2]

Bevan's name and his remarks were quoted in at least ten per cent of the Tory candidates' literature and Winston Churchill himself spoke in his Woodford constituency about the evil man who made trouble throughout the world. Here are the exact words of the former Prime Minister:

> The politician who causes most anxiety to every friend and ally of Britain all over the world. Undoubtedly his influence in the Socialist Party is great and growing. This is the man, this valuable careerist, who has called at least half his countrymen all sorts of names which have been helpful on our party platform.[3,4]

---

1 Eric Shaw, *Discipline and Discord in the Labour Party: The Politics of Managerial Control in the Labour Party, 1951–1987* (Manchester, 1988), 43.
2 D. E. Butler, *The British General Election of 1955* (London, 1955), 60.
3 *Ibid.* 78.
4 General Election results. Bevan won 26,058 votes against James E Bowen, the Conservative candidate who secured 6,822 votes in the Ebbw Vale constituency. A total of 32,880 people voted, that is 83.7% of the electorate.

Bevan did not have to worry about the Tories in Ebbw Vale. The same candidate as in 1951 – James E Bowen – stood against him in 1955 and Bevan again enjoyed a sizeable majority. But in Britain overall, the Tories won the day with 344 seats. Labour was well behind with 277 MPs.[1] Many held Bevan personally responsible for the Labour Party's defeat but the accusation was unfair: the election was lost for a number of reasons.[2] But the popular press was right in referring to the civil war within the ranks of the Labour Party. The 1955 General Election was the first time television played a key role in the democratic process. Eden had the edge over Attlee on the television screens. In its manifesto, the Labour Party called for the re-nationalisation of public transport, freight transport and the iron and steel industries, and for the country to reconsider compulsory national service. Aneurin Bevan travelled the whole country, addressing massive meetings everywhere. But he and other campaigners sensed a distinct lack of interest among the electorate. Labour policies had limited appeal at a time when the standard of living for most people was improving. In its verdict on the General Election, one newspaper, the *Sunday Dispatch*, gave its verdict in a sentence which had more than a measure of truth:

> Apart from their own impressive record as a government, the Conservative Party's greatest asset was undoubtedly Mr. Aneurin Bevan.[3]

Despite the result, Labour stalwarts had enjoyed hearing Bevan's persistent attacks on Anthony Eden. He had said of him eighteen years earlier:

> Beneath the sophistication of his appearance and manner he has all the unplumbable stupidities and unawareness of his class and type.[4]

---

1 Nicklaus Thomas-Symonds, *Nye*, 220.
2 Even Jim Griffiths, the placid moderate politician, placed some of the blame for Labour's defeat at the polls on Bevan and the Bevanites. He says of the 1955 General Election: 'We were caught rather unprepared. The "Nye" row earlier in the year – indeed the trouble ever since 1951 and, in particular, since the Morecambe conference in '52 – had split us badly. We did not have the appearance of an alternative government.' *Pages from Memory*, 141.
3 Kenneth O Morgan, Michael Foot, ibid, 158
4 Aneurin Bevan, Anthony Eden, *Tribune*, 12 November 1937, 4; Nicklaus Thomas-Symonds, *Nye*, 220.

CHAPTER 14

The new Aneurin in British politics

Aneurin Bevan was in a quandary after the 1955 General Election. He was not comfortable with his supporters and was greatly constrained by not having the opportunities he sought from the British Labour Party. In terms of popularity, there was no problem: every year he would win sufficient votes to get a place on the NEC but he knew that he was facing a losing battle trying to win the backing of the trade union barons.

Bevan is elected treasurer of the Labour Party

When the post of the Labour Party treasurer became available, Bevan decided to put his name forward. While the post carried very little responsibility or even much workload, it would bring him within Labour's inner circle again. Bevan knew Hugh Gaitskell was likely to oppose him for any official post – indeed he did on every occasion. In an article explaining why he was standing, Bevan said he believed the Labour Party had lost the last election because its manifesto contained no alternative socialist policy on foreign or home affairs.[1] He acknowledged that, because of the conservatism of the Labour Party leaders and delegates, he had no chance of getting the better of Gaitskell, but the challenge was important as Labour would not regain its power until it freed itself of the bureaucracy which stifled its administration.[2] He again lost. Bevan finally admitted to himself that if he wanted to climb the political

---

1 Aneurin Bevan, 'Why I Am Standing for Treasurer', *Tribune*, 7 October 1955.
2 *Ibid*, 2. Bevan lost once more. He was really annoyed that he could not be party treasurer and, at a rally under the auspices of *Tribune*, he criticised the hierarchy of the Labour Party, in particular Attlee and Gaitskell, calling them 'desiccated calculating machines'. See Kenneth O. Morgan, *Michael Foot*, 158. He won in 1956 and became the treasurer

ladder and be accepted by his contemporaries in the shadow cabinet, he would have to compromise his principles as he had done as Minister of Health. He was now 58, while Gaitskell was a younger man, who was gaining more support from trade union leaders every month with the help of the influential Labour politicians. Bevan continued to address rallies vigorously, while spending his leisure time on his farm, rearing pigs and growing flowers on a fairly large scale. Politically, he still craved for a prominent appointment in a Labour administration – foreign secretary at least. Early in December 1955, Bevan had another chance to try for the Labour leadership. On 7 December 1955, Clement Attlee resigned after twenty years as Labour leader. The deputy leader was Herbert Morrison, an experienced politician who, like Bevan, had failed to wrestle the leadership from Attlee. Aneurin threw his hat into the ring once more but knew any hope he had of winning had long since disappeared. He was proved right. Gaitskell won with a huge majority over Bevan and Morrison.[1] Morrison was furious and immediately resigned on 14 December. With little consideration, Bevan agreed to stand for election again, this time for the post of deputy leader to his enemy Gaitskell. This time, his opponent was his friend Jim Griffiths. It was a memorable contest. Jim Griffiths was elected with 141 votes to Aneurin's 111.[2] It was disappointing for Bevan to see the MPs from Ebbw Vale's neighbouring constituencies, Harold Finch and Ness Edwards, voting for Jim rather than for him. Other MPs from the Labour Party intelligentsia also refused to vote for him, fearful of Bevan's flamboyant utterances. In the eyes of Labour leaders, Jim Griffiths was a gentleman while Aneurin Bevan was a persistent troublemaker.

Bevan was enraged by this second failure and, two days after the vote, in Manchester, he spoke out angrily against the Labour leaders who argued for socialism from an academic point of view rather than from their understanding of morality and solidarity with the working class. It was Gaitskell he had in mind. He added:

> I know that I shall be in trouble for speaking as I have, but I am not a Communist. I am a democratic Socialist. The trouble with the movement is that decisions are taken by those who are in power and carried out by those in the square mile.[3]

Surprisingly, this honest admission caused him no trouble.

---

1 Gaitskell received 157 votes, 20 for Bevan and 4 for Morrison. Bevan had stood for deputy leader in November 1951 when he received 82 votes. At that time, Morrison was elected to the post. See Nicklaus Thomas-Symonds, *Nye: The Political Life of Aneurin Bevan*, 222.
2 Mark M. Krug, *Aneurin Bevan: Cautious Rebel* (New York and London, 1961), 232. 'Aneurin Bevan was stung and angered by this second humiliating defeat suffered in a short period of time. He bitterly resisted the implacable opposition to the trade union leaders, which continued in spite of Bevan's acknowledged effort to mend his way and to comply with Party regularity'.
3 'Mr Bevan's Broadside', *New Statesman and Nation*, February 11, 1956, 140.

Gaitskell offers Bevan a new responsibility

Soon afterwards, Gaitskell invited Aneurin Bevan to be the shadow Secretary of State for the Colonies. There were several reasons for this. Gaitskell realised that, despite their regular rows, he needed the presence of this extraordinary Welshman to strengthen his shadow cabinet and leadership, as well as gaining the backing of the moderate left wingers. Aneurin Bevan was hugely talented and brilliant speaker and having his support would be a bonus for everyone. There was no hope of winning an election if the Labour movement continued with this infighting. And while Gaitskell was not aware of it, Bevan was now ready to compromise within the ranks. Despite believing he possessed more leadership ability than Gaitskell, he had no choice but to accept the majority of his Labour colleagues did not feel the same. For them, Gaitskell was the obvious choice. Yet party unity could be possible, not least because Arthur Deakin, the hard line trade unionist leader and outspoken critic of Bevan, was dead. At the end of 1955, his successor as general secretary of the TGWU was appointed. Frank Cousins was a close friend of Aneurin and a protagonist for the left wing. Cousins was born into a poor Doncaster family and left school at eleven to work as a miner. In his lifetime, Deakin had not appreciated Cousins any more than he did Bevan. Cousins believed it was crucial to reunite the right and the left wings of the Labour Party; in his view, it was time to back Bevan as well as Gaitskell. As Mark M. Krug says:

> The new triumvirate of Gaitskell, Cousins and Bevan was ready to lead the Labour Party to an election victory, but Bevan had still to show that he would not get out of step with his new allies.[1]

The newspaper headlines began to change to 'the new face of Bevan' or 'New Nye' and he became much more constrained.[2] In February 1956, in a debate on the house-building situation – a subject on which Bevan was very knowledgeable – he spoke moderately. Such a thoughtful demeanour had not been seen since his time as Minister for Health and Housing. He was thanked by Duncan Sandys, Minister for Housing and Local Government, for being so positive.[3] The same agreeable disposition was seen in his speeches as Shadow Minister for the Colonies. These addresses were crafted effectively and showed the reading and thought that had gone into his analysis of the state of the colonies. He spoke with huge knowledge

---

1 Krug, *ibid*, 235.
2 *Ibid*. King used the caption 'The New Nye' as the title of Chapter XIV of his entertaining biography, 231–250.
3 *Hansard*, Vol. DXLVIII (1956), column 2745.

and authority. The civil service saw again another side of him and, within a short period of time, he was complimented by the Conservative politician Alan Lennox-Boyd, the Secretary of State for the Colonies.

Travels as Shadow Minister to the Colonies

In March 1956, Aneurin Bevan was assessing the situation in Cyprus.[1] He gave a detailed analysis of Cyprus that amazed all who heard him in the Commons. The main problem was that the government had not come to a decision on the future of the island and he was greatly concerned for Britain's relationship with Cyprus. Bevan argued for self-government for the Greeks, the original population of the island, on the understanding that Britain would keep a military presence there. He argued that Britain needed a presence in Cyprus to fulfil NATO's obligations to protect the oil coming from the Middle East to Britain and Western Europe. This was one of the main expectations and he believed that the world's major powers understood this. The Soviet Union and America must understand that, like Britain, they had to have absolute access to Middle Eastern oil.[2]

Bevan did not agree with the government's attitude towards Archbishop Makarios because they considered him linked to Cypriot terrorists. After all, they had in the past negotiated with Nehru in India and Dr. K. Khrumah, leader of the Gold Coast. These leaders were linked with underground terrorist movements which were inevitably promoting violence. In February, the Lord Chancellor appointed Bevan to be a member of a Round Table Conference to discuss the status of Malta.[3]

Bevan worked alongside conference members from various parties and spoke positively, with sympathy for the government, adding that he did not want to complicate matters. But he knew one thing: Malta was an important maritime position for Britain. With this in mind, he suggested Malta should be integrated into the United Kingdom so that the population of Malta could be represented in Westminster.[4] Even when discussions became heated and emotional, the eloquent Bevan kept his feelings under control. Now his was the voice of the moderate politician in the tradition of Jim Griffiths. When there was a debate on Kenya and the Mau Mau revolt, he did his homework thoroughly. He knew as much about Kenya's political, social and agricultural problems as any specialist from the Colonial Office and took care to remind parliament that Britain had faced dreadful times in

---

1 *Ibid*, Vol. DL (1956), column 387.
2 *Ibid*, column 400.
3 Krug, *ibid*, 238.
4 *Ibid*.

the colonies including Aden, Cyprus, Kenya, Malta and Singapore.[1] He made it clear that he had no radical solution and did not blame the government minister as he had done in the past. He expressed great distress for the cruelty carried out by Mau Mau terrorists, forcing the British authorities to ensure that law and order triumphed in Kenya. In August 1956, Bevan spoke on behalf of a large section of the electorate, including liberalminded Tories, when he voiced his anger on hearing that Archbishop Makarios had been brutally arrested and exiled. In his view, such action was a gift to dictators like Mao in China, Joseph Stalin and Colonel Nasser. The Speaker of the House of Commons caught a glimpse of the old, nonconformist Bevan when he delivered a typical contemptuous remark:

> Good heaven, look at the Front Bench opposite. A bigger collection of guileless ignoramuses I have never seen in my life.[2]

Fortunately, other memorable performances at Westminster increased Gaitskell's confidence that Aneurin Bevan was finally on his side .

Stands again for the post of treasurer

Such was Bevan's determination to atone that he stood a second time for the inconsequential post of party treasurer, the appointment of which would be decided by a vote at the annual conference in Blackpool.[3] the office meant automatic membership of the NEC. Political commentators believed that nobody could now have an issue with 'New Nye' except perhaps for a handful of reactionary right-wing trade union leaders, those who refused to forget his ingrained Welsh nonconformity. The National Union of Mine Workers and the National Union of Railway Workers supported him but the Amalgamated Engineering Union indicated its intention to support Charles Parnell, a Leeds MP and a great admirer of Jim Griffiths.

To complicate the situation, George Brown was nominated by the Transport and General Workers Union as an opponent. If Cousins had agreed with his union officials, it would have been the end for Bevan. The right and the left were again feuding with relish, with the trade unions divided for the first time for years, and once again by Aneurin Bevan. He was elected as party treasurer with 3,029,000 votes, with Brown receiving 2,755,000 and Charles Parnell a long way behind. When the results were announced, Bevan received deafening applause from the

---
1 *Ibid.*
2 *Hansard*, Vol. DLVII (1956), column 1474.
3 Mark M. Krug, *Aneurin Bevan: Cautious Rebel* (New York and London, 1961), 242.

conference delegates. It was an emotional moment for him, coming just a year after he was in danger of being expelled from the party. Frank Cousins' backing and friendship had helped Labour Party members again recognise the Ebbw Vale MP's worth. The electorate were in favour of him, while a million moderate trade union representatives had heeded Bevan and Gaitskell's appeal for unity. According to Barbara Castle, Cousins' predecessor Arthur Deakin would have withheld the union's support from Bevan.[1] *The Economist*, one of the finest contemporary periodicals, welcomed the result saying:

'It is a party that urgently needs Mr Bevan as a lieutenant.'[2]

The Suez crisis and the Red Army mistreating the Hungarians

A tense atmosphere was hanging over the October 1956 Labour conference. The socialist nationalist Colonel Nasser had become the undisputed dictator of Egypt in 1955 and planned to irrigate the Egyptian desert. He started by building the Aswan Dam; however, he was able to raise sufficient funds for this massive infrastructure project and so, in July 1956, he decided to take possession of the Suez Canal. As expected, France and Britain responded with military action. The British Labour Party disagreed, arguing that action should be taken through the United Nations with the support of the White House and the leadership of the US President.

Hugh Gaitskell gave an inspirational speech to the conference. He did not condone President Nasser and his violence, but neither did he support the use of British soldiers in Egypt. Following the conference, there was pressure on Bevan to represent the Labour Party on the Suez issue. By now, his speeches in Parliament were acceptable to all the opposition Parliamentarians.[3] He had demonstrated he could conduct himself as a statesman. In the House of Commons, Bevan expressed his pain at having to oppose the Conservative government policy on Egypt. The Prime Minister Anthony Eden and his colleagues were grateful to him for his understanding and sympathy.[4] The 'new Aneurin' was so different from the old, who was always laying down the law. But Bevan had his difficulties occasionally reading the signs

---

1 , Barbara Castle, 'It Could Not Have Happened in Arthur's Day', *New Statesman and Nation,* 13 October 1956, 441. She was referring to the anti- Bevan outlook of Arthur Deakin. After Deakin's death, his post was offered to Frank Cousins who admired Bevan: '(he) stuck his neck out and invited Bevan and the Bevanites to forget their old differences and work together for a united Party.' See, Geoffrey Goodman, *The Awkward Warrior: Frank Cousins, His Life and Times* (London, 1979), 20.
2 *Economist,* 6 October 1956, 20.
3 *Hansard,* Vol. DLVII (1956), column 1454.
4 *Ibid,* column 1707–1708.

of the times accurately. The Soviet Union could at times misled him on foreign affairs. Bevan voiced his opinion that the Soviet Union had used the KGB to keep its population for ever in fear of the secret police.[1] On 4 November, four days after his views on Russia, came the news that the Red Army had attacked protestors in Budapest and had taken over Hungary.[2] Bevan realised that Nasser had the goal of nationalisation within his nationalism. and, at every opportunity, he tried to adopt a moderate attitude. Even when he was addressing protestors in Trafalgar Square, he did not let his eloquence get the better of him. Even the editorial piece in the weekly journal *The Economist* praised him for his excellent speech.[3]

Aneurin Bevan's attitude towards the Soviet Union was complicated. In his speech in the House of Commons on 8 November, he failed to condemn the Soviet Union's cruel action as he was expected and as he should have done.[4] He naturally placed some of the blame for the Middle East debacle on Nasser's use force in Egypt, thus heartening and strengthening the military element in Russia. For the Russian leaders, Britain's fierce action against Nasser was responsible for what came to pass in Hungary. Bevan's conscience could not let him condemn Russia's interference. He went as far as to justify Russia's attack on Hungary because of two other things: the re-arming of West Germany and the Baghdad Pact. He felt that the British Prime Minister's invasion of Egypt took away any claim by Britain to be on the moral high ground in international affairs and he could not for a moment separate the events in Hungary from the events that happened in Egypt. He would like to see a conference of Western powers as well as Russian leaders to meet and sort out the dire situation. In truth, Bevan was wrong about Hungary, but the media, like Labour's leaders, fully supported him. To *The Economist*, he was one of the greatest men in the Labour Party and deserving of the highest office in a Labour government.[5] On the issue of Suez, Bevan had been accurate. Aneurin Bevan and Russia were dismayed by the actions of Britain and France. Anthony Eden's already poor health worsened as a result of the stress he endured over the Suez Crisis. Eventually, his illness forced him to resign and he was succeeded by Harold Macmillan, a close friend of Bevan since the thirties. The Suez Crisis was a milestone in British history and Bevan considered Britain's influence as an imperial nation was diminished by it. After 1956, the Conservatives withdrew British forces from the countries east of Suez. Nasser had gained the upper hand and was a hero in his country,

---

1 *Ibid,* column 1709.
2 *Hansard*, vol. DLVII (1956), columns 1715–1716.
3 *Hansard*, vol. DLVII (1956), columns 1715–1716.
4 *Hansard*, vol. DLVII (1956), columns 1715–1716.
5 Here is *The Economist's* praise: 'First he is so clearly one of the biggest men in the Labour movement that he ought to be given one of the biggest jobs in any Labour government. Secondly, however, any Labour MP who thinks that Mr Bevan will not some day re-open his personal feud with Mr Gaitskell is almost certainly living in a fool's paradise.' See *Economist*, 17 November 1956, 580.

while Britain still had to learn the lesson of keeping out of needless wars. Bevan had shown considerable judgement in his reaction to Suez, yet his stance towards Russia and its oppressive force in Hungary was less sound. Labour MPs acknowledged his talents but did not want him to be party leader, most preferring him to be Gaitskell deputy leader. In the election for shadow cabinet places on 29 November 1956, Bevan had to cede first place to Harold Wilson and second place to Alfred Roberts.[1] Gaitskell realised that Bevan was not likely to become leader and, to him reward for his stance on Suez, invited him to be Shadow Foreign Secretary. Gaitskell acted wisely. Some Labour leaders believed that Bevan was much more centrist than he had ever been. Editors at *The Economist* argued that Bevan had been overambitious in the past but was now ready to act as part of a team. According to the internationally read *Time* magazine, he was often talked about and praised for his parliamentary skills and potential.[2] He was by far the best speaker on Suez in the Labour Party. Scottish farmer John Mackie, one of Bevan's closest friends, recalls the agony the Suez Crisis caused him. During the crisis, Mackie had invited the Bevans, Ian Mikardo, Leslie Hale (the MP for Oldham West) and other friends to dinner. Hale and Mikardo opposed Bevan's stance on Suez but he did not give in. Bevan's debating style was always at its best around a dinner table. He appreciated the views of those who disagreed with him and would often reconsider his own opinion in the light of what had been said. The Cold War distressed him and, by 1955, he realised Russia had amassed a vast arsenal of nuclear arms including atomic and hydrogen bombs. Russia was making it very clear to the West that it would not allow any of the Eastern European countries independence from the clutches of the Soviet Union. Thousands of Hungarians were killed by soviet soldiers and tanks and at least 190, 000 fled to the Western countries , many of them coming to Britain and at least 190.000 subsequently fled to the West seeking freedom and safety, many of them arriving in Britain.[3] The Soviet Union's actions caused a rift in the British Communist Party, with many intellectuals leaving the party they had served for decades and being welcomed into the Labour Party.

---

1 Krug, *ibid*, 249.
2 This is American magazine *Time*'s tribute to Bevan on 10 December 1956, p. 27: 'He handled the assignment with humanity, indefatigable curiosity and parliamentary skill, demonstrating what his able mind can do when he checks his flamboyant gift for invective and extravagant statements. Many in the House believe that Bevan handled the Suez case against Eden more effectively than Gaitskell himself.'
3 See 'Hungarian Revolution (1956)' in *Oxford Encyclopedia of World History* (Oxford, 1997), 314. There was an uprising against communist rule from 23 October until 4 November 1956. Imre Nagry became Prime Minister but the Soviet Union did not keep its promise and Nagry and other prominent leaders were secretly executed. There is a useful summary of Hungary as a country on pages 314–15.

The result of Russia's actions in Hungary and the foolishness of Britain in Suez

Aneurin Bevan was naive enough to believe it was possible to deal with Russia as though it was a Western nation. That is why he was so ambivalent about the dreadful Hungarian situation. He considered Britain had as much right to lead the world as did the United States. His conscience meant he believed nuclear weapons should be destroyed, but not before every country which possessed arms also disarmed. Most of his friends agreed with him and supported the Campaign for Nuclear Disarmament. In fact, it was the churches and many in the Labour who initiated the campaign. There followed articles, books, and marches across Britain condemning Britain's thoughtless act in setting off a hydrogen bomb on a remote island in 1952.

The Campaign against Nuclear Disarmament (CND) was launched in London and became a familiar term in English, Scottish and Welsh communities. As the gospel of disarmament provoked great excitement and the 'Ban the Bomb' slogan became familiar, the Bevanites continued to sit on the fence over the issue. On 3 March 1955, there was a vote on the use of nuclear weapons. Megan Lloyd George felt a huge sympathy for the CND movement and felt that the Labour in opposition should at once oppose nuclear weapons. She received a letter from Clement Attlee, in which he said:

> You will, I am sure, realise that for the last week or so we have been rather taken up over the activities of your volatile compatriot from Ebbw Vale.[1]

One can see the dilemma facing Bevan. However, by the time of the Suez debate on the 5 December, he was in great form. Once again Bevan showed how, when it was necessary, he could reach the heights of oratory on a pressing issue. One of those in the gallery listening to him was Lady Megan Lloyd George, in fact it the speech was one of the reasons she soon joined the Labour Party (she had previously been the Liberal MP for Anglesey but lost her seat in 1952). Megan Lloyd George sent Bevan a letter congratulating him on his excellent speech.[2]

---

[1] Mervyn Jones, *A Radical Life: The Biography of Megan Lloyd George* (London, 1991), 247.
[2] Michael Foot, *Aneurin Bevan*, Vol. 2, 533; Mervyn Jones, *A Radical Life*, 277: 'You can judge of its revolutionary character and effect by the fact that it brought Violet Bonham-Carter and me together in almost glowing unity in the gallery. A thousand congratulations!'

The by-election in Carmarthenshire

When Megan Lloyd George fought the Carmarthen by-election as the Labour candidate in February 1957, the main concern for Labour was the Suez Crisis and its painful consequences. For the daughter of David Lloyd George, the priority was peace. Bevan feared she was taking too big a risk in making Suez the focus in a West Wales constituency; however, she knew the Plaid Cymru candidate, Jennie Eirian Davies, would certainly focus on the imperialist policies of the reactionary Tory government.[1]. It transpired that the Welsh voters were quite ready to agree with the woman they called the 'Suez candidate' and she was duly elected as Carmarthen's new MP.[2] Four thousand people paid their shilling to hear Cledwyn Hughes, Aneurin Bevan and Megan Lloyd George speak at the market hall in Carmarthen.[3] It was in fact, the first time either Bevan or Hughes had spoken in Carmarthen. That night Bevan was inspired and, in his speech, he gave a graphic description of Eden leaving Downing Street.[4]

The Road to Brighton Pier

Yet 1957 was going to be a year of losing friends and support for Aneurin and Jennie. There was disorder in Bevan's camp when, at the annual conference in Brighton, he argued against a policy of nuclear disarmament on behalf of the Labour Party. Gaitskell was firmly against any watering down of the official Labour Party policy. On the Saturday, Bevan consulted Sam Watson, a miners' leader from the Durham coalfield and an influential member on the NEC. Despite being he a hero of the party's moderate wing, Watson thought highly of Aneurin. The two men enjoyed each other's company and were proud of their mining background. Watson's only words to Bevan were: 'We need you as foreign secretary in a Labour government.'[5]

Later, Bevan went for a walk with Ian Mikardo, another of his earliest supporters, explaining to him that he was to speak on behalf of the NEC refusing the call for

---

1 Mervyn Jones, *A Radical Life, ibid,* 282.
2 *Ibid,* 283.
3 D. Ben Rees, *Cofiant Cledwyn Hughes: Un o Wŷr Mawr Môn a Chymru,* (Biography of Cledwyn Hughes: One of the Greats of Anglesey and Wales) (Talybont, 2017), 271; Mervyn Jones, *A Radical Life, ibid,* 287.
4 'And so the Prime Minister was sacrificed. But don't imagine that the lamb was dragged willingly to the sacrificial stone. He had to be hauled there'. See Foot, *Aneurin Bevan* Vol. 2, 536.
5 Mervyn Jones, *Michael Foot* (London, 1994), 221.

unilateral disarmament. He truly believed he could bring the Cold War to an end and no other foreign secretary would be ready to contemplate that. Mikardo believed that Sam Watson's influence on Bevan was obvious.[1] The debate at conference was an emotional one and of a high calibre. Judith Hart, a Labour politician from Scotland (who became the MP for Lanark in 1959), blamed the Attlee Labour government for having created the atomic bomb in the first place. The exiled Welshman Harold Davies was more controversial still and with characteristic Welsh flourish announced, to the delight of his supporters that the Labour Party needed moral and political leadership .. When Frank Cousins spoke, there was sincerity in his words and a firm suggestion that the large trade union called TGWU would vote for nuclear disarmament. When Aneurin Bevan addressed the conference, many delegates felt he gave one of the most disappointing speeches of his life. This was perhaps understandable in that he was now denying his life-long philosophy as the unofficial leader of the Bevanites.[2] The Messiah of the left had betrayed his admirers. These are the memorable words of the historian Keith Laybourn:

> Bevan effectively divested himself of the title 'Leader of the Left' at the 1957 Labour Party Conference by attacking the idea of unilateral disarmament, claiming to be unwilling to send a British Foreign Secretary 'naked into the conference chamber'.[3]

Another historian, Donald Sassoon, summarised Bevan's position in two sentences, which convey his weakest hour as a politician:

> Bevan's renunciation of unilateralism was almost certainly due to his belief that his post as Shadow Foreign Secretary would never otherwise be translated into its equivalent in a Labour government.

If such was his thinking, he was certainly correct since the unilateralist position was always seen by friends and foes alike, as an 'oppositional' posture and, at best, as a symbolic gesture of the party's commitment to a 'third way' in foreign affairs.[4]

There were two other reasons for the apparent change in Bevan's attitude, the Suez Crisis and his familiarity with Nikita Khrushchev, the leader of the Soviet Union. At the time of the Suez Crisis, Bevan realised that Britain depended too heavily for its defence on the United States. As he says in his final memoir:

---
1 *Ibid*, 222.
2 *Ibid*, 222.
3 Keith Laybourn, *A Century of Labour: A History of the Labour Party*, 104.
4 Donald Sassoon, *One Hundred Years of Socialism: The West European Left in the Twentieth Century* (London, 1996), 224.

While the H-bomb had superseded the A-bomb (Britain exploded an A-bomb in April 1957) that had not changed. If anything, Suez had reinforced Britain's junior position. To have a measure of independence from American foreign policy, and standing on the world stage, Britain needed its own H-bomb. Without it, Bevan could not even try to set about his idea of using non-aligned countries to break the deadlock of the Cold War.[1]

In September 1957, Bevan attended the Conference of International Socialists in Vienna, where there was agreement on a policy of *multilateralism*. That same month, Bevan had an opportunity to get together with Khrushchev in Russia. Richard Crossman believed Khrushchev had convinced Bevan that the Soviet Union did not want Britain to go down the path of unilateral disarmament.[2] All the major powers should disarm at the same time and that was the point of the phrase 'naked into the conference chambers of the world'. But it was the end of an era for Bevan when the result was announced at the Labour Conference : 5,836,000 voted for multilateralism and 781,000 for nuclear disarmament.[3] Bevan's friends were disappointed in him.[4] Amid the press corps, Victor Weisz, known as Vicky, was dismayed and drew a cartoon of Gandhi with the caption: 'I went naked into the conference chamber'.[5] Michael Foot, his most loyal follower, could not for a minute understand what had happened to his hero,.[6] The left wing within the British Labour party was dismayed, it was nearly destroyed .

Bevan regarded as a traitor by the leading left wingers

Aneurin Bevan had betrayed them all after a long period of campaigning. He was bitterly criticised and called a hypocrite and a traitor. According to Foot, Bevan had made the worst mistake of his life.[7] The following week *Tribune*, which was in deep financial trouble, published several letters of disappointment. These letters were

---

1 Nicklaus Thomas-Symonds, *Nye: The Political Life of Aneurin Bevan*, 229.
2 . Janet Morgan (ed.), *The Backbench Diaries of Richard* Crossman (London, 1981, 609
3 Nicklaus Thomas-Symonds, *Nye, ibid,* 233. Bevan said to his old comrades: 'You have not realised that the consequence of passing that resolution [no. 24] would be to drive Great Britain into a diplomatic purdah.'
4 NLW Huw T Edwards Papers A1/365. Letter of Aneurin Bevan to Huw T .Edwards , dated 23 October 1957
5 Nicklaus Thomas-Symonds, *Nye, ibid,* 233.See also Geoffrey Goodman, *From Bevan to Blair: Fifty Years of Reporting from the Political Front Line* (Brighton, 2010), 75–6.
6 Mervyn Jones, *Michael Foot, ibid,* 222
7 *Ibid.*

short but to the point: Nye Bevan, our stormy petrel, has turned out to be a very tame duck indeed.[1]

And this sentence from his home town:

> We are naked, without H-bombs, but fully clothed in morality.[2]

But the reader who summarises the feelings and admiration of so many of those who idolised him is this one sentence:

> Our trust in Aneurin Bevan will never be displaced, with his unequalled courage, sagacity, and brilliant thought.[3]

How did Jennie Lee feel? She came to accept his stance, seeing that the brave speech was a way forward for Labour to win the next General Election. She did not want to see her husband return to the wilderness where he had so often been.[4] When Michael Foot, Jennie Lee and Bevan met in the *Tribune* office the Monday after the conference, there was a fierce quarrel. Bevan thought the editor and staff of *Tribune* should keep out of the discord and remain neutral. There was no need to take either his side or Michael's. Unfortunately, under Bevan's influence, it was not that sort of a paper. If Michael Foot had agreed with Bevan's desire, the staff would have resigned and readers would have cancelled their subscriptions. Foot could see Bevan was more isolated than he had been in his whole career. Now he was a whipping boy for both the left and the right. Everyone knows politics can be cruel, unkind and thankless but, in October 1957, no-one experienced that cruelty and isolation more keenly than Aneurin Bevan himself.[5] Foot wrote an article for *Tribune* under the title 'Bevan and the H-bomb' in which he set out the debate clearly and acceptably, revealing respect for the Welsh MP.[6] CND was disappointed as *Tribune* and its editor Dick Clements were in favour of unilateral disarmament. The relationship between Jennie Lee and Michael Foot was not favourable. In Foot's opinion, he and his staff should decide the shape and the content of the paper; though the generous directors, Jennie and Nye and Howard Samuel had an equal right. In a matter of this sort, they had to agree with the paper's stance. In retaliation, Jennie suggested to Samuel that he should withhold his subsidy, thus killing the paper off. Foot did

---

1 *Ibid.*
2 *Ibid,* 223.
3 *Ibid.*
4 Jennie Lee, *My Life with Nye*, 235.
5 Michael Foot, *Bevan,* Vol. 2, *ibid,* 583–4.
6 Michael Foot, 'Bevan and the H-Bomb', *Tribune*, 11 October 1957, 1.

not disclose this in his biography of Bevan but Jennie did not hide her frustration.[1] Fortunately, Bevan was not prepared to let this happen. While he was unhappy with what *Tribune* had done, he did not want to bring an important platform for the Labour Party left to an end.

Serious disruption to the friendship of Foot and Bevan

Foot's wife Jill Craigie was quite ready to cause trouble and expressed her feelings to, of all newspaper titans, Lord Beaverbrook – remembering how prejudiced the *Daily Express* could be against CND. As far as she was concerned, Aneurin Bevan had bade farewell to the leaders of the left as well as to Michael Foot, though he would never acknowledge that possibility.[2] On 29 December 1957 Jennie Lee wrote a letter – very typical of her – to Beaverbrook on the unhappy situation , suggesting that Howard Samuel was completely loyal to her beloved. The CND movement was gaining ground in Wales, Scotland and England, particularly among young people and those on the left. *Tribune* could be relied on in the campaign, while the Labour Party failed to hold meetings that could compete with the calibre of those with the Revd. Donald Soper, the Revd. Daniel R. Thomas of Merthyr, Canon John Collins and Professor Gwilym Bowyer of Bangor. When Bevan himself spoke at meetings, many of the audiences would call out, 'We are the majority.' Never a speaker to shy away from a battle, Bevan replied with passion, 'Here are the moralists. Here are the saints in their purity.'[3] The relationship between Michael Foot and Aneurin Bevan remained strained. Both men were very much troubled by the conference decision: they argued fiercely and sometimes lost their tempers. After years of friendship with Foot, Bevan believed he could eventually convince him that his way was right; Foot's article in *Tribune* following the conference gave him every reason to believe this.[4] Every time, they saw each other Bevan would directly attack Foot verbally. He often left the office in a temper, slamming doors for everyone to hear. Things came to a head in July 1958 after a reception at the Polish Embassy in London. The two couples returned to Jill and Michael's home together and at first enjoyed some rational conversation, Unfortunately, Bevan soon became agitated, a situation certainly not helped by the wine he had consumed that evening. He started using the kind of vulgar, filthy words he had probably only heard at pub closing time in Tredegar. Jennie and Jill became fearful when he lifted one of

---

1 Mervyn Jones, *ibid,* 228; Jennie Lee, *My Life with Nye,* 239.
2 Leshe Hunter, *The Road to Brighton Pier,* London, 1959, 47.
3 I was part of the movement. See D. Ben Rees, *Hunangofiant Di-Ben-Draw,* (Autobiography) (Talybont, 2015), where I mention the CND movement in Wales.
4 Mervyn Jones, *ibid,* 229.

the Foots' Sheraton chairs and brought it down to the floor with such force that the chair legs shattered. He had to leave hastily.[1]

Over time, Jill managed to reconcile the two old friends, but Bevan continued to believe that he was right on the question of multilateralism rather than supporting unilateral disarmament. Foot was determined *Tribune* should continue campaigning for unilateral disarmament and the paper's slogan became 'the paper which leads the bomb campaign'. Jennie Lee maintained that Samuel could easily withhold his subsidy for *Tribune. She* wanted to start another weekly paper, but Bevan could not agree with her proposal. As Jennie Lee later said:

> It was Nye who restrained us despite the heartbreak he felt from *Tribune's* attitude.[2]

The ongoing quarrel was undoubtedly a sad one for Aneurin Bevan and Michael Foot's families, as well as their close socialist friends.[3] The crux of their conflict was how to deal with the existence of nuclear weapons. Neither man was willing to compromise and accept they would not agree. As Nicklaus Thomas-Symonds says:

> Both were unquestionably objective enough to understand the arguments of the other, but neither could appreciate why the other took the view he did. The problem was that the bomb, and what to do about it, laid bare the differences between Bevan and Foot.[4]

Bevan realised he had to understand the Labour Party's standpoint and had after years reconciled with Gaitskell for the sake of Labour's future and his own place in its leadership stakes. They agreed on many issues, including nationalisation and public ownership. This 'new Aneurin' was far more friendly towards Gaitskell than Michael Foot could ever be – Foot could not stand to wait in the green room of a television centre if Gaitskell was also present at the studio.[5]

Bevan was a pragmatist to the bone by now. Foot continued to protest while Bevan considered himself to be on the verge of a new era when, as the British foreign secretary, he would be mixing with Prime Ministers and the top tier of international politics. It was the image he cherished. As his most recent biographer says:

---

1 Mervyn Jones, *ibid*, 229–30.
2 Michael Foot, *Aneurin Bevan: A Biography, Volume II: 1945–60*, 578– 602; Patricia Hollis, *Jennie Lee: A Life*, Oxford, 1997, 181.
3 Michael Foot, *Aneurin Bevan, Volume II*, 578–602; Patricia Hollis, *Jennie Lee: A Life*, Oxford, 1997, 181.
4 Nicklaus Thomas-Symonds, *Nye: The Political Life of Aneurin Bevan, ibid*, 236.
5 Nicklaus Thomas-Symonds, *Nye, ibid*, 237

> Bevan was most comfortable as a man of power. Foot was most comfortable as a man of dissent.[1]

That is the essence of the attitude of the two former friends and politicians by 1957.

More travelling for Bevan and Jennie

1957 was a defining year for Aneurin Bevan as a politician: he changed his stance on disarmament, became reconciled with Gaitskell and crossed swords with his admirer, Michael Foot. Bevan now appreciated the opportunities for international travel which came his way. India was, in his view, a country which deserved his backing as a Western politician. Jennie Lee had met Mahatma Gandhi when he visited England in 1929 and, throughout the thirties, Bevan was one of the main campaigners for Indian independence. The office of the Indian League was across the road the one occupied by *Tribune* and Bevan regularly called in to see its secretary Krishna Menon.

Aneurin and Jennie had also known Pandit Nehru for years. Bevan visited India in 1953 and thanked the parliamentary representatives there for their efforts to secure peace in Korea. He returned to India in 1957 to ensure India remained in the British Commonwealth. The Suez Canal was an important trade route for India and so the crisis had put huge economic strain on the country, not to mention its ongoing tension with Pakistan. Jennie had also got to know Indira Gandhi well after the month she spent in the sub-continent in January 1956.[2]

Another overseas trip that was important to the Bevans was their visit to Russia, Poland and Germany, during which they spent a day at Khrushchev's second home in Crimea. Jennie was amazed to discover Khrushchev was very fond of Aneurin's speeches and was able to quote sections from memory.[3] Bevan heard from the Russians that the Soviet Union did not want Britain to give up its nuclear arms. In fact, Bevan learnt a great deal about geopolitics from Nikita Khrushchev, Stalin's successor. Khrushchev and Bevan had the opportunity to discuss Russia's foreign policy of peaceful co-existence. When he became leader in 1958, Khrushchev tried

---

1 Michael Foot, *Aneurin Bevan*, Vol. 2, *ibid*, 391.
2 Patricia Hollis, *Jennie Lee: A Life*, *ibid*, 226.
3 'We were able to talk together at length and in perfect privacy, Nye, Khrushchev, myself and a superb interpreter sat together in a shady corner of the garden overlooking the Black Sea.' See Jennie Lee, *My Life with Nye*, *ibid*, 221.

to implement a policy of de-Stalinisation as well as to allow foreign visitors to come to Russia.[1]

Bevan's trip to Russia to meet Khrushchev showed how confident he was as a politician. The unpleasantness at Chequers in April 1956, when Khrushchev and Bulganin visited England, had been forgotten. At a second meeting on 23 April, Khrushchev lost his temper after Gaitskell raised the issue of Jews in Eastern and Middle Europe while George Brown disturbed them by his belligerent attitude.[2] There was much contention between Bevan, Sam Watson and the Russian leaders. The following day Morgan Phillips and the Russian ambassador to Britain poured oil on troubled waters so that the two could return to Russia in a better mood than on the previous night.[3]

On his return from India, Bevan was given a warm welcome by the Labour Party. Gaitskell needed a deputy of the stature of Aneurin Bevan, somedy who was convincing as a leader, and so he chose Bevan as a spokesman on foreign affairs over Alf Robens. Rab A. Butler, a prominent Tory minister, made the cutting remark: 'Anything Hugh can do, Nye can do better.'[4] The moderate press, papers like *The Economist*, expected Bevan to soon oust Gaitskell, but the Ebbw Vale MP showed no interest in their prophecies. Weeks after the Brighton conference, he took advantage of his position in the Labour hierarchy and on the world stage to visit the United States, travelling on the Queen Mary. The US newspapers emphasised that it was the 'new Aneurin' who was visiting the States and that there was no need for conservative Republican politicians to fear him. Hundreds of photographs were taken of Aneurin Bevan with President Dwight Eisenhower and his secretary of state John Foster Dulles.[5] Bevan's intention was to discuss contemporary issues and he delivered eight lectures. His journey lasted for 19 days and he expressed his ideas on television, at press conferences and in public meetings. He infuriated journalists by praising Russia and China, applauding Khrushchev and for daring to tell them

---

1   In 1956, Khrushchev said, 'The idea of peaceful co-existence is gaining ground across the world . . . And this is quite natural as, under the present circumstances, we have little choice. Indeed, there are only two choices: either to co-exist in peace or war, the most destructive war in history.' See Emyr Price, *Cymru a'r Byd Modern ers 1918* (Cardiff, 1979), 189.

2   Janet Morgan (Ed.), *The Backbench Diaries of Richard Crossman*, ibid, 458.

3   Present in the third meeting were Marshall Bulganin, Nikita Khrushchev and his son Malik, an interpreter, Hugh Gaitskell, Jim Griffiths, Edwin Gooch and Morgan Phillips. Care was taken not to extend an invitation to the two who could disrupt the meetings, Aneurin Bevan and George Brown. See *Pages From Memory*, 149–51

4   John Campbell, *Nye Bevan: Mirage of Socialism*, London, 1987, 322. Bevan's first contribution as shadow foreign secretary was on 5 December. Closing the debate, Rab Butler said: 'Anything Hugh can do, Nye can do better. Nye can do anything better than Hugh'. For Bevan's speech, see *Hansard*, vol. 561, col. 1268–83 and Butler's response, col. 1471, 1570.

5   'Bevan was to denounce the capitalist press as 'the most prostituted in the world'. See, Kenneth O. Morgan, Michael Foot, 128.

the next Labour government would not be prepared to be involved in hydrogen bomb tests. He was frequently criticised for addressing the most extreme institutions such as the New York Economic Club and the New York Commerce and Industry Association.[1] Clearly, on this US visit, the 'New Aneurin' had stayed at home and the 'Revolutionary Aneurin' had come in his place. It is hard to say whether the visit was successful or unsuccessful overall. It was unsuccessful in the eyes of the US media and a large number of politicians.[2] Yet American television viewers liked Aneurin Bevan and particularly his ability to express himself convincingly.[3] Back in Britain. Bevan was said to have enjoyed a pleasant trip. When he spoke in Parliament in the debate about the NATO conference in Paris, he had the usual reception with applause and shouts from every corner of the chamber in his favour.[4] This outstanding speech was even praised by the Manchester Guardian.[5] Bevan had condemned the US for flying planes carrying hydrogen bombs over Britain, stating he did not want to lose the sovereignty of the United Kingdom he cared about just so that American planes could be harboured in Britain.[6] When Bevan sat down, he received deafening applause.

Bevan has won his place among Labour Party leaders

Throughout 1958, the Campaign for Nuclear Disarmament CND was attracting more and more members. Jennie Lee and Bevan were enraged by the headlines in *Tribune*, magazine that was being kept alive only thanks to the charity of two of Aneurin's good friends, Howard Samuel and Jack Hylton. As shadow foreign secretary, in 1958 Bevan was invited to speak at Labour's annual conference in Scarborough. There was much talk of the forthcoming election, being held in a few months. Jennie and Bevan's friends knew, however, that he had been suffering poor health in the spring and summer of 1959. At the conference, Bevan suffered several asthmatic attacks. Jennie and his friends feared he might have the miners' lung disease,

---

1 Nicklaus Thomas-Symonds, Nye, *ibid*, 240. He met President Eisenhower in the White House on 12 November. He had met with Foster Dulles and Felix Frankfurter, who was the associate justice of the US Supreme Court.
2 . *Ibid*. 'He met with some hostility, particularly at the Economic Club in New York, where he rather unwisely compared the Chinese revolution with the American War of Independence.'
3 One United States journalist went as far as to disparage him savagely, 'That British Socialist, "Nye Bevan", who hopes he will soon be Britain's next Prime Minister, is a gentleman farmer who fancies pigs and Khrushchev.
4 'Bevan arrived back at Southampton on 19 November having not only delivered his message but also displayed his personal magnetism'. See Nicklaus Thomas-Symonds, *Nye, ibid*, 240.
5 Krug, *Aneurin Bevan, ibid*, 264
6 *The Manchester Guardian Weekly*, 26 December 1957, 62.

pneumoconiosis, a condition which killed his father. Bevan was feeling rather isolated as his left-wing friends were mostly displeased with him and he found it hard to associate amiably with the centrists and right-wingers who were still occasionally critical of him. Bevan's support of Britain keeping its nuclear arms reflected the mindset of Labour's right wing and not those on the left. Noticing Bevan's isolation, Harold Macmillan compared him to one of the giants of the Old Testament: 'a shorn Samson, surrounded there by a bevy of prim and ageing Delilahs'. One of Bevan's biographers wrote of Bevan's performance at Scarborough:

> As Bevan sat down, he received the greatest ovation of his long Parliamentary career. He was on his way to become Britain's next foreign secretary.[1]

Labour needed to win the General Election for the prediction to become fact, something even Aneurin Bevan himself doubted would happen.

---

1 See Krug, *Aneurin Bevan, ibid,* 265.

CHAPTER 15

The final days of the political giant

In the spring of 1959, Aneurin Bevan was unable to attend the Paris meeting with Pierre Mendès France and Pietro Nenni, two of the most well-known socialists in France and Italy, because he was again. suffering with a bad cold. At Jennie Lee's suggestion, the meeting was rescheduled to take place at Asheridge Farm. Together, the politicians discussed the question: 'Why is the left all over Europe having difficulty in winning over the ordinary people?' Bevan did most of the talking, and the group thoroughly enjoyed the experience.[1] He was in great form with his interpretation, arguing that the right wing could not fulfil what was expected in Britain, France and Italy either politically or economically. During this meeting, the photographer Cartier-Bresson took pictures of Bevan and his friends. When the pictures were developed, he realised Bevan did not look well – his fine, strong body was slowly declining. Jennie said later:

For the first time I wondered, is there anything serious wrong with him.[2]

When the visitors from the continent left, Bevan went through the door of the farm with a glass of wine in his hand, and he stood by his favourite cherry tree that had been pruned enthusiastically. He lifted his glass to the sky and his wife heard him saying loud and clear: 'Not much more springtime left.'[3] Jennie bought

---

1 Jennie Lee, *My Life with Nye* (London, 1980), 240; for a portrait of Pierre Mendès France, see. Kingsley Martin, 'Good? Odd Man in: Pierre Mendès France' [in] *New Statesman Profiles* (London, 1958), 92–95.
2 *Ibid*.
3 Michael Foot, *Aneurin Bevan: A Biography, Volume II* (London, 1972), 616; Patrick Hollis, *Jennie Lee: A Life* (Oxford, 1997), 226.

a bigger bed for his comfort, but he was in constant pain, tossing and turning constantly as he struggled to sleep for more than an hour at a time. Consequently, the nights were long and became a time when Bevan's mind revisited his boyhood haunts. Sometimes when he couldn't sleep, he would listen to the world news programmes on the radio for hours and hours. He playfully suggested that Jennie might share the bed with him, which put her in a dilemma. Her time was extremely precious and she felt her husband knew this better than anyone. Their marriage – their socialist journey – seemed on the verge of being extinguished Would there be any more battling together for the socialist credo?[1] After all, they were no longer young but nearing the end of their middle years. But, very soon, Bevan was back in harness, challenging CND supporters, even those journalists that worked for Tribune. His vision had always to create a civilised caring society which was sympathetic to all those people who could not cope with all the demands of life and he was energised when he was invited to be a member of a parliamentary deputation travelling to Russia.[2] Bevan had come under the influence of Nikita Khrushchev and was amazed at his knowledge and mastery of world events. To Bevan, Khrushchev was an exceptional man because he was trying to change Joseph Stalin's oppressive method of ruling Russia and had also realised he could not turn his back on the world. This was the reason Khrushchev suggested to Bevan that he should not favour unilateral nuclear disarmament . That to the Russian politician was his biggest mistake till he changed his attitude. Simple answers to complex issues were not acceptable and these were irresponsible. One of Bevan's true friends said of the period from 1958 to 1959:Bevan's great anxiety was that he needed negotiating strength to deal with the Americans – not the Russians.[3]Keeping or getting rid of bombs was not just a moral question, it was was about the power afforded to a country which had them. Under President Truman, the US had killed tens of thousands of families in the cities of Hiroshima and Nagasaki with atomic bombs. Bevan believed Britain had an important role on the world stage and, as such, should provide moral leadership on disarmament. He had transformed Britain's health provision with the National Health Service; now he was equally committed to the more difficult task of advancing world peace. In 1959, the *Daily Herald*, a vocal supporter of the Labour Party, decided to back the Campaign for Nuclear Disarmament.

The *Daily Herald's* announcement was a huge disappointment for Aneurin Bevan and Jennie Lee. Aneurin Bevan had always been unusually strong mentally, emotion-

---

1 Hollis, *ibid*, 227.
2 Gaitskell ignored Bevan in the arrangement although he was the assistant leader. According to Gaitskell, Denis Healey and Edna, Aneurin Bevan and Jennie and Gaitskell and his wife Dora were to travel to Russia. Jennie did not want to go and offered Karol Kewes her place. She said of Kewes: 'As
3 Geoffrey Goodman, *From Bevan to Blair: Fifty Years of Reporting from the Political Front Line*, ibid.

ally and spiritually. He had been determined in his attitude and sincere in his dedication, but it was now evident that the political giant was declining physically. His blood pressure had soared when he was Minister of Health and Housing and his time in the colliery had left him with painful eyes and damaged lungs. He suffered from frequent colds, bronchitis and flu, which Jennie feared would become pneumonia, or even TB.[1] The couple's heavy drinking – two or three bottles of wine with dinner every night – had put a strain on his liver and overall health. Jennie constantly took to her knees and prayed for the health and future of her husband, despite not being a believer! Bevan was fortunate his doctor was the Welshman and royal physician Sir Daniel Davies, who took extremely good care of him. Sir Daniel recommended Bevan's health would benefit if he spent less time in the capital and more at Asheridge Farm looking after his animals. Aneurin Bevan was in Moscow when Harold Macmillan announced there was to be a General Election in October 1959. He rushed back to prepare his programme of meetings around the country as he was one of the main speakers in the Labour Party campaign. The *Daily Herald* had kindly offered one of its best reporters, Geoffrey Goodman, to spend the entire campaign with Bevan. At a meeting to discuss the campaign, Goodman realised the charismatic politician was not as energetic or enthusiastic as he used to be, and his characteristic pugnacity was missing from his speeches. It was also evident Bevan was unhappy with Hugh Gaitskell's leadership and felt isolated among Labour leaders. He still believed in socialist values but realised he would not see them at work in a future Labour government . The campaign timetable provided by Transport House scheduled early campaign meetings in London, a city where Bevan disliked addressing large crowds. He was happier to speak in Cannock, Jennie's own constituency, after which he would travel to the North West England, then on to Scotland and eventually south to Wales. He swallowed his whisky, wrinkled his brow and said to Goodman:

> Okay boy, let's meet next week to finish planning our journey, if that is all right with you.[2]

It was obvious to Goodman that his famous socialist friend was not in the best of health, though he struggled to put his finger on anything specific. Bevan looked pretty well, and there was plenty of life in him. Then, half-way through the campaign, he caught another cold. He spoke to a packed hall in Cannock, where even the neighbouring rooms were full of Labour supporters (indeed, every meeting in

---

1 *Ibid.*
2 *Ibid.* Geoffrey Goodman, *From Bevan to Blair: Fifty Years of Reporting from the Political Front line.*

London had been the same), but that night, under pressure from Jennie, he agreed to return to Asheridge Farm. Goodman kindly drove the unwell Bevan home in his old Rover. He went straight to bed; however, the next day, Bevan was seriously ill, weak and exhausted, with a temperature in excess of 100%. Sir Daniel Davies was called, diagnosed flu and told the politician he needed to rest for several days.

Bevan's bed rest meant there needed to be a change of plan as far as the campaign meetings were concerned. He had agreed to speak at a meeting in the Plymouth Devonport constituency in support of Michael Foot and was determined to fulfil his promise. Sir Daniel Davies as well as Bevan's companion Goodman was against motoring to Plymouth , so Bevan sent a telegram to Michael explaining the situation. When he followed this up with a written apology to the *Daily Herald*, Goodman feared Bevan was a lot worse than he, Jennie, or anyone realised, and worse was to follow.[1] When Bevan recovered, he attended three evenings of addressing large gatherings . He seems to have focused on the same theme, that is the future of mankind. He would spend his afternoons visiting the largest factories in the area. Goodman and he stayed in nearby hotels and thoroughly enjoyed one another's company – and the Scotch whisky they shared to 'warm up' Bevan. His oratory skills and performances still excited the crowds; however, in private conversations with Goodman, Bevan feared the Labour Party was likely to lose the election again because its leaders were not dealing with the most important issues of the day or offering any solutions. Despite the arrogance and supreme confidence of the Tories in their right to govern, Bevan saw little to inspire him from the Labour Party. And, if Labour did somehow manage to win, Bevan had concerns about his ability to continue to work with Gaitskell.

Bevan continued to give polished speeches. He was extremely knowledgeable on foreign affairs, particularly with regard to Cyprus, Africa (especially Kenya and Nyasaland) and the Middle East. He discussed Britain's economy authoritatively, highlighting how the use public sector could be used to promote full employment. One night after Bevan had spoken in Coventry, Goodman asked his friend how he thought the Labour campaign was going. Despite his obvious exhaustion, Bevan erupted with the hallmark anger that had marked him throughout his life. The burden of speaking at four meetings a day was clearly taking its toll. Goodman had never seen this side of the politician and later described him as similar to 'a tiger in a cage'.[2] The seasoned journalist realised Bevan distress came from his raging fury that the Tories who had been in power since 1951 were again on the verge of a victory. Here is Goodman's own explanation:

Aneurin Bevan had likely realised his health would have the last word and the

---

1 *Ibid.*, 81.
2 *Ibid.* 82.

end was swiftly approaching in his own epic story. His countrywide campaigning in 1959 was the rehearsal for that end: a time when he would no longer be pleading the gospel of socialism to the working and middle classes. To his mind, he was too young to leave the political area, which had yet to reward him fully for decades of dedication.[1] He was also disappointed at the small number of activists who turned out to hear him in some centres, particularly in North East Wales. Thankfully, the final meeting – in Corwen Pavilion – was a huge success and a worthy climax to the tour. Afterwards, Bevan and Goodman travelled to the hotel in Llangollen to relax over an expensive bottle of whisky. It was a warm, uncomfortable night even though the bar window was open. In the background, they could hear the sound of the River Dee flowing to the sea. Aneurin Bevan was at home, he was in one of his favourite places in his own beloved country. It was in Llangollen that the community had established an International Eisteddfod in 1947, attracting singers and dancers from all over the world. Llangollen symbolised to him Wales at his best. He had reached the zenith of his extraordinary oratory in the Corwen Pavilion that night. The audience mostly comprised Labour members from Merionethshire (Meirionnydd today) and Denbighshire. Bevan spoke very little Welsh – barely 150 words – but was quick to remind this Welsh-speaking community of his socialist values and the strong foundations he had inherited from Welsh nonconformity. He spoke eloquently about Britain's role in an increasingly smaller world, its huge contribution to technology and science, and the need for politicians to work enthusiastically with its international partners. He concluded with the words:

> We are moving into a world in which smaller and smaller men are strutting against narrower and narrower stages.[2]

The world was on a cliff edge but – as Bevan told his audience in Corwen – he was thankful there were still leaders of substance in the world like his heroes Pandit Nehru, Marshall Tito and Pierre Mendès France. With the election campaign now drawing to a close, Bevan travelled south through Newtown, Llandrindod and Brynmawr to Ebbw Vale, where he was idolised by at least 80% of the electorate. One of the main speakers in support of him in Tredegar and Ebbw Vale would be the gifted lawyer, Gwilym Prys-Davies.[3]

---

1 *Ibid.*
2 *Ibid,* 82–83.
3 *Ibid,* 84.

**Eirene White, Gwilym Prys-Davies
and Cledwyn Hughes**

Gwilym was much admired by Bevan's hard-working agent, Ron Evans. It was Evans who, in the run-up to the general election, had been called upon to silence the small minority who felt that Bevan, as a Labour party leader, had neglected his Ebbw Vale constituency. On 7 October 1959, the night of the General Election, Aneurin Bevan was sitting in his sister Arianwen's home, having realised earlier that evening that he was not at all well. Naturally he was also thinking about Jennie's political fate in Cannock. The Bevan family watched the election results on television and saw Macmillan being interviewed. He exuded confidence and was certain he could deal with the international challenges the new decade would bring far better than Hugh Gaitskell. When Geoffrey Goodman voiced his anger at Macmillan's hypocrisy, Bevan interrupted him for daring to insult Macmillan's good name. He defended Macmillan as a politician and a party leader, saying 'after all he manages to serve his class and his party'. Bevan was one of Macmillan's admirers, placing him on a pedestal above Churchill and especially Eden.[1] Then Gaitskell was interviewed in his Leeds constituency. The Labour Party leader promised a Labour government would decrease income tax and would keep and extend the National Health Service. Bevan was furious and turned to Goodman and said:

---

1 NLW Ron Evans' papers, Waunlwyd, Ebbw Vale. Ron Evans wrote a letter dated 28 September 1959 to Gwilym Prys Davies to invite him to speak at the public meeting in Tredegar. See. Ron Evans' papers, file 7.

> He has lost the election for us. He should never say such a thing. Every voter knows that saying things like that is madness.[1]

Bevan clearly had more sympathy for and understanding of Macmillan than Gaitskell. He could see any hope of Labour winning the General Election disappearing before his very eyes. Seeing socialism on the agenda of the Labour government in Britain now seemed a distant dream. Despite being emotionally and physically exhausted, the heavyweight Labour politician easily retained his Ebbw Vale seat.[2] The Tories won the election with 49.4% of the vote and Labour secured just 43.8%.[3] The result meant the Tories now had 365 seats in the House of Commons, with only 258 Labour MPs. After the election, Gaitskell asked Bevan to be Jim Griffiths' successor and serve as deputy leader of the Labour Party. Unfortunately, the opportunity came too late as Bevan's health was no longer up to the top tier job. Due to the election, the annual Labour conference had been delayed until 28–29 November, allowing Bevan a little time to rest and regain his stamina. At the conference, he realised it was the darling of the trade union movement, Hugh Gaitskell, who had split the party and not him. He might have been partly responsible for divisions between 1951 and 1958 but Gaitskell was equally culpable. The serious minded Gaitskell was going to stir more trouble by his effort to amend the Clause 1V of the Labour Party which favoured nationalisation . Many Labour members were upset, believing the annual conference was not the best place to discuss such a controversial question for the party faithful. Bevan felt insecure. The 1959 Labour conference was Aneurin Bevan's last and he made one of the most inspired speeches of his life. According to Goodman, in his colourful way:

> It stands in the records as one of the finest pieces of oratory in Labour's long history. It was, as in retrospect I now realise, his last will and testament to his codex of socialist beliefs. The end indeed was nye.[4]

Nowhere was Bevan's call for unity among socialists better heard. At the end of the conference, he was victorious and he returned to Jennie at Asheridge to enjoy some much-needed solitude 'far from the maddening crowd'. He needed to rest as his health problems were now very evident; he had lost his appetite and lost a great

---

1 Geoffrey Goodman, *From Bevan to Blair*, ibid. 84. Kingsley Martin said of Macmillan in the thirties: 'During the nightmare of the Depression he was a Tory Bevan – but without Bevan's glamour and without the following'. See Kingsley Martin, 'Keeper of Their Conscience: Rt. Hon. Harold Macmillan' [in] *New Statesman Profiles*, ibid, 173–178. The quotation comes from page 75.
2 Ibid.
3 Gaitskell believed he was going to win. See Philip Williams, *Hugh Gaitskell* (London, 1979), 531.
4 Nicklaus Thomas-Symonds, *Nye: The Political Life of Aneurin Bevan*, (London, 2015, 244.

deal of weight. Back in Parliament, he loved to chat and enjoy the camaraderie of the smoking room. At times the pain in his stomach was overwhelming, but he would take small pieces of ice to soothe it. Two days before Christmas, Sir Dan Davies advised him to consider surgery at the Royal Free Hospital in Gray's Inn Road, London, immediately after the holidays.[1] Bevan duly went to the hospital on 27 December and was advised by the medical team that they would have to take out most of his stomach. Now it was impossible to keep his seriousness of his health issues private. Bevan remained in hospital for six weeks, surrounded by the beautiful flowers sent by well wishers (something that would not be allowed today even for the icon who created the National Health Service). His closest friends came to see him regularly. Jennie suggested her husband's first visitor should be Michael Foot, as they had been on bad terms with each other since 1957 when Aneurin changed his opinion on nuclear armaments. Foot agreed and was advised that his responsibility was to make the patient feel better. Foot had lost his Plymouth seat a few months earlier and had the shock of his life when Aneurin said to him on his first visit, 'Why don't you consider the seat in Ebbw Vale when the time comes?'[2] Michael did not say another word but later, when he thought about his visit, he realised Bevan might have had an inkling that he was dying. Foot was not as popular in Ebbw Vale as he was with Bevan and, when the opportunity did come, he had a most difficult task in clinching the Labour nomination.

The day before Aneurin Bevan left hospital, Sir Dan Davies told Jennie Lee that he had cancer, giving him between nine and eighteen months to live. Jennie prevailed upon him not to say anything about this to his dear friend and indeed the two made a promise to each other to keep the news a secret. No-one was to know, not a word to Arianwen or to any of the brothers and sisters, not a word to his lifelong friend Archie Lush nor to his agent Ron Evans. Jennie was afraid if her husband got wind of the cancer, he would give up the struggle and live the remainder of his days in mental anguish. However, for practical reasons, there was one person to whom she would have to reveal the terrible news, that was Howard Samuel. She reasoned that their generous friend would be able to find enough sleeping tablets if Bevan's pain became unbearable. Samuel promised to do his best, but he was not uncomfortable about the situation. Sir Dan Davies' prognosis turned out to be rather optimistic. As things turned out, Bevan only had a little over six months left to enjoy the farmhouse that had become his refuge.

Once Aneurin Bevan's health issues were made public, Sir Dan Davies issued regular bulletins, which elicited sacks of letters and Get Well cards from well-wishers. Some came from quarry workers in the counties of Caernarfon and Merionethshire,

---
1 Geoffrey Goodman, *ibid,* 85.
2 Jennie Lee, *My Life with Nye*, (London, 1980), 246.

others from the coalminers of South Wales, indeed from coal fields all over Britain. Good wishes were received from Tredegar and Labour supporters, from university students across Wales, England and Scotland, from doctors and nurses, people in the building trade, and farmers who admired him as a serious farmer himself. Bevan received correspondence from supporters and admirers who were barely literate and letters from palaces and embassies. Old and sick people who had benefited from the National Health Service since 1948 and lived much longer thanks to Aneurin Bevan got in touch. His name was heard in prayers by ministers in chapels in Glamorgan and Monmouthshire and by students for the ministry in Wales. I was one of them. Archie Lush remembers visiting a shop in Gray's Inn Road, the street where the hospital was situated, to buy an ounce of tobacco. A woman rushed in from the street saying to the woman behind the counter:

> I have just seen on TV Miss Jennie Lee leaving the hospital and she was smiling.' 'Oh, thank God,' said the woman who was working in the shop, 'hope he will be better soon'.[1]

The doctors and nurses were very fond of Bevan. One of the nurses who cared for him told the MP Hugh Delargy, a true friend to Aneurin, 'Mr Bevan is a most wonderful patient.' Delargy replied: 'He must be because he is a wonderful man.'[2] One old man wrote an amazing and touching letter to him:

> Please fight and win the battle Mr Bevan. I have just come from hospital myself and have been humbled and surprised by the Health Service that you created. I beg you to live. I am praying to God that if he cannot get rid of your disease to let us suffer it for you. May God bless you Sir. Please keep alive. Many are praying for you.[3]

Messages even came from voters who called themselves 'dyedin blue Tories'. A window cleaner in Wormwood Scrubs Prison sent a letter wishing him well.[4] The letters and messages lifted Bevan's spirits and by the beginning of March there was talk of his returning to where his heart was: Parliament.

Throughout his hospital stay, Bevan had his books by his bedside. There were two quality books, in particular, that he really enjoyed and discussed at depth with Foot, namely J. B. Priestley's *Literature and the Western Man* and H. L. Mencken's

---

1 *Ibid,* 254 The seed was sown although Foot told him not to talk nonsense. Foot got the seat after a lot of struggles.
2 Hollis, *ibid,* 229
3 Hugh Delargy, 'Most Wonderful Man I have Ever known,' *Reynold's News*, 10 July 1960, 6.
4 Hollis, *ibid,* 229

Treatise on the Gods.[1] When Archie Lush visited, the conversation would turn to Tredegar and Bevan's youth. One day, Bevan asked Lush in all seriousness, 'Are they fed up with me in Tredegar?' Archie understood the close bond between Aneurin Bevan and the people of Tredegar people. The MP loved his home town and his greatest wish had been to put it on the map, something he had certainly achieved. By 1960, he was proud that a Tredegar-born nephew had been named Aneurin.

Aneurin Bevan left hospital on 16 February 1960. Before he returned to the farm, it had been arranged for him to travel by car to Brighton to enjoy the sea air and the cry of seagulls. It was a short stay for he had to turn for Asheridge due to the severity of the pain in his stomach. On the way from Brighton to Asheridge, they stopped for a quarter of an hour in Windsor Park for Bevan to stretch his legs and use the toilet. When he returned to the car, there was sadness in his voice when he said to the driver, a Welshman:

> Do you know Griff, before I go, I must go home and see the mountains.

Then he turned to Jennie with mischief in his eyes and said:

> Do you know, my love, you don't know what mountains are in Scotland. My mountains in Wales are wonderful.[2]

Many in Bevan's circle later criticised Jennie Lee for keeping Sir Dan Davies's bleak prognosis from him. There's no doubt the necessary secrecy put a huge strain on her, which led to her drinking too much wine in the evenings. On the other hand, she knew Bevan better than anyone and she did what she believed would be acceptable to him. After his death, she said to Archie Lush that hearing the truth would have ruined their relationship, as Bevan thought of her as his only hope. Jennie wrote *My Life with Nye in 1980*. In the book, she talks about why Sir Dan Davies agreed with her plea to keep the seriousness of Bevan's prognosis from him:

> There was a close bond between these two highly emotional Welshmen. Why did Dan act as he did? Was it because he could not bear to pronounce the death sentence on his friend? How can any of us ever know just how and why we behave as we do in times of uncertainty and stress? All I do know is that his only concern from first to last was to help his friend in every way he could.[3]

---

1 *Ibid,* 230
2 Interview in the *Guardian*, 29 March 1960 and quoted by Lee, *My Life with Nye, ibid.* 248–249.
3 This story is published in the *Daily Express*, 7 July 1960.

George Quist carried out Bevan's surgery and knew of the friendship between the couple and Sir Dan Davies. When he was convalescing, Bevan agreed to an interview at the farm with the *Guardian*. In the interview, which was published on 29 March. he thanked everyone for the care he had received at the Royal Free Hospital, in theatre and on the ward. He had words of praise for the surgeons , the nurses and the hospital administrators. The cards, letters and flowers had touched him no end, and he was grateful to Jennie that he was spending his difficult illness with her at the farmstead. A routine was soon established: Aneurin would get up mid-morning, shower and have a small breakfast before dressing himself for the day. He would retire to bed between ten and eleven o'clock, sometimes a little earlier. J. B. Priestley's book on English literature provided one of his intellectual comforts as he was determined not to read political autobiographies or to be tempted to write his own. As he told the *Guardian* journalist:

> I actively disapprove of people in active public life writing their memoirs. They do nothing but mischief. If they tell the truth, it is hurtful but, usually they don't tell the truth.[1]

Television provided little distraction, although he did enjoy watching the comedian Tony Hancock, whose antics were in the old-fashioned music hall tradition. He longed to return to Westminster, but Jennie wanted him to get stronger before making the journey into London. That was why she accepted Kathleen and Graham Sutherland's generous offer for a trip to France. Jennie mentions in her book nothing about the invitation except to say Sutherland was the genius who painted Winston Churchill's 80th birthday portrait and subsequently had his painting rejected by the great man. At the time, a rumour had circulated that it was Bevan himself who had urged Sutherland to adopt the controversial approach to the portrait, but he would never have done that: he thought quite highly of Churchill.[2]

Towards the end of his fascinating life, the only place Aneurin Bevan felt comfortable was at Asheridge. His health deteriorated seriously after the trip to France. His right leg swelled up and he became a prisoner in his room. Doctors suggested he should be readmitted to hospital in London, but Bevan refused and instead twenty-four-hour care was arranged at home. A loyal friend who was a physiotherapist helped to nurse Bevan and Dr Jack Buchan administered injections to help him sleep. The Bevans also accepted help from a young Australian socialist called Trude. Above all, Jennie was always there at his side, which meant everything to him. Dr Buchan and the physiotherapist cared for Aneurin during the day and then Jennie would take over at night.[3]

---
1 Jennie Lee, *My Life with Nye*, 247.
2 *Ibid*. 249.
3 *Ibid*. 250.

Every other day, Sir Dan Davies or George Quist would travel from London, sometimes together, to cheer him up. Jennie would prepare coffee and brandy, or tea and whisky, and would subsequently hear happy chattering and laughter coming from her husband's bedroom. The doctors knew their medical talents were not enough to save their friend, but they wanted to make his remaining time as pain free as possible. Knowing that Bevan would never enter 10 Downing Street ever again, they gave generously in time and care to their famous patient ,In fact, his world was extremely comfortable physically for him , and Bevan even in his distressing pain continued to plan the future. As Jennie said:

> Until almost the last days of his life, Nye would sit up in bed or in an armchair by the window planning ahead.[1]

One of Aneurin Bevan's very last visitors was, in fact, Pandit Nehru, who was attending a Commonwealth conference, and they were both full of ideas that needed to be implemented.

Dr Jack Buchan and Jack Norris, Arianwen's husband, representing the family in Wales, were staying at Asheridge when the call finally came to leave behind his precious NHS. It happened on 6 July 1960. The details were later published in the *Daily Express*. Dr Tom Wise, the local doctor, arrived after eleven in the morning in his delightful Morris car and stayed with Bevan for over half an hour. Aneurin Bevan in actual fact passed to glory that afternoon at ten minutes past four and Dr Wise returned to the farm at 4.35 p.m.

Aneurin Bevan left behind in money the sum of £23,481, the equivalent of at least half a million pounds in 2020. He also with Jennie owned a well kept farm in Buckinghamshire. In terms of wealth, Aneurin had improved his world considerably from the days he was unemployed. Jennie was comforted that afternoon by the housekeeper, Mrs McGhee, Jack Norris, Doctors Wise and Buchan and the Australian friend . The call of informing the close family got underway. Norris phoned his wife, Arianwen in Tredegar and she phoned her sister Blodwen and brothers William and Iorwerth. Norris phoned their other sister Myfanwy and Archie Lush was also informed of the news. At the time, he was the Monmouthshire's supervisor of schools; however, the next morning he travelled on his own to Asheridge.[2]

The news of Aneurin Bevan's death was difficult for so many of his admirers, friends and colleagues. Michael Foot rushed immediately he heard the news to Asheridge and Hugh Delargy left Parliament as he could not visualise socialising

---

1 *Ibid*, 251–252
2 *Ibid*, 252

with any of his fellow left wing friends .[1] For Tom Driberg, the only way to deal with Bevan's death was to drink half a dozen glasses of whisky, with a group of the Welshman's admirers.[2]

The Queen sent her sincere condolences. So too did the Prime Minister Harold Macmillan. According to Macmillan:

> He was a colleague with me on the back benches in the House of Commons for many years before the war and a real personal friend.[3]

To Hugh Gaitskell, he would be remembered as the architect of the National Health Service.[4] Earl Attlee in his tribute admired him greatly and respected his talents. To him, Aneurin Bevan was unique and one of the most important [politicians the Labour Party ever had.[5]

Arianwen Norris arranged a meeting at her Tredegar home, which was chaired by Councillor Ron Evans. Thirty of those who worked closely for Bevan in the constituency came together to share memories of the exceptional politician who was a larger than life character. According to Councillor Idris Williams, it was a dark day in his life of the county.[6] Tom Rees, a member of Ebbw Vale's executive committee, stated, 'There was not another statesman in the world with his stature.' Another Welsh Labour Party activist stated that Aneurin Bevan was equal to Pandit Nehru .Yet there was awkwardness at his passing in unexpected places. During his election campaigns, Bevan would frequent the Quarryman's Arms, an old pub on the side of the mountain in Trefil, four miles from Tredegar, which had been owned for 28 years by Margaret Evans. Aneurin and Jennie liked wandering the local hills and relaxing in the Quarryman's Arms. Mrs Evans remembered Bevan once protesting once when she had handed him half a pint of beer:

> Come on, give me a big one with a handle on it like these other boys.[7]

She cheerfully agreed. Her customers that evening shared memories of him at the pub. Some of his bosom friends including Jennie Lee, were very critical of the decision of the producers in the BBC, more than any other media outlet, for inviting

---

1 These details are available in the book by Nicklaus Thomas-Symonds, *Nye, ibid,* 246
2 For Delargy, Bevan was at the top of the list. 'The wonder of him has not passed. Nor will it ever pass. God has rest for his great soul.' See Hugh Delargy, *ibid,* 6.
3 Tom Driberg said, 'No man, it is said, is indispensable. Aneurin Bevan was as nearly an indispensable man as any I have ever known.' See Tom Driberg, 'Nye would have shrugged it all off'. *Reynold's News and Sunday Citizen,* 10 July 1960, 6.
4 Jennie Lee, *My Life with Nye, ibid,* 255
5 Delargy, *ibid,* 6
6 Nicklaus Thomas-Symonds, Nye, *ibid,* 246
7 Hugh Gaitskell, 'Nye, The Big Man', *Daily Express,* 7 July 1960, 1.

politicians who were not faith leaders helpful to Aneurin Bevan in his life to recall their memories of him. Some were vexed that the media gave Hugh Gaitskell and Harold Wilson so much opportunity rather than to Barbara Castle and Ian Mikardo. In Wales, the media went after Jim Griffiths, which was a good choice given their shared background – the same was not true of Hugh Gaitskell and even of Wilson.

Jennie arranged a service at the crematorium in Croesyceiliog in his native county for his family and herself. She left all the arrangements in the hands of the Methodist leader Rev. Dr Donald Soper, one of the most notable preachers in Britain and a *Tribune* columnist, and Bishop Mervyn Stockwood, another left-wing supporter from his time in Bristol who was now the Bishop of Southwark. She said to them:

> He was a great humanist whose religion lay in loving his fellow men and trying to serve them. He could kneel reverently in chapel, synagogue, eastern mosque, Catholic cathedral on occasions when friends called him there for marriage or dedication or burial services.[1]

Aneurin Bevan was grounded in the Christian faith as a child and the basics of that faith meant a great deal to him, especially prayer to the very end. Hugh Delargy recalled he and Bevan walking together one afternoon in Regent Street, London. Two Catholic nuns came by and greeted him, thanking him for the contribution he had made to their hospital, and they added: 'We nuns always remember you daily in our prayers.' The humanist, brought up as a Baptist, had quite a shock. He thanked them and added:

> Thank you very much, sisters, and please continue to pray for me. No-one needs prayer more than I do.[2]

His greatness was respecting the faith of others and receiving comfort in the fact that some of them were interceding for him in prayer before the throne of grace from day to day. A week after the private funeral in Croesyceiliog, a memorial service was organised in the open air by the Rev. Dr. Donald Soper. Bevan's dust was to be scattered on the hills that were so dear to him and under an ash tree where bluebells grew.

The responsibility for collecting the casket of Aneurin's ashes from the crematorium was given to his lifelong comrade Archie Lush, who was on his way to an education committee at Newport town hall.[3] He didn't have much time and in his

---

1 Lord Attlee, 'We disagreed often, but . . .' *Daily Herald*, 7 July 1960, 5. To Attlee, his judgement was not always fair and there was some grave disagreement between them.
2 George Viner, 'Sorrow at every Street Corner' *Daily Herald*, 7 July 1960, 1.
3 Basil Morgan, 'The Boy Who Spoke in Anger', *Daily Herald*, 7 July 1960, 5.

haste, he parked and forgot to lock his car. He emerged from the meeting to find his car had disappeared, and with it Aneurin Bevan's ashes. Lush ran back to the town hall for help and the police throughout the county were contacted. An urgent search followed as the remains of the giant from Tredegar were in that stolen car. In the meantime, the leaders of the Labour Party in Wales were travelling to Blaenau Gwent and only learned of the unfortunate situation when they arrived. Lush's car was eventually found in Gloucester, forty miles away, with the casket still safe. Gloucester Police drove the vehicle back to the border between Monmouthshire and Herefordshire. The five thousand or more who had assembled for the memorial service witnessed the police car breaking all speed records as it transported the mortal remains of Aneurin Bevan to his home turf. One person who was there was the Pembrokeshire based politician Gordon Parry (who later became Lord Parry) whose unforgettable words were:

> Nye was a restless bugger in life and a restless bugger in death.[1]

The huge crowd of Labour Party workers waited patiently, though some silently cursed Archie Lush for his careless mistake. This landscape had meant so much to their dead comrade; it was here he had composed many a speech and forged his plans . Jennie Lee knew that Archie Lush had inadvertently caused emotional distress to some of those who had travelled a long way, but despite her great grief she managed to say to the thousands assembled :

> In all the great battles of his life, Nye came home to you. He never left you, he never will.[2]

In just two sentences, she had crystallised the essence of the brilliant politician .

A further memorial service for the great and good took place at Westminster Abbey on 26 July 1960.[3] The Bishop of Southwark, Mervyn Stockwood, led this service of thanksgiving.[4] The abbey was full to overflowing with leading politicians of every political party, diplomats from many embassies, businessmen, artists, reporters, family, friends and socialists from the local constituencies of the South Wales valleys.

---

1 Jennie Lee, *My Life with Nye*, ibid, 255.
2 Delargy, *ibid*, 6
3 The account is available in Patricia Hollis, *Jennie Lee: A Life* (Oxford, 1997), 233.
4 Welsh National Library: Papers of Desmond Donnelly, MP for Pembroke, B15 (1960) Among his papers he kept a copy of the memorial service on 26 July 1960; there are details that are not in any of the biographies of Bevan. The Parable of the Sheep and the Goats from Matthew 25 was read and three hymns were sung: 'Guide me O Thou Great Redeemer', 'Oh God of Bethel by whose hand' and William Blake's hymn 'And Did These Feet in Ancient Time'.

The Bishop took his text, not from the Scriptures as he would normally, but from Bevan's own book, *In Place of Fear*:[1]

> The frontiers of understanding are reached when our spirit fully identifies itself with the awful loneliness and finality of personal grief.[2]

It was Mervyn Stockwood who wanted the service to be held in Westminster Abbey not in St Margaret's, Westminster because Aneurin Bevan to him was a national figure. The abbey was usually reserved for the funerals of party leaders or Prime Ministers and not cautious rebels from opposition MPs such as Bevan. Jennie Lee wanted the service to be out of the hands of the Labour Party and she knew Bevan would agree with her. There was some discussion in the Conservative government on the arrangements, but Macmillan, an admirer of Bevan, agreed with Mervyn Stockwood.

A few days later, the news came that Jennie Lee had fallen on the street and was in a clinic in Edinburgh. Married life was over for her. She and Bevan had been close friends; they had a lot in common despite being different in some ways. Jennie could not contemplate living without her husband and prayed for the angel of death to arrive . She had sufficient sleeping tablets and whisky on hand to end her life, but what would she achieve? Bevan would be furious with her such a gifted and hard-working female politician?[3] She knew she had no option but to carry on, for the sake of her late husband and her ailing mother who depended on her totally. She had responsibility for the farm and its employees, needed to rise to the demands of future Labour governments and its demands, and keep the paper *Tribune* going. Above all, she owed it to her husband to keep alive the socialist vision that had enthused them both during their youth and sustained them throughout their adult lives. Their similar coal mining backgrounds – hers in Scotland, his in South Wales – had inspired them until the mid-fifties.[4] As her grief subsided, Jennie returned to the field of politics with renewed enthusiasm.

---

1 Aneurin Bevan, *In Place of Fear* (London, 1952), 64.
2 *Ibid*.
3 Patricia Hollis, *Jennie Lee: A Life*, ibid, 233. She said: 'I wanted to die too. I had no strength left, no will to go on living.'
4 It must be remembered that Bevan compromised a great deal in his socialist vision and that at the end of his life he was quite ready to be deputy to Hugh Gaitskell and to live with right-wing leaders and scholars. See Ralph Miliband, *Parliamentary Socialism: A Study in the Politics of Labour* (London, 1979); third impression, 337. 'With his speech at the 1957 conference, Bevan unambiguously removed himself from the leadership of the Labour left and appeared to accept as final his position as Hugh Gaitskell's second in command.'

CHAPTER 16

An assessment of Aneurin Bevan as a politician

In the preface to his important Welsh language biography of Gwynfor Evans, Rhys Evans said:

> *Tair ideoleg a thri dyn sy'n bennaf gyfrifol am fowldio Cymru a'r hyn oedd hi yn ail hanner yr ugeinfed ganrif: y Rhyddfrydwr, Lloyd George; y Llafurwr, Aneurin Bevan, a'r Cenedlaetholwr, Gwynfor Evans. Nhw oedd penseiri gwleidyddol y genedl; nhw leisiodd ddyheadau a siomedigaethau eu pobl. Hebddyn nhw, ni fyddai Cymru yr hyn yw hi heddiw.*[1] (Three ideologies and three men are mainly responsible for moulding Wales and what it was in the second half of the twentieth century: the Liberal, Lloyd George; the Socialist, Aneurin Bevan and the Nationalist, Gwynfor Evans. They were the political architects of the nation; they gave voice to the aspirations and disappointments of their people. Without them Wales would not be what it is today.)

On a first reading of the quotation, I agree with the statement but I would wish to include another three: Saunders Lewis and his inspirational radio lecture *Tynged yr Iaith* (The Fate of the Language), Jim Griffiths, the greatest Welsh-speaking Welshman in the Labour party, and his successor Cledwyn Hughes, promoter of decentralisation and practical Welshness. In fact, Rhys Evans says that Cledwyn deserved to be considered as he was as important in Welsh politics as Gwynfor.[2] Bevan in the same league as David Lloyd George and Winston Churchill.

---

1 Rhys Evans, *Gwynfor: Rhag Pob Brad*, (Talybont, 2005), 19.
2 *Ibid.*

But we could go one step further; in the opinion of many people Aneurin Bevan was one of the most influential politicians in the whole of Britain in the twentieth century. He has been frequently compared with two other politicians, both of whom were Prime Ministers during the two World Wars: David Lloyd George and Winston Churchill. Three incomparable men and members of three different political parties, although at different periods in his life Churchill supported both the Liberals and Conservatives. It is incredible that of all the great men of the British electoral system so many authors still refer to the political trinity of Bevan, Churchill and Lloyd George.[1] Bevan was never given the opportunity of leading his party, nevertheless he achieved, within the limits of his remit, one of the most amazing political schemes of the twentieth century. Dora Gaitskell, widow of Hugh Gaitskell, in an interview with Geoffrey Goodman, said that Bevan should have been chosen as leader of the Labour Party rather than her husband, as he was the natural leader of a socialist party.

Aneurin Bevan certainly possessed the attributes required of a party leader and may have become Prime Minister had he only behaved and grasped all the opportunities which came his way. His working-class background meant he was perfectly placed to lead a socialist party; however, personal experience of real people's lives had never been considered important to unionists in the Conservative and Liberal parties or those on the right and left wings of the Labour Party. With the exception of Keir Hardie and Ramsay MacDonald, the Labour Party has never had a working-class leader. Like the present Labour party leader Sir Keir Starmer, the party leaders have always being successful middle-class men, most of whom had been educated in private schools or in grammar schools, followed by three years in Oxbridge.[2] They had never known first hand poverty whereas Aneurin Bevan had experienced it in his neighbourhood. His father was a collier, Welsh speaking, who persuaded his non-Welsh speaking wife to give their children Welsh names. Naming their second son Aneurin and one of his sisters Arianwen is clear evidence of David and Phoebe Bevan's adherence to the Welsh way of life. Nevertheless, David Bevan could not change the material situation of 32 Charles Street; Bevan and two of his brothers had to share a bedroom and sometimes a bed, a situation which he remembered all his life.[3] His talents were not spotted in the primary school; he was entirely the product of Sunday school.[4] Bevan was abused at primary school and he was

---

1 Richard Toye, *Lloyd George and Churchill: Rivals for Greatness* (London, 2007), 9.
2 This can be seen clearly in *British Labour Leaders* (eds. Charles Clarke and Toby S. James), (London, 2015), (especially the second section 'Assess').
3 National Library of Wales, Papers of Desmond Donnelly, 'Eulogy', B15 (1960).
4 The movement which was most influential in moulding the character of the miners in the Welsh valleys and which gave them a thirst for more education and implanted in them a desire to read widely was the Sunday school. The libraries which were installed in the miners' institutes were also immensely valuable. In 1925, 53,000 books were borrowed from the library in Tredegar. See D. J. Davies, *ibid*, 71.

caned on a daily basis. His experience at school made him militant and rebellious. It was Sunday school – and his father's encouragement –that ignited his passion for reading, first comics and later more intellectual works. Bevan read everything which came into his home, as well as borrowing a large number of books from the miners' library. His voracious love of reading greatly enlarged his vocabulary. Despite their respect for education, his parents could not afford to send him to a grammar school and Bevan began work in the colliery when he was thirteen. Yet on his way home, he took great pleasure in listening to the older socialists climbing on their soapboxes to denounce capitalism. He listened carefully to the case for socialism against capitalism.[1]

Capitalism adapts to different periods

Capitalism in 2023 is not what it was Aneurin Bevan's youth in Tredegar nor what it was in 1867, when Karl Marx published *Das Capital*. Since then, capitalism has responded and adapted itself astonishingly . Globally Marx could never envisaged the changes that took place during Bevan's lifetime. From 1897, the year of his birth, the politics of the masses and the huge growth of the Labour movement forced government leaders of all political persuasions to respond to the wishes of able working-class leaders and to recognise the basic rights of the unemployed, the elderly, the sick and the disabled. Capitalist systems operate differently throughout the world. This is illustrated in the politics of the United States, European countries and the United Kingdom. However, in the majority of countries who practice democracy, workers and their families have benefited a great deal from the actions of trade union leaders and various Labour movements. The Communist Party was relatively strong in some of the mining areas of South Wales, as well as in France and Italy, with the Labour Party gaining ground in Wales during Aneurin Bevan's career.[2] Thus, Aneurin Bevan was always in the midst of an ideological socialist battle in a capitalist country. As the most vocal politician of his day – a man who had pushed for and overseen improvements in health care, housing and the general living conditions of ordinary people – the abolition of capitalism was always on the table. In contrast, the majority of trade union leaders and those on the right wing of the Labour Party believed the important thing was for capitalism to have a human face.[3]Bevan went on to address meetings in the community and to enter politics. But it was in London, that he really developed his understanding of Marxism,

---

1 National Library of Wales, see note 911
2 Ralph Miliband, *Socialism for a Sceptical Age* (Cambridge, 1994), 7–8.
3 *Ibid.*

a key subject on the college syllabus and in the company of Jim Griffiths began to see the relevance of adapting socialism within capitalism.

His political apprenticeship

After returning to Tredegar from college, Bevan began laying solid foundations for the Labour Party in his home town. He gathered around him a number of like-minded young men to discuss issues, as he had done in Sunday school, and to influence every aspect of life in the town.[1] He became a councillor and, although the work's bosses refused to employ him, the majority of miners sincerely admired him and made sure he did not starve. Their continued support enabled Bevan to concentrate on the important practical work of representing the miners on the town council. The miners recognised they were being represented by a brilliant young man with inextinguishable socialist principles. He spoke eloquently on their behalf and for the Welsh Labour movement in the General Strike of 1926. Prior to the strike, he had been seduced by syndicalism and the ideology of Noah Ablett but, following the strike, he gave up direct action and saw his niche within the conventional political structure: the district and county councils, the Miners' Union of South Wales and the Houses of Parliament. He and Archie Lush worked hard in the constituency of Ebbw Vale and realised its MP Evan Davies was a complete failure as a spokesman for the communities and the plight of unemployed miners, It was a fair challenge and Evan Davies was given the chance of retaining his seat, but not without stiff competition from young socialists like Bryn Roberts, a future trade union leader of distinction, and Aneurin Bevan. Many Labour members with a Liberal background would have been willing for Davies to remain their MP but younger Labour members were dissatisfied with the situation. Bevan and Roberts were elected on to the list of nominees along with Davies and three others. After three elections, Bevan came first, with Roberts second and Davies third and quite a way behind.[2]

Aneurin Bevan was elected MP for Ebbw Vale in 1929 and immediately proved he was on the miners' side with his relentless attacks on the Coal Mines Bill 1929 and on Lloyd George and his dreadful slogan 'Better dearer coal than cheaper

---

1 Education for young and old had been part of the Tredegar lifestyle in Aneurin's childhood. A literary and social society had been established where lectures and mock trials were held; the politician Tom Richards and L. D. Whitehead, the works manager, were very supportive. In 1909, there were 230 members and S. Louis Harris, was the secretary. See D. J. Davies, *ibid*, 58.
2 J. Graham Jones, 'Evan Davies and Ebbw Vale: A Note', *Llafur*, vol. 3, no. 3, 97.

miners'.[1] From the beginning, Bevan showed other MPs that he was an unusual Labour politician. He recognised Sir Oswald Mosley had a fervent ideology, which attracted a following, but quickly realised he was completely misguided.[2] Bevan came to his senses but not before praising Mosley's comprehensive address in the Labour Party conference in Llandudno in October 1930. By then, Bevan had met two unusual MPs from the working class, Ramsay MacDonald and Ernest Bevin. The three were the most intelligent politicians at the beginning of the thirties, with Bevan being most talented and charismatic of them all [3] Neverthless, the MP from the Welsh valleys never really fulfilled his true potential, the exception being the five years when he was Minister of Health and Housing and Local Government. Bevan failed so many times to achieve his goals, for example, on the question of rearming Germany and his numerous attempts to become treasurer, leader or even deputy leader of the Labour Party. Herbert Morrison, who frequently crossed swords with Bevan, once warned his secretary that the Welsh politician was not acceptable even within his own party, saying, 'Never trust in that man. He is a bad one.'[4] When he resigned from the Cabinet in 1951, Hugh Dalton passed a note to Morrison saying of Bevan, 'He's like Oswald Mosley.'[5] Dalton had little patience with his fellow Welshman by then and complained in his diary about 'his evil and bad face when he's quiet or when he is addressing audiences'.[6] Hugh Gaitskell, according to Richard Crossman, compared him to Adolf Hitler of all people, remarking unfairly, 'They are demagogues of exactly the same sort.'[7] These men frequently changed their opinions, particularly Hugh Dalton and Richard Crossman. When they assessed Aneurin Bevan, they agreed that he frequently antagonised people, particularly those in authority, but also ordinary people. In the archive of his agent Ron Evans, in the National Library of Wales, there is an angry letter from an ordinary rank and

---

1 Bevan was the most enigmatic Member of Parliament to enter the House of Commons in the 1929 election. He immediately attacked Lloyd George and Winston Churchill, employing sarcasm and mocking them for looking at the problem from different standpoints. His prime accusation was that they were both lacking in responsibility and seriousness. See Richard Toye, *Lloyd George and Churchill*, ibid, 276.

2 Aneurin Bevan refused to follow Oswald Mosley as the latter had hoped, because he could not see where he would find the money and because he predicted correctly that he would eventually lead a fascist party. But Mosley succeeded in winning the secret support of the Prince of Wales, William Morris, maker of cars in Oxford, and the head of the BBC, the sanctimonious Scotsman, John Reith. See Andrew Marr, *The Making of Modern Britain*, (London, 2009), 299.

3 David Marquand, *The Progressive Dilemma: From Lloyd George to Kinnock* (London, 1991), 109. Marquand has an excellent chapter on Bevan, 'Aneurin Bevan: The Progressive Socialist', 109–122.

4 Bernard Donoughue and G.W. Jones, *Herbert Morrison: Portrait of a Politician* (London, 1973), 518.

5 Marquand, *ibid*, 109.

6 Ben Pimlott, *Political Diary of Hugh Dalton, 1918–1940, 1945–1960* (London, 1986), 539 and 650.

7 Marquand, *ibid*, 109. Note the words of Ernest Bevin. Told that Bevan was his own worst enemy, Bevin gave the immortal reply, 'Not while I'm alive, he ain't.' See Alan Bullock, *Ernest Bevin: Foreign Secretary 1945–1951* (London, 1983), 77.

file member of the Labour Party in Preston, Lancashire, dated 11 October 1954. This is what E. West wrote:

> Your party [in Ebbw Vale] may have given a note of confidence to Nye Bevan but we in Lancashire would not. Bevan will never be Prime Minister as Churchill said at Blackpool.[1]

That is just one example of the malicious comments often directed against Bevan. Furthermore, there is an anti-Welsh element in this letter from one of the citizens of Preston:

> It is evident Bevan is a rank Communist and should stay in Wales. England can well do without him. It is evident he would let Germany be overrun by Russia – which it would – but for America.[2]

Nevertheless, the hearts of even his most prejudiced opponents would soften when they heard him in a debate at the Labour Annual Conference or in the House of Commons. Listening to Aneurin Bevan in the Pavilion at Corwen or Caernarfon, in Tredegar or Nottingham was an unforgettable experience. In 1955, when he was a candidate for a Labour seat in the Denbigh constituency, the outspoken solicitor Robyn Lewis heard Aneurin Bevan speak at Corwen. He writes about his reaction in his autobiography:

> *Ar un achlysur, euthum i Bafiliwn Corwen i wrando ar Aneurin Bevan yn areithio. A minnau'n ddarpar-ymgeisydd, cefais ei gyfarfod, a sedd ar y llwyfan. Dyma'r unig dro erioed i mi ei weld yn y cnawd. Wrth gwrs, roedd hi'n araith ysgubol. Eithr dim ond un peth a ddywedodd a lynodd yn y cof. Yr oedd newydd ddychwelyd o'r Unol Daleithiau, ac meddai amdani:* 'A country of technological brilliance'. *Petrusodd am eiliadau, cyn rhoi'r swaden 'ffernol:* 'but a land of no social purpose'. *Mewn blynyddoedd i ddod, cawsom weld mor gysact-broffwydol oedd ei eiriau.*[3]

> (On one occasion, I went to the Corwen Pavilion to hear Aneurin Bevan speak. As I was a prospective candidate, I was allowed to meet him and was given a seat on the platform. That is the only time I ever saw him in the flesh. Of course, it was a brilliant oration. However, I only remember one thing. He had recently

---

[1] National Library of Wales. Papers of Ron Evans: letter from E. West, Preston, to Ron Evans, dated 11 October 1954.
[2] *Ibid.*
[3] Robyn Lewis, *Hunangofiant: Bwystfilod Rheibus* (Caernarfon, 2008), 97.

returned from America and he said: 'A country of technological brilliance'. He hesitated for a moment before adding his sharp sting 'but a land of no social purpose.' Years later, we came to understand how true his prophecy was.)

Bevan was simply the best of the Labour orators; no one could compete with his eloquence except perhaps some of the great Welsh preachers like Philip Jones of Porthcawl, James Jubilee Young of Llanelli and Howell Elvet Lewis of Carmarthenshire (who was better known by his bardic name Elfed).[1] Aneurin Bevan was a likeable character and was not politically ambitious for himself. However, one must remember that very few people in politics lack any kind of personal ambition. Perhaps the only exception in Wales was George Maitland Lloyd Davies (1880–1949), who was elected Member of Parliament for the University of Wales constituency as a Christian pacifist. He accepted the Labour whip but lost his seat a year later and only spoke on one occasion in the House of Commons. He was more like Evan Davies than Aneurin Bevan. Bevan entered local, county and national politics to have the power to improve the social environment for the people of Blaenau Gwent. He was eager to fill the most important offices, but not before he had expounded the principles he considered relevant to a socialist.

In the House of Commons, Bevan had a great influence on a number of people, some of them wealthy men like Stafford Cripps and others outside Parliament like the clever journalist Michael Foot.[2] In Foot's eyes he could do no wrong and in his biography of Bevan he is very unfair to Clement Attlee, Ernest Bevin, Herbert Morrison and Hugh Dalton, all leading lights of the Labour movement from 1930 to 1935.[3] Despite being political giants, they were not spared the lash of Bevan's tongue or Michael Foot's criticism. Bevan showed no consideration or kindness to Clement Attlee, despite the Labour leader appointing him Minister of Health and Housing. To the contrary, Bevan was very disrespectful of Attlee, criticising him on a weekly basis during the thirties and the Second World War. Bevan, Laski and Cripps were thorns in the flesh of the leader. Attlee could have chosen to deal with them harshly but preferred to accept their criticism and take the blame himself for

---

1 For James Jubilee Young (1887–1962) and Howell Elvet Lewis (1860– 1953), see *Gwyddoniadur Cymru yr Academi Gymreig* (Caerdydd, 2008), 500 and 994.
2 Bevan and Cripps had a good relationship. With his exceptional legal ability, Sir Stafford Cripps was crucial in getting all the laws through Parliament during the Labour government of 1945–50, such as Family Allowance, National Insurance and the National Health Service Acts. See Peter Clarke, *The Cripps Version: The Life of Sir Stafford Cripps* (London, 2002). For a comprehensive study of Foot see Kenneth O. Morgan, *Michael Foot* (London, 2008).
3 In the columns of *Tribune*, Bevan kept an eagle eye on Morrison, Attlee and Bevin. In the 7 April 1944 issue of *Tribune* he accused the three of being like 'Three Blind Mice'. In early May 1944, Bevan was nearly expelled from the Parliamentary Labour Party because of his disagreement with Ernest Bevin and Arthur Greenwood, but the Labour MPs voted 71 to 60 in favour of keeping him in the fold. See *Tribune*, 12 May 1944 and John Bew, *Citizen Clem: A Biography of Attlee* (London, 2016), 312.

the benefit of the Labour Party. Bevin and Morrison were less gracious. However, Clement Attlee can take credit for ensuing the Labour Party remained fairly united and stayed part of Churchill's coalition government throughout Second World War – an achievement which paid off handsomely when he won the 1945 General Election. I believe that Dr John Bew has summed up Attlee's achievement admirably:

> The underlying reality was that Attlee's political instincts were far subtler and more attuned to the mood of the country than those of his main critics, Bevan and Laski . . . Bevan was a hero for a portion of the Labour Party, but was widely regarded as hysterical, disloyal and unpatriotic by those outside it.[1]

During the thirties, Bevan supported the Socialist League and the standpoint of Stafford Cripps. But the leaders of the trade unions did not wish to cooperate with the extreme left. Bevan and Cripps wanted to include the communists and embrace a new way of looking at foreign affairs. This grew out of the idea that unity within left-wing British politics could oppose fascism, which was by now a powerful force in Germany and Italy. Instead of placing their hopes in the United Nations, it would be wiser, according to Bevan and Cripps, for the Labour Party to bridge the gap or come to an agreement with the Soviet Union in a pact which meant very little to the average working-class member of the Labour Party. This quotation sums up their frustration:

> They both failed to see that there was no need of the Communists in the United Front, as it was called, as the majority of the working class were members of the Labour Party or the Independent Labour Party or the Conservative Party. In the opinion of Right Wing supporters, the standpoint and speeches of Cripps and Bevan betrayed the solidarity of the Labour Movement and there was constant opposition and frequent demands to expel Stafford Cripps and his supporter Bevan.

One might ask why the left wing of the Labour Party, from the thirties to the mid-fifties, lost every crusade and campaign, particularly in the House of Commons. In essence, it was due to a disagreement between the Labour leadership and a handful of left wingers, with Aneurin Bevan being the most prominent. In the eyes of the leaders on the party's right, it was all very obvious , the Labour Party was the heir of the Liberal Party. That was the situation in Tredegar and every other Welsh mining community.[2] When Bevan won his Ebbw Vale seat in 1929, the Labour Party very nearly had a sufficiently large majority to rule. By 1931, Ramsay MacDonald and

---

1 John Bew, *ibid*, 361.
2 David Marquand, *ibid*, 113.

his government were tottering because of the financial problems following the Wall Street crash in New York. The impact of the economic depression which followed caused pain and suffering across the UK, particularly in regions where most people were employed in heavy industry, like coal mining and steel making.

Ebbw Vale was hit hard, with Bevan's own family suffering. The memory of those incredibly tough times would stay with Bevan for the rest of his life. These experiences made him extremely critical of Labour leaders who preferred to curry favour with the establishment – MPs like MacDonald, Philip Snowden, and the somewhat untalented Welshman Jimmy Thomas. By 1931, the Labour Party was literally in the 'Slough of Despond'.[1] The question that worried Bevan was whether MacDonald was a traitor to socialism or whether he had always been, apart from the period 1923–24 when he was Prime minister, an irresponsible politician. If that were so, how could he have deceived his fellow leaders who regarded him as the Messiah of the working class?[2] Throughout the twenties, the MacDonald-Snowden strategy was much like that of Morrison and Dalton, which perturbed Bevan so much. Labour failed abysmally in the General Elections of 1931 and 1935, but the party's left wing remained active under the lure of Marxism and Christian socialism. It was this strand of the Labour Party that provided a lantern of hope to thousands of families.[3] Soup kitchens were established by the chapels and the lodges of the collieries to prevent mothers and children from dying of starvation. By 1933, there were 2.96 million unemployed in Britain:[4]

Unemployment after the financial storm of the twenties and thirties

The Unemployment Act of 1934 established the Unemployment Assistance Board. The function of this was to have consistency and to ensure that healthy men did

---

1 *Ibid*. Marquand's bitter criticism was: 'In 1931, it was true, most of its parliamentary strength had been swept away – but that was solely due to the incompetence, cowardice and wickedness of Ramsay MacDonald, Philip Snowden and Jimmy Thomas.'

2 Andrew Marr described Ramsay MacDonald as the hero, the illegitimate child who had overcome the circumstances of his birth to become one of the founders of the British Labour Party. He also developed as a brilliant orator. 'As an orator, though no film exists of his great days, he was clearly a spellbinder.' He was called a messiah when he was MP for Aberavon, See, Andrew Marr, *The Making of Modern Britain*, ibid, 261–262.

3 Edna Healey writes about the influence of religious nonconformity in her interesting and readable autobiography: 'Nonconformist religion was the foundation of my own political belief and was the background of many Labour leaders and their wives, Harold and Mary Wilson, James and Audrey Callaghan, Tony Crosland.'

4 There is a table depicting unemployment figures in Emyr Price, *Cymru a'r Byd Modern* (Caerdydd, 1979), 27.

not receive state benefit. It was a two-tier system whereby some workers would have been entitled for financial support based on their National Insurance record, while others were mean -tested and entitled to help based on need. Bevan knew from personal experience of the financial hardship and suffering unemployment had on a family. The Act provoked Bevan and his supporters in Parliament to take action and they organised protest marches, which are still remembered in the South Wales valleys. On 3 February 1935, more than three hundred thousand people in the Rhondda, Aberdare, Pontypool and Tredegar protested. This had a far-reaching result: when Labour was elected ten years later, it established a welfare state based on the principle that benefits should be paid to all according to their needs.

During these difficult years, Aneurin Bevan met the Labour MP Jennie Lee. They were married and embarked on a unique partnership within left-wing politics.[1] Intellectual and politically engaged couples were something of a tradition in the wider Labour movement but they were generally outside Parliament itself. For example, there was Beatrice and Sidney Webb and later George Douglas Howard Cole and his wife Margaret. Bevan and his new wife agreed on most political issues and were popular with the intellectuals of the Communist Party in the South Wales valleys. Arthur Horner regarded Bevan as a close friend, as did Idris Cox, editor of the *Daily Worker* from 1935 to 1937. Around the same time, a volume of Cox's work titled *The People Can Save South Wales* was published by the Popular Front.[2] Twenty thousand copies were sold and the book was well received and appreciated by Bevan's friends.[3] Bevan regarded himself solely as a politician who represented the Welsh socialism of the coal mining areas.

He was a socialist with a poet's imagination and the conviction of David Bevan's generation, which included the emotion of his hero, and provocateur of the coal mines, Arthur J. Cook. Bevan refused to work within the framework of idle chatter, which humiliated the individual and was suspicious of any group who wanted to borrow his ideas and plans.[4] Richard Crossman, a left-wing intellectual, did his level best to criticise Bevan to the people who visited his home weekly to indulge in socialist gossip. But Bevan was no more influenced by him than he was by the capitalist Lord Beaverbrook, whose hospitality he enjoyed. Bevan liked the hospitality provided by Beaverbrook and would talk about his favourite cities: Oxford, Stratford-upon-Avon and especially the incomparable Italian city of Venice. He also made

---

1 I am indebted to Patricia Hollis for her analysis of the marriage and her perceptive account. See Patricia Hollis, *Jennie Lee: A Life* (Oxford, 1997).\ For further information, see Jennie Lee, *Tomorrow is a New Day* (London, 1939); *Our Ally Russia: The Truth* (London, 1941); *The Great Journey: A Volume of Autobiography 1904–1945* (London, 1963); *My Life with Nye* (London, 1980).
2 Gwyn A. Williams, *When Was Wales? A History of the Welsh* (London, 1985), 274.
3 *Ibid.*
4 The Welsh Labour movement has never seen a more dedicated leader than Arthur J. Cook. See Paul Davies, *A. J. Cook* (Manchester 1987), 223.

sure the capitalist propaganda, frequently expounded around Beaverbrook's dinner table, did not go unchallenged. Crossman considered Aneurin Bevan was not a Bevanite after all and that he was far superior in intelligence to them all.[1] Bevan disapproved of some of his supporters who regarded the Soviet Union as the promised land. In his opinion, the Soviet Union was a monstrous country under the leadership of Joseph Stalin. He came to that conclusion after going to Russia with E. J. Strachey and George Strauss and recording their impressions in *What we saw in Russia*, published as a pamphlet in 1931. The three of them saw the power station at Dneprostroi, spent time in the coal mining area of Schacti and actually went down a mine; they visited cooperative farms in Verbluid near Rostov and saw the treasures of the famous city of Leningrad. No-one could hide from Bevan the trouble the country was in, the lack of food and clothing for its people as a result of the shortage of cotton, and the scarcity of shoes. . He was saddened to see the shortage of houses in Moscow but gladdened to observe the opportunities provided for children in music and sport. Bevan was pleased to see children on the streets looking well and noted that begging had been eliminated. He also praised the flourishing state of the theatres and museums. Despite what he saw in the Soviet Union, Bevan was somewhat aggrieved that the only alternative to capitalism was communism. At the Central Labour College and in the South Wales valleys, he had grown tired of hearing how communism gave birth to socialism. He argued, as Ralph Miliband did later, that it was not a choice, as the Lenin inspired communism that had been created as a result of the Russian Revolution in 1917 had quickly failed.[2] It was a monolithic and oppressive system, controlled by violence, the police, the KGB and the Red Army.[3] There was no place for a nonconformist like Bevan in the Soviet Communist Party. Marxism-Leninism would have had him deported a thousand miles to the depths of Siberia. Some of the communist countries gave unnatural acclaim to their leaders and exalted them as if they were deities. Between 1945 and 1989, we have witnessed similar regimes as the Soviet Union (and more recently Russia under Putin), in China, North Korea and several Eastern European countries, like Romania and Bularia. By the thirties, Aneurin Bevan had become one of Westminster's most knowledgeable and eloquent speakers on foreign affairs. His passionate oratory was imbued with the nonconformist values of his hometown and the philosophy learnt from the books he studied in Tredegar Miners'

---

1 Eventually Aneurin Bevan became highly suspicious of Richard Crossman, a man who had bullied Cledwyn Hughes, a great friend of Bevan. Crossman was a selfish, arrogant man who firmly believed that he had no equal. He wrote in his diary 31 October1958: 'I have never felt such a strong sense of personal superiority as I have had this week, looking at Mr. Gaitskell or even poor soft Nye.' *See* Ian Mikardo, *Back Bencher* (London, 1988), 114.

2 Ralph Miliband, *Socialism for a Sceptical Age, ibid*, 45.

3 *Ibid*.

Institute. To Leighton Andrews, a politician in the Welsh Assembly for a period, Bevan was very supportive of Wales, the Welsh language, Welsh culture and Welsh identity.[1] His values were based on moral socialism and social justice, which enabled him to fearlessly challenge the Conservative establishment. Wales was different because it had its own language, a language which he understood but was diffident in speaking, although Sir Dan Davies would force him to utter a few words of Welsh. Leighton Andrews sums it up:He drew from this conception of Welsh identity to frame his oratory whilst also using it as a means of promoting those hard working values his father taught him.[2] There is no doubt that Bevan's upbringing in Tredegar formed his political character; the suffering of the miners and the poor people in Bedwellty workhouse enabled him, in spite of his stammer, to speak sincerely and honestly on their behalf without seeking any favours. This he did in a style reminiscent of the eloquence of Mabon (the trade unionist William Abraham 1842–1922), Arthur J. Cook, Jim Griffiths, Neil Kinnock and David Lloyd George. He displayed the Welsh *hwyl* (musical intonation typical of perorations formerly heard from the Welsh pulpit) at its best. What was the source of Bevan's eloquence? The answer is simple: it came from the Welsh nonconformist tradition of the South Wales valleys. He heard the very best – as did Jim Griffiths, Goronwy Roberts and Cledwyn Hughes – performing and practising their speaking skills with the chapel structure . His distinctive Welsh accent distinguished him from other outstanding Labour orators and attracted the attention of his followers, the media and his opponents alike. Two historians who studied Bevan's particular gift of oratory expressed it clearly:

> Across the arenas Bevan's Welshness textured his orations, enhanced his credibility as a speaker, providing his arguments with a forceful delivery that either enlivened or enraged his audiences.[3]

Throughout his parliamentary career he was among the most eloquent orators .[4] He maintained his reputation as a debater and rebellious orator by routinely lambasting eminent Tories like Stanley Baldwin and Neville Chamberlain and misguided Labour leaders like Ramsay MacDonald and Philip Snowden. He maintained the same profile throughout the Second World War, continuing to attack Labour and Tory leaders

---

1 For Leighton Andrews (2008), Bevan Assembly Act, 21 May 2008 see www.leightonandrews.com/2008/02) brown-assembly-art-html – read 27 November 2017.
2 *Ibid*, 15.
3 Andrew S. Crines and Keith Laybourn, 'The Oratory of Aneurin Bevan' in *Labour Orators from Bevan and Miliband*, (eds. Andrew S. Crines and Richard Hayton) (Manchester, 2015), 15.
4 From the election of 1931 to 1935 there was little competition; the situation improved in the 1935 General Election.

alike. Yet, Bevan had great respect for Winston Churchill, as Churchill had for him. Bevan was quite prepared to acknowledge the other politician's unrivalled qualities as a leader and spokesman for the British people. Despite this, Bevan believed the Labour Party should provide opposition throughout the Second World War. He had not been included in the twelve MPs who were named by Attlee to be leaders of the official opposition, thus he could be the government's severest critic, as well as criticising his own colleagues within the opposition (though others like Jim Griffiths were regularly prepared to take the lead on that score). In this respect, he was unique. During the war, the main thrust of Bevan's articles in *Tribune* was that Winston Churchill was ineffectual as a strong leader but far more effective as a propagandist.[1] In a chapter entitled 'The Problem of Mr. Churchill', he wrote that Churchill believed the war would be won through his splendid orations. Bevan was one of the few people who could make Churchill very angry. Other MPs were not at all happy with his attacks on the Prime Minister. Eleanor Rathbone, the Liverpool-born MP who had been the darling of the Liberal Party among the Liverpool Welsh, condemned him for being so disrespectful.[2] In the opinion of some, Bevan was an extremely confident speaker. He used his strength as a nonconformist politician to threaten and criticise the coalition, which incensed not only Churchill but also Attlee, Bevin and Morrison. Take for example, his speech in the House of Commons on 2 July 1942, when he described in great detail the lack of resources available to the Air Force. He hammered his message home with three points: that the British strategy for the war was wrong, that they were using the wrong kind of weapons and finally that these weapons were being given to people with insufficient training and without a thorough study of modern armaments.[3] This was his final shot:

> As I understand it, it is strategy that dictates the weapon and tactics that dictate the use of the weapon. The Government has conceived the war wrongly from the very beginning and no one has more misconceived it than the Prime Minister himself.[4]

---

1 As Andrew Marr said, Aneurin Bevan was very lonely, because most of his colleagues, with the exception of Sidney Silverman and one or two others, were afraid of supporting his hard-hitting criticism of the Prime Minister. See Andrew Marr, *The Making of Modern Britain*, ibid, 404.
2 On 23 March 1943, Eleanor Rathbone rose to her feet in the House of Commons, after Aneurin Bevan had unfairly criticised the Prime Minister and made a robust protest. According to her biographer: 'It was a brief storm, and Eleanor found the prominence accorded to it by the press a little embarrassing. She had been very angry with Mr. Bevan, as she thought rightly. But she was left with the feeling that he might, in consequence, regard himself as being very angry with her. She was both surprised and relieved, therefore, at a subsequent encounter to observe that he bore her no malice.' See Mary D. Stocks, *Eleanor Rathbone: A Biography* (London, 1949), 302.
3 Andrew S. Crines and Richard Hayton in *Labour Orators from Bevan to Miliband*, ibid, 16.
4 *Ibid,* 17.

Churchill could not escape that kind of attack. It was he who was ineffective, not the Armed Forces. Bevan asked the Prime Minister, of all people, to change his tactics. However, he took care, as a skilful debater, to ensure his colleagues that he was totally in favour of the war but hugely critical of those who were at the helm. Nevertheless, although Bevan had been highly critical of Attlee as Deputy Prime Minister, he was furious when *Tribune* published some verses on 30 March 1945 portraying Attlee as 'An Invisible Man' because he had consented to go to California as Eden's deputy:

> There is no doubt whatever that Attlee exists (Once Head of H. M. Opposition).
> But in Government circles the rumour persists that Attlee's a mere apparition.[1]

Bevan voiced his displeasure at the description of Attlee as the 'invisible man'. As general editor, he was of the opinion that the journal had not been so vulgarly lacking in respect for the Labour leader in a decade.[2] His defence of Attlee proved to be advantageous to Bevan when Labour won the General Election a few months later.[3] When it was time to choose members to the cabinet, Attlee did not deprive him of an opportunity.[4] Bevan had so much to offer and he was invited to be Minister of Health, Housing and Local Government. This proved one of the most inspired appointments of any Prime Minister, because Bevan had spent his formative years in a town, where, in the year of his birth, the Tredegar Medical Aid Society was created. The miners and iron workers paid two pence in every pound of their wages for the service, while Tredegar residents who did not work in the pits or the iron works paid a shilling a year.[5] By the time of the Second World War the society looked after the needs of 22,800 people in Tredegar, with only 12% of the population not contributing.[6] By the twenties, the medical provision included a hospital, five doctors, a surgeon, two pharmacists, a physiotherapist, a dentist and a community nurse.[7] For an extra four pence a week, hospital care was included either in the local hospital or in some of the larger ones in Hereford, London, Bristol, Newport and Cardiff. A car would be provided to take the patient to the station together with a first-class rail ticket. Later, further provision was provided for the patient to recuperate for a few weeks in a care home in one of the spas of Mid Wales. Women were able to attend maternity homes and spectacles could be

---

1 'Invisible Man', *Tribune*, 30 March 1945.
2 Bevan, *Tribune*, 30 March 1945; John Bew, *ibid*, 328.
3 *Tribune*, 20 April 1945.
4 Lord Attlee, 'Bevan as Hero', *The Observer*, 21 October 1962.
5 Steven Thompson, 'Tredegar, Birth Place of the NHS', *Wales Online*, 9 April 2012.
6 *Ibid*.
7 *Ibid*.

bought for two shillings and six pence, with false teeth and wheelchairs available at cost price. In Bevan's opinion, this was the basis upon which he would build a health service for the whole of the UK. Tredegar was not the only place that deserved commendation. In the thirties, there was also a health service in Llanelli and its surrounding areas. But it was Tredegar that provided the inspiration for Aneurin Bevan, as was suggested in the *Picture Post* under the title, 'Where Bevan got his National Health Plan'. The magazine went on to describe it as one of the most notable experiments in health care that Britain had ever seen.[1] Bevan was a politician of vision. The Beveridge Report of 1942 called for free health care but did not suggest a way forward to create a national health service. The coalition government recognised the need for a countrywide health service but its discussions were hazy and without any focus on how to successfully implement such a complex scheme. Everything became clear in January 1946, when representatives from medical aid societies and from Wales assembled to meet the minister. As someone who had played a prominent role in the provision offered by these societies, Bevan expressed his admiration for their work, 'You have shown us the way and by your very efficiency you have brought about your own cessation.'[2] The answer was to nationalise all the hospitals and to formulate a plan to maintain and run them efficiently for the benefit of the patients. This was to be a service which provided from the cradle to the grave. In Bevan's estimation, the situation was obvious, as can be seen from his speeches when the Bill was discussed in the House of Commons. He knew how many important medical institutions had been established in the Monmouthshire mining area, such as the medical aid societies in Ebbw Vale, Blaenavon and Tredegar to assist miners who had been seriously injured in the coal pits. Between 1916 and 1948, the Tredegar society had spent £61,809-16-8½ (c. £2,060 per annum) on surgical appliances, an exceptionally generous sum of money.[3] From 1936 onwards, disabled members in Tredegar enjoyed the full benefits of the medical society. Bevan realised that his constituency, albeit poor, was nevertheless rich in its provision for those who needed medical care. When he outlined his vision in the Commons, he drew attention to the lack of care for those who were suffering from depression and medical problems and those who were blind and deaf. Everyone must be included in his proposed National Health Service and there should be no curtailment on the type of service offered.[4] Bevan's argument was that all health care should

---

1 *Ibid.*
2 *Ibid.*
3 Ben Curtis, Steven Thompson, 'A Plentiful Crop of Cripples Made by All This Progress, Disability, Artificial Limbs and Working-Class Mutualism in the South Wales Coalfield 1890–1948', *Social History of Medicine*, vol. 27, no. 4, 2014, 708–727.
4 Bill, *Hansard*, 30 April 1946. See http:/hansard.millbanks systems.com/commons/1946/ap/30/national-health-servicebill – consulted 31 March 2018.

come under the administrative authority of the welfare state and should be free.[1] His argument was well-timed; many people had experienced socialism in action during the Second World War. There was now an expectation in Britain for a better world: for the soldiers who had fought in battle and the rest of society. It would be wrong to give the impression that Bevan had unanimous support for his excellent scheme across the House of Commons and within the cabinet. For example, Herbert Morrison was not in favour of his plan to nationalise the hospitals, which were then under the control of the local authorities, and opposed it at every opportunity. Bessie Braddock favoured a health system where there was just one type of ward, not some free and others to be paid for. There must be a completely comfortable bed for any patient who was seriously ill.[2] Bessie was very angry with Bevan in those days and he with her. She highlighted the voluntary work many had done in the hospitals, herself included. These volunteers were sincere socialists who had long been pressing for a better health service. Bessie feared Bevan would deprive this large cohort of volunteers of the opportunity to continue their work, because the obligation of the local authorities to govern the hospitals would come to an end. Before the National Health Service came into being, a conference of women who were active in the Labour Party was held in Weston-Super-Mare. Bessie Braddock was among the hundreds who had come to hear the health minister. Bevan reacted impatiently, 'I'm not going to be dictated to by a lot of frustrated females.'[3] The delegates of the conference were equally frustrated with him. A number approached Bessie Braddock to ask her to convey their feelings to him. Braddock refused to do so that day because she knew the press would exaggerate their frustration. The following day she requested to see Aneurin Bevan in his office, across the road from the House of Commons, any time. after 9.30 a.m. She gave him a mouthful, telling him that he would not be in parliament at all without the support of those 'frustrated women', as he had referred to the constituency supporters. The next morning, Jennie Lee went to see Braddock and asked her what she had said to her husband, saying she had never seen him so upset. Braddock told Jennie that if she wanted to know she would have to ask him herself.[4] When the National Health Service Bill was debated in parliament, it became a bone of contention between Bevan and Braddock. Bevan was furious when, along with others, she voted in favour of charging for false teeth and glasses. The two former friends did not speak to each other from 1951 until the Durham Miners' Rally in 1958.[5] Bevan

---

1 John M. Lancaster, 'Gwrthryfelwr, Realydd a Phoendod Aflan: Hanner Canmlwyddiant Gwasanaeth Iechyd Cenedlaethol: Rhodd Aneurin Bevan', *Cennad*, 1998, 102.
2 Jack and Bessie Braddock, *The Braddocks* (London, 1963), 210.
3 *Ibid*, 213.
4 *Ibid*.
5 *Ibid*, 214.

made sure he stood by her to watch the miners and their families march past and he explained to her why he had to accept three types of bed within the hospitals. The main reason was the attitude of the doctors:

> If I had stuck out for it, we would never have had a National Health Service. I daren't make this known at the time because it would have caused such a row.[1]

Another politician who disagreed with Bevan was the Conservative Richard Kidston Law, son of Bonar Law, who had been Prime Minister of the United Kingdom. Richard Law was not prepared to commend Bevan's vision, because he believed the voluntary work of ordinary people would be ignored in his proposed scheme.[2] A large section of the voluntary sector loved and supported their hospitals, and raised money to maintain the voluntary hospitals, which provided such an excellent service. Law and others like him were unwilling to see this good work come to an end. But the majority of Members of Parliament, and voters in general, did not favour Law's objection. It was very easy to quash his objections; however, the medical profession, and the BMA in particular, were a different kettle of fish. Nevertheless, Aneurin Bevan succeeded in making a revolutionary contribution to medical care in Britain; his time as Minister of Health and Housing and Local Government were the best years of his political career. In 1947, he boasted:

> All I am doing is extending to the entire population of Britain the benefits we had in Tredegar for a generation or more. We are going to Tredegarise you.[3]

As Minister for Housing, his post-war achievements were remarkable. Thousands of houses had been destroyed throughout the country, particularly in the cities and ports. There was a shortage of building materials and of people to work in the building industry. There was a constant demand for houses, shops, hospitals, schools and factories. Excluding Northern Ireland, Bevan built over a million permanent houses between 1945 and 1950, an admirable achievement. The standard of building was high; he considered that to be of prime importance. In a letter to a friend, Thomas Jones said:

Aneurin Bevan has made a very good Minister of Health and has taken a very

---

1 *Ibid*, 215.
2 Richard Kidston Law (1901–1980) was a Tory Member of Parliament who was promoted to the House of Lords in 1954 with the title Baron Coleraine of Haltemprice. He wrote a book, *Return from Utopia* (London, 1950). He says on page 9, 'Freedom is the first condition of human virtue and Utopia is incompatible with freedom.'
3 Jonathan Cox, 'A Modern Mecca' for the World', *The Welsh Agenda*, Issue 61.

firm stance on the nationalisation of steel. He has 'Welsh' outbursts in Cabinet and says things with more heat than light, sometimes.[1]

Jones, a native of Rhymney, knew how the cabinet worked better than anyone. In 1916, he had been assistant secretary of the cabinet, serving four Prime Ministers: David Lloyd George, Bonar Law, Ramsay MacDonald and Stanley Baldwin. His diligent biographer, E. L. Ellis from the University of Wales, Aberystwyth, believed that the three greatest Welshmen of the twentieth century were David Lloyd George, Aneurin Bevan and Thomas Jones. When Bevan was appointed Minister of Health in 1945, his first remark was, 'I'll go to see that old bugger from Rhymney.'[2] On his visits, Jones always had plenty of political gossip for Bevan. In his letter, he also drew attention to a very important element in Bevan's character, namely his Welshness. In the English press, Bevan and Neil Kinnock after him (both natives of the same town) were depicted with all the prejudice and filth the media often employed against the Welsh. Kinnock was labelled the 'Welsh Windbag', 'Taff the Lad', 'Teflon Taff' and 'Wild Mayor of the Valleys', which is reminiscent of the language used about Bevan forty years earlier.[3] Jon Snow, the historian and grandson of Lloyd George, said about these two men from Tredegar:

> Neither Kinnock or his advisers were able to alter what he symbolised: a traditional Welsh working-class Cwmardy ethos of community and care for the less fortunate very much out of place in the Thatcherite eightie. This was an ethos very much linked in with a Welsh culture of solidarity and community which Kinnock, like his political hero, Aneurin Bevan, very clearly represented.[4]

The truth is that eloquence, brilliant oratory and Welsh *hwyl* did not help Aneurin Bevan to succeed Attlee as leader of the Labour Party nor Neil Kinnock to be elected Prime Minister. Kinnock did not win the General Election in 1987 and did not become Prime Minister after the General Election of 1992, as had been predicted by the majority of reporters.

It would appear that the English establishment did not want a Welsh Prime Minister as there was no problem in the case of James Callaghan who represented a Welsh seat but was born English. The trouble was the two oratorical giants – Bevan and Kinnock – originated from a militant region of Wales. They were rebuked not only by English voters but by Welshspeaking communities. By Kinnock's day,

---

1 National Library of Wales, Papers of Thomas Jones, class 1, vol. 8, no. 62. Letter from Thomas Jones to Markham, dated 28 August 1945. Richard
2 *Ibid*, 494.
3 C. M. F. Dower, *Neil Kinnock: The Path to Leadership* (London, 1984), 87; Andrew S. Crines and Richard A. Hayton (eds.) *Labour Orators From Bevan to Miliband* (Manchester, 2005), 87.
4 Quoted in Simon Westlake, *Neil Kinnock* (London, 2001), 716.

Bevan's style of oratory was not suitable for the mass media and political programs on radio and television. There is no doubt that Kinnock was the best orator since Bevan; his gift as a speaker was his strength at Labour conferences. Both politicians were indebted to the Welsh *hwyl* at its best, although David S. Moon adds:

> Kinnock's *hwyl* made him a specific kind of Labour orator – one based within the movement – and like the passionate moralism of his fellow 'Bevanites', Castle, Foot (and of course Bevan himself) it is an oratory which has been rarely glimpsed since the 'New Labour' era.[1]

It is the Welsh who glory most in the exceptional gift of oratory displayed by politicians of every party, for its origins lie in the tradition of nonconformity. After entering Westminster in 1943, a Welsh academic Professor W J Gruffydd, said: In Gruffydd's opinion, three people stood out in the gallery of immortals – David Lloyd George, Jim Griffiths and Aneurin Bevan.

Soon Bevan was the most accomplished of the three. As T. Robin Chapman says:

> *Edmygai yn arbennig 'rwyddineb geiriau a beiddgarwch meddwl' Aneurin Bevan a gwnaeth ei orau i'w efelychu.*

(He particularly admired Aneurin Bevan's fluency of speech and sharpness of mind and he did his best to imitate him.)[2]

But no one could compete with Aneurin Bevan, either on the party platforms or in the House of Commons, where he was completely at home. The Welsh nation can take pride in his oratorical skills in the same way they can be proud of his pioneering work to create a National Health Service. He knew well what the situation was like. The buildings was unable to meet demand.[3] Provision varied dramatically.[4] The eternal cry was for more spending on health, as the poor and needy could not afford to pay for their treatment and, besides, the provision of medical care was excruciatingly ineffectual.[5] Jim Griffiths and Aneurin Bevan were

---

1 David S. Moon, 'The Oratory of Neil Kinnock' [in] *Labour Orators from Bevan to Miliband* (eds. Andrew S. Crines and Richard Hayton) (Manchester, 2005), 140.
2 *Ibid*, 187.
3 Aneurin Bevan was the architect of the National Health Service and he described it in these words: 'This is the Government's civilised act.' See Charles Webster, *The National Health Service: A Political History* (Oxford, second edition, 2002), 1.
4 *d*, 5. In South Wales there were 93 hospitals under the care of 46 local authorities. Totally independent of the local authorities were 48 voluntary hospitals. Every Tom, Dick and Harry could see that amalgamating all these hospitals would bring obvious advantages but the BMA and the general corpus of doctors did not agree with Bevan or his plan.
5 *Ibid*, 5.

the most prominent advocates for progress in Attlee's post-war government. Griffiths was clear that his National Insurance (1946) and Industrial Injuries (1948) laws were directly inspired by the experience of the South Wales Miners' Federation.[1] In his opinion, there was no question that the government's priority must be to establish a system which would offer free treatment to everyone in Britain.[2] Bevan knew the health provision in Wales was better than elsewhere in Britain, particularly among family and hospital doctors, but there was also greater demand for treatment.[3] There were many reasons for this: the poor housing conditions in the Welsh-speaking counties of Anglesey, Caernarfon, Merioneth and Cardigan increased the risk of tuberculosis; heavy industries like coal mining in South and North East Wales exacerbated lung disease, while accidents were rife, and there were a lot of old people. Even in the thirties and forties, Wales had communities with the highest percentage of elderly people. Therefore, the expenditure on health was 30% per head higher than in the whole of Britain.[4] Between 1999 and 2022, the Welsh government spent more on NHS Wales than on any other devolved area. First ministers Rhodri Morgan, Carwyn Jones and Mark Drakeford have consistently upheld the vision of David Lloyd George, Jim Griffiths and Aneurin Bevan. The Welsh Assembly Government's reintroduction of free prescriptions in 2007 was indeed 'an act of Aneurin', if there ever was. When he launched the NHS in July 1948 Aneurin Bevan stressed the service should enable individuals to see and read better by supplying them with glasses, to taste their food better with the provision of false teeth and to hear better by providing them with hearing aids. He revealed that the teeth of Britain's lower classes were in a deplorable condition. Bevan knew the chancellor would be quite prepared to overturn the basic principle of his NHS, which was that every UK resident could receive health services free of charge.[5] Bevan regularly defended his NHS, but when Attlee asked him to be Minister for Labour and National Service he knew there would be a storm ahead.[6] Unfortunately his friend Stafford Cripps betrayed him. He allowed Hugh Gaitskell, rather than Aneurin, to succeed him as Chancellor of the Exchequer. The ensuing clash between the two did great harm to the Labour Party's aspiration of gaining power. In the fifties, there was continual rivalry between the two politicians and Gaitskell always gained the upper hand .

---

1 D. Ben Rees, *Cofiant Jim Griffiths: Arwr Glew y Werin* (Talybont, 2014), 152.
2 'Gwladwriaeth Les' in *Gwyddoniadur Cymru yr Academi Gymreig, ibid*, 409.
3 *Ibid*.
4 *Ibid*.
5 K. O. Morgan, *The People's Peace: British History Since 1945* (Oxford, 1992), 102.
6 Bevan had spoken regularly about his support for the National Health Service he had created. At a Labour rally in Staffordshire on 25 September 1949, he was not in favour of decreasing expenditure. He said: 'I have made up my mind that the National Health Service is not going to be touched and there is no disposition by the Government to touch it . . . the health service is sacrosanct. See Keith Laybourn, *A Century of Labour: A History of the Labour Party* (Stroud, 2001), 80.

Bevan even failed in his bid to become the Labour Party's treasurer, later admitting in a letter to his agent Ron Evans that it was a worthless office:

> For your information, my own view is that the treasurership of the Party should be allowed to lapse. It is an out-moded institution with practically no work at all to do.[1]

Bevan realised that there was a strong body of ministers who were determined to keep him out of the leadership contest and who favoured Gaitskell. As he said to his agent:

> This is just another squalid conspiracy similar to the one that was hatched last year, designed to get Morrison on the Executive, after he had been defeated by the Constituency parties.[2]

But the main reason Bevan could not resist the temptation to stand for the office was his loathing of Gaitskell. In Bevan's opinion, it was obvious that Thomas Williamson and Arthur Deakin, not to mention the Labour Party as a whole, were out to teach him a lesson for challenging their standpoint. The only consolation Bevan had was that the Leeds Labour Party had nominated him rather than Gaitskell for the office of treasurer and agreed with his opposition to rearming Western Germany. He said to Ron Evans:

> As you know, this City is represented by a group of the most reactionary members in the Labour Party, including Gaitskell himself.[3]

In the fifties, Bevan had developed into a statesman who was known all over the world. He was invited to visit the Far East, the Middle East, the United States of America and Russia. He told Ron Evans in the summer of 1954 that he was leaving for China and had also been invited to visit New Zealand and Japan.[4] He had to omit New Zealand from his schedule as the Labour members were very anxious

---

1 *Ibid*.
2 National Library of Wales, Papers of Ron Evans, Ebbw Vale. Letter from Aneurin Bevan to Ron Evans, dated 26 July 1954.
3 *Ibid*. Letter from Aneurin Bevan to Ron Evans, dated 6 July 1954.
4 Letter from Aneurin Bevan to Ron Evans, dated 23 September 1954. He was looking forward to attending the general meeting in Tredegar and genuinely hoped that it would be widely advertised. Ron Evans wrote to him after the meeting (Letter from Ron Evans to Aneurin Bevan, dated 17 October 1954) saying that he looked tired but extolled his scintillating speech. He criticised a local man named Evan Rees for saying that there were empty seats in the hall. In fact, there were only two empty seats, but he believed that for the next meeting the constituency party should print tickets and open the hall in good time.

to see him in his constituency. He was very fortunate to have had agents and constituency secretaries of the calibre of Ron Evans, and Archie Lush before him, to defend him, cover up for him and represent him when necessary. When a prominent Labour Party worker died, Aneurin should have made an effort to attend . But he hardly ever attended the day of celebration, the funeral. One such hard worker in the constituency was Gomer Jones, from Rhymney, and it was arranged for Dai Moseley, another industrious worker, to represent the MP at the funeral. He was continually having to apologise for cancelling meetings in his constituency, a failure which has not been mentioned in his biographies until now. But by the winter of 1955, there was a great deal of criticism, as Ron Evans reported to him:The couple of critics present had a very hot time and we were able to pull one out who had been sitting on the fence.[1] Ron Evans was aggrieved that prominent Members of Parliament were so fickle in their support of his hero and he wrote of Hugh Gaitskell's triumph in these words:

> I am sure Mr. Gaitskell must be feeling pleased with himself, his friends inside and outside of the Party canvassed well for him. It seems to me that some of the MPs voted in this ballot like they vote in the Parliamentary Labour Party completely disregarding the wishes of the Constituency Labour Parties. It's a secret, and they take advantage of it.[2]

He was referring to the two-faced Members of Parliament who gave the impression they were in favour of Bevan but then transferred their allegiance to Gaitskell in the secret ballot. Another issue was worrying Bevan too: more people were coming to hear him speak at public meetings outside his constituency than in Ebbw Vale itself, where there would be at times one or two empty rows. It was a reality the press referred to frequently. At the end of 1957, four hundred attended a successful meeting in Ebbw Vale but the empty seats annoyed Bevan. Without concealing his feelings, he said to his agent:

> My meetings elsewhere are invariably crowded and the propaganda effect of having empty seats at an Ebbw Vale meeting is a serious disadvantage.[3]

Archie Lush and Ron Evans agreed the public meetings in Bevan's constituency were no longer as successful as they used to be and were expected to be. Ronald Haines, the Labour Party candidate in Darwen in 1950, 1951 and 1955, was all too

---

[1] National Library of Wales, Papers of Ron Evans, Ebbw Vale. Letter from Ron Evans to Aneurin Bevan, dated 17 December 1955.
[2] *Ibid.*
[3] *Ibid.* Letter from Aneurin Bevan to Ron Evans, dated 17 December 1957.

aware of the Party problems in the town. He pleaded on Bevan to come and unite them. He was expected to do everything before he performed his unexpected U-turn at the 1957 Labour Party conference and supported Gaitskell on the question of arms and disarmament. After that the invitations mushroomed. In the end, it had been the argument of Sam Watson, a Durham miner, that had changed his mind. Watson persuaded Bevan that it was not only Britain but the entire world which needed him as foreign secretary in a Labour administration but that this would not be possible unless Bevan abandoned his stance on unilateral nuclear disarmament.[1] The effect of Bevan's change of heart was an immediate increase in the membership and effectiveness of the Campaign for Nuclear Disarmament. Nearly all the Bevanites joined the movement. His decision did not cause a rift between Bevan and his constituency because their declaration on the matter to the conference was one he could agree with. Thereafter, a rift developed with Donald Soper and Michael Foot; however, after being embroiled in a civil war for seven years, the relationship between Bevan and Gaitskell drastically improved. As Chris Mullin said of Bevan:

> He developed a visceral loathing of Hugh Gaitskell, whom he saw as a usurper and openly undermined Attlee despite being a member of the Shadow Cabinet.[2]

In February 1955, Bevan came within a whisker of being expelled unceremoniously from the Labour Party and was only saved when Mikardo returned specially from Israel to vote. By 1957, Bevan was willing to compromise and support his arch enemy. For a while, foe became a friend, though the partnership between Bevan and Gaitskell was rooted in sand and not in rock.

Despite being superficially close, the men remained suspicious of one other. Bevan believed Gaitskell was too uncompromising in his ideas but too weak to make a dynamic leader who could defeat the Tories. Ian Mikardo claimed they were like a husband and wife who hated one another but stayed together for the sake of the children.[3] The constituency party in Ebbw Vale and readers of *Tribune* never forgave Gaitskell for three reasons. First, his unsuccessful bid to expel Aneurin Bevan from the Labour Party. Secondly, his announcement in the General Election of 1959, without any consultation with his deputy Bevan, that the Labour Party would not raise the level of taxation.[4] Lastly, they were angry that he blamed Labour's failure to

---

1 Sam Watson and Aneurin Bevan had a good relationship. See D. Ben Rees, *Cofiant Jim Griffiths, ibid*. 193.
2 Chris Mullin, 'Nye: The Political Life of Aneurin Bevan – Lucid Account of a Flawed Hero', *The Observer*, 28 December 2014. Review by Chris Mullin of the biography by the politician Nicklaus Thomas-Symonds, *Nye: The Political Life of Aneurin Bevan* (London, 2014).
3 Ian Mikardo, *Back-Bencher* (London, 1988), 161.
4 *Ibid*, 162.

win in 1959 election, not on himself but on the Labour Party for being too socialist. By the time the Labour Party conference was held in Blackpool, Gaitskell was in deep trouble. He was saved from the wrath of the delegates by Bevan of all people, who delivered what was to be his last – and one of his most memorable – speeches. The political cartoonist Vicky (Victor Weisz) depicted Gaitskell throwing himself off the Blackpool Tower and being rescued by Bevan. In his panic, Gaitskell was screaming, 'Help! Help! He is saving me.'[1] Ian Mikardo believed that if Bevan had not been afflicted by cancer, Gaitskell would not have been elected leader in his stead. He had a strong argument: The question one should ask is how Hugh Gaitskell succeeded in being elected leader in the first place and I believe we have given the answer. But the tragedy was that there was no comparison between the two men at any level – personality, background, conviction, administrative ability, contribution or vision.[2] It was by accident that Gaitskell joined the Labour Party in the first place, but Aneurin Bevan had been born into it, as had Neil Kinnock, coming as they did from a family of miners and servants; and both men were successful pioneers in the Labour Party.[3] Aneurin Bevan strove above all else to remain true to his working-class, cultured Welsh background. He was a nonconformist rebel who could not escape the allure of socialism – not Marxism. According to the English historian John Campbell, Bevan died in failure because socialist Marxism had failed. That was only part of the truth, because in *In Place of Fear*, Bevan reveals that he was far from being a Marxist thinker. He is consistently nonconformist, some of his ideas clear, but in his best passages he refers to his own pilgrimage in the Sirhowy Valley. Bevan could not understand the mentality of those born with silver spoons in their mouth who joined the Labour movement, politicians like Hugh Gaitskell, Tony Crossland, Roy Jenkins, Richard Crossman, Douglas Jay and others of their ilk.[4] Bevan complicated the issue because of his hatred of public schools. Hugh Gaitskell had been educated at Wykeham, and nearly all his contemporaries in Attlee's cabinet had received a better education than him. One could describe the relationship between Bevan and Gaitskell as a personal battle between conviction on the one hand and ambition on the other. Bevan was never wholly comfortable with his well-to-do supporters, although he became a country gentleman himself when he moved to Asheridge Farm. Ian Mikardo and Michael Foot were dedicated Bevanites but Bevan never was. He had a foothold in

---

1 *Ibid*, 163.
2 One must consider the opinion of experienced journalists like Geoffrey Goodman and David G. Rosser from the *Western Mail*. Rosser said: 'As a politician he ranked with the foremost as an administrator. Those who served under him had only the highest praise for his ability. He was a tough and resolute ally and, in most ways, a true symbol of the Left.' See David G. Rosser, 'Death of a Rebel', *Western Mail*, 7 July 1960.
3 Neil Kinnock on 'Leadership, the Labour Party and Statecraft Theory' in British *Labour Leaders*, *ibid*, 336.
4 Nicklaus Thomas-Symonds, *Nye: The Political Life of Aneurin Bevan* (London, 2015),158.

both camps. While he remained true to *Tribune*, in his latter years he became reconciled to the right-wing of the Labour Party and their literature. Despite being highly critical of reviewers like Tony Crossland and the journal *Socialist Commentary*, he ultimately became one of them. It is difficult to give a fair appraisal of Aneurin Bevan. Michael Foot portrayed him as a saint whereas John Campbell thought he had more weaknesses than virtues, an unsuccessful prophet who was forced to pay a high price and abandon his socialist principles. Bevan is frequently portrayed as a flawed and foolish man who failed to achieve his potential. Campbell thought the rift between him and Gaitskell was Bevan's fault. But is that a fair assessment? Not at all. Hugh Gaitskell insisted on putting a charge on prescriptions for teeth and glasses because he was sufficiently right wing to know that it would annoy Bevan. The money he accrued for the Treasury that way was pitifully small in the light of the need. He had much in common with those who chastised the right wing of the Labour Party. However, by 1957, Bevan realised that Britain would not benefit through the Bevanites, a group influenced by his charisma but which he did not lead, and which made unsubstantiated allegations. Bevan and Gaitskell believed in a mixed economy and could not tolerate what they had seen in the Soviet Union. In his opinion, the way forward was to have communities cooperating with each other, caring for one another, defending the values of his upbringing with an underlying nationalism as a basis for everything. He enjoyed enormous influence. It was he who inspired Neil Kinnock to join the fray, as Kinnock himself acknowledges:

> There was also the inspiration of Aneurin Bevan who was our Member of Parliament and who I saw performing compellingly in public several times, even if I only met him a couple of times. That's the way I became political and that's why I joined the Labour Party.[1]

Hattersley and Kinnock

---

1 See note 104.

Aneurin Bevan's comparatively early death in 1960 was a loss to the world, Britain, Wales, Monmouthshire, Ebbw Vale and the Labour Party. The loss was crystallized in the letters of his close friend Sir Eugene Cross, who was in charge of Ebbw Vale steelworks and Henry F. Spencer, managing director of Richard Thomas and Baldwins steelworks. Spencer came under the influence of Eugene Cross, a good friend to Aneurin for many years.[1] To Spencer Aneurin was an original thinker, who looked after the places he loved: I have known and admired him for many years as a thinker, a prophet and an irresistible impulse on reform, life, politics and the great events of the times, and only over a comparatively short time in a more intimate personal way in which I have felt his tremendous realness, warmth, sympathy and genius.[2] To the people of the Welsh valleys and men like Eugene Cross, Ron Evans, Bill Harry, Archie Lush, Aneurin Bevan was a constant source of inspiration. Spencer and Cross were determined to erect a memorial for Bevan. Together with Ron Evans, Michael Foot and the committee established to oversee the effort, three granite stones were to be erected in the Gwaun Valley pointing towards the main towns of his constituency – Ebbw Vale, Tredegar and Rhymney – the places where some of the most memorable meetings of his political career had taken place. A fourth stone was added to symbolise that Aneurin Bevan spoke for people across the world. These stones in the Gwaun Valley are the main memorial to the great man but there are others. It took a long time for this to be implemented for there were other events to organise, such as in Tredegar Public Library in 1964. The unveiling of the stones in 1972 was not easy as Jenny Lee admits to the local agent :I think you know why I cannot walk over the hills Nye and I walked over together so often. But this is a speech and different occasion.[3] It was a special day. The trustees of the memorial to Aneurin Bevan had wished to invite Mrs. Indira Gandhi, Prime Minister of India or U Thant, the secretary of the United Nations to unveil the granite stones. Neither of them could come, so the honour was given to Michael Foot, his first biographer and successor. It was wonderful to hear a choir of a thousand voices singing songs of praise and delighting the assembled crowd. The following year, councillors in Chesham decided to call a new road near Asheridge Bevan Hill in his honour. Other areas followed with their own memorials to the Welsh politician. In 2010, the Aneurin Bevan Hospital opened in Ebbw Vale, while in Queen Street, Cardiff there is a life-size statue of him. In Hengoed, there is Aneurin Bevan Avenue, while Aneurin Bevan Place exists in Rugeley, London W5. Maes Aneurin Bevan is to be found in Sirhowy and Ffordd Aneurin Bevan is situated in the middle-class suburb of Sketty, Swansea where the Welsh poet Dylan Thomas spent his childhood and

---

1 National Library of Wales, Papers of Ron Evans. Letter from Henry F. Spencer, managing director of Richard Thomas and Baldwins, London, to Eugene Cross, dated 18 July 1960.
2 *Ibid.*
3 *Ibid,* Letter from Jennie Lee, 67 Chester Row, London, dated 29 September 1972.

youth. In Brynmenyn, near Bridgend, there is an Aneurin Bevan Avenue. In Merthyr, there is even a think-tank – the Bevan Foundation – which pursues Bevan's values and concerns. It's certain the man who created the National Health Service will not be forgotten.

The Anglo-Welsh author Gwyn Thomas wrote a play *Return and End*, which deals with Bevan's relationship with his native town. Gwyn Thomas even had a discussion with the late Welsh actor Richard Burton about playing Bevan. Burton had always wanted to portray Aneurin Bevan and said of him:

> He was one of the most eloquent of men I have met and my admiration for him was immeasurable.[1]

Burton was quite right. In the fifties, Bevan was the only politician who could attract audiences of five or ten thousand people. The journalist Fred Majdalany wrote about the experience of hearing him speak in Margate. He described Bevan's blue eyes and the way he would pucker his face, a young face, thus intimating his feelings. On that occasion, Bevan spoke for forty-five minutes and Majdalany was sorry when he finished. Michael Foot was a very different speaker, and one with a tendency to shout. Bevan, on the other hand, was 'an artist of words'. His final assessment: 'But what a charmer! And what a performance!' There was also Bevan the organiser, the inspired Minister of Housing and founder of the National Health Service.[2] One thing was certain: how fortunate Bevan was in his wife Jennie. She suffered 154 many disappointments, particularly when he supported the right-wing on the question of disarmament. In the words of one journalist:

> Nobody will ever know what turmoil it must have caused Jennie when Nye deserted the Left over the H-bomb issue.[3]

In assessing Aneurin Bevan, we must not underestimate his contribution to international affairs. In the thirties, he gained the goodwill of several overseas leaders. At conferences, meetings and summer schools, he established friendships with Pandit Nehru, Krishna Menon, Jomo Kenyatta, Kenneth Kaunda, to name but a few

---

1 Swansea University, archive of Richard Burton, Box 4.
2 At the 1951 Labour conference, Bevan was congratulated on his achievements in housing and health. High standards had been set for the new National Health Service and Britain had built more houses in five years than any other country in Europe. There was still opposition to the notion of nationalising the building industry, even though the nationalisation of hospitals had been accepted. This is the opinion of Mark Krug, the American who wrote a biography of him under the title *Cautious Rebel* (New York, 1961), 54. The journalist David G. Rosser talks of people travelling fifty miles to hear him speak: 'No politician since the turn of the century attracted so many enemies and admirers. With amazing fluctuation.' See David G. Rosser, ' Death of a Rebel', *Western Mail*, 7 July 1960, 1.
3 Arthur H. Booth, 'Nye and the Loving Tigress', *Daily Herald*, 7 July 1960, 5; George Viner, 'Sorrow at Every Street Corner', *Daily Herald*, 7 July 1960; Ian Smith, *Western Mail*, 17 July 1970, 7.

prominent people. From 1951 onwards, he enjoyed visiting Yugoslavia; he and Jennie spent a month's holiday there with the poet and politician Milovan Djilas, who got into trouble between 1954 and 1957 for daring to criticise Tito and his government. In Britain, not everyone on the left wing in favoured him as much as Nye and Jennie. But in 1952, these troubles were in the future and they were welcomed by Tito and were granted the privilege of swimming with him and his friend Djilas, who was Yugoslavia's Deputy Prime Minister at the time. Aneurin used some of these lazy, relaxing days to complete the first draft of *In Place of Fear*. He had great faith in the fortunes of Yugoslavia and he hoped that, like India, it would refuse to support the major powers: the United States and the Soviet Union. Tito showed great respect to the Bevans and Aneurin Bevan saw him as the conscience of the poor countries of the world, a leader of neutral countries. Jennie had a tribute to Tito published in *Tribune* as early as 1953.

When Djilas was imprisoned, Aneurin worked hard alongside Socialist International in support of him and his friend Vladimir Dedifer, while Jennie travelled to Belgrade to help their families and to plead on their behalf with the heedless authorities. Bevan wrote to Tito and invited the families of Djilas and Dedifer to come to Britain for a holiday [1]. At a meeting in the House of Commons in January 1959, Milovan Djilas paid a lavish tribute to them both for their kindness and pastoral care. He said he could not pay them back but that was not necessary as there were no debts or debtors in the battle for freedom.[2] He visited the Middle East over Christmas 1953, first to Egypt and then to Israel to stay with their friends, the Sieffs. Aneurin had upset the Tories (as was his wont) in an article in which he argued that it was a pointless exercise to send an army to a country which did not welcome them in the name of imperialism and the only sensible way ahead was to recall the soldiers. The article was reproduced in the Egyptian newspapers and Downing Street was incensed. There followed a furious debate in Parliament when Bevan was accused of being a revolutionary who challenged the Egyptians to attack British soldiers. In the eyes of the Tories, he was no patriot. Nevertheless, the Bevans went ahead with their travel plans and spent a few days in Neguib. Unfortunately, Bevan was confined to his bed with flu, an infliction which assailed him regularly. When he recovered, they were able to visit the Sphinx and other places of historical interest, before going to the Suez Canal with a British army escort. After arriving in Israel, Bevan could not keep quiet and told a reporter from the *Daily Express* that Britain had violated the sovereignty of Egypt. He was never going to be a statesman who curbed his tongue; he was a rebel at heart.

In the fifties, the couple had an opportunity to travel to India, visiting the country

---

1 University of Swansea, Archive of Richard Burton, Box 4. Letter from Aneurin Bevan to Tito, 1 February 1954. Tito and other leaders in Yugoslavia were friends of Bevan.
2 Nicklaus Thomas-Symonds, *Nye: The Political Life of Aneurin Bevan*, 199. .

twice, in 1953 and 1957.¹ The purpose of the second trip was to ensure that India would remain a member of the Commonwealth after the Suez Crisis and the tension created in its wake. Reference has already been made to Bevan's journey through Poland to Russia and his friendship with Nikita Khruschev and how he came under his influence on the question of nuclear arms. It was from Khruschev that Aneurin learned the Soviet Union did not want Britain to get rid of the bombs, as possession of them would act as a deterrent to the Americans. In Jennie Lee's opinion, her husband's stance at the 1957 Labour conference was the beginning of their personal troubles. She insisted the pernicious attitude of his friends, including Michael Foot and Ian Mikardo, was responsible for breaking his heart and intensifying his grief and bad health. Bevan was the symbol of a Welshman who was acceptable in Third World countries, the neutral ones and the Soviet Union.² He enjoyed the fine life he achieved, mixing with wealthy individuals, artists, doctors, talented Jews and Welsh people, and newspaper magnates in London restaurants. He received many invitations from the great, but only once was he welcomed to Buckingham Palace. George Thomas and Cledwyn Hughes were far more acceptable to the royal family than Aneurin Bevan. It has been said that Bevan betrayed Wales, but I cannot find any evidence of that. After all, it was he who ultimately enabled Gaitskell and Jim Griffiths to have their way on devolution. He saw devolution as the way ahead but, like the majority of Welsh politicians of his day, viewed Wales in terms of its place in the United Kingdom, despite being regarded as a 'Welsh boy'.³ In 1997, BBC Wales spent £800,000 on a production of *Food for Ravens*, the excellent play by Trevor Griffiths.⁴ During the course of his research, Griffiths discovered the vast majority of people under the age of forty had never heard of Aneurin Bevan and, even those who had, did not realise he was passionately Welsh. Yet in the opinion of

---

1 A Welshman who had befriended Nehru in the thirties D. R. Grenfell, Member of Parliament for Gower. See *Partha Sarathi Cupta, Imperialism and the British Labour Movement, 1914–1964* (London, 1975), 257–258. Cupta frequently mentioned Bevan and the respect in which he was held in the Indian subcontinent. Kingsley Martin includes two glowing profiles of them both. See 'Heir to Two Worlds: Jawaharlal Nehru' and 'Camden Town to Delhi: Krishna Mennon' [in] Martin Kingsley, *New Statesman Profiles, ibid,* 106–111 and 132–137.
2 *Ibid.* 343. When Bevan was moved from being minister of health and housing to minister of labour, his real desire was to become minister for foreign affairs
3 After his death, the *Daily Herald* said, 'He was a Welsh Boy' and that is how he was known to many. Kevin Williams is the one who wrote of Bevan as a traitor to Wales, 'The End is Not Nye', *Planet,* 127, February/March 1998, 318–342, (39).
4 *Food for Ravens* was a television drama made for BBC Wales and first screened in 1997. It was written and produced by Trevor Griffiths. Aneurin was memorably played by Brian Cox and Jennie Lee by Sinead Cusack. The play won a Royal Television Society Award for the best programme of the year from the provinces and won the Gwyn A. Williams Award in the BAFTA Cymru Awards in 1997. Subsequently the play was published as a paperback edition (80 pages) by Oberon Books on 9 February 1998.

Cledwyn Hughes that is what Bevan always was: a Welshman through and through.[1] In spite of his Welsh identity, he lost his command of the language and, like many of his fellow countrymen, missed the opportunity to speak out against the flooding of Tryweryn, which would have deafened the English establishment. With regard to the Welsh language, we must remember the words of Dyfnallt Morgan, (It was not easy to bring up a child to be Welsh speaking in Merthyr Tydfil after the First World War.'). It was equally true in a town like Tredegar; if anything, it would have been even more difficult.[2] However outstanding Welsh poets had a high regard for him .One of these was R Williams Parry. Born in Nantlle Parry came to live to Bethesda, where the quarrymen stayed out on strike for three years (1900–1903). When Bevan accepted a cabinet post, Parry composed an *englyn* for him (a four-lined rhyme containing alliteration).[3] But undoubtedly, Aneurin Bevan's finest hour was in 1945 when he created the National Health Service.[4] Little wonder that an anonymous Welshman said about him: 'In retrospect, he appears to have been the most dazzling exponent of democratic socialism ever produced in Wales.'[5] Mervyn Jones, who knew him well when he was a reporter on *Tribune*, wrote of Aneurin Bevan's lasting contribution to the UK in his book *Chances*:

The Health Service was ours, the new social services built on the wreckage of charity and the Poor Law was ours, the well-planned Council Estates and the New Town.[6]

Bevan is still with us in spirit . Every biography of him adds to our understanding. Perhaps it was Lord Beaverbrook who came nearest to the truth with regard to Nye when he said that 'he was the most original and visionary politician ever produced by the British working-class movement ' I would agree with his insight.[7]

---

1 Cledwyn Hughes, Member of Parliament for Anglesey, counted Aneurin Bevan as one of his main heroes. See D. Ben Rees, *Cofiant Cledwyn Hughes:*

2 The failure of every Welsh politician is to allow their Britishness to take precedence over their Welshness. See the publications of the philosopher and patriot, Professor John Robert Jones (1911–1970). His main work *Gwaedd yng Nghymru* (A Cry in Wales) was published in 1970 by Modern Welsh Publications of Pontypridd and Liverpool. See also J. R. Jones, 'Need The Language Divide Us?' *Planet*, no. 49/50, January 1980, 23–33.

3 *Cerddi R. Williams Parry: Y Casgliad Cyflawn* (Gol. Alan Llwyd) (Denbigh 1998), 14.

4 Jennie scattered her husband's ashes on the wild bleak mountain above Tredegar, Jennie Lee told the assembled crowd of Welsh people, 'He gave blows, he took them, and he didn't whine. Don't think, because he held his

5 'Aneurin Bevan (1897–1960)', *The Oxford Companion to the Literature of Wales* (ed. Meic Stephens) (Cardiff, 1986), 38.

6 Mervyn Jones, *Chances: An Autobiography* (London, 1987), 220

7 Kenneth O .Morgan, Michael Foot, (London , 2006) , 97.

A Detailed Bibliography

Sources from the National Library of Wales and other archival centres: Press Reports

BBC archives in Wales
Labour Party archives, Manchester
Richard Burton archive, Swansea University
PRO, Kew, London

WITHIN THE NATIONAL LIBRARY

Papers mostly of politicians :

Leo Abse
Aneurin Bevan, correspondence, from 1951–1961
General correspondence, 1956–1961
Electorate files 1954–1961
Blaenau Gwent Constituency, Labour Party Papers, 1951– 1961
Desmond Donnelly
Idris Cox
Councillor Ron Evans (1944–1987)
Iorwerth Cyfeiliog Peate
Alwyn D. Rees
Lord Cledwyn Hughes
Lord Goronwy Roberts
Lord Gwilym Prys-Davies
Lord Tudor Watkins
The Labour Party in Wales
The Labour Party in Ebbw Vale
Clement Davies
Brinley Richards

Professor Gwyn Thomas, the Anglo-Welsh writer
Gwynfor Evans
James Griffiths
Cassie Davies
Cliff Prothero
David Lloyd George
David Rees Griffiths (Amanwy)
Caradog Jones
Professor Sir Deian Hopkin
Eirene White
E.T. John
Lord George Thomas
Huw T. Edwards
Ithel Davies
John Morris
Kate Roberts
Lewis Valentine
Sir Goronwy Daniel
T. E. Nicholas
W. J. Gruffydd
W. H. Mainwaring
Plaid Cymru
John Tripp ('Homage to Aneurin Bevan')
Emlyn Williams
Illingworth's cartoons at the National Library, number 003381773 where Bevan is portrayed as an owl.

Newspapers, weeklies and magazines

Aberdeen Press and Journal
Aneurin
Baner ac Amserau Cymru
Barn
Belfast News Letter
British Medical Journal
Blaenau Gwent Heritage Forum Journal
Cymro, Y
Daily Express
Daily Herald
Daily Mail

Daily Mirror
Daily News
Daily Sketch, The
Daily Telegraph, The
Economist, The
Goleuad, Y
Guardian, The
Independent, The
Jewish Chronicle, The
Lancet
Llafur
Marxism Today
Merthyr Express, The
Municipal Journal, The
New Statesman and Nation
News Chronicle and Daily Despatch
Observer, The
Planet
Reynold's News
Socialist Commentary
South Wales Argus
South Wales Daily News
South Wales Echo
Spectator, The
Sunday Times, The
Time and Tide
Times, The
Traethodydd, Y
Tredegar Valley District Monthly Report
Tribune
Tribune Weekly
Welsh History Review
Western Daily Press, The
Western Mail, The

BIOGRAPHIES AND VOLUMES ON ANEURIN BEVAN in Welsh and English

Beckett, Clare and Beckett, Francis, *Bevan* (London, 2004)
Brome, Vincent, *Aneurin Bevan* (London, 1953)

Campbell, John, *Nye Bevan and The Mirage of British Socialism* (London, 1987)

Foot, Michael, *Aneurin Bevan*, Volume 1, 1897 to 1945 (London, 1962); Volume 2, 1945 to 1960 (London, 1973)

Goodman, Geoffrey, *From Bevan to Blair: Fifty Years of Reporting from the Political Front Line* (Revised Edition) (Brighton, 2010)

Idem, (ed.), *The State of The Nation: The Political Legacy of Aneurin Bevan* (London, 1997)

Hollis, Patricia, *Jennie Lee: A Life* (Oxford, 1997)

Jenkins, Mark, *Bevanism: Labour's High Tide, The Cold War and The Democratic Mass Movement* (London, 1977)

Krug, Mark M., *Aneurin Bevan: Cautious Rebel* (New York, 1961)

Laugharne, Peter J. (Ed.), *Aneurin Bevan: A Parliamentary Odyssey*, Volume 2, 1945–1960 (Liverpool, 2000)

Lee, Jennie, *This Great Journey: A Volume of Autobiography 1904–1945* (London, 1963)

Idem *My Life with Nye* (London, 1980)

Morgan, Kenneth O., *The Red Dragon and The Red Flag: The Cases of James Griffiths and Aneurin Bevan* National Library of Wales, Aberystwyth 1989)

D.Ben Rees, *Cofiant Aneurin Bevan: Cawr o Gymro a Thad y Gwasanaeth Iechyd* (Lerpwl, 2021)

Smith, Dai, *Aneurin Bevan and The World of South Wales* (Cardiff, 1993)

Thomas-Symonds, Nicklaus; *Nye: The Political Life of Aneurin Bevan* (London, 2015)

SOME OF ANEURIN BEVAN'S OWN WRITINGS

Bevan, Aneurin, Strachey, E. J., Strauss, George, *What we saw in Russia* (London, 1931), 30

Idem, 'Plan for Work' in *Plan for Britain: A Collection of Essays,* Prepared for the Fabian Society (ed. G. D. H. Cole) (London, 1943), 34–52

Idem, (Celticus), *Why Not Trust the Tories?* (London, 1944), 89

Idem, *In Place of Fear* (London, 1952; second edition 1978) Idem, *Democratic Values* (London, The Fabians, 1950), 15.

Idem, 'Angers Long Ashton', *Western Daily Press*, 18 October 1950, 6

Idem et al, 'One Way Only', *Tribune* (London, 1951)

Idem et al, 'It Need Not Happen: The Alternative to German Rearmament', *Tribune* (London, 1954)

Idem, 'Labour Must Take the Offensive', *Times,* 27 October 1952, 2

Idem, 'Labour Must Stay in Government', *Tribune, (314)* 5 March 1943, 6–7

Idem, 'Labour Has Been Tricked', *Tribune* (268), 13 February 1942, 1–2

Idem, 'What Churchill Must Do', *Tribune* (269), 20 February 1942, 1–2

Idem, 'Consider Coal', *Tribune* (279), 20 March 1942, 1

Idem, 'The Movement Away from the Party'; *Tribune*, 3 April 1942, 1–2

Idem, 'The Palace Revolt Against Churchill', *Tribune* (278), 24 April 1942, 1–2

Idem, 'Labour Must Lead Now', *Tribune* (282), 22 May 1942, 6–7

Idem, 'Labour and The Coalition', *Tribune* (311), 11 December 1942, 6–7

Idem, 'How do we Keep Germany Disarmed, *Tribune* (420), 12 January 1945; 6–7

Healey, Denis (ed.), *The Curtain Falls: The Story of the Socialists in Eastern Europe*, Preface by Aneurin Bevan (London, 1951)

SHORT BIOGRAPHIES OF ANEURIN BEVAN

'Aneurin Bevan' in *Dictionary of British History* (Aylesbury, 1981), 65

Breverton, Tony, 'Aneurin Bevan' in *100 Great Welshmen, Volume 1* (Saint Tathan, 2001), 41–44.

Edwards, Huw T., 'Aneurin Bevan' in *Aneurin, Vol 1* (1) (1961)

Laybourn, Keith, 'Aneurin Bevan (1897–1960)' in *Encyclopaedia in the Age of War and Reconstruction, Vol 1* (eds. John Merriman and Jay Winter), (Detroit, 2006), 361– 362

Llewellyn, David, *Nye: The Beloved Patrician* (Cardiff, 1960), 1–31

Mafdalany, Fred, 'Nye Bunter', *Daily Mail,* 4 October 1955

Magee, Bryan, *Confessions of a Philosopher* (London, 1997), 266, 271–278

Marquand, David, 'Aneurin Bevan, stormy petrel of the Labour Left', *New Statesman*, 19 March 2015

Moran, Lord, Tribute: 'Aneurin Bevan', *The British Medical Journal*, Vol 2 (No 5193), 16 July 1960, 236

O'Neill, Dan, 'Great Orator who would have changed our lives', *South Wales Echo* (11), 1997, 23

Portillo, Michael, 'The Bevan Legacy', *British Medical Journal*, Vol 37 (No 7150), 4 July 1998, 37–40

Rees, D. Ben *'Aneurin Bevan'* in *Cymry Adnabyddus 1952–1972* (Liverpool and Pontypridd, 1978), 22–24

Rees, Ivor Thomas, 'Aneurin Bevan PC 1945, JP 1928' in *Welsh Hustings 1885–2004* (Llandybïe, 2005), 25–26; picture of Bevan on the cover.

Sheen, Michael, 'Aneurin Bevan: The Man who made the NHS', BBC World Service, 11 July 2018 (radio programme) Speed, Nick, 'Legend Recalled', *South Wales Echo*, 14 November 1997, 29

Idem, 'Political hero for a young Kinnock', *South Wales Echo*, 15 November 1997, 27

Stephens, Meic (ed.), 'Aneurin Bevan 1897–1960' in *Cydymaith i Lenyddiaeth Cymru* (Cardiff, 1986), 41–42

Thomas-Symonds, Nicklaus; 'Golwg ar Aneurin Bevan' in *Maniffesto 48 National Library of Wales* (Aberystwyth, 2017), 13–16

Williams, Chris, 'Aneurin Bevan and the World of South Wales', *History Workshop Journal, Number 41* (Spring 1996, 266–276

Viner, George, 'Nye Bevan: the man between two worlds', *The Miner*, September/October 1960

VOLUMES AND ARTICLES ON TREDEGAR: THE TOWN, NATIVE AREA AND PLACE OF ANEURIN BEVAN'S YOUTH

Alderman, Geoffrey, 'The Anti-Jewish Riots of August 1911 in South Wales: A Response'; *Cylchgrawn Hanes Cymru, Volume 20*, No 1 (June 2001), 565–571

Idem, 'The Jew as Scapegoat? The Settlement and Reception of Jews in South Wales Before 1914', *Transaction of the Jewish Historical Society of England*, XXVI (1974–1978), 62–70

Harrison, Rev. J. J., 'History of the Political Minister in Tredegar, *Merthyr Express*, 7 May 1921

Holmes, C., 'The Tredegar Riots of 1911: Anti-Jewish

Disturbances in South Wales, *Cylchgrawn Hanes Cymru, Volume 11* (1982), 214–215

Jones, Oliver, *The Early Days of Sirhowy and Tredegar* (Risca, Fourth Edition, 1975); A preface was written by Michael Foot, Oliver Jones being one of Aneurin Bevan's best friends. The two had been together from their childhood until the end of the twenties.

Parry, Jon, 'The Tredegar Anti-Jewish Riots of 1882', *Llafur*, vol.3, no 8, 20–23

Prosser, Philip, *A Look at Old Tredegar in Photographs* (Swansea, 1990)

Idem, A Look at Old Tredegar in Photographs, Volume 12 (Swansea, 1998). See pictures of Aneurin Bevan on page 70.

Powell, Evan, *The History of Tredegar* (Tredegar, no date), a formidable work.

Rubinstein, W. D., 'The Anti-Jewish Riots of 1911 in South

Wales: A Re-examination'; *Cylchgrawn Hanes Cymru*, Volume 18 (1997), 667–699

Scandnett, W., *Old Tredegar, Volume 1* (Rogerstone, 1990)

Yates, F. E. A. (ed.), W.C. Smith, *Tredegar, My Town* (Risca, 1976); It is interesting to make note of all the boxers that existed in Tredegar in the thirties, such as Kid Harris, Tommy Price, Tommy Dowlais and Jack Phillips

TRIBUTES TO ANEURIN BEVAN ON HIS DEATH

Account of Bevan during the First World War before the

Magistrates, *Merthyr Express*, 22 June and 20 July1918; *Western Mail*, 19 June and 16 July 1918

Anon., 'The Man They Idolised', *The Western Mail*, 7 July 1960, 4

Anon., 'Salute to Bevan'; *News Chronicle and Daily Despatch;* 7 July 1960, 1

Anon., 'Nye: We Lose a Giant in an Age of Pygmies', *Daily Sketch*; 7 July 1960, 2

Attlee, Earl Clement, 'We Disagreed Often, but . . .', *Daily Herald*, 7 July 1960, 5

Booth, Arthur H., 'Nye and the Loving Tigress', *Daily Herald*, July 1960, 5

Delargy, Hugh, 'Most Wonderful Man I Have Ever Known', *Reynolds News and Sunday Citizen*, 10 July 1960; 6

Driberg, Tom, 'Nye Would Have Shrugged It All Off', *Reynold's News and Sunday Citizen*, 10 July 1960, 6

Eaton, Edward, 'Tredegar', *Western Mail,* 7 July 1960

Eden, Guy, 'So Near to No. 10'; *Daily Sketch*, 7 July 1960, 6

Evans, Trevor, 'Bevan's Secret', *Daily Express*, 7 July 1960, 1

Fairlie, Henry, 'Why I Class Him with Winston Churchill', *Daily Mail,* 7 July 1960

Foot, Dingle, 'The Constant Rebel', *Observer,* 10 July 1960, 10

Fagence, 'Rebel With a Dream', *Daily Herald,* 7 July 1960, 4

Gaitskell, Hugh, 'Nye, The Big Man', *Daily Express,* 7 July 1960, 1

Griffiths, James, 'World Figure Still Remained a True Son of the Valley', *Western Mail,* 7–8 July 1960

Hastings, Somerville, *Aneurin Bevan: an appreciation of his services to the Health of the People* (Socialist Medical Association, 1960)

Levy, Benn W., 'Aneurin', *Observer,* 10 July 1960, 3 Llewellyn, David, 'Nye – The Beloved Patrician', *Western Mail,* 8 July 1960, 6

Marks, Derek, 'Bevan: The Man Destiny Passed By', *South Wales Echo*; 8 July 1960

McLeare, Hugh and Bennett, Stanley, ' Bevan Dead', *Daily Mail,* 7 July 1960, 1

Morgan, Basil, 'The Boy Who Spoke in Anger', *Daily Herald,* 7 July 1960, 5

Owen, Frank, 'When I Lived with Nye in Cromwell Road', *Daily Mail,* 7 July 1960, 6

Phillips, Peter, 'Tredegar: A Town in Mourning', *South Wales Echo,* 7 July 1960, 7

Rosser, David, 'Death of a Rebel', *Western Mail,* 7 July 1960, 4

Smith, Jan, 'Jennie', *Western Mail,* 7 July 1960, 7 Terry, Walter, 'Power That was What Fascinated Aneurin Bevan, *Western Mail;* 7 July 1960, 7

Viner, George, 'Sorrow at Every Street Corner', *Daily Herald,* 7 July 1960, 1

Westgate, 'Wales and the World', *Western Mail,* 7 July 1960, 8

Wyatt, Woodrow, 'A Magic Personality', *Sunday Times,* 10 July 1960, 4

RESEARCH DISSERTATIONS

Barclay, M., 'Aberdare 1880–1914: Class and Community' (M.A. dissertation, University of Wales, 1985)

Demont, Susan E., 'Tredegar and Aneurin Bevan: A Society and its Political

Articulation 1890–1929' (D.Phil. dissertation, University of Wales, March 1990). A most valuable study.

Lowe, Keith William, 'The State and Medical Care in Britain: Political Process and the Structuring of the National Health

Service' (D.Phil. dissertation, Oxford University, Wolfson College).

BOOKS, ARTICLES AND PAMPHLETS

Abse, Leo, *Margaret, Daughter of Beatrice: A Politician's Psycho-biography of Margaret Thatcher* (London, 1989)

Acland, Richard, *The Next Step* (Exeter, 1974)

Addison, Paul, *The Road to 1945: British Politics and The Second World War* (London, 1994)

Allen, V. L., *Trade Union Leadership: Based on a Study of Arthur Deakin* (London, 1957)

Andrews, Leighton, 'Written Out of History', *Bevan Foundation Review*, No 4, Spring/Summer 2004, 33–37.

Anon., *Taith treftadaeth Aneurin Bevan*, (Cyngor Bwrdeisdref Blaenau Gwent, 1999)

Arnot, R. Page, *South Wales Miners, Glowyr De Cymru: A History of the South Wales Miners' Federation 1914–1926,* (Cardiff, 1975)

Idem, *The Miners, One Union, One Industry: A History of the National Union of Mineworkers 1939–46* (London, 1979)

Attlee, Clement R., *The Labour Party in Perspective* (London, 1937)

Idem, *As It Happened* (London, 1954).

Ballard, Paul H., 'The Changing Chapels', *Planet*; June 1978, 54–59

Bassett, Reginald, *Nineteen Thirty-one Political Crisis* (London/New York, 1955)

Beers, Laura, *Your Britain: Media and the Making of the Labour Party* (Boston, 2010)

Bellamy, Joyce and John Saville, Sir John (Jack) Bailey (1896–1969), in *Dictionary of Labour Biography, Volume 2* (edited by Joyce M. Bellamy and John Saville) (London and Basingstoke, 1974), 25–30

Beveridge, Sir William, *Social Insurance and Allied Services*, (London, 1942)

Bew, John, *Citizen Clem: A Biography of Attlee* (London, 2016)

Brivati, Brian, *Hugh Gaitskell* (London, 1996

Brookes, P., *Women at Westminster: An Account of Women in the British Parliament 1918–1966* (London, 1967)

Bullock, Alan, *The Life and Times of Ernest Bevin, Volume 1; Trade Union Leader 1881–1940* (London, 1960)

Idem, *The Life and Times of Ernest Bevin, Volume 2; Minister of Labour 1940–1945* (London, 1967)

Butler, D. E., *The British General Election of 1955* (London, 1955)

Burgess, Simon, *Stafford Cripps: A Political Life* (London, 1999)

Braddock, Jack and Bessie, *The Braddocks* (London, 1963) Bryant, Chris, *Possible Dreams: A Personal History of the British Christian Socialists* (London, 1996)
Callaghan, James, *Time and Chance* (London, 2006)
Campbell, John, *Roy Jenkins: A Well-rounded Life* (London, 2014)
Idem, 'Demythologising Nye Bevan', *History Today, Volume 37* (April 1987), 13–18
Idem, Pistols at Dawn (Liverpool, 2009), 195–243
Castle, Barbara, *Fighting All The Way* (London, 1994)
Catterall, P., 'Morality and Politics: The Free Churches and the Labour Party Between the Wars', *Historical Journal 3*, 3 (1993), 677–679
Chapman, T. Robin, *Dawn Dweud: W.J. Gruffydd* (Cardiff, 1993)
Church, Ian (ed.), *Official Record (Hansard) House of Commons Centenary,* Volume 1909–2009 (London, 2009)
Citrine, Walter, *Men and Work: The Autobiography of Lord Citrine* (London, 1964)
Crines, Andrew S. and Hayton, Richard, *Labour Orators from Bevan and Miliband* (Manchester, 2015)
Cronin, A. J., *Adventure in Two Worlds: Autobiography of a Doctor and Writer* (London, 1952)
Cole, G. H. D., *Great Britain in the Post-War World* (London, 1942)
Cole, M., *The Life of G. D. H. Cole* (London, 1971).
Craik, W. W., *Bryn Roberts and The National Union of Public Employees* (London, 1955). There is a preface to the book by Aneurin Bevan.
Idem, The Central Labour College 1909–1929 (London, 1964)
Idem, Sydney Hill and the National Union of Public Employees (London, 1968)
Crosland, Anthony, *The Future of Socialism* (London, 1956)
Dalton, Hugh, *The Fateful Years: Memoirs 1931–1945* (London, 1957)
Davies, A. J., *We, The Nation: The Conservative Party and the Pursuit of Power* (London, 1995)
Davies, D. J., *Ninety Years of Endeavour: The Tredegar Workmen's Hall 186–1951* (Tredegar, 1952)
Davies, E. Hudson, 'Welsh Nationalism', *Political Quarterly*, 39 (1968), 322–332
Davies, Geraint Talfan, 'Cofio Leo Abse', *Barn* No. 548 (September 2008), 17–18
Davies, John, 'Cymreictod cymhleth Aneurin Bevan', *Barn* 570/571, July/August 2010, 38–9
Davies, Paul, *A. J. Cook* (Manchester, 1987)
Idem, High Tide and After: Memoirs 1945–1960 (London, 1962)
David, Wayne, *Remaining True: A Biography of Ness Edwards* (Caerphilly, 2006)
Davidson, Peter (ed), *George Orwell: A Patriot After All, 1940–1941* (London, 2000)
Demont, Sue, 'From Localised Necessity to Universal Ideal: Tredegar and Aneurin Bevan', *Llafur,* vol. 12, no. 3 (2018), 171–186

Document No. 003366279, 'Hiraeth yn Nhredegar ar ôl marwolaeth Aneurin Bevan', 14 July 1960 (National Library of Wales, Aberystwyth)

Donoghue, Bernard and Jones, G.W., *Herbert Morrison: Portrait of a Politician* (London, 1973)

Djilas, Milovan, *The New Class: An Analysis of the Communist System*, (New York and London, 1957)

Dutt, Rafani Palme, *India Today and Tomorrow* (Bombay and London, 1955)

Eagleton, Terry, *Why Marx Was Right* (New Haven and London, 2011)

Eckstein, Harry, *Pressure Group Politics: The Case of the British Medical Association* (London, 1960)

Edwards, Andrew, 'Aneurin: Reinventing Labour, The Voices of a New Generation', *Llafur*, vol. 9, no. 1 (2004), 71–84

Idem, *Labour's Crisis, Plaid Cymru, The Conservatives, and the Decline of the Labour Party in North-West Wales, 1960– 1974* (Cardiff, 2011)

Edwards, Hywel Teifi, *Arwr Glew Erwau'r Glo: Delwedd y Glowr yn Llenyddiaeth y Gymraeg 1850–1950* (Llandysul, 1994)

Edwards, Ness, *History of the South Wales Miners' Federation, Volume 1* (London, 1938)

Edwards, Wil Jon, *From the Valley I Came* (London, 1956)

Ellis, T. I., *Crwydro Mynwy* (Llandybïe, 1958)

Evans, E. W., *Miners of South Wales* (Cardiff, 1961)

Evans, Gwynfor, *Aros Mae* (Swansea, 1971)

Evans, John Gilbert, *Devolution in Wales: Claims and Responses 1937–1979* (Cardiff, 2006)

Evans, Rhys, *Gwynfor: Rhag Pob Brad* (Talybont, 2005)

Finch, Harold, *Memoirs of a Bedwellty MP* (Risca, 1972)

Fishman, Nina, *Arthur Horner: A Political Biography, Volume 1: 1894–1944* (London, 2010)

Foot, Michael, *Debts of Honour* (London, 1980)

Idem, *Loyalists and Loners* (London, 2011)

Idem, *Parliament in Danger* (London, 1959)

Idem, Crossman, Richard and Mikardo, Ian, *Keep Left* (London, 1947)

Francis, Hywel and Smith, Dai, *The Fed: A History of the South Wales Miners in the Twentieth Century* (Cardiff, 1980; second edition 1998)

Goodman, Geoffrey, 'What would Nye Think?', *Bevan Foundation Review*, No. 5 (Autumn/Winter 2004), 23–4

Gorsky, Martin, *Public Health in Interwar England and Wales*, (Dynamis 2008), 28, 175–198

Grant, John, *Member of Parliament* (London, 1974)

Grigg, John, *Lloyd George: The People's Champion 1902– 1911* (London, 2002)

Gwyddoniadur Cymru yr Academi Cymreig (Cardiff, 2008), 71, 76–77; 182, 226, 295, 299, 384, 409, 462, 494, 725, 746, 788, 841, 862, 909 and 997

Hancock, W. C., 'No Compromise: Nonconformity and Politics 1893–1914'; *Baptists' Quarterly* (1995), 36 (2), 56– 69

Hardie, Keir, *The ILP and All About It* (London, BLA, 1909)

Idem, The Red Dragon and The Red Flag (Merthyr, BLA, 1912)

Harris, Kenneth, *Attlee* (London, 1984)

Harris, William, 'Labour and Home Rule for Wales', *The Welsh Outlook*, June 1919

Hutchinson, George, 'Near-socialist Macmillan', *The Spectator*, 25 February 1978, 10

Hawking, Stephen; 'How to Solve the NHS Crisis – Significantly', *The Guardian*, 19 August 2013, 35

Hattersley, Roy, *David Lloyd George: The Great Outsider* (London, 2010)

Heffer, Eric S., *The Class Struggle in Parliament. A Socialist View of Industrial Relations*, (London, 1973)

Hill, D. (ed.), *Tribune 40: The First Forty Years of a Socialist Newspaper* (London, 1977)

Honingsbaum, F., *The Division of British Medicine: A History of the Separation of General Practice from Hospital Care 1911–1968* (London, 1979)

Idem, Health, Happiness and Security: The Creation of the National Health Service (London, 1989)

Hodges, Frank, *My Adventures as a Labour Leader* (London, 1925)

Honeyman, Victoria, *Richard Crossman: A Reforming Radical of the Labour Party* (London, 2007)

Horder, M., *The Little Genius: A Member of the First Lord Horder* (London, 1966)

Howell, David, *The Rise and fall of Bevanism* (Leeds, 1978), 43

Hughes, Lord, *The Referendum: The End of an Era* (Cardiff, 1981)

Humphreys, Emyr, *The Taliesin Tradition: A Quest for the Welsh Identity* (London, 1983)

Hunt, Allen, *The Post-War History of the British Working Class* (London, 1937)

Jeffreys, K., *The Labour Party Since 1945* (London, 1993)

Jenkins, Gwyn, *Cofiant Huw T. Edwards: Prif Weinidog Answyddogol Cymru* (Talybont, 2003)

Jones, J. Graham, 'Evan Davies and Ebbw Vale: A Note', *Llafur*, vol. 3, no. 3, 93–99

Idem, 'Welsh Politics Between the Wars: The Personnel of Labour', *Trafodion Anrhydeddus Cymdeithas y Cymmrodorion*; 1983, 164–183

Idem, 'Rift and conflict within the Labour Party in the 1950s', letters from Aneurin Bevan *Llafur*, vol. 7, no. 2, (1997), 31–40

Idem, 'Aneurin Bevan and the Establishment of the National Health Service' in *Healthcare in Wales, An Historical Miscellany* (eds. Colin Baker and John Lancaster London , 2000), 127–41

Jones, Jack, *Unfinished Journey* (London, 1938)

Kantanka, Michael (ed.,) *Radicals Reformers and Socialists from the Fabian Biographical Series* (London, 1974)

Kennan, George F., *Soviet Foreign Policy 1917–1941* (New York and London, 1960)

Kennedy, Thomas, *The Hound of Commerce: A History of No Conscription Fellowship 1914–1919* (Arkansas, 1981)

Khrushchev, Nikita, *For Victory in a Peaceful Competition with Capitalism* (New York, 1960)

Idem, *Khrushchev Remembers* (London, 1971), 335.

Klugman, James, *History of the Communist Party of Great Britain, Volume 1* (London, 1938)

Koss, S., *Nonconformity in Modern British Politics* (London, 1975)

Lee, Jennie, *Tomorrow is a New Day* (London, 1939)

Idem, *Our Ally Russia: The Truth* (London, 1931)

Lewis, John, *The Left Book Club: An Historical Record* (London, 1970)

Liddell Hart, Basil, H., *The Other Side of the Hill: Germany's Generals, Their Rise and Fall with Their Own Account of*

Military Events 1939–1945 (London, 1948; new edition, 1951)

Idem, *Defence of the West* (London and New York, 1950)

Lovell, R.; *Churchill's Doctor: A Biography of Lord Moran* (London, 1992)

Matthews, Ioan,' Hen Arwr Maes y Glo Carreg: John James 1869- 1942' in *Cwm Aman* (ed. Hywel Teifi Edwards), (Llandysul, 1996), 320–349

May, Timothy C., *Trade Unions and Pressure Group Politics* (Westmead, Hants, 1975)

Miles, Gareth and Griffiths, Robert, *Cymru, Marcsiaeth a'r Cwestiwn Cenedlaethol* (Cardiff, 1988)

Moran, James, NATSOPA: *Seventy Five Years* (London, 1965)

Morgan, Austen, *Harold Wilson* (London, 1992)

Morgan, Kenneth O., *Labour in Power 1945–1951* (Oxford, 1984)

Idem, *Labour People: Leaders and Lieutenants, Hardie to Kinnock* (Oxford, 1987)

Idem, *The Red Dragon and The Red Flag: The Case of James Griffiths and Aneurin Bevan* (Aberystwyth, 1989)

Idem, *Michael Foot: A Life* (London, 2007)

Idem, *Wales in British Politics 1868–1922* (Cardiff, 1980)

Idem, *Ages of Reform* (London, 2011), 314

Marr, Andrew, *The Making of Modern Britain* (London, 2009)

Martineau, Lisa, *Politics and Power: Barbara Castle, A Biography* (London, 2000)

Marwick, William H., *A Short History of Labour in Scotland* (Edinburgh, 1967)

McLaine, W., 'Fifty Years in the Labour Movement', *Plebs*, *Vol. 49*, No. 6, June 1957, 132–34.

McKibbin, Ross; 'Why Was There No Marxism in Great Britain?', *English Historical Review* (1984), *Vol. 99* (391), 297–331

Macfarlane, Leslie. J., *The British Communist Party: its origins and development until 1929* (London, 1960)

Mikardo, Ian, *Back-bencher* (London, 1988)

Miliband, Ralph, *Parliamentary Socialism: A Study in the Politics of Labour* (London, 1972)

Morgan, Janet (ed.); *The Back Bench Diaries of Richard Grosvenor* (London, 1981)

Morris, Jan, *The Matter of Wales: Epic Views of a Small Country* (London, 1998; first edition Oxford University Press, 1984)

Morris-Jones, H., *Doctor in the Whips' Room* (London, 1955) Morrison, Herbert, *Herbert Morrison: An Autobiography* (London, 1960)

Newman, Michael, 'Democracy versus Dictatorship: Labour's Role in the Struggle Against British Fascism 1933–1936', in *History Workshop*, No. 5, Spring 1938, 69–88

Pearce, Brian, *The Communist Party and The Labour Left 1925–1929*, Introduction by John Saville (Hull, 1957)

Pelling, Henry, *The British Communist Party: A Historical Profile* (London and New York, 1958)

Idem, 'The 1945 General Election Reconsidered', *Historical Journal*, Vol. 23, 2 (1980), 413–423

Perry, Matt, *'Red Ellen' Wilkinson: Her Ideas, Movements and World* (Manchester and New York, 2014)

Pater, John E., *The Making of the National Health Service* (London, 1981)

Idem (ed.), *The Political Diary of Hugh Dalton 1918–1940, 1945–1960* (London, 1980)

Idem (ed.), *The Political Diary of Hugh Dalton 1940–1945* (London, 1986)

Pikoulis, John, *Alun Lewis: A Life* (Bridgend, 1984)

Pimlott, Ben, *Labour and The Left in the 1930s* (Cambridge, 1977)

Idem, *Harold Wilson* (London, 1992)

Porter, R., *The Greatest Benefit to Mankind: A Medical History of Humanity* (New York, 1998)

Price, Emyr, *Cymru a'r Byd Modern ers 1918* (Cardiff, 1979)

Idem, *Yr Arglwydd Cledwyn o Benrhos* (Penygroes, 1990)

Pugh, Martin, *Speak for Britain: A New History of the Labour Party* (London, 2011)

Idem, 'The Daily Mirror and the Revival of Labour 1935– 1945'; *Twentieth Century British History* (1998), vol. 9 (3), 420–438

Prys-Davies, Gwilym, *Llafur y Blynyddoedd* (Denbigh, 1990)

Idem, *Cynhaeaf Hanner Canrif: Gwleidyddiaeth Gymreig 1945–2005* (Llandysul, 2008)

Rees, D. Ben, *Wales: The Cultural Heritage* (Ormskirk, 1981)

Idem, 'Casglu Aneurin Bevan', *Casglwr*, no. 62 (1998), 15.

Idem, 'Fy Arwr Gwleidyddol', *Cristion*, no. 124 (May/June 2010), 38–9

Idem, 'Gwasanaeth Iechyd Aneurin yn 70'; *Barn*, Rhif 666/667, July/August 2018; 24–25

Idem, 'Aneurin Bevan a'r Gwasanaeth Iechyd Cenedlaethol'; *Y Goleuad*; Vol. CXLVI, no. 30, 27 July 2018; 8

Idem, Cofiant Jim Griffiths: Arwr Glew y Werin (Talybont, 2014)

Idem, Cofiant Cledwyn Hughes: Un o Wŷr Mawr Môn a Chymru (Talybont, 2017)

Rees, Dylan, Jones, Morgan; 'Educationist and Labour Politician'; *Morgannwg*, vol. XXXI, 1987, 66–83

Roadhouse, Mark, 'Nye Bevan, black marketeer,' *History Today, Vol.55* (July 2005), 2–3

Roberts of Conwy, Lord; *Right from the Start: The Memoirs of Sir Wyn Roberts* (Cardiff, 2006)

Rogers, W. and Donoughue, B., *The People Into Parliament: A Concise History of the Labour Movement in Britain* (New York, 1966)

Rintala, Marvin, *Creating the National Health Service* (London, 2003), 163.

Samuel, Ralph, 'North and South: A Year in a Mining Village', *London Review of Books,* vol. 17 (12) (22 June1995), 3–6

Samuel, Stuart, 'The Left Book Club', *Journal of Contemporary History, Vol. 1*, No. 2 (1966), 65–86.

Sassoon, Donald, *One Hundred Years of Socialism: The West European Left in The Twentieth Century* (London, 1996)

Sissons, M. and French, P. (eds.), *Age of Austerity 1945–1951* (Harmondsworth, 1984)

Smart, Nick, 'Four Days in May: The Norway Debate and the Downfall of Neville Chamberlain', *Parliamentary History*, vol. 17, no. 2, (1998), 215–243

Smith, Dai, 'Bevan the cutting edge of inexperience', *The New Statesman* (19 April 1987)

Idem, 'Bevan a'i bobl', *Golwg, Vol. 6*, No. 5 (30 September 1993), 12–13

Idem, 'Speaking the Word', *New Welsh Review,* vol. 4, no. 2 (1991), 31–43

Smith, J. Beverley (ed.), *James* Griffiths *and His Times* (Ferndale, 1979)

Idem, 'Pan alwodd Bevan a Robeson heibio', *Barn*, 572 (September 2010), 30–1

Stevenson, John, 'Arwr yn y Glorian (Aneurin Bevan)', *Barn*, 418 (November 1997), 18–19

Stewart, John, 'The backroom boys of state medicine', *Journal of Medical Biography,* vol. 4, no. 4, (November 1996), 279–235

Tanner, Duncan, 'The Development of British Socialism 1900–1918'; *Parliamentary History* (1997), vol. 16, no. 1, 48–66

Taylor, A. J. P., *Beaverbrook* (New York, 1972)

Thompson, Steven, *Unemployment, Poverty and Health in Interwar South Wales* (Cardiff, 2006)

Toye, Richard, *The Labour Party and the Planned Economy* (Woodbridge, 2003)

Idem, Lloyd George and Churchill: Rivals for Greatness (London, 2007)

Watkin, B., *The National Health Service: The First Phase 1948–1974 and After* (London, 1978)

Webster, Charles, *The Health Services Since the War, Volume 1: Problems of Health Care: The National Health Service Before 1957* (London, 1988)

Idem, *The Health Services Since the War, Volume 2: Government and Health Care: The British National Health Service 1958–1979* (London, 1996)

Idem, *The National Health Service: A Political History* (1998)

Idem, 'Birth of the Dream: Bevan and the Architecture of the National Health Service', *The State of the Nation: The Political Legacy of Aneurin Bevan* (ed. Geoffrey Goodman); (London, 1997), 106–129

Idem, 'Healthy or Hungry Thirties?' in *History Workshop: A Journal of Socialist and Feminist Historians;* no.13, Spring 1982, 116–129

Wertheimer, Egon, *Portrait of the Labour Party* (London and New York, 1929)

Williams, Frances, *A Prime Minister Remembers: The War and Post-War Memoirs of the Rt. Hon. Earl Attlee* (London, 1961)

Idem, *Ernest Bevin* (London, 1953)

Williams, Kevin, 'The End is not Nye', *Planet*, 127 (1998), 38–42

Williams, P. M., *Hugh Gaitskell: A Political Biography* (London, 1979), 1007

Wilson, Harold, *A Prime Minister on Prime Ministers* (New York, 1977) Witts, L., 'Thomas Jeeves Horder' in E. Williams and H. Palmer (eds.), *The Dictionary of National Biography 1951–1960* (Oxford, 1971)

Wood, Ian, *John Wheatley* (Manchester and New York, 1990)

Woolton, Earl of, *The Memoirs of the Rt. Hon. The Earl of Woolton* (London, 1959)

Wyatt, Woodrow, *The Peril in Our Midst* (London, 1956)

Young, James D., *Socialism and The English Working Class: A History of English Labour 1883–1939* (New York, 1989)

Idem, 'Daniel de Leon and Anglo-American Socialism', *Labor History*, vol. 17, no. 3, 1976, 329–350

Hansard, House of Commons, vol. 422, col. 63, 30 April 1946.

Aneurin Bevan, "In Place of Fear" (1952; London; Quartet Books, 1978).

Nicklaus Thomas-Symonds, "Nye: The Political Life of Aneurin Bevan" (London: I.B.Tauris, 2014).

"Winston Churchill and Aneurin Bevan," by Rt Hon Nick Thomas-Symonds, MP, International Churchill Society, Finest Hour 193, Third Quarter 2021, "Churchill and Wales" available at: https://winstonchurchill.org/publications/finest-hour/finesthour-193/winston-churchill-and-aneurin-bevan/

Report of the Forty-Eighth Annual Conference of the Labour Party Held in Empress Ballroom, Winter Gardens, Blackpool, June 6 to June 10, 1949 (London: The Labour Party, 1949), p.172.

INDEX

A.

Abercynon xvi
Abersychan xviii, 68
Ablett, Noah xxvi, 25-6, 41, 43, 45, 47, 100, 293
Abraham, William (Mabon) 74
Abse, Leo 153
Aggex, David 10
Andrews, Leighton 301
Aneurin (Socialist magazine for students) xv
Arnot, Robin Page 328
Asheridge Farm 111, 118, 121, 124-5, 251, 274, 276, 280, 313, 315
Attlee, Clement ix, x, xix, 93, 106, 132, 136, 145, 149, 159, 172, 177, 181, 197-8, 204, 218, 221, 233, 249, 252, 255, 286, 296-7, 303
Australia 51, 116

B.

Balderston, Marion 113
Baldwin, Stanley 76-7, 82, 92, 108, 131, 301
Bargoed 21, 231
Beaverbrook, Max (Lord Beaverbrook) 97, 129, 132, 268, 299, 319
Bedwellty 30-1, 57
Bevan, Aneurin passim
Bevan, Arianwen (his sister) 7, 50, 111, 117-21, 279, 281, 285-6
Bevan, Blodwen (his sister) 17, 35, 285
Bevan, David (his father) 11-2, 14, 19, 22, 52, 57-8, 100, 174-5, 205, 227, 299
Bevan, Iorwerth (his brother) 7, 285
Bevan, Margaret May (his sister) 7, 35
Bevan, Myfanwy (his sister)
Bevan, William (Nye's eldest brother) 7, 17, 22, 30, 285

Bevan, Phoebe (née Protheroe) 7, 13-6, 21-2, 116-120
Beveridge, William 150-2, 304
Bevin, Ernest 163, 186, 197, 294, 296-7
Blackwood 8, 31, 37, 54, 73
Blair, Tony xxi, 154
Bondfield, Margaret 90
Bowen, Henry 10, 67, 74-5
Bowen, James E. 254
Braddock, Bessie 89, 176, 305
Bristol 14, 287, 301
Brome, Vincent 224-5, 245-6
Brynmawr 91, 99, 278
Buchan, John 209, 284
Burton, Richard 316
Butler, David 246, 253

C.

Caerphilly 21, 46, 154, 237
Campbell, John xviii, 105, 135, 271, 313
Campbell, Reverend R. J. 28
Cardiff 34, 61, 75, 153, 315
Castle, Barbara 111-2, 135, 246, 249, 260
Chamberlain, Neville 56-7, 77, 136, 143, 163, 301
Churchill, Winston 24, 87, 97-8, 103, 131, 147, 160, 162, 204, 230, 284, 290
Citrine, Walter 134, 245
Cole, G. D. H. 52, 151, 299
Communism 52, 107-8, 121, 236
Conservatives 23, 29, 77, 103-4, 144-6, 160, 254, 292, 301, 316-8
Conway, Walter 23, 27, 32
Cook, A. J. 60-1, 63-4, 299, 301
Corwen 278, 295
Cousins, Frank 265
Cove, W. C. 83

Cox, Idris 299
Craigie, Jill 116, 268-9
Craik, W. W. 42-3, 52
Cripps, Sir Stafford 91-3, 100, 106, 131, 134, 136-9, 164, 296-7
Cronin, A. J. 59-60
Cross, Sir Eugene 57, 240, 315
Crossman, Richard 190, 217-8, 224-5, 244, 249, 271, 294, 299-300, 313
Cummings, A. J. 108
Cyprus 258-9, 277

D.
Daggar, George 46
Daily Express 122-3, 151, 202, 218, 317
Daily Herald 48, 148, 151, 275-6, 277
Daily Mail 105, 151, 202
Daily Mirror 123
Daily Worker 47-8, 299
Dalton, Hugh 146, 164, 166-7, 244, 294, 296
Darwin, Charles 23
David, Wayne 21, 41, 238
Davies, Clement 205
Davies, Dan 122, 129, 209, 276-7, 281, 285
Davies, D. J. (Rhondda) 44, 46
Davies, David (Llandinam) 34, 132
Davies, Evan 48, 53, 57 75-6, 293
Davies, Harold 246, 256, 265
Davies, Idris 97
Davies, James D. 6
Davies, John 76
Davies, Rhys J. 73, 150
Davies, S. O. 97-8, 232, 235
Deakin, Arthur 244, 251, 257, 260
Delargy, Hugh 282
Demont, Susan 10, 32, 35, 68, 73
Devolution 153, 236-8
Dietzgen, Joseph 46
Driberg, Tom 132, 249, 258, 286
Dukestown 230
Dunn, Clara 42

E.
Ebbw Vale xii, xiv, 1, 56-7, 96, 107, 131, 163, 295, 298, 315

Ede, James Chater 198, 213-4
Eden, Anthony 262, 275
Eden, Guy 85
Edwards, Charles 73
Edwards, Clem 33
Edwards, Huw T. 153, 181
Edwards, Ness 21, 32, 41, 44, 46, 237, 256, 266
Ellis, Robert (Cynddelw) 3
Evans, Glyn 44
Evans, Gwynfor xx, 58, 290
Evans, Rhys 290
Evans, Richard 94
Evans, Ron 279, 294-5, 315
Evans, Reverend Towy 28

F.
Fabians (a society of intellectual socialists) 169-170, 196
Fascism 133-5
Finch, Harold 31, 34, 37, 41, 79, 84, 256
Finlay, Graeme 215
Firth, Sir William 107
Fisher, Sam 48-9
Foot, Michael 18, 30, 63, 113, 116, 144-6, 174, 232, 266-8, 274, 296, 313, 316
Freeman, John 199, 221, 242

G.
Gaitskell, Dora 275, 291
Gaitskell, Hugh xviii, 200, 217, 221, 223, 235, 252, 255-6, 260, 262, 275-7, 287, 291, 311-4
Gallagher, Willie 107-8, 137
George, David Lloyd 16, 24, 27, 34, 39, 47, 74, 88, 90, 98, 144, 155, 163, 171, 224, 230, 290, 301
George, Megan Lloyd 83, 112, 146, 238
Goodman, Geoffrey 104, 266, 276-7, 291
Griffiths, David (Tredegar) 35, 54-5, 72
Griffiths, James xiii, xvi, 41, 43, 49, 100-2, 133, 140, 144, 221, 223, 231, 233, 235, 237, 249, 251-2, 256, 271, 290, 301
Gruffydd, W. J. 233-4

H.
Hacking, Alfred J. 42
Hale, Leslie 262
Hannington, Wal 134
Harcourt, William 12
Hardie, Keir xxii, 26-8, 291
Harris, Oliver 87
Harrison, J. J. (Tredegar) 48, 74
Hart, Judith 265
Hastings, Dr Somerville 202
Healey, Denis 156, 219, 275, 298
Henderson, Arthur 27, 107, 113
Hengoed 315
Hitler, Adolf 101, 131, 135, 137-40, 144, 294
Hollis, Patricia 68, 299
Holloway, Lewis 23
Horner, Arthur 45, 63, 101, 165, 230
Hughes, Cledwyn 126, 153, 231, 238, 290, 318
Hughes, John Ceiriog 8-9
Humphreys, Emyr 227, 230
Hylton, Jack 128, 272

I.
In Place of Fear 104-5, 174, 313
Independent Labour Party (ILP) 25-8, 32, 43
India 251, 270, 315-8,

J.
James, Graham xiii
Jamison, Sir William 189
Jay, Douglas 313
Jeffreys, Len 67-8
Jenkins, Arthur (Pontypool) xviii, 67-8
Jenkins, David (Neath) 86
Jenkins, Gwyn 233
Jenkins, Roy xviii-xix, 313
Jones, Aneurin (Aneurin Fardd) 16
Jones, Arfon (co-editor of *Aneuri*
Jones, Evan (Ieuan Gwynedd) 3, 231
Jones, John Graham 76, 83
Jones, Lewis 102, 230
Jones, Mervyn 263-4, 319
Jones, Morgan (Caerphilly) 21
Jones, Oliver 53, 74
Jones, Sydney 32, 73-4
Jones, Thomas (Rhymni) 34
Jones, Tom (Rhosllanerchrugog) xv-xvi

K.
Kandell, Eduard 211
Kaunda, Kenneth 316-7
Kenyatta, Jomo 258-9, 316
Kinnock, Neil xxi, 21, 294, 301, 313-5
Kruschev, Nikita 265, 270-1, 275, 318

L.
Labour Party xv, 20-1, 23, 25, 26-7, 39-41, 66, 74, 86, 136-9, 141, 192-5, 217, 223, 227, 229, 231, 235, 245, 277, 292, 305-10, 315-7
Labour-Liberal 12
Lang, Gordon 76
Lansburg, George 93, 106
Laski, Harold 131, 151, 182, 195
Lee, Euphemia 115, 117, 209
Lee, Jennie 107, 110, 115, 117-20, 166, 176, 240, 246, 251, 264, 267-70, 274, 276, 281, 283-4, 286, 299, 315-6
Levy, Ben 115
Lewis, John Saunders xvi-xvii, 7, 290
Lewis, Lewis 37
Lewis, Richard 44-5
Lewis, Robyn 295
Lewis, Watkin 27
Leyburn, Keith 265
Liberal Party 12-4, 23-7, 39, 73-4, 76, 140, 293
Liverpool 39, 89, 99, 162, 167-8, 183-4, 186
Llangollen 278
London 33, 45, 93, 97, 106, 277, 292
Lowther, Sir William 244, 246
Lush, Archibald 21, 75, 78, 80, 111, 113, 115, 281-3, 287

M.
MacDonald, Ramsay 27, 53, 83, 92-3, 109, 261, 294
Mackie, John 124, 262
Macmillan, Harold 165, 273, 276, 286, 289
Magee, Bryan 53

Mainwaring, W. H. 42, 46-7
Mallalieu, J. P. W. 248
Marx, Karl 43, 104-5, 174, 292
Marxism 29, 44, 104, 292-3, 298, 313
Mathias, Ron xvi
Maxton, James 87
May, W. H. (Pontypridd) 101
Meir, Golda 251
Mellor, William 115, 134-6
Mencken, H. L. 282-3
Menon, Krishna 316, 318
Merthyr Express 35, 53, 62, 73-4, 78
Merthyr Tydfil 316
Mikardo, Ian 224, 246, 249, 300
Miliband, Ralph 221, 249, 289, 292, 300
Miners Minority Movement 63-5
Minton, David (Blaina) 51
Morris, John (Lord John Morris) 155
Morgan, Kenneth O. 12, 27, 144, 227, 246, 296, 319
Morrison, Herbert 88, 90, 136, 139, 146-8, 163, 167-8, 221
Mosley, Sir Oswald 90-2, 94, 294
Mussolini, Benito 101, 137

N.
Norris, Jack 285
Norris-Bevan, Arianwen 285-6, 291

O.
Onions, Alfred 28, 33
Orchard, William 17-18, 20
Orwell, George 140, 147, 181
Owen, Robert 100
Oxford xviii, 78, 186, 193, 217, 221, 247-8, 262, 299

P.
Pages from Memory 249-50, 253
Paget, Reginald 192
Parnell, Charles 259
Parry, Gordon 287-9
Parry, R. Wiliams 319
Parry, Sir Thomas 232-3
Paynter, Wil 63, 230

Peate, Iorwerth Cyfeiliog 232-3
Phillips, Ben 9-10
Phillips, Morgan 46, 223, 237, 271
Plaid Cymru xx, 58, 233, 264
Plebs League 29
Pollit, Harry 104
Powell, Oliver 32, 54-5
Price, T. J. (magistrate) 35
Prichard, Caradog 185
Priestley, J. B. 282-3
Protheroe, Cliff xvi, 237
Prys-Davies, Gwilym 278-9

R.
Rees, Evan (sailor) xxv
Rees, Noah 25
Religious Revival of 1904-6 11
Reynolds, Thomas 30-1
Rhymney 1, 28, 32, 41, 315
Rhys, Keidrych 152-3
Richards, Tom 27-8, 32-3, 37, 74-5
Rintala, Marvin 160, 164, 167
Roberts, Bryn (Rhymni) 24, 41-2, 80-1, 188
Roberts, Samuel (S.R.) 3
Robertson, Alec (Glasgow) 42
Robeson, Paul xxv, 230
Rosen, Greg 155

S.
Samuel, Howard 128, 267, 272
Sankey, John 47, 91, 93
Sassoon, Donald
Shinwell, Emanuel 93, 140
Snowden, Philip 73
Socialism 19, 23, 25, 27, 29, 37, 46-9, 60-4, 74, 88, 100-4, 174, 217, 227, 224-5, 251-3, 275-6, 285-9, 291, 296, 305, 318-9
Soper, Reverend Donald 133, 180-1, 287
South Wales Miners' Union 13, 19, 22, 24, 26, 28, 30, 33, 38, 40, 44, 46, 63, 67, 76-80, 82-3, 86-7
Spencer, Henry F. 315
Stalin, Joseph, 140, 142, 219, 243-4, 300
Starmer, Sir Keir xxi, 291
Stockwood, Mervyn 115-6, 132, 287-8

Strachey, John 106, 300
Strauss, George 100, 111, 135, 139, 300
Symonds-Thomas, Nicklaus ix, xi, 20, 58, 156, 190, 192, 242, 246, 260, 266, 313
Syndicalism 24, 33

T.
Tawney, R. H. 82
Taylor, Bernard 52
Tewson, Sir Vincent 252-3
Thatcher, Margaret 188
Thomas, Dr Ceinwen xx-xxi
Thomas, David xvi
Thomas, Dylan I. 315-6
Thomas, George 132, 217, 251, 318
Thomas, J. H. 88, 90, 92
Thomas, John (WEA) 42-3
Tonypandy 24
Tredegar 1-16, 27, 32, 49, 54-5, 58-9, 61, 72, 74, 78, 97, 110, 119-20, 128, 164, 195, 218, 227-30, 245, 293, 303-4
Tribune 128, 139, 144, 146, 148-9, 232, 249, 266, 272, 275, 289, 317
Tryweryn 235

V.
Valentine, Reverend Lewis 83
Vaughan, Janet (Somerville College, Oxford) 96, 186, 188-9
Vaughan, Kathleen (Tredegar) 72-3
Vermin 196

W.
Wakefield, W. W. 67
Watkins, Tudor 238
Watson, Sam 264-5, 271
Webster, Charles 95, 163, 193
Wells, H. G. 31, 97, 129
Weekly Argus 55, 76
Welsh Outlook 58
Western Mail 61-3
Wheatley, John 55-7
White, Eirene (née Jones) 155, 279
Why Trust the Tories? xiii, 149-50, 210
Williams, D. J. (Neath) 43
Williams, E. J. (Ogmore) 46
Williams, Emlyn 220
Williams, John Lloyd (Glasgow) 36, 46, 68-9
Williamson, Sir Thomas 244, 251
Wilson, Charles, Lord Morgan 175, 178-9
Wilson, Harold xviii, 165-6, 199, 224, 242, 251, 287
Wise, E. F. 110-2, 116, 119
Wise, Dr Tom 129, 285
World War 1 27, 32, 36, 38, 40, 46
World War 2 123, 145-8, 150-5, 245, 303-5
Wyatt, Woodrow xix, 244